St. Anne in Renaissance Music

Devotion to Saint Anne, the apocryphal mother of the Virgin Mary, reached its height in the fifteenth and early sixteenth centuries. Until now, Anne's reception history and political symbolism during this period have been primarily discussed through the lens of art history. This is the first study to explore the music that honored the saint and its connections to some of the most prominent court cultures of Western Europe. Michael Alan Anderson examines plainchant and polyphonic music for Saint Anne, in sources both familiar and previously unstudied, to illuminate not only Anne's wide-ranging intercessional capabilities but also the political force of the music devoted to her. Whether viewed as a fertility aide, wise mother, or dynastic protector, she modeled a number of valuable roles that rulers reflected in the music of their devotional programs to project their noble lineage and prestige.

Michael Alan Anderson has taught at the Eastman School of Music, University of Rochester, since 2008. In 2012, he won the Noah Greenberg Award, given by the American Musicological Society for outstanding contributions to historical performing practices. In the same year, he received the Deems Taylor Award from the American Society of Composers, Authors and Publishers for an article published in the journal *Early Music History*. Since 2008, he has been the artistic director of the professional early music ensemble Schola Antiqua of Chicago, which he cofounded in 2000. The group's albums include previously unrecorded music by Leonin, Du Fay, La Rue, Guerrero, and Lassus.

St. Anne in Renaissance Music

Devotion and Politics

MICHAEL ALAN ANDERSON
Eastman School of Music, University of Rochester

CAMBRIDGE
UNIVERSITY PRESS

32 Avenue of the Americas, New York, NY 10013-2473, USA

Cambridge University Press is part of the University of Cambridge.

It furthers the University's mission by disseminating knowledge in the pursuit of education, learning, and research at the highest international levels of excellence.

www.cambridge.org
Information on this title: www.cambridge.org/9781107056244

© Michael Alan Anderson 2014

This publication is in copyright. Subject to statutory exception
and to the provisions of relevant collective licensing agreements,
no reproduction of any part may take place without the written
permission of Cambridge University Press.

First published 2014

Printed in the United States of America

A catalog record for this publication is available from the British Library.

Library of Congress Cataloging in Publication data
Anderson, Michael Alan, 1975–, author.
St. Anne in Renaissance music : devotion and politics / Michael Alan Anderson.
  pages cm
Includes bibliographical references and index.
ISBN 978-1-107-05624-4 (hardback)
1. Anne (Mother of the Virgin Mary), Saint – Songs and music – History and criticism.   2. Motets – 16th century – History and criticism.   3. Masses – 16th century – History and criticism.   4. Sacred vocal music – 16th century – History and criticism.   5. Church music – Catholic Church – 16th century.   I. Title.
ML3003.A53   2014
781.71'209–dc23   2013040591

ISBN 978-1-107-05624-4 Hardback

Cambridge University Press has no responsibility for the persistence or accuracy of URLs for external or third-party Internet Web sites referred to in this publication and does not guarantee that any content on such Web sites is, or will remain, accurate or appropriate.

For Julie

Contents

List of Illustrations   [*page* viii]
List of Tables   [x]
List of Examples   [xi]
Acknowledgments   [xiii]
List of Abbreviations and Conventions   [xvii]

1 Mary's Mother: Devotion, Politics, and Music   [1]

2 Heritage and Progeny in an Office for St. Anne   [26]

3 Of Widowhood and Maternity: La Rue's *Missa de Sancta Anna*   [66]

4 Devotion and Letters: St. Anne in Pre-Reformation Wittenberg   [104]

5 A "Divine Favor" at the French Court: In Pursuit of a Motet for St. Anne   [143]

6 Devotion without Borders: The Afterlife of *Celeste beneficium*   [176]

7 The French Royal Trinity, Biblical Humanism, and Chanted Mass Propers for St. Anne   [212]

Postlude   [247]

Appendix A   [251]
Appendix B: Complete Text of the Mass for St. Anne *(Paris, Bibliothèque nationale de France, MS fr. 1035)*   [261]
Notes   [271]
Bibliography   [317]
Index   [341]

Illustrations

1.1 *The Holy Kinship* from an Anonymous Book of Hours (Rouen, Use of Paris), ca. 1500   [*page* 8]
1.2 Brabant, Mechelen, Anna-te-Drieen, 1515–24   [11]
1.3 Choir breviary   [13]
1.4 Bernhard Strigel, *Portrait of Maximilian and His Family*, 1515   [18]
2.1 (a) Opening of the office for St. Anne; (b) Illuminations of St. Hilarion (left) and St. Anne (right) in the Turin Codex   [27]
2.2 *St. Anne Trinitarian* in the Book of Hours for Duke Louis of Savoy   [63]
3.1 Vienna, Österreichische Nationalbibliothek, Musiksammlung, MS Supplementum Musica 15496   [73]
3.2 *Master of Mary of Burgundy*, from the Register of the Guild of St. Anne (Ghent, 1477)   [82]
3.3 Bernard van Orley, *Portrait of Margaret of Austria as a Widow*, after 1518   [92]
4.1 Jena, Universitätsbibliothek, MS 7   [105]
4.2 Lucas Cranach the Elder, Relics of Saint Anne, woodcut from the Wittenberger Heiligtumsbuch. Buch 581/82. S. 69 Kupferstichkabinett, Staatliche Museen, Berlin, Germany. 1509   [112]
4.3 Lucas Cranach, *Altarpiece of the Holy Kinship*   [114]
4.4 Lucas Cranach, *Altarpiece of the Holy Kinship* (wings in closed position)   [117]
4.5 La Rue, *Missa Conceptio tua*   [136]
4.6 La Rue, *Missa Conceptio tua*   [138]
5.1 Anne of Brittany with St. Anne, St. Ursula, and St. Helena. Jean Bourdichon, *Grandes Heures of Anne of Brittany*   [166]
5.2 *Education of the Three Marys* in the Prayer Book of Anne de Bretagne   [168]
5.3 (a) *A Girl Kneels at a Desk with the Virgin and Saints*, from a Primer, c.1500–10 and (b) *St. Claude Presents a Kneeling Girl to St. Anne and the Virgin*, c.1500–10   [170]

5.4 St. Anne teaching the Virgin Mary to read and the Annunciation to St. Anne. Master of Claude of France, Prayer Book of Queen Claude of France, ca. 1517   [172]
6.1 *Adjutorium nostrum*, superius part   [177]
6.2 Anonymous, *Anna matrona nobilis*, opening of superius partbook. Used with permission of Biblioteca Apostolica Vaticana, with all rights reserved   [193]
6.3 Jan Cornelisz Vermeyen, Emperor Ferdinand I and Anna of Hungary, after 1531   [195]
7.1 *Portrait of Marguerite of Navarre*, attributed to Jean Clouet, ca. 1527   [215]
7.2 Leonardo da Vinci (1452–1519), *Virgin and Child with Saint Anne*, ca. 1510   [219]
7.3 Dedication to Louise of Savoy, miniature on paper from *Petit livret faict à l'honneur de Madame Sainte Anne*   [225]
7.4 Dedication of the *Mass for St. Anne*   [228]
7.5 The Introit *Noli timere mater filiorum* (opening) from the *Mass for St. Anne*   [233]

Tables

2.1 Contents of the Office for St. Anne in the Turin Codex   [*page* 33]
2.2 Themes of the St. Anne Office in the Turin Codex   [42]
3.1 Comparison of La Rue's works in the manuscripts VienNB Mus. 15496, MontsM 773, and JenaU 7   [68]
4.1 Tonal transitions between *Gaude mater anna gaude* (JenaU 34) and *Alma parens anna gaude* (JenaU 30)   [127]
5.1 Sources of the motet *Celeste beneficium* by Jean Mouton   [144]
5.2 Select sources of the antiphon *Celeste beneficium*   [156]
5.3 Children of Anne of Brittany between 1492 and 1512   [163]
6.1 Opening group of motets in Vatican City, Biblioteca Apostolica Vaticana, MSS Palatini Latini 1976–9   [179]
7.1 Proper texts in the *Mass for St. Anne*   [231]
7.2 Melodic modes and sources of the Propers in the *Mass for St. Anne*   [234]

Examples

2.1 *Anna parens matris* (WE) from the Turin Office for St. Anne, fol. 19r [*page 45*]
2.2 *Genealogie christi* (MR6) from the Turin Office for St. Anne, fol. 16v [48]
2.3 The hymn *Lucis huius festa*, from the Turin Office for St. Anne, fols. 14r–v [53]
2.4 *Abrae beati senis* (MA4) from the Turin Office for St. Anne, fol. 16r [56]
3.1 Opening of the (a) Kyrie and (b) Gloria of La Rue's *Missa de Sancta Anna*, after VienNB Mus. 15496 [70]
3.2 Excerpts of the paraphrased motive in the interior of La Rue's *Missa de Sancta Anna*, after VienNB Mus. 15496; (a) Gloria, "Qui tollis"; (b) Credo, "Confiteor" [71]
3.3 Beginning of antiphon *Felix Anna quedam matrona* from Paris, Bibliothèque nationale, MS 15182, fol. 269v [75]
3.4 The antiphon *Felix Anna quedam matrona* from Mainz, Bischöfliches Dom- und Diözesanmuseum, Codex C, fol. 226v [76]
3.5 Costanzo Festa, *Felix Anna quedam matrona* (opening) [78]
3.6 Anonymous, *Felix Anna quedam matrona*, Cambrai, Mediathèque Municipale, MSS 125–8, fol. 47r [79]
4.1 *Alma parens anna gaude* in JenaU 30 (mm. 149–end) [129]
5.1 Mouton, *Celeste beneficium* (opening) [149]
5.2 Mouton, *Celeste beneficium*, mm. 59–82 [151]
5.3 Févin (or Mouton), *Adjutorium nostrum*, mm. 62–78 [153]
5.4 Synoptic transcription of select versions of *Celeste beneficium* [158]
6.1 Anonymous, *Anna matrona nobilis*, mm. 55–69 [182]
6.2 Anonymous, *Ave mater matris Dei*, mm. 36–57 [191]
7.1 (a) *Alleluia V. Multiplicabitur* from the *Mass for St. Anne* (fols. 12r–13r), compared with (b) *Alleluia V. Dilexisti iusticiam et odisti iniquitatem* [235]
7.2 The Introit *Noli timere mater filiorum* in Paris, Bibliothèque nationale de France, MS fr. 1035, fol. 8r (opening) [238]
7.3 The Communion *Gaudium et leticia invenietur* in Paris, Bibliothèque nationale de France, MS fr. 1035, fols. 14r–15r [238]

Acknowledgments

Although I spent some of my youth at a church named St. Joseph and St. Anne in Chicago's Brighton Park neighborhood, only within the past decade have I been drawn into the lore of Jesus' extended family, given my interest in the music of late medieval devotion. This book expands on topics raised in my dissertation and develops arguments that exceeded its scope. The project owes intellectual and personal debt to numerous individuals, institutions, and agencies. I am deeply grateful to all of those who, in ways large and small, have improved this book-length study of St. Anne or simply enabled it to reach its final form, not least of which is Victoria Cooper at Cambridge University Press. Vicki believed in this project from the start and guided it for more than two years. For this, I am very thankful. Rebecca Taylor has also ensured that the book's final preparation was a smooth one.

No study of this magnitude would have been conceivable without the financial support of a number of institutions. As a graduate student at the University of Chicago, I received generous dissertation write-up grants from the American Musicological Society (Alvin H. Johnson AMS 50 Dissertation-Year Fellowship), the Mrs. Giles Whiting Foundation, and the Medieval Academy of America (the Grace Frank Dissertation Grant). These grants, along with funding from the university's department of music, allowed me to complete my initial findings on the subject of St. Anne that form the basis of this study. Since my arrival at the Eastman School of Music (University of Rochester) in 2008, I have been fortunate to receive support from the school's professional development funds, which subsidized trips to research libraries and assisted with the cost of purchasing images for use in this book. Two particular sources of funding accelerated the completion of the book in its final stages. A summer stipend from the National Endowment for the Humanities allowed an important trip to the Bibliothèque nationale de France in June 2011 to complete work on the seventh and final chapter of the monograph. I would like to acknowledge further the Eastman School of Music (Jamal Rossi in particular) for granting a semester-long faculty leave in the fall of 2011 to complete this book's remaining chapters. I am indebted to the Office of the Provost at the University of Rochester for a generous publication subvention that defrayed expenses associated with images and photographic rights. Finally, I am grateful for a similar publication subvention from the Martin Picker Endowment of the American Musicological Society, funded in part by the National Endowment for the Humanities and the Andrew W. Mellon Foundation.

Countless individuals have facilitated my work over the past several years. I am grateful to Daniel Zager, the associate dean of the Sibley Music Library, for never hesitating to purchase resources that could benefit my research. Robert Iannapollo and Alan Lupack also deserve thanks for being steadfastly attuned to my plentiful requests. Colleagues of all stripes have been a source of encouragement and inspiration, especially Virginia Nixon and David Rothenberg, who have given me much needed assurance. My Eastman colleagues Patrick Macey, Ralph Locke, and Honey Meconi have been models and confidantes throughout the writing process. Andrew Hughes has shared his resources freely, and Sherry Reames and Catherine Saucier have selflessly cheered my work on St. Anne. I am sad that Rev. James Boyce (O. Carm.), who died in 2010, will not get to see the fruits of this study, as his substantial work on the Carmelite liturgy provided unexpected solutions to some key questions I had about works for St. Anne.

Several colleagues have had a direct impact on the shape of this book, no matter the stage at which they encountered the work. I am most appreciative of the time that each has lent to this project. I would especially like to thank Karl Kügle, Honey Meconi (again), Jennifer Bloxam, Hannah Mowrey, Timothy Shephard, Jonathan Reid, Robert Kendrick, Rachel Fulton, Erika Honisch, and Eric Lubarsky, who each read substantial amounts of my work on St. Anne. Thomas DiPiero, Timothy Scheie, Anna Zayaruznaya, and Leofranc Holford-Strevens assisted with some pesky translations in the final stages. Elizabeth L'Estrange, Margaret Hadley, Debra Lacoste, Michael Peppard, Steven Saunders, and Klara Broekhuijsen each helped with issues that arose in the research process and provided quick answers that saved much time.

On a more personal note, I wish to make special mention of Calvin Bower, who was the first to suggest that musicology might make a good career for me. He is a consummate scholar and a genuine friend. I hope that some of Calvin's profound understanding of plainchant and careful attention to detail are reflected in my work. The principal advisor for my dissertation and the project at hand has been Anne Walters Robertson. While it is merely a coincidence that I am writing about her namesake, Anne is the main reason that I enrolled at the University of Chicago, and she has proven an unfailing mentor. Her collegial spirit and generous attention to my scholarly growth – well after the dissertation was complete – have been rare gifts that will not soon be forgotten. She has had a substantial impact on the shape of this book for which I will be ever grateful.

I am thankful to my parents, David and Virginia Anderson, as well as my mother-in-law, Patricia Brubaker, for their constant support of my work and music making, but I must single out the unique contribution of my mother to this study. As Latin teacher extraordinaire, she sat many hours with me and provided the helpful perspective of a classicist on the versified office texts with which I was working. Her expert command of the Latin language was invaluable and directly impacted more than a few areas of this study.

Finally, I owe the greatest thanks to my family for showing great patience and love as I compiled this book on St. Anne. My two beautiful children, Madison and Alex, have been astonishingly understanding about the time it took to complete this work. I am most grateful, however, to my wife, Julie, whose sacrifices I can never repay in my lifetime. She has been the most supportive spouse one could ask for and has shown an unwavering commitment to helping me succeed at work and at home. She alone afforded me the necessary time and resources to pursue this project, and it is to her that I dedicate this book.

Abbreviations and Conventions

AH   *Analecta hymnica medii aevi.* 55 vols. Ed. G. Dreves, C. Blume, H. Bannister. Leipzig, 1886–1922 (volume [dot] number is used to indicate the office, sequence, or hymn number, instead of page numbers).

AM   *Antiphonale monasticum pro diurnis horis.* Paris, 1934.

CAO   *Corpus antiphonalium officii.* 6 vols. Ed. René-Jean Hesbert. Rerum Ecclesiasticarum Documenta, Series maior, Fontes 7–12. Rome, 1963–79.

NG   *The New Grove Dictionary of Music and Musicians.* Second edition. 27 vols. Ed. Stanley Sadie. New York, 2001.

PL   *Patrologiae cursus completus: series latina.* 221 vols. Ed. J. P. Migne. Paris, 1844–79.

RISM   *Répertoire International de Sources Musicales.* Series A/I.

Abbreviations for most polyphonic manuscripts follow those given in the *Census-Catalogue of Manuscript Sources of Polyphonic Music 1400–1550*. 5 vols. Renaissance Manuscript Studies. Neuhausen-Stuttgart, 1979–88. Prints are given using the nomenclature from RISM Series B (*Répertoire International des Sources Musicales*).

The system of representing single musical pitches in this study will begin with capital letters for the lowest register, while the octave above will be lowercase letter names. Prime and double prime marks will be included for successive octaves. "Middle C" on the keyboard would be written c. The possible pitches on F ascending in octaves would be F, f, f′, and f″. Harmonies are listed simply as capital letters.

1 | Mary's Mother: Devotion, Politics, and Music

> Anna floret ut lilium
> In summi regis curia,
> Thronum adepta regium
> Cum immortali gloria,
> Inter matronas rutilans,
> Ut sol mundum illuminans.
>   (MR6, AH 25.19)
>
> Anne blossoms like a lily in the highest court of the king, having obtained the royal throne with immortal glory. Like the sun lighting the world, she is the one shining among mothers.

Anna floret ut lilium, the sixth Matins responsory from a widespread versified office for St. Anne, brings forth in song a rich variety of suggestive images for the intent listener. St. Anne, the apocryphal mother of the Virgin Mary, is celebrated through a series of comparisons that appropriates some of the vocabulary of Marian symbolism. Anne is first compared to a lily, widely understood as signifying the Virgin's undefiled purity. She is also situated allegorically within an imperial court, "having obtained the royal throne with immortal glory." This regal imagery co-opts another attribute of her illustrious daughter, who held the epithet "Queen of Heaven" (*Regina caeli*). The responsory closes by casting St. Anne as a beacon for mothers, reflective of her popular status as the "Mother's mother" (*Mater matris*). As is well known, she was a guiding light for women wishing to conceive and for those already with children, even surpassing her daughter to some extent as an intercessor for matrons. How did Mary's mother, a woman not mentioned in the New Testament, rise to this lofty status, on par with royalty and well suited to aid in maternity? This study presents several cases from the early fifteenth century to the early sixteenth century that demonstrate the value of musical devotion to St. Anne mainly by female nobles in some of the leading courts in Western Europe of that time. This inimitable Christian saint has received considerable scholarly attention over the past century, but the cultural embrace of her multifaceted character (whether as a wise mother or powerful progenetrix) has yet to be assessed through the medium of music. The survival of both plainchant and polyphony in her honor indicates that music was an essential component of the devotional life of the nobility and offered an important means of invoking – and indeed, interacting with – the mother of Mary. In focusing on the sonic expressions of devotion to St. Anne in elite court contexts, these cases not only illuminate new ways of understanding Christ's legendary grandmother, a figure known for her remarkable intercessory capacity, but also unveil the values that the saint offered to several unusually powerful noblewomen in this period.

In the history of the Latin Church, the fifteenth and early sixteenth centuries represent an intense period of sanctoral devotion, some of which can be attributed to a revived emphasis on salvation. Symptoms of the attention to individual deliverance can be seen at the close of the Hundred Years' War with the growth of clergy and mendicant orders, the rise of confraternities, the economics of indulgences, and the emergence of devotional aids such as the Rosary. These phenomena increased lay anxiety about redemption. Permeating society from the aristocracy to the peasantry, the saints – holy models of Christian living – kept the focus on salvation, providing supplicants valuable intercession with Christ to calm their worries about the hereafter. Saints' lives were retold in widely circulated legends, especially in Jacobus de Voragine's *Golden Legend* (*Legenda aurea*) from the mid-thirteenth century, an encyclopedia of saints and feasts that became one of the most broadly disseminated books of the late Middle Ages. Key episodes of saints' *vitae* were also the subjects of visual art. Their *historiae* were further highlighted in the celebration of the Divine Office, which set their lives in poetry and song. Works of polyphony in honor of saints, such as choral motets and themed settings of the Mass Ordinary, were more elaborate musical creations available to wealthy patrons and opened up avenues for imprinting saints' merits in the soundscape.[1] This period of high cultural awareness of soteriological matters gave rise to significant artistic production that served to strengthen the movement.[2]

As suggested by the floral and royal analogies presented here, St. Anne was a figure validated by association with her daughter Mary, whose role as the most powerful *Mediatrix* of Christianity is well known. Marian devotion gained considerable traction in the late Middle Ages, coinciding not just with the renewed emphasis on salvation but also with the establishment of purgatory, the unknown region of waiting where one's sins that had accumulated on earth could be expiated. Because of her sinlessness, Mary could naturally be called upon to help purify sinful lives, and composers played an important part in supplying patrons with bountiful chant and polyphony for the Virgin.[3] Believers thought that an appeal to the very source of Mary – her mother, Anne – could also help secure the redemption of human souls.

There were even more advantages to venerating Mary's mother. As scholarship has emphasized, St. Anne is polysemic, though her image was anchored by several key character attributes that defined her numerous intercessory capabilities. An impressive matriarch over Christ's extended family, which was known as the Holy Kinship, St. Anne was pivotal in establishing the virtuousness of marriage and the value of progeny.[4] As *Mater matris*, she was also tapped as an intercessor promoting fertility and aiding in the dangerous experience of childbirth. Given Anne's role as nurturer of the Virgin Mary, Christians further revered her as a master teacher, an advocate for female literacy in particular. Although she appealed to supplicants of all social ranks, St. Anne had a physical connection to Mary and to Christ, as well as to generations of distinguished kin, and this network of relationships attracted the attention of the nobility, whose claims to magnificent antecedents defined their place in society. It is these devotees of St. Anne (especially queens and duchesses) who could request – or were showered with – visual and aural works in honor of the "grandmother saint" to help shape their own images as rulers, in addition to earning her protection.

In *The Autumn of the Middle Ages*, Johan Huizinga observed that late medieval art was essentially functional in nature.[5] The idea of a masterpiece, a piece of "art for art's sake," was completely foreign to both the artist or composer and his noble patron. Art instead had a job to perform, one that shifted according to circumstances. This principle would be easily grasped if the texts of the music for St. Anne to be studied simply announced their functional intent. But such music does not exist. What remains instead is a body of liturgical music in commemoration of the *Mater matris*, some of it with detectable political undertones. By focusing on this music for St. Anne prepared for some of the most important sovereigns of Renaissance Europe (many of them female), the reader will witness a wide range of sacred genres under consideration. Motets and more extensive polyphonic settings of the Mass Ordinary, along with newly composed plainchant for the Mass and Office, are all represented in this study. These genres are seemingly bound together by their role in the liturgy, the work or duty of the Church in the service of God; however, such works also offer a glimpse of a devotional atmosphere that may also construct or reinforce noble identities in the declamation of rich texts.[6]

Where are the politics in music geared for liturgies? Importantly, the sonic works for St. Anne were both collected by noble houses and sent as gifts to courts to curry favor, usually in lavish manuscripts.[7] The music was likely experienced in private liturgies, but it is also possible that these works simply lay in "coffee table"-type volumes for display, still efficacious for fashioning regal self-images. In possession of music for St. Anne, rulers established their own identities by associating with the powerful mother of Mary. The function of the sacred music identified in this study, I argue, transcended its obvious role in the liturgy. It was an emblem of prestige that reflected the values and ambitions of its patrons or dedicatees, mostly women in uncharacteristically powerful positions.

As Roman Hankeln has written, the celebration of the liturgy, particularly services in honor of saints, has typically mediated between religious ideals on one hand and historical reality on the other.[8] The components of the liturgy that achieved this balance (namely, the variable texts and music) echoed human values and could have political weight, no matter how veiled that weight may be. Of course, nearly all of the items in the Mass and Office were sung, which draws attention to the multitude of chanted texts and their meaning for the recipients of music for St. Anne. Since the fourteenth century, motets in particular – not exclusively bound to the liturgy – developed a reputation as the genre of choice for ceremony and even for political statements, a feature that was carried through at least to the end of the sixteenth century in the music of William Byrd, whose politically tinged motets are well known.[9] Over the course of the fifteenth century, the so-called cyclic mass, which draws together the texts of the Mass Ordinary into polyphony, became the most ambitious form of composition for cultural elites, eclipsing the motet as the "highest" genre of sacred music.[10] Plainchant too, as will be shown, cannot be dismissed as incapable of performing cultural work toward political ends, despite (or conversely, because of) its pervasiveness and ancient roots.

As much as secular works, sacred music participated in the formation of identities for patrons, sometimes mapping their personal and political concerns onto pieces as communicated by composers. This added subjective layer of meaning and the reception of the music (whether performed in private or in public) intensified what some may perceive as a humble act of devotion. As difficult as it may be for the modern mind to admit politics into the sacrality of the liturgical ritual, this book demonstrates that the boundary between ecclesiastical conventions and secular wishes was as porous as ever in the fifteenth and early sixteenth centuries. It is in this light that the case studies ahead must be viewed to unlock fully the perceived potency of Mary's mother in the soundscape of Western Europe's noble courts. This study endeavors not only to determine those aspects of St. Anne's character that were being proclaimed in the sound world, but also to address the impact of this music on the rulers who requested, sent, received, or experienced it. Only a few of the nobles under consideration were women named Anne, thus suggesting that devotion to Mary's mother was not as simple as an invocation of a patron namesake.[11] The political value surrounding St. Anne undoubtedly extended into the sound world as a complement to – or sometimes in conflict with – the impressions from visual culture and devotional life. In addition to a wide social view of sacred musical settings, materials of their construction will also be investigated, often shedding light on their political capacity, whether it is a musical gesture in plainchant underlining a particular word, a freshly identified cantus firmus that brings a new interpretive dimension to a Mass Ordinary setting, or the network of associations unfolded in a polytextual motet.

St. Anne and Her Family

The Gospels reveal very little about the life of the Virgin Mary, and so it comes as no surprise that her mother, Anne, receives no mention in canonical sources. In this way, Mary's mother survives as a "constructed" saint, as nothing was officially known about Jesus' historical grandmother. However, some details of the life of Anne and her husband Joachim are documented in the second-century *Protoevangelium of James*, which enjoyed widespread circulation in the early Christian world. Responding to the silence in the New Testament on the subject of Mary's childhood, this apocryphal account supplied Christians with minutiae on the Virgin's early life.[12]

According to the *Protoevangelium*, Anne and Joachim, a rich man from the tribe of Judah, lived for many years without offspring and made a vow to God that if granted progeny, they would dedicate the child to the service of God. The righteous Anne and Joachim gave generously of their possessions, keeping only one-third of their wealth for themselves. Another third of their assets was given to the poor, and the remaining third was earmarked for the temple and its servants. While Joachim was at the temple one day, a priest criticized him about his childless marriage. Reflecting contemporary associations of fertility with heavenly approbation, the priest argued that a sterile man should not be in the company of those blessed with children. The humiliated Joachim fled to the desert. There, he was visited by an angel, who announced that his wife would bear an extraordinary daughter named Mary. The same angel then appeared to Anne and proclaimed the glorious news. Anne and Joachim reunited at the Golden Gate of Jerusalem and returned home in anticipation of the divine promise to receive Mary.[13] This legend of Mary's parents remained strongly in the Christian collective memory for at least the next millennium and a half, and the figures of Anne and Joachim, if not the particulars of the story, have survived to the present day. Places like Sainte-Anne-de-Beaupré, a major pilgrimage site in Quebec, Canada, continue to sustain the legend around St. Anne and testify to the power of her intercession.

The chronicle of Anne in the *Protoevangelium* follows a common Hebrew narrative of a barren woman who pledges a long-awaited child to God and then miraculously conceives at an old age. The account most closely resembles the Old Testament story of Hannah, the mother of Samuel, who issued a plea to God at the temple and conceived after remaining childless for a long time. The orthographical and aural proximity in the name (Anna/Hannah) strengthens the analogy between the two mothers. Anne's circumstances may also be compared to those of Sarah, the wife of Abraham from the book of Genesis.[14] The legend also finds a parallel in the New Testament: the angel's announcement of the birth of John the Baptist to Elizabeth and Zechariah echoes the angel's declaration of the conception of Mary to Anne and Joachim.[15] As shown later in this study, the modeling of Anne on the ancient Hebrew mothers was not only reinforced in the texts of musical works but also provided noblewomen – and men – with a potent social use for the saint.

Having no basis in Scripture, the apocryphal life of St. Anne as transmitted in the *Protoevangelium of James* was unacceptable to the Church Fathers, and their disapproval delayed Anne's immediate acceptance into the sanctoral canon.[16] Amid the slow and uneven reception history of St. Anne in the early Middle Ages, one of the Church Fathers, Jerome, was indirectly drawn into the apocryphal legend in his writings on Mary's lineage, specifically in his explanation of the "brothers" of Christ named in the gospels of Mark and Matthew.[17] Jerome assumed Jesus' "brothers" to be the sons of Mary's sisters (i.e., his cousins), and not the sons of Joseph by some other woman.[18] The ninth-century biblical commentator Haimo of Auxerre (d. 853) went a step further, connecting these presumed sisters with women named "Mary" mentioned in the Gospels at the scenes of the sepulcher and the resurrection.[19] His theory gave rise to Anne's "three marriages" (known as the *trinubium*), and the saint was henceforth held up as the mother of the "Three Marys." According to the popular trinubium belief, Joachim must have died soon after Mary was born, so that Anne – already eighty years old in some versions of the legend – could marry her second husband, Cleophas (sometimes called Jacob or James), by whom she bore "Mary Cleophas" (also known as "Mary Iacobi"). Anne then married a third man, named Salome, following Cleophas's death. By Salome, she bore the third Mary, known as "Mary Salome." From these three Marys, the theory continued, came Jesus and all six of his "brothers" or cousins named in the Gospels. James the Less, Joseph the Just, Simon, and Jude were positioned as the sons of Mary Cleophas, who had married a man named Alphaeus, while James the Greater and John the Evangelist were said to be the sons of Mary Salome, who had married Zebedee. In this way, Anne became the grandmother to some of Jesus' most prominent disciples, all members of the Holy Kinship.

Depictions of the Holy Kinship were common in northern continental Europe in the fifteenth century. A book of hours from Rouen dated around the turn of the sixteenth century shows the core members of the Kinship (Figure 1.1). St. Anne and the Virgin Mary (with the Christ Child) occupy a central position flanked by Mary's two sisters, who hold open books. Four men stand behind the throne, their undifferentiated representation – what Pamela Sheingorn has aptly described as an "awkward clump" – typical of the male figures in Holy Kinship iconography.[20] Presumably, the background features an arrangement of Joachim and the husbands of the Three Marys (Joseph, Alphaeus, and Zebedee), though technically one or more of the men could instead be a husband of Anne (Cleophas or Salome).

The theory of the trinubium took some time getting off the ground. Thomas Aquinas (1225–74) for one rejected the idea of Anne's three marriages.[21] But Jacobus de Voragine secured St. Anne and the "Three Marys" in the pantheon of holy figures in his *Golden Legend*. By the thirteenth century, a tradition had developed associating St. Anne with Mary's early childhood, and Voragine followed suit, providing her legend as part of his entry on the Nativity of Mary (September 8). Reflecting a cultural appetite for the lineage of the Virgin in particular, he offered a mnemonic for the reader to keep track of the Holy Kinship, of which Anne and Mary were crucial members:

Anna solet dici tres concepisse Marias,
Quas genuere viri Joachim, Cleophas, Salomeque.
Has duxere viri Joseph, Alpheus, Zebedeus.
Prima parit Christum, Jacobum secunda minorem,
Et Joseph justum peperit cum Simone Judam,
Tertia majorem Jacobum volucremque Joannem.[22]

Anne is usually said to have conceived three Marys, / Whom her husbands Joachim, Cleophas, and Salome begot. / The Marys were taken in marriage by Joseph, Alpheus, and Zebedee. / The first Mary bore Christ, the second bore James the Less, / Joseph the Just with Simon and Jude, / the third, James the Greater and John the Wingèd [the Evangelist].

Figure 1.1 *The Holy Kinship* from an Anonymous Book of Hours (Rouen, Use of Paris), ca. 1500. Photo: The Pierpont Morgan Library, New York. MS M.175, fol. 17v. Purchased by J. Pierpont Morgan (1837-1913) in 1902.

In addition to his validation of Jesus' extended family in the *aide-mémoire*, Voragine took a bolder step of criticizing the evangelists Matthew and Luke for tracing Jesus' lineage through Joseph instead of Mary.[23] The *Golden Legend* did much to raise the status of St. Anne, and she would be celebrated with unusually fervent devotion during the three centuries following.

The details of Anne's legend also circulated in *vitae* across the continent, particularly in the Low Countries and in Germany during the fifteenth century. As believers eagerly soaked up as many particulars on the early life of Mary as possible, the legends accrued new layers of biographical trivia related to St. Anne. In some late fifteenth-century *vitae*, Anne was given a mother named Emerentia, a father called Stollanus, and a sister known as Esmeria.[24] The creation of these and other ancestors in this period should give an indication of the fascination not just with the saints but specifically with those related to Christ and his mother. As the genetrix of Jesus and his holy relatives, Anne earned a reputation that extended far beyond that of a local or regional saint. And while veneration of Mary's mother took more than a millennium to gain momentum in Western Europe, the value of the "Mother's mother" in the distinguished company of the Holy Kinship spread rapidly throughout the Latin West after the twelfth century. Urban VI's official papal approval of her feast day (July 26) in 1378 recognized formally the value of Jesus' grandmother whom Christians had been celebrating for years.[25]

Intercessory Flexibility

It is said that one can't be all things to all people, but Christians deployed St. Anne in a surprisingly broad devotional scope in the late Middle Ages and the early modern period. Her plasticity as a saint with powerful and wide-ranging intercessory capabilities made her an attractive subject of veneration in this period, particularly for women. For more than two decades, visual representation of St. Anne has drawn the attention of scholars, especially those attuned to issues of cultural meaning and shifting reception contexts for the saint. Her principal areas of intercession, right down to her assistance with salvation itself, derived from the intersection of her apocryphal life story and the social dynamics of the fifteenth and early sixteenth centuries. Further, she served gendered and nongendered functions alike, well beyond the warm, matronly role that many Catholics assign to her today. A review of St. Anne's polysemic nature and her functional value in society will lay the foundation for an investigation into her ability to convey political power.

The central event in the life of Mary's mother is of course the conception and birth of her daughter. The topic of St. Anne often calls to mind the doctrine of the Immaculate Conception in particular, a raging debate that peaked in the mid-fifteenth century concerning the precise moment of the Virgin's attainment of sinlessness in her mother's womb (a subject addressed more fully in Chapter 4). Recent scholarship, however, has downplayed a long-held view that St. Anne's cult was a direct product of the late medieval controversy over Mary's purity.[26] Rather, studies have emphasized that St. Anne had a hand in the "humanation" or "enfleshing" of Christ, because she gave birth to his earthly mother. While Christ's divinity came from God the Father, he owed his physical presence to his mother, Mary, who in turn owed her existence to her mother (and so on). St. Anne, as much as the Virgin Mary, was a reminder of the corporeality of Christ, the "Word made flesh." In addition to his divine qualities, Christ's bodily nature – a "low Christology," as modern theologians are wont to call his humanity – was a prevalent theme in visual art of the late Middle Ages and the Renaissance, as demonstrated by the countless Renaissance paintings in which Jesus touches his genitals.[27] The imagery of the Holy Kinship also went far to capture Jesus' connection to humanity, his grandmother often playing the dominant figure in the "family portrait."

Jesus' physicality and the value of his matrilineage achieved through St. Anne combine in a single iconographic representation known as the St. Anne Trinitarian. Often taking the form of a handheld statue especially popular in the Rhineland, this image features St. Anne holding miniaturized versions of her daughter and grandson in her arms or lap. The German equivalent *Anna Selbdritt* (literally "Anne, herself the third") suggests a subsidiary role for Anne compared to the core figures of Mary and Jesus.[28] But the generally oversized mother of Mary is clearly the focal point of the image, ironically making her two glorious descendants seem subordinate to her powerful maternity (Figure 1.2).[29] The Anglicized "St. Anne Trinitarian" is a more evenhanded term for this image, though it too fails to capture the idea that Mary and Jesus appear quite diminished in size. The divinity of Christ is hardly in evidence in the St. Anne Trinitarian iconography; rather, the viewer would be attracted to St. Anne as the corporeal source of the Virgin and her most holy son. Together with the Holy Kinship imagery, the St. Anne Trinitarian illustrates the "correction" of Christ's lineage that was issued in Voragine's *Golden Legend*. The image was emblematic of

Figure 1.2 Brabant, Mechelen, Anna-te-Drieen, 1515–24. Museum Catharijneconvent, Utrecht.

the feminine "power" to produce flesh, potentially resonant with (female) sovereigns in their quests to sustain precious dynasties.

St. Anne's miraculous conception of the Virgin and her role as progenetrix of a glorious lineage made her a logical intercessor to aid Christian women in fertility and in the act of childbirth, especially given the high rate of infant mortality.[30] The creation of such a mediator reflected a cultural need for assurance in matters of fertility and delivery. Mothers-to-be fervently venerated St. Anne along with St. Margaret. In the city of Apt in

Provence (a center of the saint's veneration), the association between St. Anne and women's fertility was enacted in ritual. In the city's cathedral dedicated to the grandmother saint, women placed grapes in the bosom of a statue of St. Anne as a sign of her fruitfulness (and in hopes of their own fecundity); they also flocked to the cathedral to rock a special cradle, which was supposed to promote conception among infertile women.[31] The appeals to the fertility powers of Mary's mother were also in full force in the Rhineland city of Düren. Not only was it a popular destination for pilgrims seeking the precious relics of the saint, but women wishing to become pregnant also wore "Anne girdles" around their waists.[32] These are just a few examples of the kinds of charms and rituals that produced women's physical interaction with St. Anne.

Anne's oversight of women did not cease once the children of these expectant mothers were born.[33] Early modern Christians looked to Mary's mother in particular as a model for raising a family. Again, her apocryphal biography furnished the materials of devotion. Anne was obviously a key player in the childhood of the Virgin Mary, and thus she was absorbed as a protectress of families, especially valuable for the upbringing of children. To some extent, the St. Anne Trinitarian image would have registered this aspect of Anne's patronage, but it was the depiction known as the "Education of the Virgin" that directly showcased Anne in her daughter's formative years (Figure 1.3). An image revealing the saint's tutorial abilities, the "Education" scene features Mary's mother engaged with Mary, who may be shown either as a young child or a teenager. In the scene, Mary usually holds open a book (presumably the psalter or a book of hours) and is sometimes seen pointing to the volume to convey a sense of curiosity for learning. Remember from Figure 1.1 that Mary's sisters held open books, an extension of the core "Education" image, providing another layer of meaning to the popular Holy Kinship icon.

As Pamela Sheingorn and Miriam Gill have independently argued, the iconography of the "Education of the Virgin" did much more than inspire mothers to instruct their children just as Anne taught Mary: the imagery seems to have been a force to promote literacy among women. As it is today, literacy was a form of power during the late Middle Ages and the Renaissance, and women equipped with the ability to understand written texts – often the nobles of society – could hold substantial intellectual, political, or possibly spiritual advantages in their lives in an otherwise androcentric world. Despite the strong emphasis on females and the campaign for the written word, the "Education" scenes were not widespread and could be found mainly in England. Scholars have explained that the

Figure 1.3 Choir breviary. The Bodleian Libraries, University of Oxford, MS Laud Misc. 93, fol. 105v.

absence of Jesus in the image might have caused the constricted reception of the "Education of the Virgin."[34] That St. Anne imparted great wisdom, however, was a facet of her sanctity that northern European humanists took up and extolled in the late fifteenth and early sixteenth centuries, especially those involved in the formation of urban confraternities honoring St. Anne (*Annenbruderschaften*). To humanists such as Rudolf Agricola, Arnold Bostius, and Cornelius Aurelius, the saint represented a classic mother-goddess (*Magna mater*) and wise teacher, two persuasive attributes for humanists in pursuit of ancient wisdom.[35]

Rounding out St. Anne's role in family life is her easily overlooked patronage of the institution of marriage. Virgin saints such as Barbara, Margaret, and Katherine had long been revered as models for Christian women, but during the later Middle Ages, the degree to which women should emulate the lives of these saints came into question, as marriage steadily accrued a positive, unsullied connotation for one's course of life. A particular emphasis on the sacramental definition of marriage (conjugal love as a sign of God's grace) by twelfth-century theologians, together with the rise of the urban patriciate, played no small role in the shifting perceptions of the institution. Yet again, the biography of the thrice-married St. Anne emphatically drives this point home. Her story demonstrated that living a married life was no longer incompatible with living a holy life; she made the once inferior life of marriage as attractive as the life of chastity. It was a thoroughly realistic paradigm for lay women, at least more realistic than her daughter's marriage, because Mary miraculously remained a virgin with Joseph in the conception of Jesus. Along with saints such as Birgitta of Sweden and Elizabeth of Hungary, Anne became one of the venerable "marrying saints," a key protectress of the sacrality of matrimony.[36]

According to the legend of the trinubium, Anne witnessed the deaths of two husbands to enable her three marriages. Not surprisingly, she could be called on to comfort widows following the death of a spouse. Here too, her biography was in step with cultural norms. Despite the perils of childbirth that awaited medieval and early modern women, husbands typically predeceased their wives, by about a decade on average.[37] As a patroness of widows, Anne truly spanned the full arc of a woman's life to a degree that her own daughter could not achieve. One would indeed be hard-pressed to identify a saint who so closely mirrored the experiences of contemporary women and yet ran against the inherited (patriarchal) ideals of feminine sanctity. From a loyal wife and mother to a teacher and widow, St. Anne reflected several core values of the period, seeming to fit the bill at every turn and bringing a sense of empowerment to these sociocultural roles.

And this was just for women. As scholars have been quick to point out, Mary's mother was available to serve nongendered roles in lay devotional life at all levels of society. The embrace of St. Anne by humanists and confraternities has already been mentioned. By the late fifteenth century, more than two hundred urban confraternities in the saint's honor were scattered across northern and central Europe.[38] These confraternities often welcomed men and women alike, especially those who were capable of charitable giving, and it was in these institutions that anxiety regarding salvation was cultivated. In these contexts, St. Anne, as progenetrix of the Holy Kinship with a fleshly connection to Mary and her son, held tremendous sway in interceding for these Christians of the merchant and higher classes. Virginia Nixon's monograph on the veneration of St. Anne in the late fifteenth and early sixteenth centuries emphasizes how religious guilds (particularly in the Rhineland) as well as cultural elites (e.g., clerics and humanists) promoted the salvational power of St. Anne, effectively controlling lay piety.[39]

Mary's peerless mother, the hope of salvation, and the saint's long list of quotidian areas of intercession had economic implications. As confraternities reaped enormous benefits from the saint's patronage, churches took St. Anne as their dedicatee, and countless side chapels emerged in her honor during the late Middle Ages and the Renaissance. All were poised to collect endowments and special contributions in honor of the potent mother of Mary. Cities with institutions that hosted relics of the *Mater matris* could also expect economic boons. That some interpreted the legend of Anne as a lesson in financial security and well-being did nothing to slow the devotional deluge. Joachim's wealth was noted in the *Protoevangelium of James*, but another important detail – reiterated often in the Divine Offices for St. Anne – involves the couple's tripartite distribution of their assets (also mentioned earlier) as dutiful servants of God. This purported disbursement of Anne and Joachim's possessions seems to have fueled the notion that St. Anne was to be associated with wealth and could suddenly make one rich.[40]

St. Anne's fashionability as a saint touched almost every aspect of early modern culture, from issues specific to women to aiding in the salvation of souls. As the mother of the most important mother in the Christian faith, St. Anne interceded foremost on behalf of matriarchs, regardless of social rank, from the moment of conception through the raising of a family. As a rare married saint, she conferred legitimacy on the institution of marriage, which, until that time, bore a blemished reputation for those seeking the spiritual high road. Anne's legendary fruitfulness at an old age also made her a patron saint of woodworkers (trees bearing fruit) and grape growers, as well as a protectress from drought. Seamstresses further revered the saint for her domestic reputation.[41] St. Anne's fanciful biography thus proved to have distinct applications to life during this period.

While one can account for these broad areas of intercession, a profitable direction in studies of St. Anne concerns her appropriation by sovereigns for political purposes. As much as queens, kings, and nobles reached out to the grandmother saint to resolve everyday concerns, several cases reveal how the ruling class in Europe strategically petitioned Mary's mother as a sign of its dynastic ambitions. A brief examination of how politics and devotion intersected in the name of St. Anne is in order. The political repurposing of St. Anne will prepare an investigation into the music composed and compiled in honor of Mary's mother.

The Politics of Devotion to St. Anne

With her intercessory capabilities extending to seamstresses and woodworkers, St. Anne – not unlike other saints – was easily assumed into secular life, which throughout the late Middle Ages and the Renaissance was itself difficult to demarcate from purely sacred experiences. Indeed, it would be anachronistic to try and separate the two, as the distinction between sacred and secular was not articulated during these historical periods and was only recognized as a dichotomy after the seventeenth century.[42] The invocation of the holy in the service of expressly political displays was commonplace by the fifteenth century but had roots in prior centuries. Consider the coronation tradition of the *laudes regiae* ("the king's praises"), the royal acclamations used at a French monarch's installation mass dating back to Carolingian times. The *laudes* began with a chanted trifold declamation: *Christus vincit, Christus regnat, Christus imperat* ("Christ conquers, Christ reigns, Christ rules"). Then in the "litany" section of the acclamations, the ceremony called for the king's name to be inserted into the roll call of saints. The orchestrated intersection of the hallowed liturgy with the majesty surrounding the earthly ruler's coronation is both obvious and inseparable. As defender of the French people, the monarch was implicitly the guardian of their faith. He was expected to make good on the title "most Christian King" (*Rex christianissimus*), a formal recognition that the sovereign had a sacerdotal or ministerial role as much as a governing one. His anointing at the royal inauguration further recalled ancient Hebrew ceremonies of kingship and blurred traditionally sacred ritual acts with political theater.[43]

While there is nothing like the *laudes regiae* in the surviving music for St. Anne, there are still ways to witness a political hue in devotional music in the saint's honor.

Saints broadly mediated between religion and society, sometimes with political force. They were often local heroes who rose to canonical status by their intrepid actions. As holy figures who were considered physically present in their remains, saints' relics were constantly available to Christians and could be acquired by nobles for prestige or even political (and certainly economic) gain. In addition to relics, patron saints of cities protected their people, whose ambitions for the locality rested in the domain of their holy defender. As it concerns St. Anne, the city of Florence is a case in point. Here, the grandmother saint was in fact commemorated for entirely political (and arbitrary) reasons. On St. Anne's then unofficial feast day (July 26) in 1343, a great revolt by the citizens of Florence saw the overthrow of Walter VI of Brienne, a military leader in the city who was championed by the nobility. This defeat began an important period of republicanism in Florentine culture, causing St. Anne, not normally a subject of intense devotion in Italy, to be venerated as a de facto custodian of the city, second to its eminent patron saint, John the Baptist. From that decisive day through at least the sixteenth century, July 26 was an official public holiday in the city, considered by one chronicler to be on par with the celebration of Easter.[44]

While the Florentine veneration of St. Anne was an accident of history, the case for mixing politics with Mary's mother grows more simply out of the saint's apocryphal biography, a story of a woman on whom God bestowed momentous privileges. Monarchs and nobles commonly called upon Mary's mother to aid with fertility, a point that does not separate them from their subjects. But it was the perception that St. Anne presided over the noblest of dynasties – the Holy Kinship – that often encouraged the high-ranking members of society to adopt her into their devotional lives. In short, the grandmother saint provided noble supplicants with precious access to an unrivaled lineage, in the process conferring her "royal" attributes on rulers who sought her protection. For any aristocratic family, the conception of a male heir defined the success of a dynasty, and the notion of the Holy Kinship did much to highlight the production of magnificent descendants.[45]

A family portrait of the Habsburgs that Bernhard Strigel painted for Maximilian I in 1515 clearly demonstrates the power of association with the Holy Kinship (Figure 1.4). In addition to depicting the members of the family, the court painter made clear allusions to figures of the Holy

Figure 1.4 Bernhard Strigel, *Portrait of Maximilian and His Family*, 1515. Kunsthistorisches Museum, Vienna.

Kinship. An inscription on the portrait curiously identifies the Holy Roman Emperor Maximilian – the central figure of the family – as "Cleophas" and his wife, Mary of Burgundy, as "Mary" (Cleophas), allegorical appellations that actually confuse the analogy within the Holy Kinship. (Cleophas was said to be the second husband of Anne, not a husband of Mary. Recall that Mary Cleophas was the purported daughter of Anne and Cleophas.) Strigel further provided analogical names for Maximilian's progeny, including the grandchildren (and future emperors) Charles and Ferdinand, discussed in the course of this book.[46] None of these epithets of course would have been possible without the grandmother St. Anne, who is strongly implied as hovering over these genealogical allegories. Strigel unmistakably situated Maximilian and his family as honorable descendants of Mary's mother, indeed as members of a privileged heritage.

Representing a physical connection to Jesus and Mary, St. Anne played an unambiguous role as the Holy Kinship's progenetrix. She offered a secure model and untouchable space for noble women (and men) to pursue the goals of a dynasty with the help of a figure who radiated the merits of matrilineage and forged a new archetype for feminine sanctity. Who better to call on to oversee a ruling family than the woman who not only conceived miraculously like her daughter and matrons of the Old Testament but also powerfully presided over an extended family of unparalleled progeny? As much as, if not more than, the Virgin Mary, St. Anne was one to relieve dynastic anxieties that consumed sovereigns especially in fifteenth- and early sixteenth-century Europe. The value of noble lineage, an idea suggested in the image of the Holy Kinship, may also spring from heightened attention to demonstrating ancestry and proving kinship in the late Middle Ages. As R. Howard Bloch has explained, aristocrats in particular sought to prove their long and distinguished heritage as a sign of their nobility.[47]

To be sure, the exploration of genealogy was entangled in changes to the institution of marriage. In the early and central Middle Ages, marriages between closely related kin ensured that property stayed with a given family. The church, however, discouraged this practice, instead advocating "exogamy," or marriage outside of one's family. Marriage between first cousins or closer blood relatives was considered a violation of this premise. The Fourth Lateran Council (1215) formalized this position, although enforcing the decree would remain an ongoing problem, especially in rural areas.[48] The increasing pressure to substantiate genealogical relationships before marriage thus brought an increased awareness of kinship, with nobility often seeking relatives to preserve dynastic bloodlines. Family continuity was essential at all costs, usually to prevent the passing of a title to another ruling family or branch. As musical artifacts for a variety of Western European sovereigns show, poets and composers participated in this social phenomenon by going to some lengths to establish St. Anne as a woman with an illustrious pedigree.

Noble devotees of St. Anne were given precious access not just to the ancient heritage of the faith, but specifically to a lineage that was both royal and priestly at the same time. These assets were further political insurance for aristocrats who aimed to demonstrate their prestige. The claim to regal and sacerdotal ancestry stems from commentary traditions surrounding the Nativity of the Virgin Mary. Already a feast bound up with Mary's lineage from the Carolingian era, the Virgin's nativity commemoration received a strong boost in the early eleventh century from Fulbert, a bishop of Chartres, who propagated the view that Mary synthesized two critical strands of lineage from the Old Testament – a royal one from the house of David (of Abrahamic descent) and a priestly one from the house of Levi. According to Fulbert's exegesis, these distinct lines of heritage uniquely converged in the familiar image of the "rod of Jesse" (*stirps Iesse*), an idea that was transmitted in offices for the feast of the Nativity of Mary in Chartres.[49] The impact of these strengthened filial perceptions was felt in later centuries in the versified offices for St. Anne, which grew out of the Nativity offices. Just one generation away from Mary, St. Anne conveniently rode the coattails of her daughter's outstanding heritage. Virginia Nixon has noted a German office for St. Anne that described the saint's royal and priestly lineage, but more incisive proof can be found in at least four different offices for Mary's mother, which contain phrases linking St. Anne directly to the precious heritage of Jesse (e.g., *virga Iesse, stirps Iesse,* and *Iesse plantula*).[50] The political utility of a figure with access to a doubly impressive royal and priestly heritage was no doubt attractive to sovereigns of the late Middle Ages and the Renaissance.

Politics in Music for Mary's Mother

This study seeks to chart the political force of the *Mater matris* through the medium of music, in forms ranging from the simplest of plainchants to opulent settings of the Mass Ordinary inspired and underpinned by melodies for St. Anne. As the preceding pages have suggested, the past century of scholarship has brought unusually high interest in explaining the significance of St. Anne during the late Middle Ages and the Renaissance; however, it has been art historians who have dominated these studies of cultural expression to the saint. At the same time, this is not the first investigation to make mention of Mary's mother in music. Paul-Victor Charland was the first to include the texts of the Divine Office in his study of devotion to St. Anne, extracting examples of the hymns, sequences, and rhymed offices from *Analecta Hymnica* (AH) and categorizing the musical output by monastic order and region. He did not attempt, however, to synthesize and comment on the repertory as a whole, nor is there mention of the music that was set to these texts.[51]

Research on musical works honoring St. Anne has also appeared, though in contexts not explicitly including Mary's mother. For instance, Stephen Bonime's archival study of repertory and musicians at the court of Anne of Brittany demonstrates an appeal to Mary's mother in Jean Mouton's motet *Celeste beneficium*, possibly in thanksgiving for the conception of what would become her second surviving child, Renée of France.[52] (This motet will be examined more thoroughly in Chapter 5.) Working on a later period, Robert Kendrick also noted that Barbara Strozzi's motet *Mater Anna, quisquae personat* for solo soprano reflects not just the patron saint of the work's dedicatee (Anna de' Medici), but also perhaps the archduchess's devotion to the saint in light of her miscarriages, stillbirths, and future efforts to produce an heir at a relatively advanced age for motherhood.[53] No broader study has accounted for the social function of the music written for the grandmother saint. This investigation explores for the first time the breadth of meanings and uses of St. Anne specifically in music destined for fifteenth- and early sixteenth-century nobles for political as much as devotional ends.

A complete set of plainchants from a versified office for St. Anne is the center of investigation in Chapter 2. These chants for Mary's mother were a product of the court of King Janus I in Cyprus of French Lusignan descent, and the early history of this office, which has eluded scholars, will be brought to light. More important, the potential meaning of this music, based on a close reading of the office texts, will be explored from multiple perspectives. Indeed, this office, which is transmitted in the so-called Turin Codex (Torino, Biblioteca nazionale, MS J.II.9), would have been encountered by nobles in contrasting circumstances. This source is filled with sacred and secular music to be enjoyed by any court and represents one of the central collections of music from the early fifteenth century because of its comprehensive scope. The compiler of the Turin Codex prominently placed the office of St. Anne in the first fascicle of the manuscript along with an office for St. Hilarion. The extensive chants for St. Anne await interpretation as an expression of dynastic greatness and the promise of offspring in more than one courtly context, namely the Lusignan court on the island of Cyprus (where the music was heard in an early stage), the Avogadro family of Brescia (for whom the Turin Codex was prepared), and the court of Savoy (the apparent final destination of the manuscript).

The same court of Savoy returns to view some three generations later, in connection with musical devotion to St. Anne by Margaret of Austria (1480–1530), the subject of Chapter 3. As a child, Margaret was sent to the French royal court to be reared by Anne de Beaujeu (i.e., Anne of France) in preparation for marriage to Charles VIII. It was here that Margaret encountered a boy from the Savoyard court (Philibert II), who in time would become the last of her three husbands. Anne of France exposed Margaret to the power of St. Anne at the French court, but it was not until the untimely death of her husband Philibert that Margaret – as sole regent of the Netherlands – would have begun to flee to the *Mater matris* for wisdom and comfort. At her court in Mechelen, likely between the years 1508 and 1514, Margaret received a polyphonic mass for St. Anne from her esteemed court composer, Pierre de La Rue. In each of its five movements, the mass paraphrases a heretofore unknown melody to be identified as a plainchant from an office for St. Anne. The full text set to this melody seems to encode a message about how Margaret understood St. Anne and how the mother of Mary could reenergize the regent's image. Though her profile as a twice-widowed noble in many ways mirrors the legend of St. Anne, the text of the underlying chant, along with other biographical and artistic evidence, suggests that Margaret wanted to portray her "eligibility" for marriage to the political elite of Western Europe.

Margaret's court eventually sent La Rue's mass in honor of St. Anne to Frederick the Wise, Elector of Saxony and famous protector of Martin Luther. Chapter 4 considers the function of this mass and several other pieces of polyphonic music for St. Anne in the context of the Castle Church of Wittenberg between approximately 1507 and 1519. The Castle Church was the elector's signature institution, one that quickly developed into a major center of Christian devotion in Western Europe during the early sixteenth century. In conjunction with art historical evidence, this chapter shows that St. Anne was revered for her versatility and diplomacy, a direct reflection of the elector himself, known for his evenhandedness as a peace negotiator within the Holy Roman Empire. St. Anne also appealed to both the humanistic and devotional pursuits of the citizens of Wittenberg, and her domestic family-centric qualities reinforced her sanctity in the early stages of the Reformation that occurred in that city.

The French court – the site of Margaret of Austria's first exposure to St. Anne – forms the backdrop to Chapter 5. This chapter highlights a single motet (*Celeste beneficium*) in honor of Mary's mother, written by French royal composer Jean Mouton probably between 1508 and 1511. Dedicated to Anne of Brittany, the twice-crowned queen of France, *Celeste beneficium* served as no ordinary piece of liturgical music. Instead, this motet acted foremost as a devotional vehicle encouraging fertility and progeny for the queen and her second husband, Louis XII, who failed to produce an heir.

The queen's veneration of St. Anne will be shown in the wider context of her devotional life (particularly in prayer books), and the political force of Mouton's motet for the grandmother saint is all but confirmed by the presence of a second related motet (possibly by Mouton's colleague), with which *Celeste beneficium* was sometimes paired in extant sources.

Between 1528 and 1534, Mouton's *Celeste beneficium* reappeared in a set of partbooks, known as the "Palatini Partbooks" (Vatican City, Bibliotecha Apostolica Vaticana, MSS Palatini Latini 1976–9). These books were compiled by the famous Alamire scriptorium for Queen Anne of Bohemia and Hungary (1503–47), whose husband was the future Holy Roman Emperor Ferdinand I of Habsburg descent. In this extraordinary collection of music, *Celeste beneficium* was grouped together with other motets expressly for St. Anne, and this section was significantly positioned at the beginning of each of the partbooks. Chapter 6 features the first formal evaluation of this group of works as a whole and proposes how these pieces of music for St. Anne – three of them anonymous – would have resonated with the Austrian Habsburgs in general and with this "other" Queen Anne in particular. Because Anne of Bohemia and Hungary was already blessed with children before the partbooks arrived, the motets for St. Anne could not have functioned as a fertility appeal as in the case of Anne of Brittany; instead, they seem to act as a gesture of thanksgiving for offspring, a vehicle for establishing a royalty identity in fragile political times, and even a point of connection with the northern Christian humanists, so eagerly sought at court in the late 1520s.

Christian humanist theology plays a much stronger role in the final case study presented in Chapter 7, which returns to the French court and draws attention to an overlooked document of musical devotion to St. Anne during the reign of Francis I. Just as the grandmother saint held appeal in Wittenberg even in the advent of the Reformation, she became a figure of interest at the French royal court and took on demonstrable political overtones. In the early stages of the biblical humanist movement in France, the fascination with the Holy Kinship waned, similar to its demise in the north German estates. But the political appeal of Mary's mother remained, thanks in part to the cultural perception of Louise of Savoy, her daughter Marguerite of Navarre, and her son the French monarch Francis I as a kind of "St. Anne Trinitarian" in visual culture. Along with Mary Magdalene, St. Anne further underwent an identity transformation at the hands of biblical humanists, who held unusual sway at the French court (with Marguerite in particular). Although the saint's three marriages came under attack, reformers never abandoned devotion to St. Anne. This concluding chapter explores a hitherto unstudied set of Mass Proper chants for St. Anne dedicated to Marguerite, the influential sister of the French king and author of *The Heptaméron* (1558). With texts selected from the Old Testament, the *Mass for St. Anne* on the surface presents a plea for fertility, fitting for Marguerite, who did not conceive a child until 1528, well after the likely appearance of the mass (ca. 1518–19). But an underlying political strategy emerges in the mass's loquacious preface, as the anonymous author explains that St. Anne can serve to rally Christian unity, effectively settling internal divisions and allowing Christians to fight against their persistent common enemy, the Turks.

A topical study of music such as this has inherent advantages. As it concerns St. Anne, the transmission of her legend and its political use can be observed in a number of accessible scenarios. Not beholden to a composer or to a particular geography, one is free to explore the multivalent meanings attached to the grandmother saint at some of the most pivotal European courts of the fifteenth and early sixteenth centuries. Taking stock of her appearance across disparate court contexts, we are in an auspicious position to compare the musical findings with the interpretations established in other cultural media, modifying the understanding of Mary's mother as it has been received in scholarship.

The evidence examined and the approach taken in this investigation productively expose larger musicological issues. The question of periodization is peripheral to this study but constantly hovers over scholars' identities and pursuits. The music surveyed here covers approximately 1410 until 1530, resisting – despite the book's title – the increasingly uncomfortable labels of "late medieval" and "Renaissance" commonly associated with music produced in this interval. The decision to operate within this chronology is of course a result of the extant music for St. Anne in court circles that can be assembled coherently. This is not to say that there is a lack of music exceeding the limits of the study. From a wider perspective on St. Anne, it is known that devotion to her began about two centuries prior to the early boundary of this study and that veneration of the saint did not slow after the Reformation, contrary to the usual historical narrative.[54] This study also profitably examines multiple musical genres circulating during this period. This book is framed by chapters on plainchant, from both Office (Chapter 2) and Mass (Chapter 7), defying the familiar privilege given to polyphony by historians of fifteenth- and sixteenth-century music. Some of the interior chapters also discuss how plainchant undergirds pieces of decorative polyphony. As scholarship has increasingly shown, plainchant lost no momentum during the sixteenth century, polyphony still being the exception of the liturgical day. The versified offices for St. Anne are a source of unrecognized poetic treasures and in some ways can provide the most extensive and immediate insight on the perception of Mary's mother. The reader should sense the balance of plainchant and polyphony in the course of this investigation and should come to the realization that the precise genre of a work (so critical to musicologists) may not reliably indicate how it will function socially or politically. Indeed, the first case study demonstrates the premium put on plainchant – for St. Anne no less – in a manuscript that has overwhelmingly attracted musicologists' attention for the extent of its polyphony. The journey begins in the French outpost kingdom of Cyprus, with a manuscript compiler who prominently positioned chants for Jesus' esteemed grandmother in a prestigious collection of music for a court. This case is an important starting point for illustrating the powerful and multi-faceted role that St. Anne played in the politics of the era.

2 | Heritage and Progeny in an Office for St. Anne

Appropriately, this study of a special saint begins on the island of Cyprus, known as the "Island of Saints." It is here that a large body of plainchants forming a versified office in St. Anne's honor fortunately can be connected with a time, a place, and a court context – ideal for beginning to understand the array of meanings associated with Mary's mother. While it may seem odd to venture away from continental Europe and into an unexpected (though pervasive) musical genre, the evidence initially points toward the court of King Janus of Cyprus of the Lusignan family, an expatriate dynasty from western France (Poitou) that ruled the island and the Kingdom of Jerusalem from the late twelfth century until the late fifteenth century. In this milieu of the Cypriot court, we can examine a significant array of chants for St. Anne. These appear in the manuscript Torino, Biblioteca nazionale, MS J.II.9 (hereafter, the "Turin Codex").[1]

The Turin Codex comprises 334 monophonic and polyphonic entries spread across five principal sections organized by musical genre and dominated by complex mensural polyphony.[2] In the aggregate, the manuscript represents a full complement of music for a court, spanning liturgical plainchant to French vernacular songs. It can be dated no earlier than November 1413, a *terminus post quem* deduced from an extract of a papal bull attached as a flyleaf to the manuscript. The bull grants the Lusignan court the privilege of developing a versified office for St. Hilarion, the patron saint of Cyprus.[3] Other early fifteenth-century manuscripts containing large amounts of polyphony – such as Bologna, Civico Museo Bibliografico Musicale, MS Q15 and Oxford, Bodleian Library, MS Canonici misc. 213 – do not approach nearly the breadth of the repertory in the Turin Codex. But it is the large opening section of the manuscript occupying the first twenty-eight folios that will be of concern in this study of St. Anne, for therein lies a versified office of plainchants for Mary's mother (Figure 2.1a), paired with the office for St. Hilarion.[4]

The opening folio of the St. Anne office features an illumination of Mary's mother, which would normally be a clue to its function and reception. However, the straightforward pose of St. Anne clasping a red book

Heritage and Progeny in an Office for St. Anne 27

Figure 2.1 (a) Opening of the office for St. Anne. Torino, Biblioteca nazionale, MS J.II.9, fol. 14r. Ministero per I Beni e le Attività Culturali, Biblioteca Nazionale Universitaria di Torino; (b) Illuminations of St. Hilarion (left) and St. Anne (right) in the Turin Codex. Detail: fols. 1r and 14r, respectively. Ministero per I Beni e le Attività Culturali, Biblioteca Nazionale Universitaria di Torino.

Figure 2.1 (*continued*)

(presumably either a psalter or a book of hours) reveals very little about the circumstances surrounding this manuscript (Figure 2.1b, right). The absence of a miniaturized Virgin Mary to accompany St. Anne and her book separates it from the English iconographic tradition of the "Education of the Virgin"; rather, the image of St. Anne appears to be a mere status symbol establishing the nobility of the donor or the recipient of the manuscript. Though Mary's mother is easily identifiable from her blue, heavily flowing attire, one notices that the book actually connects her to St. Hilarion (fol. 1r), who also holds a red book. Unlike the St. Anne miniature, the illumination of Hilarion shows him actively engaged with the book (Figure 2.1b, left).[5] This devotional duo may symbolize a noble couple that received the Turin Codex. As it stands, these pictures are hardly worth a thousand words, yet the contents of the office, as will be shown, provided social utility for those who likely encountered it.

Although it is the largest source of music in the French-inspired tradition between the "Ars nova" manuscripts of the late fourteenth century and the Franco-Burgundian sources of the late fifteenth century, the Turin Codex has attracted less attention in the musicological literature than have comparable early fifteenth-century manuscripts. Karl Kügle has remarked that the Turin Codex is "without a doubt the most neglected major source of late medieval polyphony that has come down to us."[6] This neglect Kügle noted concerning one of the principal sources of the "Ars subtilior" style doubtless stems from the fact that no composer attributions exist; furthermore, all of the pieces seem to be *unica*. Still, the past two generations of scholars have completed a few major studies of the codex. Richard Hoppin produced extensive research on the manuscript, publishing editions for all of the polyphony found in the source. He further provided a thorough stylistic analysis of the music from the opening fascicle of plainchant; this accompanied a (poorly resolved) facsimile reproduction of the offices and supplementary cycles of plainchant.[7] More than two decades after Hoppin's groundbreaking studies of the manuscript, considerable progress was made with the musical contents and context of the Turin Codex as part of an international congress devoted to its study in 1992. These studies continued to focus on stylistic qualities of the music to help establish potential dates and lines of musical influence in the creation of the manuscript.[8] A beautiful color facsimile reproduction followed in 1999, updating the state of scholarship on the manuscript.[9]

Most recently, Kügle made a major breakthrough with the Turin Codex by identifying the hitherto inscrutable dynastic emblems adorning the border of the manuscript's first folio. In short, he found that the crest belongs not to the Lusignan house, but to the Avogadro family of Brescia in northern Italy, which suggests that this family was the likely dedicatee of the manuscript. In addition to contextualizing some Dominican ties to the Turin Codex, Kügle's study amplified the centrality of one Jean Hanelle, a *petit vicaire* from Cambrai who traveled to Cyprus in the retinue of Charlotte of Bourbon in 1411. Hanelle was effectively the master of royal music at the Cypriot court from 1434 to 1436 and a likely composer of some of the repertory. He possibly oversaw the copying of the manuscript in the mid-1430s and, more importantly, may be the key transmitter of the music between the Cypriot court and the Avogadro family.[10]

In spite of, or even because of, these important discoveries, numerous opportunities remain for understanding the wider context of this repertory, including a perspective on the function and meaning of the plainchant offices for the two honored saints (Hilarion and Anne), who are featured at the beginning of the manuscript. The neglected texts and chants for St. Anne will serve as a lens through which devotion to the saint can be assessed in this chapter. But devotion from whom? There are at least three court contexts for which the office for Mary's mother could have had resonance, and the versatility and universality of the music for St. Anne will also be addressed in this chapter. After an introduction to the versified plainchant office provided for St. Anne and its untold history, this chapter explores the peculiar aspects of this office and its political utility for different audiences. A close reading of the individual texts in the Turin office for Mary's mother will uncover ideas that could be useful for both the Lusignan court (where the repertory originated) and the Avogadro house (to whom the music was dedicated). Another key figure who undoubtedly encountered this music – King Janus's daughter, Anne of Cyprus – will also be investigated.

The copying history of the Turin Codex is shadowy at best, but it is easier to speculate that the cultivation of the office repertory began not long after King Janus received papal permission. Because these plainchants might well have been compiled before the birth of Anne of Cyprus, the symbolic importance of the office for the Cypriot court under King Janus will be considered with an eye toward the dynasty's waning dominion in the Latin East. Following the compilation of the repertory for the Avogadro family, the survival of this manuscript in Turin also demands that the book of music itself be assessed in light of its appearance at the court of Savoy, as suggested by its presence in a 1498 inventory of books held at Chambéry castle.[11] Anne of Cyprus left the island in 1433 to marry Louis of Savoy, the second son of Amadeus VIII; she is best remembered for her acquisition two decades later of the Holy Shroud of Turin, the cloth that is said to have wrapped Christ's body and that is believed to hold an imprinted image of his face. Before gauging the meaning and political impact that emerges in multiple contexts from the music for St. Anne in the Turin Codex, some background on the versified office in general and the office for the *Mater matris* in particular is in order.

The Office for St. Anne in the Turin Codex

Far more impressive than the liturgical hymn and sequence, the versified office (also called rhymed office) was a musico-poetic super-genre primarily geared toward the recognition of new saints and feasts that developed around the turn of the eleventh century.[12] While daily masses for saints tended to borrow stock chants based on a common category of sainthood, the texts and music of the office allowed a saint's life (*vita*) to be distinguished in a narrative (*historia*) unfolded in time across the liturgical day. At the same time, it is critical to remember that the office was celebrated as an act of devotion, indeed of duty to God, on a daily basis. This imposing liturgical genre prescribed the performance of musical texts and readings, along with private prayer. Despite some fifteen hundred versified offices in the late medieval repertory, serious study of the genre has attracted relatively few musicologists. This is perhaps understandable because the corpus is not only large, but also highly provincial. Only a few of the newly minted saints' offices widely circulated, such as the offices of St. Thomas of Canterbury, St. Francis, St. Dominic, and indeed St. Anne.[13] Musicologists have instead tended to follow the more innovative (and alluring) sounds of polyphony from the late Middle Ages, while classicists have maligned the versified offices as mutilated Latin poetry and a last gasp at classical verse.[14] More than twenty distinct versified offices for St. Anne survive, which represents a staggering amount of new poetry and musical composition, indicative of her widespread popularity.[15] While all are worthy of study in their own right, a set of historical circumstances accompanies the text and music of the St. Anne office in the Turin Codex, thereby permitting a contextualization of these pieces.

It is difficult to plunge into the versified office for St. Anne without some background on the structure of the office in general. The components of the office are usually straightforward. Notable feasts, such as those for saints, begin on the evening preceding the feast day itself (the vigil) with two services, First Vespers and Compline. In the middle of the night on the appointed feast day, Matins is celebrated with an elaborate array of antiphons, lections, and responsories. At daybreak, the service of Lauds takes place. Four short services run approximately every three hours across the day (Prime [~6 A.M.], Terce [~9 A.M.], Sext [~noon], None [~3 P.M.]). These "Little Hours" do not offer as much as do the previous observances in terms of texts and music, sometimes repeating music found in other offices. The Mass – not properly part of the Office – is the central event of the liturgical feast day, and its placement varies by location and festal rank. The feast concludes with a service of Second Vespers. It should be noted that the most consuming part of these prayer services is spent singing the psalms, which are framed by the numerous antiphons organized throughout the office. While psalm singing took place regardless of the feast day, the services of First Vespers, Matins, Lauds, and Second Vespers provided the majority of texts and music proper to the feast and are indeed the focus of the office from the Turin Codex.

Within the four principal services, lections, psalms, antiphons, responsories, hymns, and other prayers establish not just the solemnity of the feast but also a narrative and thematic emphasis surrounding a particular saint. These genres could be fully brought together in a breviary, a liturgical book that provides all the necessary parts to carry out an office. With the bulk of its contents devoted to intricate polyphonic music, the Turin Codex on the whole is no breviary. But the offices in the first fascicle have the requisite components to execute the services without recourse to another liturgical book. (The office for St. Hilarion even contains a full plainchant mass for the saint.) The most salient devotional vehicles of the office were those texts set to music; these were chiefly antiphons and responsories, whose arrangement could differ among institutions. In the office, the music of the antiphons and responsories can both prepare and echo the lections, constantly reinforcing the themes of the day with musical enchantment. In contrast to the simple intonation of the readings, the antiphons and responsories have built-in repetitive structures that intensify key ideas and bind them to musical gestures in the process.[16] Because of their brevity (usually four poetic lines), antiphons are repeated in their entirety after the psalm, whereas the more elaborate musical expressions of responsories permit only a "short repeat" using the *repetendum*, usually the last half of the responsory. The consistent repetition in these genres, to say nothing of strophic hymns, has the potential to strengthen a particular image, mantra, or ideology over the course of a service or liturgical feast day.[17] Set as monophony, the texts were comprehensible, free from distortion that might occur, say, with the scattering of texts in a polyphonic or polytextual musical setting, so common in this period. The rich and varied expressions of the antiphons and responsories constitute the substance of this examination of the office for St. Anne found in the Turin Codex.

Table 2.1 captures the complete musical contents and melodic modes of the more than thirty plainchants contained in the Cypriot office for St. Anne. The principal observances of First Vespers, Matins, Lauds, and Second Vespers carry the simple abbreviations of V, M, L, and W, respectively, employing the nomenclature Andrew Hughes developed for his electronic database of late medieval offices. The initial letter indicates the service but neither the genre nor the position of that item in the office for St. Anne. Clarifying the genre, the letters A and R correspond to antiphon and responsory, respectively. The genres of Invitatory (I) from Matins and canticle antiphon (E), sometimes called the antiphon *ad Evangelium* or *ad Magnificat*, can also be used. Finally, an Arabic numeral denotes the position within the ceremony.[18] For example, the designation MA4 would be the fourth antiphon of Matins. The music of the office for St. Anne in the Turin Codex – originally heard at the chapel of the Lusignan court – largely conforms to the standard practice of ecclesiastical institutions. The particular organization of material in the Matins service in the manuscript signals a secular (i.e., non-monastic) cursus for the office.[19] The Turin office also has an abbreviated service of First Vespers for St. Anne, lacking a set of five antiphons to precede the responsory *Inter legis sacramenta*, the first piece of music in the office.[20]

Table 2.1 Contents of the Office for St. Anne in the Turin Codex

Service/Genre/Position	Title (Incipit)	Melodic Mode
VR	*Inter legis sacramenta*	5
VH	*Lucis huius festa*	6
VE	*Ad felicis Anne*	1
MI	*Adoremus Christum regem*	4
MH	*O quam mirifica luce*	3
MA1	*Sol eternus Annam Christus*	1
MA2	*De stirpe patriarchali*	3
MA3	*Ex hac olla*	5
MR1	*Celebremus hodiernam*	2
MR2	*In redemptionis nostre*	4
MR3	*Bethlehem natale solum*	6
MA4	*Abrahe beati senis*	6
MA5	*Hic ager, quem de supernis*	7
MA6	*Annam Iuda germinavit*	8
MR4	*Mediante nobis Anna*	1
MR5	*Sindonem virginitatis*	3
MR6	*Genealogie Christi*	7
MA7	*Hec ad opus matris Christi*	5
MA8	*Linea virginitatis*	7
MA9	*Dignum genetrici sue*	4
MR7	*Felix Anna quae prophetam*	5
MR8	*Omnia prophetans longeva*	6
MR9	*Rex dilecte matris Anne*	1
LA1	*Ad legis metas*	1
LA2	*Concives, late regi domino*	2
LA3	*Anna Deo vigilat*	3
LA4	*Eximia celebris*	5
LA5	*Laudem de celis*	6
LH	*Gaudet chorus fidelium*	1
LE	*Hodie splendor eterni patris*	1
WR	*Genealogie Christi*	7
WH	*Lucis huius festa*	6
WE	*Anna parens matris*	5

In the late Middle Ages, many versified offices exhibited a deliberate systematization of musical material; the antiphons and responsories, particularly for newly recognized feasts and saints, began to be ordered in serial succession according to the eight melodic modes that governed plainchant composition. Both antiphons and responsories progress separately through the melodic modes, typically in the service of Matins (and sometimes continuing into Lauds). Compared to the older "Gregorian" repertory, modal identification in the late versified office is relatively uncomplicated, especially as mode became an increasingly prescriptive parameter of monophonic designs.[21] Whether this type of organization functioned as an intellectual game among composers, a challenge or means of edification for singers, or simply a systematic means of ensuring tonal variety in the office is not known. For the analyst, breaks in modal succession amidst these serial arrangements can sometimes reveal how offices were compiled, transmitted, and reorganized over time to suit different institutions.[22]

The compilers of the Turin Codex were evidently no strangers to modal organization, as Hoppin showed in the highly ordered successions in the office for St. Hilarion.[23] However, Table 2.1 demonstrates that a clear arrangement of the melodic modes is not to be found in the St. Anne office. Still, a few patterns do emerge in short bursts. Most striking is the succession that surfaces in the service of Lauds, in which LA1 through LA5 ascends through modes 1, 2, 3, 5, and 6. This series contains a modal interruption with the lack of a fourth mode antiphon – admittedly one of the more unpopular modes for medieval composition, but not one insurmountable for a composer. In the office of Matins, MA4, MA5, and MA6 reveal the progression of modes 6, 7, and 8 respectively; similarly, the contiguous MA9, MR7, and MR8 unfold the sequence of modes 4, 5, and 6. Further in Matins, the six musical items between MA1 and MR3 contain the pattern 1, 3, 5, 2, 4, 6 – almost certainly an intentional progression of modes, despite lacking modes 7 and 8. The effect of this kind of sequence, then, is one that introduces the authentic (higher) ranges of each ascending mode and then returns to the plagal (lower or constricted) ambitus. The arrangement here contrasts with the typical ascending modal succession, which would achieve the alternation of authentic and plagal modes.

The short strings of ascending mode in the St. Anne office could be a clue that it derives from a larger, more consistently ordered office. The versified office for St. Hilarion likewise shows some coordinated progressions of mode combined with some nontraditional series, but of course special permission was sought in this case to develop his office.[24] The variable arrangement of modes also might simply indicate that the compilers (or commissioner) of the St. Anne office cherry-picked the music from an exemplar (or exemplars) that suited the needs of the court or that would have particular resonance with the recipient of the manuscript. The office for St. Anne found in the Turin Codex might have an ancestor in Western Europe, but until now, a model for this office has remained mysteriously unidentified.

Concordances in the North

In his 1968 facsimile edition of the plainchant from the Turin Codex, Richard Hoppin unveiled a single source that was concordant with the St. Anne office.[25] In particular, he noted that the texts of the Turin office are closely related to an office cataloged in *Analecta Hymnica* (AH 5.37). While it is often the case that the versified offices shown in *Analecta Hymnica* can be traced to several sources, AH 5.37 has been curiously associated with just one source – a breviary from Odense (Denmark). Surviving today in excellent condition in the Royal Library of Copenhagen (Royal Library, L.N. MS 30), this breviary was printed in Lübeck in 1497 and designed specifically for the usage of Odense. This version of the St. Anne office, which was celebrated on December 9 (following the newly established feast day of the Immaculate Conception) instead of July 26, provides only the texts (no music) for the hours of the liturgical day.[26] With its nine antiphons and responsories in the service of Matins, the Odense office reveals the secular cursus as found in the Turin Codex. Although the two offices for St. Anne are most certainly related, closer analysis reveals significant variance between the two sources, especially in the office of First Vespers and in the Matins responsories.[27]

At minimum, the evidence suggests that the office for St. Anne in the Turin Codex, which predates the Odense office by some three generations, is part of a different strand of the tradition (or transmission) of this basic office template. Given the geographical and chronological separation between the sources, it is virtually impossible that the office in the Turin Codex could have served as a model for the Danish breviary. Naturally, there must have been intervening sources to arrive at the variants present in these two versions of an office for St. Anne. Giulio Cattin rightly argued that the discrepant arrangements between the St. Anne office in the Turin Codex and that of the Odense breviary should "oblige us to postulate other sources" predating the Turin office.[28] He also suggested that, with the number of legends written about the life of St. Anne in northern France and England, some of the inspiration for the office texts must derive from Western Europe in general, if not those places in particular. Though it turns out that Cattin was correct, he had no evidence to substantiate his point at the time. Fortunately, the story does not end with the Odense breviary as the sole relative of the St. Anne office in the Turin Codex.

In an essay published as part of a festschrift for Andrew Hughes, Sherry Reames contributed an illuminating study on some of the earliest known pre-Sarum offices for St. Anne. Beginning with an office in the early fourteenth-century Stowe Breviary (London, British Library, MS Stowe 12), Reames demonstrated the early English and northern French cultivation of offices for St. Anne, well before the feast day for Anne was codified for the universal church by the Roman pope Urban VI in 1378.[29] Her work revealed important relationships among a dozen sources of a particular tradition of office texts for St. Anne mainly from the fourteenth century; little did Reames know, however, that she was unveiling the very tradition that musicologists had long sought for the office of St. Anne in the Turin Codex.

One of Reames's major discoveries was a single "master" source that contains the full stock of chants found scattered across both ancestor and descendant sources with an early office for St. Anne. This "master" manuscript, against which eight others were compared, is Oxford, Bodleian Library, MS Rawlinson C. 489 – a two-volume Benedictine breviary from 1424, copied by William Vincent at St. Swithun's in Winchester, the wealthiest diocese in England at the time. Representing the monastic cursus described earlier, the Winchester source provides the expected thirteen antiphons and twelve responsories at Matins, some of which would have been omitted in the abbreviated secular cursus seen in the Stowe breviary from about a century earlier. Reames thus set forth the reasonable hypothesis that the known French and English versions of this early office for St. Anne probably descended from a Benedictine model resembling the one found in the Rawlinson manuscript.[30]

Reames's study fortuitously included the Odense breviary as one of the sources surveyed. However, the contents of this breviary, though part of the tradition of office texts that she was exploring, were not critical to her particular project. Being a later printed source and a geographic outlier when viewed against the other concordant sources in northern French and English territories, the Odense breviary did not occasion much discussion in Reames's work. Fortunately, the source still fell within the scope of her study and could be compared with a considerably larger tradition of similar offices for St. Anne from the dozen sources in her essay.[31] At the very least, an ancestry for the Turin Codex has now come to light: the office in the Turin Codex can now be connected with the broad set of offices Reames studied. This newly discovered relationship surfaced because of the shared connection to the Odense office, an office that, ironically, was a dead end for both Hoppin and Reames.

Comparisons in the studies mentioned have only included texts (or worse, only text incipits), but we would seem to be in a position to account for the musical relationship between the melodies of these northern offices and those in the Turin Codex. Unfortunately, data from more sources would be needed before any conclusions can be reached. However, notated sources are not entirely lacking. One of the liturgical books in the network of sources from Reames's study is a fourteenth-century antiphoner presumably from the Abbey Notre-Dame of Lyre, a monastery founded in the mid-eleventh century in Normandy.[32] Reames was unable to consult this manuscript for her study, but, significantly, it is the only remnant of this group of offices for St. Anne except for the Turin Codex that contains musical notation. Examination of the melodies from the Lyre antiphoner and the Turin Codex reveals no concrete concordances. Less than 30 percent of the antiphons and responsory texts common to both manuscripts is composed in the same melodic mode, leaving little hope of any internal musical resemblance. Even when liturgical items do show agreement in melodic mode, the relationships at the musical surface are very weak overall and are more likely attributable to the conventions of modal composition than to recognizable variants of a shared tradition.[33]

While a direct stemmatic relationship between the Turin Codex and the Lyre antiphoner can be ruled out, one may still investigate the melodies of the two sources, which potentially aid in determining the more musically stable or dominant tradition as transmitted in these offices. Take for example the only hymn text common to both sources, *Lucis huius festa*. This hymn represents one of the oldest hymns known for St. Anne with no shortage of sources, the earliest dating from the twelfth century.[34] *Lucis huius festa* was associated with four different melodies, the most widespread of which was the Marian hymn *Ave maris stella*.[35] Indeed, the melody supplied for this hymn in the Lyre antiphoner matches this popular first-mode hymn tune.[36] The setting of *Lucis huius festa* in the Turin Codex, however, is in sixth mode, an *unicum* according to Bruno Stäblein. This piece of evidence might suggest that the compiler of the Lyre antiphoner, not that of the Turin Codex, followed a more established musical tradition for the St. Anne office.

To recap briefly, Hoppin's studies of the Turin Codex found only one concordance for the St. Anne office – the Odense source. Reames's essay revealed a slew of English and northern French offices for St. Anne, one of which was the same Odense print. While the Turin texts can now be connected with the larger network of office texts, a musical link has yet to be found. The only manuscript from Reames's study that contained music (the Lyre antiphoner) does not match the plainsong of the St. Anne office from the Turin Codex. In the absence of other notated sources with these texts in honor of Mary's mother, it cannot be positively known whether the St. Anne office in the Turin Codex was newly composed or whether it derives from a larger musical tradition. In his study of the plainchants of the Turin Codex, Hoppin saw a distinct compositional difference between the chant settings of the office for St. Anne and those for St. Hilarion, the former being considerably more modest in their melodic profile.[37] If the office for St. Anne was newly composed, one can assume that it was not written by the composer of the Hilarion office (also newly composed). On the other hand, the office for Anne might have emerged out of a distinct or rare musical branch associated with a relatively stable set of office texts for Mary's mother. With what little evidence survives, it can be said at minimum that the compilers of the St. Anne office transmitted in the Turin Codex took great liberty in setting a stable core of liturgical poetry in honor of the *Mater matris*.

The Search for Meaning(s) in the St. Anne Office

Previous scholarship dealing with the office for St. Anne in the Turin Codex, whether directly or indirectly, has been content to address the musical style, general structure, and origins of the texts. Hoppin fashioned an elaborate analysis of the offices for both St. Hilarion and St. Anne, which included a detailed "note-per-syllable" measurement of the chants by genre. Cattin transcribed the texts of the full offices of Hilarion and Anne and provided general background on these saints. He also located the sources of some of the material in the office, finding, for instance, that several lections in the Turin Codex could be traced to passages in Jacobus de Voragine's *Golden Legend* and other hagiographical sources. Also on the hunt for textual origins, Reames, as mentioned, unearthed an early fourteenth-century tradition of the versified office for St. Anne. She was even able to link the text of several chants from the office (and also lessons in some sources) to a sermon on the feast of St. Anne by Osbert of Clare, a twelfth-century English Benedictine monk. This single sermon was disseminated quite quickly after 1136 to a large number of English churches and probably across the channel.[38] With the identification of Osbert of Clare as the progenitor of several parts of the versified office and the observations made with the Lyre antiphoner, the origins of the office material for St. Anne found in the Turin Codex can hardly be penetrated further. To this finding, I have supplied a network of English and French sources not known to Hoppin in his groundbreaking work with the Turin Codex nor to those who investigated the office for St. Anne in later studies. Close analysis of the plainchants honoring Mary's mother and the question of the reception history of this music remain unexamined, however, and deserve fuller attention in the study of this versified office.

In theory, the two versified offices at the head of the Turin Codex were fit to be sung once per year on the saints' respective feast days. But on a practical level, this music was broadly emblematic of noble prestige and offered social benefits to its elite listeners. The exploration of its context begins with the Lusignan court, where the liturgies were ostensibly written or copied prior to the appearance in the Turin Codex. In these two offices, the compilers selected sanctoral subjects as templates for creativity. The motivation for developing an office in honor of St. Hilarion seems clear enough. Hilarion was the chief patron saint of the island of Cyprus, where the family dynasty had been stationed since around the turn of the thirteenth century. It is generally conceded that the Hilarion office, which contains far more liturgical items than does the office for St. Anne, was developed as a generous acknowledgment of the island's most beloved saint. St. Hilarion died in Cyprus on October 21, 371, and was immortalized by St. Jerome, who compiled a biography of the saint.[39] The presence of the Byzantine saint's office at the Cypriot court might also have reflected the relatively peaceful coexistence between the Latin Christian hierarchy and the indigenous Greeks, especially those serving in the royal administration.[40] In addition to the royal family's summer home at the castle of St. Hilarion on a mountain above the city of Lampousa, the Lusignans housed the body of St. Hilarion at the court in Nicosia, thus keeping the saint and hero of the island unusually close to them.[41] Though this broad study of St. Anne is no place to probe the contents and context of St. Hilarion, the Lusignan court evidently celebrated the patron saint of the island with great pomp and unusual specificity, not only in the extensive versified office and mass for Hilarion, but also in a motet found in the third fascicle of the Turin Codex (*Magni patris magna mira/Ovent Cyprus*). A thorough investigation of the hagiographical texts in conjunction with the newly composed music for the Cypriot saint in this manuscript and its reception awaits further study and will no doubt repay with interest.

Not unlike many places in Europe, St. Anne was beloved on Cyprus as an intercessor for women in childbirth, and the island was home to several of her relics,[42] but the reason for providing a versified office in her honor at the Lusignan court in particular is not precisely clear. At first blush, the birth of Anne of Cyprus might have provided the impetus for the office. She was the oldest daughter of King Janus and Queen Charlotte of Bourbon and represented both the future of the Lusignan dynasty and its extension of influence back to the European continent whence it originated. Hoppin and others have argued that the office for St. Anne was likely compiled to honor the namesake saint of Janus's daughter, who would later become Duchess Anne of Savoy. This is one possible scenario, but it assumes that she was alive at the time of the creation of this repertory. Unfortunately, there is no definitive date for Anne's birth. Testimony concerning this date is inconsistent from the chief informant during the reign of King Janus I, Leontios Makhairas. In an extant Venetian copy of Makhairas's *Chronicle of Cyprus*, Anne's birth is set in 1418; yet, in another copy of the same book from Oxford, this event was said to happen in 1415.[43] Further, Wipertus Rudt de Collenberg has pointed to evidence that may place the birth of Anne of Cyprus closer to 1419.[44] The matter remains unsettled.

The codex, as mentioned earlier, contains a flyleaf providing papal permission for King Janus to create an office for St. Hilarion. There is no reason to assume that the musical setting of the office for the Cypriot saint was delayed much after the approval from (antipope) John XXIII. If it too was newly composed, the musical setting of the office for St. Anne could reasonably have been accomplished around 1413/1414, a time that precedes even the earliest of dates provided for the birth of Anne of Cyprus (1415, from the Oxford copy of Makhairas's *Chronicle of Cyprus*). If it was copied from an existing office, it most certainly predates her birth. The fact that the St. Anne office probably predates its assumed dedicatee forces a consideration of meaning in the music across multiple scenarios. In the likely event that the office developed in advance of Anne's birth, one may first ask why King Janus and his court would call on St. Anne. While the office repertory transmitted in the Turin Codex suggests development and use in the Lusignan court, Kügle's identification of the Avogadro coat of arms on the manuscript's first folio demands consideration of the impact of this music as a repurposed gift for the Avogadro family of Brescia. Though this music originated in Cyprus and was evidently intended for Brescia in the mid-1430s, the manuscript would arrive shortly thereafter in Savoy, though how and to whom it was delivered remains a mystery. In the end, it is hard to envision that the office for St. Anne, so prominently positioned in the codex, would not have been encountered in one form or another by Anne of Cyprus, who ventured to the continent for her new life with Louis of Savoy.[45] These diverse contexts will be considered later in this chapter in the transmission of this single office for St. Anne.

In the versified office tradition celebrating saints, the poetic texts typically narrate the life of the holy figure, trumpeting the merits of the individual at every turn and offering universal praise for the saint's achievements. When one carefully examines the texts and music of the office for St. Anne in the

Turin Codex, a well-formed narrative does not appear, nor do any simple generic gestures of devotion to the grandmother saint. Rather, the office bears a series of scattered ideas, revealing particular aspects of St. Anne that do not always relate to one another. That this office comprises selections from a larger master template (texts only) still does not explain its disjunct nature. Often abstractly presented as simple reflections, many of the selective messages in the office for St. Anne have a political hue that would been advantageous to a noble family. The substance of the St. Anne liturgy will now be investigated with attention to the social utility of the texts in light of the multiple parties who might have experienced this music.

Maternal Allegories

With a full view of the plainchants in the office for St. Anne in the Turin Codex, it is time to examine the contents of individual liturgical items. A closer look at the plainchants in this office (Table 2.2) reveals a myriad of thematic areas in an arrangement that is impossible to condense into a single, coherent chronicle. While the versified office for St. Hilarion in the Turin Codex rather methodically traces the life of the saint, the office for St. Anne is no simple *historia* recounting the life of Jesus' grandmother, about which little was known in the first place. In stark contrast to the office for St. Hilarion, the wide array of topics in the St. Anne office divulges various images, ideas, and metaphors, each offering a small window into the multivalent meanings behind Mary's mother, as if a quilt presenting miniature portraits were being pondered from both close and far range. Each item is heard in force within its own liturgical space and moment, but across the day, a variegated picture emerges from the numerous images that escape into the sound world. Though a few themes predominate in the office, some seemingly uneventful topics could have been received as affirmations with political subtext. Indeed, this office for the *Mater matris* can be read not only as a gesture of devotion but also as an allegorical plea for political gain.

Curious references emerge in Table 2.2, such as allusions to textiles and the natural world, but poetry concerning Anne's offspring and her lineage (sometimes rooted in figures from the Old Testament) dominates the collection of plainchants. The emphasis on Anne's matronly role as supreme genetrix is unsurprising across the spectrum of associative possibilities in a versified office, but this kind of thematic focus establishes the clearest path to a political reading of the devotion.

Table 2.2 Themes of the St. Anne Office in the Turin Codex

Service/Genre/Position	Title	Themes / Figures mentioned [or implied], besides St. Anne	Keywords and phrases
VR	*Inter legis sacramenta*	**OT*** / Mary, Xt	*patriarchis, virgo sine viro*
VH	*Lucis huius festa*	**OT**(Mary from Jesse) / Anne in Trinity	*radix Yesse, carnis planta*
VE	*Ad felicis Anne*	Natural imagery / Mary, Xt	*in horto sponsi*
MI	*Adoremus Christum regem*	Praise / Xt, Mary	–
MH	*O quam mirifica luce*	**Lineage** / Eve, David, Mary	*proles regia, stirpis davitice*
MA1	*Sol eternus Annam Christus*	Anne as chosen mother / Mary, Xt	*carnaliter*
MA2	*De stirpe patriarchali*	**Lineage**	*stirpe patriarchali*
MA3	*Ex hac olla*	**Offspring**, pottery metaphor	*olla…figulis*
MR1	*Celebremus hodiernam*	Celebration / Mary	–
MR2	*In redemptionis nostre*	**Fertility**, nature metaphor / Mary, Xt	*Anna felix velut radix*
MR3	*Bethlehem natale solum*	Anne as nourishment	*domus eterni panis*
MA4	*Abrahe beati senis*	**Lineage** / Abraham, David, Mary, Xt	*Abrae…et David promissio*
MA5	*Hic ager, quem de supernis*	Beauty of Nature	–
MA6	*Annam Iuda germinavit*	**Lineage** via nature metaphor / Judah, [Mary, Xt]	*Virgo [germinavit] florem*
MR4	*Mediante nobis Anna*	Anne as mediatrix / Xt	–
MR5	*Sindonem virginitatis*	Textile metaphor / Mary, Xt, God [Father]	*contextuit, sindonem*
MR6	*Genealogie Christi*	Heritage, textile metaphor / Xt	*genealogie, texit*
MA7	*Hec ad opus matris Christi*	**Offspring**, via textile metaphor / Mary, [Xt]	*contexitur, toga…preciosa*
MA8	*Linea virginitatis*	**Offspring**, via textile metaphor / [Mary, Xt]	*linea, caro factum, carne*
MA9	*Dignum genetrici sue*	Heavenly vision (no mention of Anne) / [Mary, Xt]	–
MR7	*Felix Anna quae prophetam*	Anne as new "Hannah" from **OT** / Hannah, Mary, [Xt]	–

42

MR8	Omnia prophetans longeva	**Lineage** / Jacob, Phanuel, Xt [Anna the Prophetess from NT, Mary]	proles…Phanuel, mater…matris,
MR9	Rex dilecte matris Anne	Praise / [Xt]	Genetricis matris
LA1	Ad legis metas	**Lineage** / David	Cum genus…David
LA2	Concives, late regi domino	Praise / Xt	–
LA3	Anna Deo vigilat	Anne's Obedience, **Offspring** / [Mary]	lucis alumna
LA4	Eximia celebris	Following Christ pleases Anne / [Xt]	pacificare nepotem
LA5	Laudem de celis	Intercession	–
LH	Gaudet chorus fildelium	Praise / Mary, Xt	matronam unicam, parentes nobiles
LE	Hodie splendor eterni patris	Praise on the feast day / God the Father, [Mary]	sumere carnem, desiderabilem…. pulcritudinem
WA1	Ad legis metas	**Lineage** / David	Cum genus…David
WA2	Concives, late regi domino	Praise / Xt	–
WA3	Anna Deo vigilat	Anne's Obedience, **Offspring** / [Mary]	lucis alumna
WA4	Eximia celebris	Following Christ pleases Anne / [Xt]	pacificare nepotem
WA5	Laudem de celis	Intercession	–
WR	Genealogie Christi	Heritage, textile metaphor / Xt	genealogie, texit
WH	Lucis huius festa	**OT** (Mary from Jesse) / Anne in Trinity	radix Yesse, carnis planta
WE	Anna parens matris	Intercession / [Mary, Xt]	parens matris

*Old Testament.

In several liturgical items in this St. Anne office, the compilers ensured that ample attention was paid to Mary and Jesus, as much as to the grandmother saint. The trio of Anne, Mary, and Christ takes hold from the first antiphon of the night office of Matins, *Sol eternus Annam Christus*. In this brief chant, it is the Messiah who paradoxically chooses Anne to be his mother's mother. The emphasis on maternity (*matris, genetrix*) and incarnation (*carnaliter*) is unmistakable and would have resonated with any dynasty in its encounters with this music, presumably in a private chapel setting.

MA1	MA1
Sol eternus Annam Christus	The eternal sun, Christ,
Preelegit taliter	preselected Anne in such a way
Ut matris sue genitrix	that the Mother might be made
Fieret carnaliter.	in the flesh of her mother.

A separate paradox involving the grandmother saint appears in the third antiphon of Lauds, *Anna Deo vigilat*. This antiphon presents St. Anne as both a child of God and the bearer of the one who would bear Jesus.

LA3	LA3
Anna Deo vigilat	Anne watches out for God,
Eo quod sit lucis alumna,	and therefore, is a child of the light.
Hunc [sic] genuit, quem virgo	She, in turn, bore the one who was
Sue viteque columna.	the virgin and pillar of her life.

As the last formal antiphon of the liturgical day and the most musically elaborate expression in the service of Second Vespers, *Anna parens matris* continues to direct the listener beyond St. Anne and toward her splendid progeny. Anne is addressed as the mother's mother (*parens matris*), and she is beseeched to pray expressly to her grandson (*nepotis*) on behalf of those who are trapped in their earthly lives (Example 2.1). Outside of the melodic apex that occurs at the command of the supplicants (*collige*) and the invocation of Anne in the first phrase, the most elaborate musical gesture of the antiphon takes place in reference to Anne's offspring (*nepotis*). Among the melodic turns accompanying the word *nepotis* is the vaulting triadic gesture f-a-c, which not only constitutes stock rhetoric of the fifth melodic mode but also references the opening of the antiphon that hails St. Anne (*Anna*).

Example 2.1 *Anna parens matris* (WE) from the Turin Office for St. Anne, fol. 19r.

WE	WE
Anna parens matris	O Anne, the mother's mother
De qua sapientia Patris	from whom the wisdom of the Father
Incarnata dedit fidei	granted the incarnate one to the faithful,
Quod mundus habebit,	which the world will hold;
Collige nos retis	In a net, gather us up
Inter sacra membra nepotis	among the holy members of your grandson.
Anna, beatorum comes,	O Anne, companion of the saints,
Esto memor famulorum.	be mindful of your servants.
Magnificat.	My soul magnifies …

As Susan Boynton has demonstrated in her revealing study of the plainchant tradition at the medieval abbey of Farfa, the organization of an office's liturgical items can carry different meanings in diverse contexts. Boynton has expressly pointed toward the powerful effect of office texts when themes are reinforced by juxtaposition in the office.[46] The office for St. Anne from the Turin Codex contains an unusual metaphor connecting Mary's mother with the craft of weaving, but one that ultimately reconnects to the idea of offspring so prominent in this office and so valuable for a noble family. That the analogy extends through several contiguous liturgical items in the Turin office is cause for analysis. This peculiar series emerges in the middle of the Matins service in the versified office, beginning with the fifth responsory *Sindonem virginitatis* (MR5) and progressing through the eighth antiphon of the service (MA8) *Linea virginitatis*. The arrangement comprises two responsories, two antiphons, and one lection, passing from the second to the third nocturn of Matins in the process. The component parts are conceptually bound together by the allegorical references to the craft of weaving and its apparent connection to procreation.

MR5	MR5
Sindonem virginitatis	Anne wove
Anna contexuit,	**a shroud** of virginity,
Quam enixa maris stella	which the star of the sea brought forth
Deo patri vendidit,	and sold to God the Father.
V. Ut in carne matris verbum	V. In the flesh, may the Mother's word
esset vite precium. (Quam)	be the prize of life.

Lectio VI
Quapropter, ut Deus novit, **beata et gloriosa Anna semen inclitum germinavit, ex qua spiritu sancto cooperante granum ex Bethleem processit**, quod factum est panis angelorum et hominum, et vita et resurrectio mortuorum. Anna quoque, *providente* divina gratia, virum habuit Ioachyn cuius domus ex Galilea et ex Naçareth erat. T[u autem.]

Lection VI
For this reason, as God knows, **blessed and glorious Anne germinated this famous seed, out of which proceeded the seed from Bethlehem together with the Holy Spirit**, which was made from the bread of angels and men, and the life and the resurrection of the dead. Anne too, foreseeing with divine grace, had a husband Joachim whose house [stock] was out of Galilee and Nazareth. But you O Lord …

MR6
Genealogie Christi
Dum texit hystoriam,
Ad Annam ex abundanti
Respicit egregiam,

V. Et sit meta tersa nube
Et legis et gratie. (Ad Annam)
Gloria patri. (Ad Annam)

MR6
While the **genealogy of Christ**
weaves a history,
it looks back to the extraordinary Anne,
out of an abundance of figures.

V. So there might be the perfect goal
with the cloud of both law and grace.
Glory to the Father …

In III° Nocturno

MA7
Hec ad opus matris Christi
Purpura contexitur,
De qua **toga** summo regi
Preciosa conditur.

Ps. *Cantate* i.

Third Nocturn

MA7
This **purple cloth is woven**
for the need of Christ's mother,
from whom the precious **garment**
of the highest king was made.

Ps. Sing to the Lord [Ps. 95]

MA8
Linea virginitatis
Ex hac stella prodiit,
Verbum Dei caro factum
Quod in carne subiit.

Ps. Dominus regnavit exultet terra.

MA8
The **linen** of virginity
proceeds out of this star,
the word of God made flesh
which goes into flesh.

Ps. The Lord has reigned, let the earth rejoice [Ps. 96]

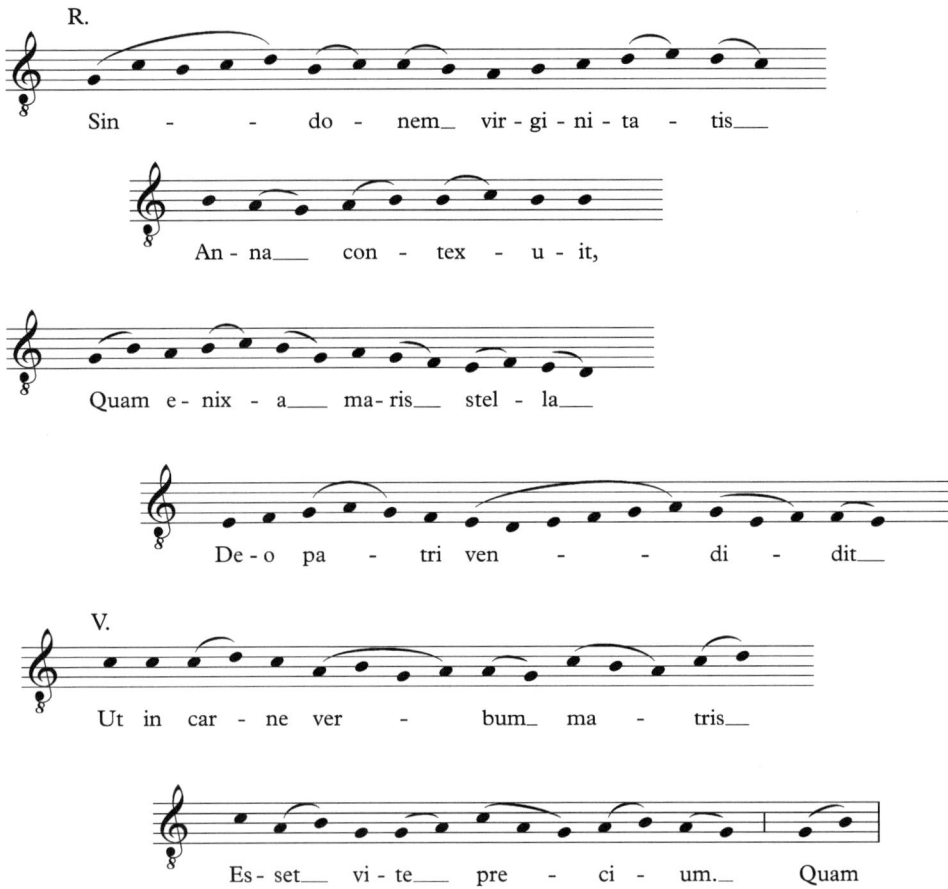

Example 2.2 *Genealogie christi* (MR6) from the Turin Office for St. Anne, fol. 16v.

The allusions to the textile arts are too many to dismiss as mere coincidence in this succession of liturgical items. MR5 opens the string of metaphors by announcing that "Anne wove a muslin cloth of virginity" (*Sindonem virginitatis Anna contexuit*). Lection VI follows with a short discourse on the lineage brought forth from Anne, the implications of which will be clear shortly. The ensuing responsory *Genealogie Christi* (MR6) continues the theme of lineage, but interestingly uses the verb *texit* ("weaves") to prolong the analogy of weaving begun in the previous responsory. The word *texit* is even marked for importance in the music as it (1) ascends to the octave above the final and (2) employs an uncharacteristic e ♭ – two striking aspects that are neither assumed nor elaborated on in the more soloistic verse of this responsory (Example 2.2).[47] With a text that traces back to Osbert of Clare's twelfth-century sermon on St. Anne, the antiphon *Hec ad opus matris Christi* opens the third nocturn (MA7) and features the boldest use of the weaving allegory yet (*purpura, contexuit*), securing the connection to precious lineage with references to both Mary and Christ. The final member of the group above *Linea virginitatis* (MA8) may also be included in this list, reconnecting with MR5 as it alludes to a spotless "linen of virginity" proceeding from St. Anne, another metaphor indebted to Osbert.[48]

Kathleen Ashley and Pamela Sheingorn have called attention to the ability of St. Anne to serve both gendered and nongendered functions for her devotees. It is not difficult to see a gendered connection to the household through the extended references to weaving in the office items listed earlier. Anne's legend is silent on her domestic pursuits, making the images of weaving a striking diversion from the typical stories and general praises for her found across all offices for St. Anne. Indeed, a subtler gendered function lies within the analogy. Early fifteenth-century French writer and proto-feminist Christine de Pizan, discussed in Chapter 3 as a model for widowhood, placed the art of weaving high on the list of the duties of an expressly aristocratic wife. While a noblewoman would not have performed the act of weaving, she was expected to be knowledgeable about the craft in order to oversee the process in the noble household.[49] In the case of St. Anne, the meaning behind needlework and textile production may, however, have a more precise connotation. In her studies of the history of women, Olwen Hufton has noticed that in some sixteenth-century artwork, St. Anne is shown winding wool, from which the Virgin Mary knits a fabric. Hufton interprets the raw material as both the instrument to achieve perfection and the foundation that is transmitted from a mother to her daughter. Studies of the history of textiles further reveal that cloth production was an occupation that celebrated the virtue and even prestige of women.[50]

These perspectives, while valuable in their association between female achievement and the art of weaving, do not entirely account for the broader concept of lineage that the texts of the versified office from the Turin Codex suggest. There is, however, evidence from early Christian history that may shed light on the symbolism of textiles suggested in this office. In his study of the writings of St. Proclus (a fifth-century archbishop of Constantinople), Nicholas Constas demonstrated that Proclus associated the craft of weaving with the production of human flesh, which seems to resonate more with the thrust of the analogy in the office for St. Anne. One of the archbishop's recurrent symbolic images for the Virgin Mary was a textile loom. Mary's womb is likened to a "workshop" containing a loom on which the flesh of God is magnificently laced together, giving texture to the divinity of Christ.[51] This allegorical act of incarnation is seen even earlier in the *Protoevangelium of James*, wherein the lives of St. Anne and other noncanonical figures were expounded. In a scene from Mary's infancy, the Virgin spins purple thread following the annunciation by the angel Gabriel.[52] The act of spinning purple thread in particular was juxtaposed and thus associated with the moment of incarnation. The color of purple represents the royal heritage imbued in the cloth,[53] and this analogy can transfer seamlessly to Anne, Mary's *progenitrix*, in the Turin office. When Anne is said to weave a fine cloth of virginity in *Sindonem virginitatis* (MR5, echoed in MA8), this means that she will bear the mother of the Lord, cued in the intervening lection. Garments for Mary and Christ appear in *Hec ad opus matris Christi* (MA7), invested with the regal color of purple. By associating St. Anne with textile production, the office draws attention to the goal of every dynasty – to produce kin. With the help of Mary's mother, bearer of the Holy Kinship, a noble household would not be left to fend for itself.

As Hufton has explained, St. Anne in some ways signals the institution of motherhood even more strongly than does her daughter: "Mary's role as mother is directed to infant care: that of St. Anne is to raise a woman fit to be the mother of God. She rather than Mary therefore represents long-term working maternity."[54] The second responsory of Matins, *In redemptionis nostrae*, is a final example of the maternal accentuation in the St. Anne office from the Turin Codex, one that secures the notion that St. Anne functioned as a kind of "fertility insurance" not just for women in general, but more pointedly for nobles to produce illustrious dynasties. The poet of this responsory describes the grandmother saint as fertile (*felix*), comparing her to a root that nourishes the full tree. Using references to the natural world, the verse prolongs the arboreal metaphor, as the tree yields a branch (i.e., Mary), which in turn produces an almond (Christ).

MR2	MR2
In redemptionis nostrae	In the need of our redemption
[Et] salutis opere	and salvation,
Anna felix velut radix	Anne was fertile, just as the root
Vivit in arbore,	lives in the tree,
V. Ex qua virgo traxit ortum	V. Out of which a branch emerged,
Pariens amigdalum. (Anna)	Bearing an almond.

In this responsory, the image of the tree has the power to symbolize both fertility and lineage as a source of growth. Right down to our present notion of the "family tree," the tree has long served as an indelible icon of both human origin and continuity. In the book of Genesis (2:9), the Tree of Knowledge of Good and Evil is the source of sin. But beginning in twelfth-century exegesis, the connotations of the tree were expanded to include Christocentric piety, as the wood of the tree was said to be responsible for both the incarnation and the crucifixion of Christ, a point confirmed by references to trees in biblical commentary and other treatises with a Christological bent. As Sara Ritchey has put it, "To imitate Christ in either his human capacity or his death was to acknowledge the presence of a tree."[55] Thus the humanity of Jesus was bolstered by the arboreal allusion. St. Anne could participate in this imagery, but it becomes immediately clear that the wood of the anthropocentric tree must stand for life and incarnation (rather than death) when the grandmother saint is involved, because she plays no role in the crucifixion scene. References to the familiar Tree of Jesse solidify the arboreal imagery applied to St. Anne while also shifting attention to the other intercessory advantage of Mary's mother apart from her role in producing her daughter, grandson, and the rest of the Holy Kinship – the retrieval of royal heritage that reaches back to Old Testament figures.

The Tree of Jesse: Looking Forward, Looking Back

The Turin office for St. Anne and its relatives were not the only offices to draw on the arboreal tradition to allegorize St. Anne. In some cases, the saint was compared to an olive tree.[56] More often, however, she is associated with the well-known image of the Tree of Jesse from the Old Testament. The Tree of Jesse was based on the prophecy from Isaiah 11:1–2: "A shoot shall come out from the stem of Jesse and a branch shall grow out of its roots. And the spirit of the Lord shall rest upon him." In the late Middle Ages, the Tree of Jesse was understood to depict the impressive royal legacy that naturally brought forth the Virgin Mary and Christ. Christian exegetical tradition, beginning with the third-century apologist Tertullian, viewed Jesse's son David as the foundational stem or root (*radix*) and the Virgin Mary as the shoot or branch (*virga*); to continue the exegesis from Isaiah, the flower (*flos*) would thus represent Jesus, emerging by extension from the branch.[57] The imagery embodied in the Tree of Jesse helped settle the double paradox of Christ's heritage as both God and man, born of both a virgin and a mother. The arboreal imagery was central to explaining how original sin was impeded in Mary's conception, therefore rendering her sinless and capable of generating a magnificent and untainted "flower."[58]

Many different offices for St. Anne propagated the Tree of Jesse icon, exploiting the rich meaning of the arboreal image. Poets of these liturgical offices generally positioned St. Anne as either the root (*radix*) or the branch (*virga*), giving her a familiar but flexible position of symbolic importance in the holy line of descendants and allowing her to borrow iconography associated with both the weighty figures of the Old Testament and her own glorious offspring, Mary.[59] As mentioned earlier, several invocations of the rod (also root, stem, tree) of Jesse appear across the full array of offices for St. Anne, in which Mary's mother is identified with appellations that could easily pass for epithets of the Virgin Mary. The hymn *Lucis huius festa* (Example 2.3) contains the lone reference to the Tree of Jesse imagery in the office for St. Anne from the Turin Codex. While the second stanza of this hymn hails the life-giving benefits of devotion to St. Anne, the third strophe more pointedly declares that the root of Jesse (*radix Yesse*) produced Anne to make visible (*expresse*) the lineage of Mary and Jesus, who are also referenced with imagery from the natural world (i.e., plant, fountain, stone, mountain).

VH	VH
Lucis huius festa	Let the honest people
Colat plebs honesta	promote the feast of this light,
Deum celo dignis	celebrating God in heaven
Confrequentans hymnis	with worthy hymns.
Mater matris Christi	The mother of the mother of Christ,
Ex hoc mundo tristi	going away from this sad world
Migrans fide bona	with good faith,
Sumpsit vite dona.	took up the offerings of life.
Annam sic expresse	The **root of Jesse** put forth Anne
Fudit **radix Yesse**	thus making her visible, so that she might
Ut sit mater matris	become the mother of the mother of the
Nati Dei patris.	Son of God the Father.
Ex hac carnis **planta**	Out of this **plant** of flesh
Surgit virgo sancta	the holy virgin arose.
Ex hoc fluit **fonte**	Out of this **fountain** flows the **stone** cut
Lapis cesus **monte**.	out of the **mountain**.
Celo iam sublata	Now lifted from heaven,
Mulier beata	may the blessed woman
Suo nos precatu	cleanse us from our guilt
Purget a reatu.	in her prayer.
Trino laus et **uni**	Praise be to God,
Deo sit communi,	joined **three-in-one**,
In quo vivit Anna	in which Anne lives
Simul cum Maria. Amen.	together with Mary. Amen.

Example 2.3 The hymn *Lucis huius festa*, from the Turin Office for St. Anne, fols. 14r–v.

If one of the benefits of a saint was making that which is numinous visible on earth, St. Anne and her daughter went a step further by making Christ himself visible to the world. The hymn *Lucis huius festa* confirms this notion with help from the root of Jesse icon. The final stanza of the hymn presents a striking image of Anne and her daughter mysteriously dwelling amidst the Holy Trinity, the entity that is typically praised in a hymn's ultimate strophe. Remember that the devotional trio of Anne, Mary, and Jesus (concretized in the image of the St. Anne Trinitarian) may be regarded as a kind of "earthly" or "fleshly" alternative to the traditional Trinity (God, Son, and Spirit/Dove), a concept with political implications addressed more fully in Chapter 7 in the context of the French royal court of a century later.[60] As a hymn, *Lucis huius festa* presents stanzas sung to a recurring and uncomplicated musical tune, thereby drawing more attention to the text than would befall an ordinary antiphon or responsory. That this particular hymn was to be sung twice in the complete liturgical day (First and Second Vespers, according to instructions in the Turin Codex) allows the rich texts of this unassuming melody to collectively become impressed upon singers and listeners alike.

Other Biblical Heritage

The Tree of Jesse allusion is part of a larger thematic strand in the St. Anne office from the Turin Codex involving the value of noble lineage and its relationship to biblical heritage, a valuable asset for any dynasty. The recovery of holy ancestry for St. Anne stems from broad cultural trends of the time. The widespread devotion to the Virgin Mary, about whom so little is said in Scripture, prompted investigation into her life, particularly her upbringing and pedigree. Indeed, it is in the context of the nativity story of Mary that her parents, Anne and Joachim, first appear in the *Protoevangelium of James*. Amid the exploration of the life circumstances of Mary, momentum was gathering behind the theology of incarnation, which stressed the "humanation" or "enfleshing" of God in Christ. Jesus' humanity was a product of his maternal side, so any commemoration of his incarnation reached back not just to Mary but, more broadly, to her forebears.[61] At the same time, the conscious effort to locate St. Anne in the line of ancient biblical figures may stem from the general cultural endeavor to substantiate kinship that gained special favor during the thirteenth century, as explained earlier. The compiler of the office for St. Anne went to some lengths to acknowledge the precious human interconnections of Jesus' grandmother, naturally to a much greater extent than one would typically claim for a saint. After Jacobus de Voragine alerted Christians to the importance of Jesus' matrilineage in the thirteenth century, securing Mary's ancestors in the holy line of descendants became a concern and a project of the next two centuries.

With these general theological and cultural trends in mind, the multiple references to figures of ancient biblical lineage – of which Mary and St. Anne were necessarily offspring – can now be examined. Allusions in the Turin office to particular individuals of the Old Testament help to chisel an image of Christ's grandmother that accesses the esteemed lineage of the Virgin Mary. Some of the poetry appeals very generally to Jewish ancestry, as in the Matins antiphon *De stirpe patriarchali* (MA2). In a characteristically short space, this antiphon encapsulates the bifurcated notion of Anne both inheriting and bequeathing the prized stock of a great dynasty.

MA2
De stirpe patriarchali
Contraxit originem
Et sanctorum proles regum
Ornavit originem.

Ps. Celi enarrant.

MA2
Out of the patriarchal lineage
[Anne] brought about the source
and she provided the descendants
of the holy kings.

Ps. The heavens shew forth. [Ps. 18]

The ancient lineage in the St. Anne office becomes more precise as one progresses through the night office of Matins, first with Hannah from the book of Samuel, the namesake of Mary's mother (Anna). The two share more than their Latin homonymic property: the legend of Anne, it turns out, is patterned to some extent after the story of Hannah. In the narrative from the first book of Samuel, Hannah is presented as the second of the two wives of Elkanah the Zuphite. Unlike the first wife of Elkanah

(Peninnah), who bore a child, Hannah remained barren for years. At the temple before Eli the High Priest, Hannah prayed silently for a child, and her wish would be granted that night as she conceived a child, Samuel, who would become one of the major figures in the development of the line of David.[62] Similar to Hannah, St. Anne was said to be barren for much of her life until God allowed her to conceive at an old age. The ninth responsory of the Matins *Felix Anna quae prophetam* features an explicit comparison between Hannah and Anne.

MR9

Felix Anna quae prophetam	**Blessed** was the **Anna** [Hannah],
Samuelem genuit,	who bore the prophet Samuel,
Sed felicior est ista,	but more blessed is she [Anne]
Quae Mariam edidit:	who gave birth to Mary.
V. Illa vocis [*sic*] impetratum	V. That one [Hannah] produces for us
Nazarenum generat,	the sought-for Nazarean.
Ista matrem Nazareni,	This one [Anne] begets the mother of
Qui Nazarenos generat.	the Nazarene, who bears the Nazareans.

The incipit may confuse the listener at first, because it is not a reference to St. Anne but to Hannah, obviously playing on the ambiguity of the Latin. The poet of this responsory saw the connection between the two Annas, but wanted to ensure that St. Anne effectively surpassed her predecessor, even though the saint's name is only implicit in the short responsory by virtue of the larger context of the office. Also, note that the first word, *felix*, although translated as "blessed" here (a typical adjective used with both male and female saints),[63] may retain some of the connotations of fertility or productiveness witnessed earlier in the Matins responsory *In redemptionis nostrae*.

While some late medieval offices for St. Anne highlight Sarah (wife of Abraham) even more than Hannah among Anne's alleged ancestors from the Old Testament, the office liturgy connects the *Mater matris* directly with Abraham himself.[64] In the fourth antiphon of Matins *Abrae beati senis* (Example 2.4), the text reveals Anne's heritage reaching back to the forefather of the Israelites, as well as to King David. The Davidic ancestry is a clear appropriation of a Marian trope, not unlike the invocation of the root of Jesse for St. Anne found in the hymn *Lucis huius festa*. Because Anne directly precedes Mary in the holy line of descendants, she must share in the royal lineage of Israel that began with Samuel, Saul, and David.[65] In *Abrae beati senis*, the composer draws the most musical attention to the third line

Example 2.4 *Abrae beati senis* (MA4) from the Turin Office for St. Anne, fol. 16r.

of poetry (*adimpleta est per Annam*) – the line that speaks expressly of Anne in the noble lineage set forth. In this third line, the musical range of the antiphon reaches its apex, pushing through the confines of an otherwise constricted ambitus of the sixth-mode melodic scale in which it operates. The psalm prescribed for this antiphon (Ps. 44 *Eructavit cor meum*) speaks directly to a king and even the life of a new bride, a possible hint at its political efficacy.[66]

MA4
Abrae beati senis
Et David promissio
Adimpleta est per Annam
In Marie filio.

Ps. Eructavit.

The promise to blessed, old Abraham and David
was fulfilled through Anne
in the son of Mary.

Ps. My heart has uttered… [Ps. 44]

Just one antiphon separates *Abrae beati senis* from another that hails the precious Jewish lineage of Mary's mother. *Annam Iuda germinavit* calls on Judah in particular, though it is not clear whether the poet is referring to the fourth son of Jacob and Leah (great-grandson of Abraham) or, more broadly, to the Tribe of Judah (or even the Kingdom of Judah). Still, the purpose of the allusion – either to the figure or to an ancient people – is to connect the grandmother of Christ with distant roots in the Old Testament. The antiphon *Annam Iuda germinavit* engages imagery from the natural world to substantiate St. Anne's existence. The familiar image of a flowering plant, akin to the root of Jesse icon, allegorizes Anne's lineage and her biological connection to Jesus.[67]

MA6

Annam **Iuda** germinavit,	**Judah** sprouted forth Anne,
Anna virgam regiam,	Anne [sprouted forth] the royal branch,
Virga florem, flos decorum,	The Virgin [sprouted forth] the flower,
Decor vitam coelibem.	the beautiful flower,
	Grace [sprouted forth] the celibate life.

The St. Anne office as transmitted in the Turin Codex seems to have something for everyone and reflects the wide areas of intercession that were attached to Mary's mother. The idea of maternity and the power of women to produce flesh is given no small emphasis in the office. St. Anne is also promoted as a gateway to illustrious heritage. Both themes had universal resonance with the early modern nobility. The most elite families typically traced lineage as a sign of honor. The objective of a dynasty in turn was to produce progeny to sustain the line. With a firm grip on the subject matter of this particular liturgy for the grandmother saint, we are now in a position to survey how the office might have functioned in the multiple court contexts to which it was likely connected.

Political Utility in Cyprus, Brescia, and Beyond

Although the St. Anne office appears in a manuscript prepared for the Avogadro family of Brescia, the contents were almost certainly exposed to the Lusignan court of Cyprus, as this is the family that sought permission for the companion office for St. Hilarion. Beyond these circumstances, the Turin Codex had an afterlife in Savoy that must be considered in the transmission of this office for Mary's mother. In each case, the thematic accents of the office would have found a welcoming noble audience eager to reap the benefits of devotion to the *Mater matris*. To begin, a brief review of the gradual weakening of the Lusignan claims in Cyprus during Janus's reign can help explain why St. Anne would be a key figure of veneration at his court.

After the assassination of King Peter I of Cyprus in 1369 and the capture of the eastern port city of Famagusta in 1373 by the Genoese, the Lusignan kingdom suffered a steady decline until its demise more than a century later in 1489.[68] Janus I was crowned king of Jerusalem, Cyprus, and Armenia in Santa Sophia in November 1399, and his first wife, Heloise (Visconti), died within five years of their marriage in 1401. The king's advisor Raymond de Lescure was dispatched to the continent in 1407 to negotiate the Cypriot king's second marriage, this one to Charlotte of Bourbon, with the French court. The latter marriage in 1411 brought a large French retinue into service at the Lusignan court, including composers Jean Hanelle and Giles Velut, the first of which, as mentioned earlier, probably had a hand in the compilation of the Turin Codex and maybe some of its compositions.[69]

Queen Charlotte was seen as a harbinger of better fortunes for the island, as plagues, locusts, and the losses of vegetation began to subside within the first year after her arrival. Unfortunately, both uncontrollable and man-made woes crippled Cyprus in the years ahead. Pestilence revisited the island in 1419, 1420, and 1422, and the debt of the Lusignans mounted during this time, which hampered the king's attempts to retake Famagusta.[70] Charlotte died in 1422, but even more devastating for Janus was the damage delivered by the raids of the Egyptian Mamluks in the following years, culminating in a full-scale attack in July 1426. That same month at the battle of Khirokitia, the Mamluk invaders ransacked the island and captured King Janus, who consequently had to pay a large ransom for his freedom. Deemed a tributary to Mamluk interests and increasingly dominated by Italian merchants with whom the island engaged in trade, the Lusignan kingdom dwindled to nothing when Queen Catherine Cornaro was forced to sell the island to Venice in 1489.[71] Remember that the offices for St. Hilarion and St. Anne were probably compiled soon after Janus received permission in 1413 for his court to develop texts and music for the former saint. If this assumption is true, the repertory would have been present in the early years of the king's second marriage, precisely in the advent of heirs to the Lusignan throne.

The office for St. Anne would have been closely held at Janus's court and almost certainly had personal meaning for Queen Charlotte and him, particularly in light of its references to maternity and heritage. Well known as a patroness of fertility and childbearing both in the Lusignan court and in Byzantine art on Cyprus, St. Anne could heed the call of a dynasty to produce heirs to a noble lineage, as she had accomplished with the Holy Kinship. Rich with symbolism, the office likely functioned as a medium to express the desire of the royal couple to construct an enduring dynasty with multiple children of regal stock under the sponsorship of St. Anne. Such a model would have been especially pertinent as the political clout of the Lusignans was thinning in the region and heirs for the kingdom were a priority. The Tree of Jesse icon from the office of St. Anne is particularly apt for the Lusignans wishing to extend their domain. The image encapsulates the dual emphasis in the versified office on both illustrious progeny and the magnificent heritage from past generations. The office for Mary's mother known at the Cypriot court indeed had something to offer for any family dynasty, and its usefulness was not confined to the Lusignan house. As this liturgy traveled to northern Italy and appeared formally in the Turin Codex, the circumstances of its reception necessarily changed, but the noble ideals embedded in this particular office for Mary's mother remained very much intact.

Although the music of the Turin Codex reflects a repertory known to Janus's court, the coat of arms in the manuscript suggests that the source was initially dedicated to the Avogadro family of Brescia. Pietro Avogadro in particular was pivotal during the second quarter of the fifteenth century, as he rid Brescia of perceived persecution from the Milanese (Visconti), allowing the Venetians instead to control the north Italian city. For this, he was hailed as a hero in Venice and received numerous honors and entitlements.[72] In his study of the Brescian connection to the Turin Codex, Kügle posited a program of sanctoral devotion in the manuscript that would have appealed to Pietro Avogadro and his wife, Brigida, the assumed dedicatees of the manuscript. St. Anne participates in this program, projecting the values of procreation and mature femininity. These qualities could complement those of the wise virgin saint Katherine of Alexandria, who is honored with two motets in the codex. In Kügle's view, the full range of female gender roles revealed in these female saints is balanced by attention to three masculine figures – Christ, John the Baptist, and St. Hilarion. The first two represent exemplary male ideals in early and middle adulthood, while Hilarion, who lived an ascetic lifestyle into his eighties according to the legend, completes the spectrum.[73]

The versified offices for the elder saints Hilarion and Anne, notably positioned at the opening of the Turin Codex, were liturgies for two figures well suited to the noble Pietro and Brigida, who were probably between forty and fifty years of age when the manuscript was compiled. As *pater* and *mater familias* over their aristocratic house, Pietro and Brigida might have viewed these saints as models to be emulated on earth, quite possibly for their wisdom. Recall that both are holding books in the manuscript's only miniatures. St. Anne, a wise mother for having instructed the Virgin Mary, offered an even wider array of intercessory realms than did St. Hilarion, including the oversight of noble families. This area also would have realistically appealed to the Avogadro duo, eager to sustain its position in Brescian society in the face of continuing struggles with a reconquest by Milan. That very political unrest in mid-1430s Brescia might explain why the Turin Codex was apparently never presented to the Avogadro family and is now found in connection with the House of Savoy.

Documents suggest that Jean Hanelle, the Lusignan court chapel master and likely transmitter (or even composer) of the repertory found in the Turin Codex, was present at the Savoy court in Thonon in 1434 and 1436, receiving significant disbursements of ten and six ducats respectively in those years.[74] Concurrent with the second payment of 1436 is an expense in the amount of eighteen ducats for a book purchased by the court. The expenditure for this evidently extravagant book was recorded alongside several other luxury items obtained during the court's summer stay at Lake Geneva.[75] It is possible that the Turin Codex was this very book. After what appears to be a failed attempt to provide a manuscript to the Avogadro family, Jean Hanelle seems to have succeeded in finding a home for the manuscript at the court of Savoy. It is in this last set of circumstances that the office for St. Anne from the Turin Codex merits final consideration.

Anne of Lusignan had been resident in Savoy since early 1434 with her marriage to Louis, prince of Piedmont. The young woman's arrival concluded a protracted set of marriage negotiations between the Lusignan and Savoyard courts, which began in 1431. Anne was originally betrothed to the firstborn of Amadeus VIII (Prince Amadeus of Piedmont), but he died shortly after the arrangements were made. By January 1432, Anne was affianced to Louis (brother of Amadeus), the next in line to the duchy. Following a marriage ceremony by proxy on the island of Cyprus, Anne and her entourage of more than sixty traveled to Chambéry, arriving February 7, 1434 for a grand ceremony in the Sainte-Chapelle, officiated by the uncle of the bride Cardinal Hugh de Lusignan.[76] Upon arriving at the court of Savoy, Anne of Cyprus stepped into a musical culture that rivaled the cultures of the major courts across Western Europe, one modeled after the celebrated Burgundian court. Set in a strategically advantageous position in the French Alps, the cosmopolitan Savoyard court drew on artistic talents and trends from both northern Europe and Italy. The most important composer of the first half of the fifteenth century, Guillaume Du Fay, maintained strong ties to the court of Savoy and served as maître de chapelle in no fewer than three multiyear stretches during his long career (1433–5, 1437–9, 1452–8).[77] Though its resources ultimately were no match for the Burgundian court, the court of Savoy maintained a number of competent musicians in its large domestic retinue during the fifteenth century, and the nobles themselves showed interest in attaining skills on various musical instruments. Jean Hanelle must have been aware of the significant investment in the Savoyard court's musical life.[78]

Hanelle might have peddled the Turin Codex to several individuals at Savoy. Anne of Cyprus is a strong candidate to have received the office of her patron saint at the Savoyard court and harvested the benefits of this music in the elegant Turin Codex. Although the duchess might have encountered the music for St. Anne in her youth, the office would have taken on special meaning for her in Savoy. The death of Anne's mother in 1422 must have impacted the young girl. (She would have been between three and seven years old at the time of her mother's passing.) Except for the Virgin Mary, St. Anne can hardly be matched as an intercessor to provide solace and comfort for the motherless Anne of Cyprus for more than a decade. The emphasis on maternity and the promise of offspring in the St. Anne liturgy would have resonated with Anne and Louis, as much as it likely did some twenty years earlier in the Lusignan court chapel, or for any dynasty in search of heirs. Indeed, Anne and Louis were in a position to generate a line of possible successors to the duchy of Savoy, with the hope of spreading Savoyard dominion in the process. Surely, antiphons such as *Sol eternus* (MA1) and *Anna Deo vigilat* (LA3) would have tapped into the procreational ambitions of the young couple. As witnessed earlier, the substantial emphasis on weaving and textiles in the office further sustains a metaphor for the bearing of offspring.[79]

That the duty of Anne of Cyprus, like any noble wife, was to bear and raise children can also be viewed retrospectively through the visual culture of the Savoyard court, specifically in the famous book of hours (Paris, Bibliothèque nationale, MS lat. 9473) made for her husband, Louis, in the mid-fifteenth century, well after Anne had established herself in Savoy. The beautifully decorated *livre d'heures* features seventy miniatures and forty-one embellished initials.[80] Of the illuminated miniatures, two images directly involve St. Anne, one of which is a classic example of the "St. Anne Trinitarian" (Figure 2.2). This icon is not only a powerful marker of Christ's matrilineage and physicality, but also one that embodies the tripartite entity raised in the hymn *Lucis huius festa* from the St. Anne office. This miniature follows one for St. Louis, King of France (fol. 181v), making the obvious association with the noble couple's patron namesakes in this section of the book of hours. In contrast to the various scenes surrounding the Louis illumination, several angels are involved in music making (both playing and singing) as they encircle St. Anne, her daughter, and her grandson.

The other image of St. Anne in the presentation-style book of hours for Louis of Savoy is a miniature of Mary's mother and her husband Joachim at the Golden Gate (fol. 187v), the traditional scene foretelling the birth of the Virgin Mary. Directly following the Golden Gate image is an illumination featuring the two daughters of St. Anne from her legend, Mary Iacobi and Mary Salome (fol. 188v). The opening miniature of the entire manuscript shows scenes from the life of King David in medallions (fol. 2r), and a depiction of the Tree of Jesse falls later in the manuscript (fol. 102r). One can imagine that all of these suggestive images in this book of hours were likely not read as quotidian devotion to the duchess's namesake or these figures from the Old Testament; rather, they combine allegorically as a reminder of a sacred dynastic family par excellence, whom Anne of Cyprus and Louis could revere and emulate as a model for producing a terrestrial dynasty. When this book of hours was compiled, Anne had already experienced a fruitful run in her childbearing years, giving birth to no fewer than eighteen children, most of them surviving past their delicate first year.[81]

Having traversed well over a thousand miles by sea and land, Anne and her retinue of some sixty members (notably including Jean Hanelle) were very much strangers in a new cosmopolitan world when they arrived in Chambéry. Moreover, Anne slowly took control of the duchy's administration, not in a power grab, but rather as the result of the weakness of her husband, Louis of Savoy, who in the end cared less about politics and diplomacy than the pursuit of letters and the thrill of hunting.[82] As a young outsider in new environs, the duchess could have benefited from assurance of a strong heritage, whether expressed abstractly in the office for St. Anne, in the distinctly Cypriot office for St. Hilarion, or in motets that directly referenced her father, Janus (he died just after Anne married).[83]

Outside of the woman with direct Cypriot ties (and her husband, Louis), the Duke of Savoy Amadeus VIII (the future antipope Felix V) would have been another viable candidate to obtain the Turin Codex. Amadeus entered into quasi-retirement after November 1434, living in solitude at his palace in Ripaille. Naturally, the emphasis on heritage and dynastic oversight found in the St. Anne office could have conceivably attracted his interest in the manuscript. He was a passionate bibliophile and had one of the most extensive libraries among fifteenth-century nobles. Such an impressive

Figure 2.2 *St. Anne Trinitarian* in the Book of Hours for Duke Louis of Savoy. Paris, Bibliothèque nationale de France, MS lat. 9473, fol. 182v. Photo: Bibliothèque nationale de France.

volume of music would have been a logical addition to his collection.[84] Kügle has also suggested the possibility that the Turin Codex might have come into the possession of the Visconti of Milan. Not only was this noble house (especially Gian Galeazzo [d. 1402]) an avid patron of "Ars subtilior" music, but a mass cycle added late to the Turin Codex lacks an Agnus Dei, a potential gesture to the Ambrosian rite of Milan.[85] A connection to Savoy can also be found in Milan, as Mary of Savoy (the sister-in-law of Anne of Cyprus) married Filippo Maria Visconti (Duke of Milan) in 1427, setting in motion a generation of musical exchange.[86] Again, the notions of maternity and noble heritage found in the St. Anne office would have had resonance with the Duke and Duchess of Milan, as much as it might have for the noble couple in Savoy or others along the way.

In his studies of noble families in the Middle Ages, modern French historian Georges Duby wrote, "To be noble is to be able to refer to a genealogy."[87] St. Anne could help the sovereigns of Western Europe by reminding them of the sacrality of a venerable heritage. With references to her lineage traced to Abraham, David, and Judah as well as responsories like *Genealogie christi* (MR6), the office on the whole produces a strong sense of nobility on those who encountered the saint's office in the Turin Codex. It is not hard to imagine the utility of these sentiments for any of the personages mentioned.

In his seminal studies of the plainchant in the Turin Codex, Richard Hoppin noted that, in addition to the office for St. Anne being modest in its offerings when compared to the Hilarion office (and mass), it is the more highly syllabic – and thus less musically elaborate – of the two.[88] The unspoken corollary to the relatively syllabic disposition of the St. Anne office is that the text would have been quite comprehensible in performance, declaimed in a more natural and conversational manner than could be achieved in a comparatively neumatic setting. This style of delivery produces a directness and lucidity that a noble could grasp at first hearing. Despite the clarity of the text in the St. Anne office, the ideas and images of any office are spread in theory over the course of the liturgical day. But the variegated images of Mary's mother also collapse across the hours or even perhaps in a noble's casual thumbing through the repertory of this deluxe manuscript. Words of devotion to a saint or feast are reduced to a few key intercessory emphases; and if performed, they are heightened by monophonic expression and cast into the ineffable sound world.[89] Ancient biblical lineage feels less distant, especially when paired with forward-looking images of holy progeny and posterity.

The versified office for St. Anne in the Turin Codex has exposed two basic areas of political usefulness guided by Mary's mother: the prospect of noble offspring to extend dominion and the retrieval of genealogy to legitimate noble heritage. This is not the last stop in Savoy, nor is this the last reference to the Tree of Jesse, Christine de Pizan, or the offices that honor St. Anne. As the next chapter considers St. Anne in the Habsburg-Burgundian court culture of the late fifteenth and early sixteenth centuries, the issue of patronage becomes more focused, while the meanings associated with St. Anne in early modern music begin to proliferate. In the case that follows, the saint's highly customizable areas of intercession combine with a set of political circumstances in a volatile period of Western European history to produce a nuanced reading of the *Mater matris* for another female noble and her ambitions.

3 | Of Widowhood and Maternity: La Rue's *Missa de Sancta Anna*

As models of Christian living, the saints were venerated by secular authorities for their protection, as well as for the power and prestige that they could offer symbolically. Though extraordinary individuals, saints could also be adopted for quotidian use. Believers routinely implored saints to provide communities with protection for land and crops, and saints could also intercede to combat a range of human ailments. If a foundation for the political usage of St. Anne is suggested in the fifteenth century, the benefits of invoking Mary's mother expanded into the sixteenth century. In the present case, the saint's intercession is noticeably personal. It will quickly be seen how the saint's own story intersected on an individual level with that of a celebrated female of the early sixteenth century, a woman with substantial political influence and aptitude. The reader will also witness how music could be used not only as a sign of dynastic repute but also as a document of introspection in court culture.

Under consideration is a polyphonic mass for St. Anne by one of the most important composers of the late fifteenth and early sixteenth centuries, Pierre de la Rue (ca. 1452–1518).[1] La Rue's *Missa de Sancta Anna* (hereafter, *St. Anne Mass*) survives in three sources (VienNB Mus. 15496, MontsM 773, and JenaU 7), all copied before 1516 in the workshop of Petrus Alamire.[2] The latter two manuscripts place the *St. Anne Mass* at the beginning of their respective collections, undoubtedly indicative of the importance of this work, while in the manuscript VienNB Mus. 15496 the mass comes second in the order. Only VienNB Mus. 15496, a manuscript devoted exclusively to works of La Rue, holds a complete version of this mass.[3] The *St. Anne Mass* contains many of the hallmarks of the composer's style, including fluid melodic lines, rhythmic vitality, and unexpected cadences. Yet it does not share some of the more forward-looking aspects of La Rue's masses from this period. All five sections of the relatively conservative mass move from *tempus perfectum* to *tempus imperfectum* internally; the major third is never present at the final cadence; and there is no use of canon at any point during the mass. These more archaic compositional traits could explain the general lack of scholarship addressing this work.

A substitution motet *O salutaris hostia*, which explicitly takes the place of the first Hosanna of the Sanctus of La Rue's *St. Anne Mass*, has drawn scholarly attention.[4] While a typical mass setting would repeat the first Hosanna at the second Hosanna, in this case a new Hosanna was introduced for the second Hosanna, because it would not be appropriate to repeat the substitution motet. Motets around the elevation characteristically displayed a simple homophonic texture, and the composer's *O salutaris hostia* is no exception. But the presence of this substitution motet has essentially diverted scholarly focus away from the five principal sections of the *St. Anne Mass*. The curious tenor rubric that accompanies this mass – "Felix Anna" – has attracted far less scrutiny in the literature and has clouded a fuller understanding of this mass.[5] The remainder of this chapter not only reopens inquiry into the musical inspiration for the *St. Anne Mass*, but also more broadly endeavors to situate St. Anne as a subject of devotion in Burgundian circles, particularly in the milieu of Margaret of Austria, the likely patroness of the work.

Before delving into the melodic underpinning of La Rue's *St. Anne Mass*, some comments on the transmission and structure of the mass are in order. While all three manuscripts were assembled in a short window of time (probably between July 1515 and March 1516), La Rue most likely composed the masses contained in these manuscripts between 1508 and 1514, a "quiet period" for the composer in the court's *Grande chapelle*, which remained relatively stationary in the cities of Mechelen and Brussels, as opposed to the more itinerant stretches preceding 1508.[6] Two of the three manuscripts strictly contain music by La Rue (Table 3.1) and seem to have been held exclusively at the court: VienNB Mus. 15496 was compiled for the future Holy Roman Emperor Charles V, and MontsM 773 was possibly intended for Margaret of Austria (Charles's aunt). JenaU 7, which contains the arms of Austria, features three masses by La Rue (out of seven total), and Frederick the Wise eventually obtained it. The two "in-house" manuscripts have considerable overlap in repertory: of La Rue's seven masses found in VienNB Mus. 15496, six occur in MontsM 773, a manuscript that includes nine masses by the composer.[7]

With no small credit to Margaret's prestigious and well-connected court at Mechelen, La Rue's works circulated widely in manuscripts, not to mention in some of the earliest musical prints. His music was disseminated well beyond court circles and was recorded in sources (mainly Italian ones) surviving as late as the mid-sixteenth century. La Rue's mastery of the polyphonic style was certainly on display when the court undertook its many travels, thereby magnifying the works of the composer as a symbol of the

Table 3.1 Comparison of La Rue's works in the manuscripts VienNB Mus. 15496, MontsM 773, and JenaU 7

VienNB Mus. 15496	MontsM 773	JenaU 7
Missa Alleluia*	*Missa Alleluia* (lacks Sanctus and bits of other mass sections)	
Missa Ave Maria	*Missa Ave Maria* (parts of Kyrie and Agnus missing)	
Missa de Sancta Anna	*Missa de Sancta Anna* (only Credo is complete)	*Missa de Sancta Anna* (parts of Kyrie and Agnus missing)
Missa de sancta cruce	*Missa de sancta cruce* (missing parts of Kyrie)	
Missa de Sancto Job	*Missa de Sancto Job* (attr. page missing)	*Missa de Sancto Job* (attr. page missing; parts of Agnus missing)
Missa Inviolata	*Missa Inviolata* (parts of all sections missing)	*Missa Inviolata*
Missa Sub tuum presidium		
[*O salutaris hostia*] (no attr. as motet; to be sung as Hosanna I of *St. Anne Mass*)	[*O salutaris hostia*] (no attr. as motet; to be sung as Hosanna I of *St. Anne Mass*)	[*O salutaris hostia*] (no attr. as motet; to be sung as Hosanna I of *St. Anne Mass*)
	Missa de feria (missing part of each mass section)	
	Missa O gloriosa domina (text: *O gloriosa margareta*; missing two small sections of the mass)	
	Missa O salutaris hostia (portions of Gloria, Credo, and Agnus missing)	
		Missa Ave Maria (Févin, incomplete)**
		Missa de Venerabili sacramento (Prioris, incomplete)
		Missa de Nostra domina, i.e., *Missa de Beata Virgine* (Josquin)
		Missa Si dedero (Divitis)

*Contents are arranged alphabetically for comparison, not in the order presented in the manuscripts.
**Masses not by La Rue in JenaU 7 have composers in parentheses.

powerful Habsburg-Burgundian dominion. Considering that Margaret of Austria quite possibly requested these three key manuscripts, it would further be no exaggeration to say that this mass represented a taste of her preferences at the Mechelen court. Most manuscripts copied in the Alamire workshop were eventually sent to other courts and nobles, not just as gifts to procure relations during travels, but also as emblems of prestige, touting the court's most distinguished composer. Discussion of the JenaU 7 manuscript will be postponed until the next chapter, but the fact that VienNB Mus. 15496 and MontsM 773 were guarded internally is noteworthy and will frame the findings of the present investigation. These domestic "mass favorites," among them La Rue's *St. Anne Mass*, expose not only the court's musical predilections, but also its vehicles of self-presentation in the early sixteenth century.

In Search of a Musical Model

La Rue's mass for St. Anne has long been considered a standard devotional work in honor of Mary's mother for the Habsburg-Burgundian court chapel.[8] But it will be shown that the invocation of St. Anne through music could have served a number of strategic purposes at Margaret of Austria's Mechelen court, not least of which was the regent's personal identification with the *Mater matris* and the dynastic protection that the grandmother saint offered. Part of the meaning in this mass may be embedded in the musical model for the work, which has heretofore remained unidentified. The proposal of a musical foundation for the *St. Anne Mass* will open up new possibilities for interpreting the work and determining its function within and outside court quarters.

The editors of the La Rue critical edition have noted the "accessibility" of the *St. Anne Mass*, relative to his other masses, on account of its duet textures, transparent imitative passages, and general harmonic "suavity" around an unambiguous F tonal center.[9] Typical of his masses, La Rue also obscured the musical underpinning of the *St. Anne Mass*. It might best be described as a paraphrase mass or even a motto mass: each section seems to refer to an existing melody, but there is no long-note cantus firmus to signal an explicit monophonic model.[10] Instead, there is a consistent head motive at the outset of most major junctures, echoed in imitation and transformed in different ways through some or all of the vocal texture. The incipits of the Kyrie and Gloria are given in Example 3.1.

Example 3.1 Opening of the (a) Kyrie and (b) Gloria of La Rue's *Missa de Sancta Anna*, after VienNB Mus. 15496.

The unifying motive can be represented by the syllables *ut-mi-fa-sol*, with the syllable *la* often appended to the gesture as decoration of the fifth scale degree. Many duets throughout the mass reiterate the head motive (*ut-mi-fa-sol*, etc.), and even subsections in the interior of the mass reaffirm this principal opening gesture. Example 3.2 illustrates two such internal moments ("Qui tollis" of the Gloria; "Confiteor" of the Credo), each of which revives this simple motive.[11] All suggestions of the recurring gesture (including transpositions) are indicated with a dashed line above the staff.

No matter if the gesture occurs as a four- or five-note head motive (*ut-mi-fa-sol-[la]*) in each major section or in the interior of the mass, it disintegrates quickly into diminution, clouding the source melody for the analyst. This is by no means the first time that La Rue's inclination toward paraphrase in his masses has stifled scholarly quests to locate preexistent models.[12] As Honey Meconi has explained, the fact that the composer worked amid numerous chant traditions in his life complicates the search for the origin of some of his melodies.[13] Raised and trained in Tournai, La Rue might have had a particular fondness for melodies learned during his formative years; he must

Example 3.2 Excerpts of the paraphrased motive in the interior of La Rue's *Missa de Sancta Anna*, after VienNB Mus. 15496; (a) Gloria, "Qui tollis"; (b) Credo, "Confiteor".

have also encountered a distinct tradition during his canonicate at the collegiate church of St. Ode before joining the Habsburg-Burgundian court in 1492. Further, the court of Maximilian (and consequently his chapel) was quite itinerant in the mid-1490s, making brushes with other plainchant settings inevitable. In short, these shifting circumstances no doubt provided new and variant melodies in La Rue's collective memory, further obfuscating the sources of some of his models.

The scholarly community has not been entirely silent on a possible musical basis for La Rue's *St. Anne Mass*. In 1954, Jozef Robyns conjectured that the head motive bears a similar profile to the Marian antiphon *Alma redemptoris mater*.[14] A decade later, Martin Picker independently recognized the resemblance of the governing mass melody to this Marian antiphon, even pointing to a section of the Credo in the *St. Anne Mass* where the tenor is "easily identifiable as *Alma redemptoris mater*."[15] It is true that some of the most notable masses and motets of the fifteenth and sixteenth centuries were developed with *Alma redemptoris* as a model.[16] And indeed, certain gestures of the antiphon are adumbrated in the tenor during a part of the Credo. But any passing resemblance is short-lived, nonpervasive, and muddied by ornamentation. It is telling that *Alma redemptoris* was not accepted as a model for this mass by the editors of the La Rue critical edition, who themselves have spent decades trying to identify some of the enigmatic sources of La Rue's works. As it concerns the *St. Anne Mass*, the editors cautiously noted that the condensed melodic contour was in fact shared with many fifth-mode models and thus could not be connected definitively to the Marian antiphon.[17] Were the tenor of this mass rubricated with the words "Alma redemptoris," the stock head motive *ut-mi-fa-sol-*[*la*] could then be decisively linked with a rubric, and one would not hesitate to declare the antiphon the source of this mass. The fact remains that the only known inscription associated with the *St. Anne Mass* is not a reference to Mary, but to St. Anne herself in the tenor of the opening Kyrie, where the words "Felix Anna" are inscribed between the initial *Kyrie* and *eleyson* (Figure 3.1).

With the seemingly generic fifth-mode head motive *ut-mi-fa-sol-*[*la*] forming the basis for La Rue's *St. Anne Mass*, it is no wonder that the melodic underpinning has remained unidentified. Yet the succinct rubric "Felix Anna" encourages the pursuit of a more satisfying source of musical inspiration for this mass. This inscription in the tenor from VienNB Mus. 15496 likely refers to an actual plainchant, as scribes typically – and often accurately – rubricated for borrowed material in the Habsburg-Burgundian court manuscripts.[18] And while it may seem pithy in nature, such a chant could potentially hold symbolic meaning for the composer or his patron, not unlike many other cantus firmi set during this period. The musical basis for the mass was not likely chosen at random from the melodies for St. Anne; instead, the terse label "Felix Anna" could possibly encode personal or spiritual meaning within the work.[19]

In the *New Grove Dictionary* under the catalog of La Rue's works, Honey Meconi raises the question of whether the *St. Anne Mass* arose from an antiphon called *Felix Anna*.[20] Indeed, it is not unreasonable to suspect that the musical model for this mass was a plainchant entitled *Felix Anna*, probably taken from a versified office for St. Anne. Several plainchants named *Felix Anna* appear in the office repertory, including one discussed in Chapter 2 (the Matins responsory *Felix Anna quae prophetam*), but the possibilities from which La Rue might have generated his mass for the *Mater matris* can be narrowed down quickly. Among the eleven *Felix Anna* texts found in *Analecta hymnica*, two liturgical items with this title occur with a fair amount of frequency. The Second Vespers antiphon *Felix Anna quedam matrona* and the Matins responsory *Felix Anna cuius tres filie* are each found in a considerable number of sources (at least forty-eight and twelve

In Search of a Musical Model 73

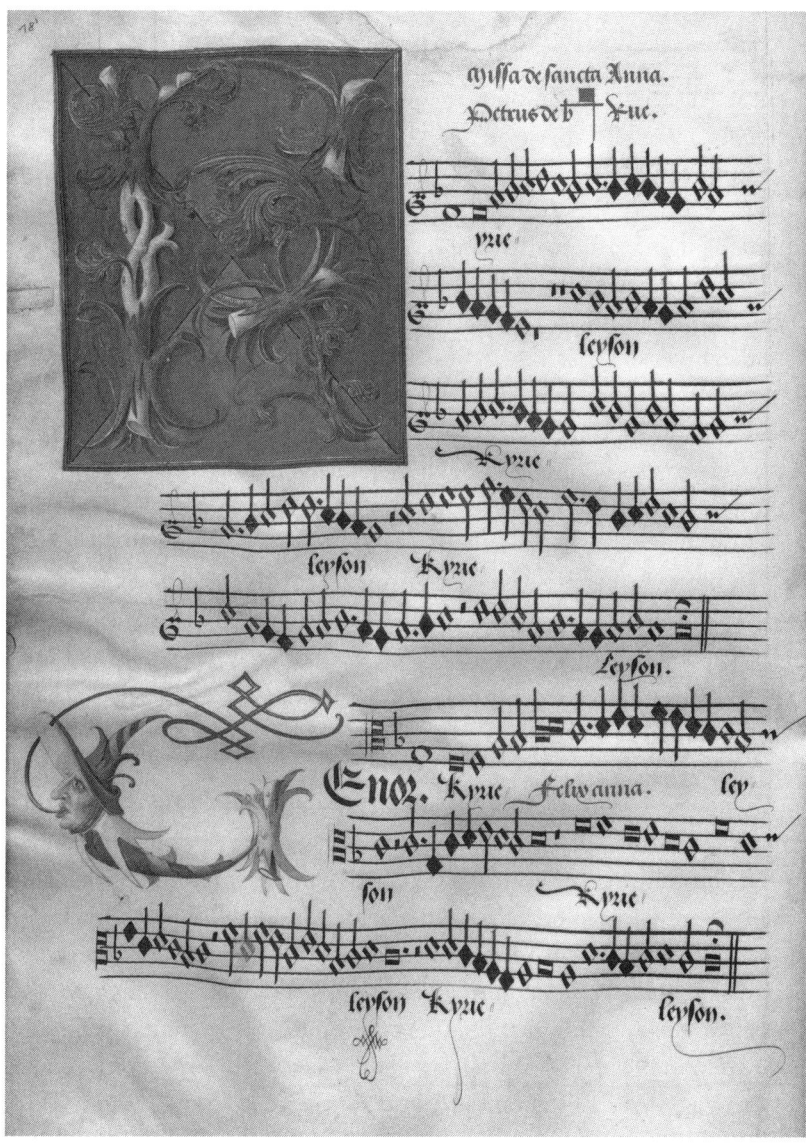

Figure 3.1 Vienna, Österreichische Nationalbibliothek, Musiksammlung, MS Supplementum Musica 15496, fol. 18v.

sources, respectively).[21] Perhaps one of these texts can be connected with a melody that suggests the basic shape of the mass's head motive, allowing the proposal of a possible foundation for the mass. In this study of the context of music for Mary's mother, it is high time to revisit the suspicion that an office melody was associated with the rubric "Felix Anna."

Finding "Felix Anna"

In an article-length definition of the medieval rhymed office from the *Dictionary of the Middle Ages*, Andrew Hughes predicted that the late medieval offices would likely hold the key to identifying many elusive cantus firmi in the polyphonic repertory of this period.[22] The technological advances in the cataloging of texts (and, more recently, melodies) in the Divine Office have facilitated navigation of these liturgical items, and substantial amounts of chant are beginning to accrue for other feasts and saints in electronic chant databases to assist in searches of this kind.[23] Still, the office antiphons and responsories remain an unwieldy and highly variant repertory that has understandably escaped widespread scholarly attention, despite the opportunities the corpus affords. Although melodies can be surprisingly difficult to find for the versified offices for St. Anne, Hughes's own database of melodies from more than 100 versified offices of the late Middle Ages reveals two new liturgical items called "Felix Anna" (*Felix Anna cella mundicie* and *Felix Anna flos hortorum mira*), which derive from the same rhymed office (AH 5.39). Neither of these tunes, however, remotely resembles La Rue's principal motive.[24] Further, the Matins responsory *Felix Anna cuius tres filie* identified earlier is an E-mode melody, again with no hint of the recurring tune from the *St. Anne Mass*.[25]

The liturgical rite of Paris may witness a melody "Felix Anna"; the Burgundian court chapel was to follow that usage, specifically that of Notre-Dame, during the years in question.[26] Two "Felix Anna" plainchants from different Parisian breviaries emerge for consideration, both transmitting nearly identical versions of the widespread Magnificat antiphon from Second Vespers *Felix Anna quedam matrona*.[27] Example 3.3 illustrates the first part of this Magnificat antiphon common to both manuscripts. In her 1994 review of the first three volumes of the La Rue critical edition, Jennifer Bloxam suggested that the cantus firmus for the composer's *St. Anne Mass* might indeed be this *Felix Anna quedam matrona*.[28] Upon closer inspection, however, this melody does not appear to be the one La Rue paraphrased in the *St. Anne Mass*. The frequent and awkward skips in particular would seem to discount it as a candidate for a cantus firmus. The antiphon is in the seventh mode, which at least offers the potential of an *ut-mi-fa-sol-[la]* gesture. And while there is a fragment *ut-mi-fa* on the word *legitima* (labeled **X**), this three-note succession is insufficient evidence to claim a connection to La Rue's paraphrased model, especially because the motive is displaced from the incipit "Felix Anna." Such a short motive is simply too

Example 3.3 Beginning of antiphon *Felix Anna quedam matrona* from Paris, Bibliothèque nationale, MS 15182, fol. 269v.

uncoordinated and fleeting in nature to be considered a strong candidate for the governing melody of the *St. Anne Mass*.

Although the cases of *Felix Anna quedam matrona* from the rite of Paris do not yield a glimmer of hope for the cantus firmus of the *St. Anne Mass*, one hesitates to fold up the tent with such a pervasive text. This widespread antiphon situated at the musical climax of Vespers (the Magnificat) was associated with yet more melodies from sources not of the Parisian rite. Two surviving melodies with possible Habsburg connections sadly do not correspond to the head motive.[29] But another promising Magnificat antiphon *Felix Anna quaedam matrona* does turn up in a Carmelite liturgical book from Mainz. Although this particular source has no direct connection to the Habsburg-Burgundian court, it might channel a version of this melody found in sources known to La Rue that have not survived.[30] The Carmelites were among the earliest devotees of St. Anne and could have impacted the development and diffusion of melodies for the saint.[31]

The resting tone (*finalis*) of this Magnificat antiphon from Mainz is C, rather than one of the four traditional plainchant finals (D, E, f, or g); however, the opening gesture *ut-mi-fa-sol* on the word "Felix" (labeled **X** in Example 3.4) matches the initial paraphrased melody of the *St. Anne Mass*, a crucial link that has eluded scholarship to date. This important motive is revived halfway through the short antiphon, as the melody reveals the pentachord *ut-mi-fa-sol-la* at the word *promeruit* (marked **X'** in Example 3.4), a gesture that even more closely follows the contour of La Rue's head motive. Directly following this reengagement of the key melodic fragment, the antiphon takes an unexpected turn, again restating the *ut-mi-fa-sol* motive, but instead ascending through the hard hexachord beginning on g (marked **X"** in Example 3.4).[32]

Example 3.4 The antiphon *Felix Anna quedam matrona* from Mainz, Bischöfliches Dom- und Diözesanmuseum, Codex C, fol. 226v.

Because La Rue's mass only divulges a few notes of an unknown model, it is unrealistic to compare note by note with the chant at hand. But let this not detract from the fact that this melody more than once unveils the head motive of La Rue's mass, set to the text "Felix Anna" at its first presentation.[33] This version of *Felix Anna quedam matrona* clears an important hurdle in this search. Unlike the Marian antiphon *Alma redemptoris mater* or the antiphon *Felix Anna* Bloxam identified, the opening melodic fragment of the Carmelite melody (and its refreshed interior iterations, unusual for an antiphon) recalls the opening of La Rue's *St. Anne Mass* with a melodic gesture that coincides with the rubric "Felix Anna" supplied by the Alamire workshop.

During the late Middle Ages and the Renaissance, polyphonic compositions using preexisting musical materials were crafted not only from plainchant models but also from polyphonic works (in part or whole). While a likely candidate melody (or better, melodic tradition) for La Rue's *St. Anne Mass* can now be proposed, the polyphonic realm cannot be left behind as a possible treasury for the composer. Motets by Dunstaple, Gombert, and Clemens non Papa with a form of the text "Felix Anna" in their title do not seem to be motivated by the *ut-mi-fa-sol-*[*la*] motive that underpins La Rue's mass.[34] But two motets of the same name found in sources later than the manuscripts that contain the *St. Anne Mass* stand closely related to the suggested parent chant. The four-voice motet *Felix Anna quedam matrona* by Costanzo Festa is found in three early sixteenth-century sources, none earlier than 1521.[35] Important for these purposes, the motet is set in imitative polyphony with a clear, isolated head motive, which happens to be *ut-mi-fa-sol*. Example 3.5 provides the opening of Festa's G-mode *Felix Anna* motet.[36] The long notes of the tenor, amidst the diminution of this melody in the surrounding voices, suggest a monophonic model for the motet, one that appears to paraphrase something like the Carmelite melody surveyed earlier. The motive *ut-mi-fa-sol* begins on C in long deliberate notes in the altus (mm. 1–3, labeled **X**), and the remaining three voices echo this simple melodic fragment (with superius and tenor transposed to g' and g, respectively, and marked **X'**), bringing the polyphonic fabric to a full, four-voice texture. In addition to other similarities throughout Festa's motet that echo the chant model, the proximity of the head motive statements on c/C (altus/bassus) and g'/g (superius/tenor) calls to mind that large, linear gesture in the parent plainchant on the suggestive words *promeruit generare*.

Another motet – the anonymous *Felix Anna quedam matrona* from the partbooks Cambrai, Mediathèque Municipale, MSS 125–8 (fol. 47r) – seems to match La Rue's principal motive even more closely than that of Festa's motet. Unlike Festa, this composer set the opening gesture on f (not c) with a flat in the signature, and he has provided a motive that ascends through the hexachord (*ut-mi-fa-sol-la*) and then reaches the octave, at least in the discantus and tenor parts (Example 3.6), which are located in the same range. The syllable placement of the initial text also resembles the Carmelite chant identified earlier. The motive dissipates quickly, however, not fully echoed through the entries of the four voices. Owned by Bruges

Example 3.5 Costanzo Festa, *Felix Anna quedam matrona* (opening).

merchant Zeghere van Male (1504–1601), the partbooks offer a relatively favorable provenance when considering the Mechelen court as the likely site of the composition for La Rue's *St. Anne Mass*, but a firm date of 1542 distances the source from the mass in question by more than a generation.[37]

Example 3.6 Anonymous, *Felix Anna quedam matrona*, Cambrai, Mediathèque Municipale, MSS 125–8, fol. 47r.

The anonymous *Felix Anna quedam matrona* further contains a *secunda pars* that sets a brief supplicatory text "O Saint Anne, pray to the Lord Jesus Christ for us. Amen" (*Sancta Anna ora pro nobis, Dominum Jesum Christum. Amen*), not known to be associated with the antiphon outlined earlier. Still, the fleeting exposure of the proposed source melody in this motet is more evidence that the Alamire workshop seems to have had it right when rubricating the tenor of La Rue's *St. Anne Mass* with the words "Felix Anna."

The antiphon *Felix Anna quedam matrona* was part of a pervasive office for St. Anne in the late Middle Ages, even though the melody for this text can be quite difficult to trace with its scattered sources.[38] While the antiphon from the Carmelite manuscript in Mainz cannot be directly linked to La Rue's mass, the multiple iterations of the motive *ut-mi-fa-sol-*[*la*] of the plainchant, along with the concordant incipit "Felix Anna," establish that fragment as the likely basis for the mass. Additional evidence from two different motets with the title *Felix Anna quedam matrona* (one by Festa, one anonymous) indicates that they too are almost certainly drawing on a model that is suggested in the Carmelite antiphon.[39] In the case of the *St. Anne Mass*, La Rue obscured the model with such a high level of diminution that a much wider collection of melodies for *Felix Anna quedam matrona* would be necessary to help account for the precise provenance of his model. In the meantime, the antiphon *Felix Anna quedam matrona* not only illuminates the hitherto enigmatic rubric "Felix Anna" that accompanied the tenor of this mass but also explains the heavily foregrounded melodic idea that pervades La Rue's composition in all voice parts.

As mentioned earlier, pithy tenor rubrics – like that found in one of the manuscripts bearing the *St. Anne Mass* – have the potential to reveal a range of symbolic meanings and occasionally a clue to historical context, once the full extent of the texts is unlocked. The clear but ephemeral references to the plainchant in the incipits that echo throughout the *St. Anne Mass* may serve a synedochic purpose, registering (with the listener or dedicatee) the full force of the antiphon as music and text. With the antiphon *Felix Anna quedam matrona* freshly connected to the "Felix Anna" rubric, the text of the entire antiphon should be examined to see if any special allusions might throw light on the origin or reception of La Rue's mass.

Felix Anna	Blessed Anne
Quedam matrona	one certain
Legitima	rightful Mother,
Beato Ioachim	deserved to produce,
Promeruit generare	with blessed Joachim,
Felicem filiam	the blessed daughter
Nomine Mariam.	with the name Mary.

The antiphon describes the uncomplicated image of St. Anne as a mother, chosen along with her husband, Joachim, to bear the Virgin Mary. The words *quedam* and *legitima* bring marked rhetorical emphasis to St. Anne as one of God's elect, underscoring the import of her maternity. Further, remember that the music highlights the text *promeruit generare* ("deserved to produce") with a peculiar sweeping gesture through the natural and hard hexachords. These cues bring the notion of motherhood to the front and center in suggesting the context for the once vague "Felix Anna" rubric. How did St. Anne and her matronly role impact the creation and reception of this mass? What other social and political qualities of the multifaceted saint resonated with the recipients of La Rue's mass? With some firmer footing for the basis of the *St. Anne Mass*, the court environment that fostered and sponsored this mass can now be explored, allowing for a richer contextual understanding of this work in the Habsburg-Burgundian domain.

St. Anne in the House of Burgundy

Although devotion to St. Anne reached its zenith in Christendom during this time, the choice to adorn multiple manuscripts with polyphony for this saint was no mere part of a customary checklist of sanctoral patronage for the Mechelen court. Once the importance of St. Anne in Habsburg-Burgundian culture is established, one can begin to understand the selection of Mary's mother in the polyphonic realm as both a marker of self-awareness by the court and a conscious assertion of nobility and dynastic promise after a politically volatile period in Western Europe.

The search for a context for La Rue's mass begins in the Burgundian territory of Flanders in the city of Ghent. For the moment, the concern will not be with Margaret of Austria, the presumed patroness of the mass, but with another Margaret – the English princess Margaret of York (d. 1503), the third wife of Charles the Bold – and her stepdaughter, Mary of Burgundy, the mother of Margaret of Austria.[40] Ghent was dealt a devastating blow in 1453 when Philip the Good, Duke of Burgundy, sent in forces to defeat a major popular uprising in this fiercely independent city. As a result of this bloody endeavor, Ghent's population significantly diminished, and city authorities campaigned to stimulate population growth; widows in particular were urged to remarry and produce children quickly. To this end, a cult dedicated to St. Anne developed at the heart of this movement, with the city of Ghent issuing statutes for a Guild of St. Anne in 1470.[41] Shortly after the founding of this guild, Margaret of York and Mary of Burgundy were listed as members of the institution.[42] By 1477, Margaret and Mary's support for the St. Anne Guild was captured in visual culture, specifically in the frontispiece to the new register of the guild. In this miniature from the workshop of the Master of Mary of Burgundy, the two women kneel in prayer in front of the St. Anne altar in the Church of St. Nicolas in Ghent (Figure 3.2).[43] The imposing figure of Anne holds miniaturized renderings of Mary and Christ in her arms, and the center panel of the triptych below the statue shows the scene at the Golden Gate, where Joachim learns of Anne's conception of Mary. The overall effect emphasizes the importance of children

Figure 3.2 *Master of Mary of Burgundy*, from the Register of the Guild of St. Anne (Ghent, 1477). Windsor Castle, Royal Library, inv. RCIN 1047371 (fol. 2v). Reproduced with permission of the Royal Collection Trust. © Her Majesty Queen Elizabeth II, 2013.

(*in* and *ex utero*) for the guild, whose primary function was to pray for the achievement of an accelerated birth rate for the city of Ghent.

Burgundian devotion to St. Anne also grew tangentially from loyalty to a different female saint, Colette of Corbie. A member of the Franciscan suborder called the "Poor Clares," Colette was well known for a series of visions that she had in the course of her devout life.[44] Following traditional models of veneration employed during the late Middle Ages, she confined her adoration of female saints to the virgin type. Colette openly refused to tender devotion to St. Anne, expressing disgust at the idea of praying to a saint who had married multiple times. According to Colette's *vita*, she even censured her own mother for having married twice. However, in one of her most remarkable visions, Colette is "corrected" by St. Anne, who justifies her notorious three marriages by demonstrating the powerful effect of producing the Holy Kinship.[45] Colette then saw the merit in honoring Mary's mother and would include that saint in her program of devotion.

Philip the Good's successor as Duke of Burgundy, Charles the Bold (d. 1477), was well aware of the Colette-Anne vision. In 1475, Charles commissioned a copy of Colette's *vita*, which appears in one of the two extant manuscripts of the saint's life with accompanying miniatures. In the Burgundian *vita*, Colette's vision of St. Anne is depicted in miniature.[46] More important, however, it is in this vision of St. Colette that the illuminator placed Charles and his wife, Margaret of York, directly within the image. Notably, the duke and duchess kneel and gaze at St. Anne and her kin along with Colette, herself attended by St. Francis. Colette's vision of St. Anne underscores, at minimum, the value of marital sanctity in the Burgundian house.[47] Further, Margaret of York was the third wife of Charles the Bold, a biographical coincidence with the thrice-married St. Anne that was probably not lost on the duke. As the guardian of Margaret of Austria, Margaret of York likely educated the young regent about Colette's vision of St. Anne. In fact, the younger Margaret's library contains an abridged version of the *Vie de Sainte Colette*, copied expressly for her. At the end of the copy of Colette's *vita*, Margaret even made a special appeal to St. Anne and her family (namely, Anne, Joachim, Mary, and Jesus).[48] This is but one clue to the centrality of feminine sanctity and the merit of matrilineage in the life of Margaret of Austria. A more complete assessment of the place of St. Anne in the realm of Margaret of Austria will come with a thorough understanding of the unusual course of her life and her deliberate and profound patronage of the arts at her Mechelen court.

The Burgundian Succession Crisis and Margaret's French Years

The death of Charles the Bold at the Battle of Nancy in 1477 left the duchy of Burgundy without a male heir, raising urgent questions concerning who would control the coveted territory. Following a controversial interpretation of the specifications of the original gift of Burgundy to Philip the Bold from 1363, the French king, Louis XI (cousin of Charles the Bold), seized the Burgundian lands. Subjecting the territories to Salic law, French royalists claimed these holdings should pass to the crown in the absence of a male Burgundian heir. In contrast, those who recognized Charles's daughter Mary of Burgundy as the rightful successor to these lands did not view male succession as imperative in this situation, because it had never been stipulated in the gift to Philip the Bold. Moreover, while Salic law strictly forbade women from succession, no such prescriptions appeared to apply to regions outside of France. Burgundian apologists faced an uphill battle, however: by acknowledging Mary of Burgundy as the heiress to the lands, the Flemish implicitly opened themselves to Habsburg rule, because Mary wed Maximilian I as a strategic counter against the French effort to acquire her land.[49]

The crisis in the duchy came to a head in 1482 with the death of Mary of Burgundy, who was thrown from a horse while pregnant with her fourth child. She never recovered from the accident. Three days before her death, the duchess had authored a will declaring her children (Margaret of Austria and Philip the Fair) heirs to the Burgundian lands and naming her husband, Maximilian, protector of the region until the age of majority of her son.[50] Habsburg control, however, was viewed suspiciously as foreign occupation, which had the ironic effect of making former supporters of Mary of Burgundy favorable to French rule and Salic law. The political vacuum was temporarily filled in 1482 with the Treaty of Arras, an agreement whose terms were largely dictated by Louis XI. The treaty conceded Picardy and the duchy of Burgundy to the French king, while Maximilian would retain regency over Franche-Comté and the Netherlands. With the Flemish uneasiness over Maximilian's stake in their cities, battles would be fought for the next decade over the legitimacy of his regency.[51] But as part of the treaty, two-year-old Margaret of Austria was transferred to the French court for her education and affianced to the thirteen-year-old dauphin, Charles (later Charles VIII of France). Margaret would be reared under Louis XI's daughter, Anne de Beaujeu ("Anne of France"), Duchess of Bourbon. Less than a year after the treaty was enacted, Louis died, leaving Madame la Grande, as Anne was known, to act as the regent of France for her brother, the dauphin.[52] At the Château d'Amboise in the Loire Valley, two more children would eventually be entrusted to Anne of France. The two – Louise and Philibert – were sent from the House of Savoy, orphaned by the death of their mother, Margaret of Bourbon.

Although Anne of France was known to have commissioned artwork in honor of the grandmother saint for political gain, Margaret's early encounters with St. Anne while in the care of the French regent are not known.[53] Better understood is Anne's rigorous education of the young Margaret beginning in 1484, a process that presented the young princess with ambitious lessons in female empowerment, a devotional domain of St. Anne. In forming Margaret as an astute, future member of the nobility, Anne of France arranged instruction for the young northerner in the fine arts, from painting and dance (*danses basses*) to music, specifically singing and the lute. The regent further cultivated the craft of embroidery with Margaret.[54] As explained in Chapter 2, needlework was not merely a sign of domesticity but also a potent metaphor for expressing the inimitable power of women to create the fabric of humanity.

Anne of France provided her four entrusted "children" with an expressly French education unmatched at any other court of the late fifteenth century. As Margaret of Austria and Louise of Savoy grew, Anne's zeal to raise them particularly rigorously was exemplified in two important books on feminine virtue. Both written around 1405, Christine de Pizan's *Le Livre de la Cité des Dames* (*The Book of the City of Ladies*) and *Le Livre des Trois Vertus* (*The Book of the Three Virtues*) presented allegories that highlighted problems women faced in society.[55] Christine's books were well-reasoned guides for all women – from princesses to peasants – to live honorably as indispensable members of society; both pieces of literature chipped away at misogynic attitudes firmly embedded in culture. In *The Book of the City of Ladies*, Christine constructed a symbolic "city" exclusively for women under the auspices of three female Virtues (Ladies Reason, Rectitude, and Justice). In this imagined city, females were to cultivate their unique qualities as individuals, an idea extended into *The Book of the Three Virtues*.[56] Christine inspired women to advance their valuable contributions to society through fervent lives of divine contemplation and dedicated public service. Although mainly intended as "words to live by" for the daughter of Anne of France (Suzanne of Bourbon), the book not only had a profound impact at the French court, but also had the broader potential to be a volume that women at all levels of society could consult for encouragement at many stages of life.[57]

The impact of Christine's writings, especially the *Book of the Three Virtues*, on Margaret of Austria cannot be overstated. Often turning to the book's uplifting advice over the next generation, Margaret relied on these forward-looking ideas throughout her unpredictable and increasingly independent life. While two copies of the *Book of the Three Virtues* survive in the Bourbon library at Moulins, no fewer than three copies were held in Margaret's own library.[58] As will be shown, the "self-help" *Book of the Three Virtues* and explicit devotion to female saints were available to Margaret to counterbalance the erratic changes in her life that would take place after the years she spent at the French court.

Although her mother engaged with St. Anne through the Ghent guild, Margaret's first encounter with the iconography and meaning of St. Anne more likely occurred at the French court under Anne of France. It was here that the regent's patron saint would have been immediately visible to the future Queen Margaret. Two extant pieces of visual art at the French court demonstrate the place of the regent's namesake in the French royal household. First is a large sculpture of St. Anne and the Virgin that was located at Anne of France's chapel at the court château in Chantelle.[59] Drawing on a familiar motif, the sculpture features Mary's mother intently watching over her young daughter (approximately in her early teens) as the latter learns to read. This typically English depiction of St. Anne teaching Mary may be understood as a reflection of rising feminine literacy, a trend highly valued by the court. Though the young Margaret left the French court in 1493, a later piece of art featuring St. Anne – the triptych "Bourbon Altarpiece" (ca. 1498) by Jean Hey, known as the "Master of Moulins" – conveys something about the feminine strength of that time and place. In the triptych's right wing, Hey presents an enlarged figure of St. Anne presenting his patroness Anne of France and her daughter Suzanne, and all three women gaze at the central image of the coronation of the Virgin Mary.[60] Like the large sculpture, the Bourbon altarpiece omits reference to Christ, again registering the characteristically English understanding of St. Anne as nurturer and instructor, a role that Anne of France imitated. More broadly, the representations of St. Anne at the French court in both pieces of visual art suggest a special focus on women.

Margaret of Austria's acquaintance with the influential writings of Christine de Pizan and her awareness of the power of the *Mater matris* were a crucial part of the strong foundation that the young princess received at the French court under Anne of France. With this education, Margaret was ready to rule France with honor, prepared to exemplify the image of a modern, empowered noblewoman. However, Margaret's life would take bizarre and lamentable turns. For some time, she would remain a political pawn, not yet the chess master she might have boldly envisioned herself as a highborn princess. Her string of setbacks was just about to begin, as she learned as a young teenager that she was not destined to be queen of France.

Fortune – Infortune – Fort une

Despite her early exposure to St. Anne, Margaret likely fled to the protection of the saint only retrospectively as a young adult. A careful review of her circuitous life events, the adversities that would befall her, and her patterns of patronage will go far toward establishing a context for venerating the powerful mother of the Virgin Mary. In 1488, the Duke of Brittany, Francis II, perished in a horse-riding accident, leaving his eleven-year-old daughter Anne of Brittany as his heiress. (She will be studied in more detail in Chapter 5.) In an effort to maintain long-standing Breton independence from France, the young woman sought a powerful husband who would share her anti-French sentiment. Margaret's father, Maximilian, fit the bill, and the two were married by proxy in 1490. The French royal house, feeling the encroachment of the Habsburgs on more than one border, sent its army to invade Brittany. The weak marriage by proxy between Maximilian and Anne of Brittany was dissolved, paving the way for a wedding between the king and the Breton duchess of a province that long escaped French control. This new arrangement – the skilled political calculation of Anne of France – would necessarily annul the unconsummated marriage of Charles VIII and Margaret of Austria. Eager to have a strengthened France make peace with the north before he set his sights beyond the Alps, Charles VIII signed the Treaty of Senlis in 1493 with Maximilian, not only yielding the disputed Burgundian territories to the House of Habsburg, but also sending Margaret back to her father.[61]

Together with her brother Philip, Margaret served as a vehicle for extending the Habsburg domain through marriage alliances, embodying the house mantra *Bella gerant alii, tu felix Austria, nube*! ("Let others wage war, but you, O blessed Austria, marry!"). As Margaret obtained her French education, Philip remained in the disputed northern territories under the guardianship of his father. But the siblings would reunite in connection with two strategically arranged marriages joining the Habsburgs with the children of Ferdinand and Isabella of Spain. In November 1495, Margaret was betrothed to Juan, prince of the Asturias and heir to the throne of Aragon-Castile, an arrangement that marked Maximilian's most significant political achievement. A ceremony by proxy in Mechelen was formalized in Burgos by 1497. Meantime, Philip was wed in Antwerp to the Spanish princess, Juana of Castile.

The Spanish royal court offered Margaret another base of forward-looking intellectual culture, but her marriage to the Spanish prince would not last more than five months. Though he had always displayed fragile health, Juan died suddenly in October 1497 at nineteen years of age. The widow Margaret, still just seventeen years old, was expecting a child. She bore a daughter prematurely, but the child did not survive long after the delivery.[62] Juana and Philip's marriage would fare better, the princess giving birth to the eventual Holy Roman Emperor Charles V. But for Margaret, the experience in Spain was a disaster: if the annulled marriage to Dauphin Charles VIII was not disappointing enough, the death of her next husband and the lost hope of a child with the House of Castile would be devastating for the former princess of Spain. The hardships that Margaret experienced during her teens are captured in her most famous personal motto – *Fortune – Infortune – Fort une* ("Fortune makes one very unfortunate," to use Picker's translation).[63] The calamity at the Spanish court could have driven Margaret to St. Anne, but she also might have realized that her plight paralleled that of Christine de Pizan, who was widowed at age twenty-five. Christine wrote extensively as a means to support her household, which included three children, her mother, and other relatives.[64] Incorporating her own experiences in her books of advice, Christine's writings include counsel and encouragement for widows. With the *Book of the Three Virtues* close at hand, Margaret had some meaningful literature within reach as she weathered these unusual setbacks.

Misfortune would strike yet again in the next chapter of Margaret's life, requiring strength that exceeded the limits of Christine's handbooks of advice. The widowed daughter of Maximilian I would once more be used as a pawn to serve political ends. Margaret's father, with the support of the reigning French king Louis XII, arranged a marriage to secure peace with the Duchy of Savoy, a crucial Alpine buffer territory for both the French and the Holy Roman Empire. In 1501, it was arranged for Margaret to wed Duke Philibert II of Savoy, her childhood companion from the French court under Anne of France. This marriage would set Margaret in the midst of an ongoing rivalry between the Habsburgs and the French: not only was she the aunt of her brother's son Charles V, but she also became the aunt of the son of Louise of Savoy (Philibert's sister), the future king of France, Francis I.

Duke Philibert of Savoy – Margaret's third husband – represented an opposing image to the fragile prince of Asturias. Athletic and well suited for battle and tournament, Philibert eschewed the responsibilities of government and was content with leaving administrative and diplomatic busy-work to others (not unlike the aloof Louis of Savoy from three generations earlier, surveyed in Chapter 2).[65] After the duke's brother and lieutenant-general René (the Grand Bastard of Savoy) was charged with conspiring with the Swiss against the state of Savoy, Margaret removed him and assumed an unusually prominent role as chief diplomat for the Savoyard court, a role she evidently enjoyed and one in which she excelled.[66] It may not have been lost on the Duchess of Savoy that she was well exceeding the place of a woman as set forth in Christine de Pizan's writings. Margaret went quite beyond her prescribed duty as manager of the estate and advisor to her husband. She surrounded herself with capable counselors, several of whom would remain by her side over the next generation.[67] But Margaret's curiously public role in the House of Savoy would last just a few years. In 1504, Philibert met with a disastrous fate: after some rigorous exercise, he died suddenly from heat stroke at twenty-four years of age.[68] In an instant, Margaret was widowed again; to that point, each of her three marriages had dissolved, not one through any fault of her own.

Recent studies of early modern widowhood have drawn attention to the complex and ambiguous feelings surrounding a woman who (not atypically) outlives her husband. At once a devastating blow and an empowering opportunity, most widows for the first time in their lives controlled their own destiny, shedding the notion of a *feme covert*. The church even reserved moral high ground for widows, citing their ability to attain or regain virtue and moral strength.[69] Margaret likely turned to her copy of Christine's *Book of the Three Virtues* for consolation and reassurance, where the author recommends that widows who are not in dire financial ruins continue to live off their lands. On the question of whether widows should remarry, Christine was particularly wary:

But for all those who have passed their youth and who are sufficiently comfortable financially so that poverty does not oblige them, remarriage is a complete folly! Though some who want to remarry say there is nothing in life for a woman alone, they have so little confidence in their own good sense that they will claim that they don't know how to manage their own lives. But the height of folly and the greatest of all absurdities is the old woman who takes a young husband: There a joyful song is rarely heard for long. Although many pay dearly for their foolishness, nobody will sympathize with them – for good reason![70]

With Maximilian continuing to view Margaret as a political pawn, the option to accept widowhood was not necessarily hers. Still, Christine gave comfort to widowed women like Margaret, reminding them of the strength and stamina required to carry on with their lives. In the *Book of the City of Ladies*, Christine again counsels widows directly: "May there be integrity in your dress, conduct, and speech; piety in your deeds and way of life; prudence in your bearing; patience (so necessary!), strength, resistance in tribulations and difficult affairs; humility in your heart, countenance and speech; and charity in your works.... [Women,] show forth your virtue."[71] Whatever turns her life would take next, Margaret would let her virtue shine through and humbly accept her fate, which was still in the hands of her father.

With the untimely death of her brother Philip in Burgos in 1506, Margaret departed the House of Savoy for Rothenburg to confer briefly with her father. Because Philip left a vacancy in the Netherlands by his death, Maximilian agreed to place Margaret in the Netherlands as a *princesse naturelle*. In March 1507, her father appointed her his *Procureur général*, and she received the oath of the States General.[72] Despite the administrative potential of her appointment, the newly minted Margaret was becoming a victim of cruel Fortune, reaching depths that Christine de Pizan could not have envisioned for an adult woman – childless and twice widowed. It was at this time that the Archduchess of Austria turned to even more exemplary models of strength and encouragement, finding comfort in the arts, which she enlisted not just for her own personal solace but also as an outward expression of her new court to her constituents and the world.

Regent of the Netherlands and Patroness of the Arts

Margaret of Austria established her court residence in the city of Mechelen, where her step-grandmother (and godmother) Margaret of York had flourished during the last quarter of the fifteenth century. It was a home base that she called the House of Savoy (*Hof van Savoyen*), an obvious gesture to her most recent marriage. Midway between Brussels and Antwerp and away from the characteristically independent Bruges and Ghent, Mechelen was a place in which the widowed archduchess could live peacefully and from which she could govern effectively. Her life experiences to this point made Margaret well suited to ruling over the territory. Not only did she witness powerful and influential females at various courts (including, for a time, her own guardian, Anne of France), but she also got "on-the-job training" in the duchy of Savoy, managing administrative affairs of the court in light of the carefree and negligent attitude of her late husband Duke Philibert.

Maximilian, still despised as a foreigner in the Netherlands, was eager to reinstall a Burgundian or Valois descendant in the region. Well aware of both Margaret's fortitude and abilities emerging from her brief period in Savoy, Maximilian believed his daughter would receive a warmer reception than he had experienced two decades earlier.[73] The new Holy Roman Emperor Maximilian raised Margaret's rank to the title of Regent of the Netherlands, which gave her considerable power to govern the constituent duchies and territories. She soon became the mother figure to a once hostile people, lauded by Baldassare Castiglione for her wise and just leadership.[74] Appointed to the guardianship of Archduke Charles (the future Holy Roman Emperor) upon the death of her brother Philip, Margaret also became a de facto mother within her "House of Savoy." As a widow (Figure 3.3), Margaret was resigned to her new course of life and would establish a steady and fulfilling regency in Mechelen.[75] It was here that she placed newfound value on her own lineage and continued belief in feminine virtue, which included devotion to holy women like St. Anne.

In light of her rich education at the French court, it is no surprise that Margaret of Austria fostered an atmosphere at her Mechelen residence that promoted literature and the fine arts. She encountered many important luminaries of the day, most notably the great Christian humanist Desiderius Erasmus and the influential painter Albrecht Dürer.[76] Her time in Savoy, with its extensive ducal library, did nothing to diminish her status as a bibliophile, and soon she found herself in rare company among women of the time for having assembled such a robust library and collection of artworks.[77] Through her enthusiastic and unceasing patronage, the regent used texts, images, and sounds not only to reaffirm her own beliefs, but also to extend her influence and establish the foundation for a second golden age of Burgundian rule. Margaret mobilized the arts to serve as objects of prestige and to support her strategies for political propaganda. Works on view for her allies encompassed ideology as much as personal taste. As the last ruler of the Netherlands who could claim natural Valois descent, she commissioned art to emphasize her noble heritage, in particular the lineage from her mother's side. By accentuating this pedigree, she gathered popular sentiment to bolster her delicate regency.[78] La Rue's *St. Anne Mass* must be counted as one of the vehicles that underscored the value of the maternal legacy.

Margaret's court housed one of the most impressive collections of visual art in Western Europe. She owned the famous *Arnolfini Wedding* by Jan van Eyck and the Passion cycle by Juan de Flandes, while her remarkable collection of secular portraiture alone numbered more than 100 pieces at the time of her death.[79] The *première chambre* of the Mechelen court offered the

Figure 3.3 Bernard van Orley, *Portrait of Margaret of Austria as a Widow*, after 1518. Brussels, Museés royaux de Beaux-Arts de Belgique, inv. no. 4059. © IRPA-KIK, Brussels.

most public forum for artistic display. As a high-profile gathering room for court visitors and powerful allies, this room reflected family portraits on the surface, but a political agenda as a subtext. With nearly thirty portraits of past and present rulers beginning with John the Fearless (d. 1419), the overwhelming emphasis in the *première chambre* was on Burgundian ducal lineage. The concomitant suppression of Margaret's agnatic heritage – the

Habsburgs – further highlighted the regent's maternal Valois pedigree reaching back either by blood or by marriage to the end of the fourteenth century. Her calculated commissions (and striking omissions) allowed her to seize popularity with both her allied leaders and the Netherlandish people at large.[80]

The projection of the dynastic power of the maternal side of Margaret's family extended into aspects of genre and style within visual works of art. Nearly all of the commissioned portrait miniatures in the court manuscripts assumed the format of the diptych, a deliberately archaic format that symbolically connected with the past. From a very young age, Margaret herself appeared often in diptychs and usually in conjunction with family or heraldry as markers of a cherished lineage.[81] Further gestures to a bygone era can be found in Margaret's funerary tribute to her late husband Philibert.[82] As the custodian of a magnificent lineage, the regent sought protection and solace with visual cues that summoned the generations preceding her. But this secular assembly of artwork was not enough: as a widow in extraordinary circumstances, Margaret turned to strong and impressive female models, St. Anne among them.

Feminine Sanctity, St. Anne, and Mechelen

The theme of time-tested, dynastic legitimacy that Margaret oversaw in the visual culture of the court was matched with artistic emphasis on feminine strength and virtue in devotional works of art, a reflection in sacred terms of the empowering, worldly literature that the regent encountered in the writings of Christine de Pizan.[83] Beyond the standard Marian and Christological pieces of art, Margaret's collection of sacred objects included several artistic items on the subject of the Jewish heroine Judith. In one of the more dramatic biblical stories of the Old Testament, Judith used her beauty to seduce the general Holofernes and cut off his head, saving the Jewish people from an Assyrian assault on the city of Bethulia. Margaret owned a tapestry depicting the heroine, which she had saved from her marriage to Juan of Castile. In the *Book of the City of Ladies*, Christine specifically exalts Judith – among other courageous biblical figures like Esther – as a noble woman who saves her people.[84] Toward the end of her life, Margaret commissioned an alabaster statuette of Judith from Mechelen court artist Conrad Meit for court display.[85] Margaret seems to have recognized not only the inherent power of such a virtuous and widely known female character, but also the implicit political authority gained by choosing to represent a figure like Judith.[86] There was even more to Margaret's favoring of this Jewish heroine: inextricable from her feminine virtue, beauty, and heroism, Judith was a widow, thus making her accomplishments all the more unexpected and potentially appealing from the regent's perspective. Implicit in the legend of St. Anne – herself constructed after an Old Testament prototype – is of course the idea that she too was widowed, not once but twice. While not known for her physical acts of strength, St. Anne was believed to have the efficacy to protect dynasties, in light of her own oversight of multiple generations of holy progeny. St. Anne and other select female saints were no small entities in Margaret's devotional roster.

Margaret of Austria venerated a limited group of female saints. St. Margaret naturally had a special place as the patron namesake of the regent.[87] But after St. Margaret, the regent channeled devotion to three female saints – St. Clare of Assisi, St. Colette of Corbie, and St. Anne.[88] These holy women are not unrelated. In the early thirteenth century, Clare of Assisi founded an important female-only monastic branch of the Franciscans (the aforementioned "Poor Clares"); more than a century later, Colette of Corbie, another member of the "Poor Clares," became an important voice for reform within this religious order. With authorization from Pope Benedict XIII, Colette began to establish reformed convents for Franciscan nuns. The House of Burgundy had a personal connection to Colette through her confessor, the Franciscan priest Henri de la Baume, whose family had ties with the Burgundians. The dukes and duchesses of Burgundy of the early and mid-fifteenth century supported the many convents that Colette founded across Flanders. They further campaigned for Colette's beatification by urging another confessor and fellow Franciscan, Brother Pierre de Vaux, to write her biography.[89] In exchange, the Burgundians could draw on Colette's powerful example of feminine spirituality to advance their political ambitions.

The third female saint, St. Anne, was reaching the pinnacle of her popularity in Christendom in the early sixteenth century, around the time that La Rue composed his *St. Anne Mass*. But the saint's favor by the Burgundian court actually developed through the filter of the Colette narrative with an oblique, but important connection that cannot be missed. As explained earlier, Colette was dedicated to the merits of virginity and only fled to St. Anne through a vision that changed her unforgiving view of the thrice-married *Mater matris*. The result of this vision alerted Colette to the virtues of married life, childbirth, maternity, even widowhood, and she would eventually cast her net wider to recruit widows into the Colettine convents.[90] As Nancy Bradley Warren has described it, "St. Anne, in effect, thus becomes for Colette on a celestial plane what Colette is for the Burgundians on earth – that is, a way of tapping into divine authority to legitimate one's own authority and advance one's own political agenda."[91] Colette would go on to found several convents dedicated to St. Anne,[92] which is not only proof of her newfound devotion to the popular grandmother saint, but also a signal to the Christian faithful of where devotion should be directed – a signal not lost on the Burgundian court. Saints Clare, Colette, and Anne thus formed a "progression" that culminated in St. Anne as the supreme intercessor and model of feminine sanctity.

Even after Colette's death in 1447, the House of Burgundy did not waver in support of the Franciscans. Margaret of York and Queen Isabella, step-grandmother and mother-in-law respectively to Margaret of Austria, continued patronage of the order of religious women with a passion that regent seems to have acquired.[93] Margaret even solicited support for Colette's canonization.[94] That a *Vie de Sainte Colette* was copied for Margaret and contained her appended appeal to St. Anne and her family reinforces the devotional interconnections between the saints for the Burgundians. The implication that St. Anne effectively trumped Colette and her Franciscan predecessor Clare could not have gone unnoticed by Margaret. The regent also held an embroidered work featuring the grandmother saint amid the Holy Kinship.[95] The highly personal nature of Margaret's devotion to St. Anne finds an analog in La Rue's mass, in which a seemingly enigmatic melodic underpinning (the "Felix Anna" tune) was rigorously clouded, but a fragment of which was also repeated heavily on the surface. The connection was doubtless comprehended only by a small circle of individuals at the Mechelen court. In St. Anne, Margaret likely found more than an uncanny self-reflection and a compelling archetype to direct her spiritual fervor: she found a symbol of her own ambitions.

Margaret's Biography in Music

The regent Margaret strategically commissioned art with an eye toward politics, displaying works that reflected favorably on her and offered a careful subtext of power and sanctity for those who encountered the products of her court. In Mechelen court culture, music played an important role beyond providing entertainment or augmenting devotion. As a complement to the extensive visual culture procured by the regent, music was also a medium for projecting an appropriate image of the regent to audiences internal and external. But not all repertories had a public showing. Margaret's personal songbooks in particular were notable objects of self-reflection, rather than outward political statements, as demonstrated in the case of the well-known chansonnier Brussels, Royal Library, MS 228 (BrusBR 228). While this manuscript has attracted much scholarly attention, recent interest has raised questions about the extent to which the songbook encodes biographical connections to its owner.[96]

Though compiled at the end of her life, the bulk of the music in Margaret's chansonnier of almost sixty songs was written between 1508 and 1516,[97] in nearly the same interval as La Rue's *St. Anne Mass*, as her court established its position in the region. Several of the songs in the collection, many by La Rue, express the melancholy of a dejected lover, which one would expect after her denied marriage with Charles VIII and the compounding loss of two husbands thereafter. More than one chanson can be read with reference to the beginning of Margaret's fateful course of life. Though the chansonnier is "consecrated" with a token Marian motet,[98] two pieces in the songbook by La Rue set parts of the large poem (*complainte*) on the departure of Margaret from the French court in 1493, written by French court poet Octavien de Saint-Gelais (*Tous les regrets* [the opening secular work of the manuscript] and *Tous nobles cueurs*).[99] The third song in the collection (La Rue's *Ce n'est pas jeu*) is written from a female vantage point and may also ironically hint at the dissolved marriage between Margaret and Charles VIII.[100] The preceding work in the collection, *De l'oeil de la fille du roy* (again by La Rue), dates before Margaret's venture to Spain in 1497 and can further be read biographically as pertaining to her (daughter of the "King [of the Romans]," Maximilian).[101] As Meconi has shown, the majority of the remaining songs in the collection express the woeful emotions of an unlucky lover.[102]

Margaret's sources of distress, all before she reached the age of twenty-six, are clear – namely, the deaths of her mother, brother, daughter, and two husbands. The losses of Juan and Philibert were especially devastating, to say nothing of the broken-off marriage with Charles VIII following Margaret's edifying experiences in France. If the songs contained in BrusBR 228 had personal meaning for the regent, they may not have completely captured the range of sentiments that Margaret might have felt as a political pawn and widow now hoisted to a new powerful governing role. The protection of saints and the presence of sacred music on meaningful subjects could have further ventriloquized the regent's response to her dynamic course of life.

In each of the three sources that contain La Rue's *St. Anne Mass* (Table 3.1), there is a polyphonic *Missa de Sancto Job* by the same composer. While the St. Anne masses were either first or second in the manuscript, the masses for St. Job were invariably tucked near the back of each collection.[103] The St. Job mass seems to have encapsulated Margaret's despair from the events of the previous two decades. Not usually classified as a saint, Job was an indelible figure from the Old Testament, the embodiment of a just sufferer. While he was formally commemorated in certain areas of northern Italy, he was best remembered through his appearance in the Office of the Dead, which became widespread in the proliferation of books of hours.[104] The saint was also widely venerated in the Low Countries, where Margaret's influence was most concentrated. Jennifer Bloxam has suggested that La Rue's mass for St. Job might have reflected the plight of Margaret, who seems to have taken refuge in the most notable sufferer of the Bible.[105] This appeal of the saint seems to be confirmed in the regent's commissioning of an altarpiece of St. Job from her court painter Bernard van Orley in 1521.[106]

Job and Anne are indeed the only saints except for the Virgin Mary celebrated with a mass across the three manuscripts in which they occur together.[107] If a mass for St. Job captured some of Margaret's inauspicious past, what explains the devotion to St. Anne? While it is easy to linger over Margaret's widowed status and the subtle portrayal of her plight in music, she was still very much available for marriage, an attractive woman and a descendant of a powerful lineage. She steadily wielded political influence and was eager to govern strongly to restore Burgundian rule. The time for Margaret to call on St. Anne was ripe and coincided with the composition of La Rue's *St. Anne Mass*, which was probably completed after 1508 but before 1514, not unlike her cherished chansonnier. It was a period that demanded a robust protectress for Margaret, one who could preserve the regent's grace under pressure.

If Margaret found a strong widow in Christine de Pizan, a noble sufferer in Job, and feminine paragons in Clare and Colette, she might well have seen an even closer image of herself in the figure of St. Anne. As already shown, Margaret knew the *Mater matris* well from her Burgundian relatives in the often rehearsed life of St. Colette. But after the death of Philibert in 1504, it must have occurred to the young princess that her biography to date had striking correspondence to the legend surrounding St. Anne and her three husbands. To generate the extensive kinship of holy figures and yet still conform to Christian principles, St. Anne had to witness the deaths of the first two of her husbands to achieve the feat. The details of the trinubium theory required that Anne's first husband, Joachim, die, which facilitated her next marriage, to Cleophas, who in turn would have to pass to provide Anne with a third husband (Salome). As noted in the introduction, each of Anne's three marriages produced a daughter named Mary. And these

"Three Marys" accounted for the births of Jesus and his six "brothers" or cousins named in the Gospels. Margaret of course could only relate to part of this legend built around St. Anne, but it was no insignificant detail: St. Anne married exactly three times and was widowed twice, a mirror reflection of the regent's fate, with the understanding that her first marriage to Charles VIII was never consummated.

Margaret might have realized her unusual connection to the legend of St. Anne and the trinubium through the lens of Colette of Corbie, the Franciscan beloved by the Burgundians. Colette's precise opposition to Anne's three marriages and the vision in which St. Anne admonished Colette was a story well known to the regent. Further, Colette was a reformer of Franciscan life. Along with the Carmelites (and most religious orders except the Dominicans), the Franciscans became staunch defenders of Anne's trinubium. They were also supporters of the Immaculate Conception, a complex theological question on the nature of the Virgin's relationship to sin explained in Chapter 4. This church dogma peripherally involved St. Anne as the vessel that carried the Virgin Mary, but it was an image that was perpetuated in Burgundian artistic culture.

La Rue's *St. Anne Mass* was another node in the network of Margaret's devotion to Mary's mother. The regent's obvious biographical connection to the saint remains the three marriages and the dignity of widowhood. The virtues of female power and sanctity, as well as esteemed lineage, also accompanied the vulnerable regent's invocation of St. Anne. But the likely cantus firmus of La Rue's mass encourages a more selective interpretation of Anne's intercessory power, not surprising given her flexibility and "customizability" as a saint. The melody that governs the mass speaks neither of widowhood nor noble descent, but of marriage and maternity.

"One Certain Chosen Mother"

While the precise circumstances giving rise to the composition of the *St. Anne Mass* remain unclear, numerous attractive reasons still exist for Margaret of Austria to invoke Mary's mother in artistic production between the years 1508 and 1514. Certainly, the Flemish region at large had developed outlets for lay devotion to St. Anne, but La Rue's mass was not meant for broad circulation.[108] Sadly, the privately held court manuscripts do not divulge illuminated miniatures with the *St. Anne Mass* to assist with the search for a more circumscribed meaning: miniatures are missing in JenaU 7 and MontsM 773, while VienNB Mus. 15496 provides various coats of arms in place of illuminations.¹⁰⁹ But the paraphrased melody *Felix Anna quedam matrona* is a musical picture in itself, inviting a more specific interpretation for this mass, beginning with Margaret's own perspective. Any number of melodies for St. Anne could have conceivably served as the basis for La Rue's mass setting for this saint. Why this particular antiphon?

Returning to the full text of the chant that undergirds this large work, one finds special emphasis on Anne's worthiness to bear the Virgin Mary ("O blessed Anne, one certain chosen Mother, with blessed Joachim, deserved to produce the blessed daughter with the name Mary"). The antiphon highlights Anne's matronly role, and, together with the mention of her husband, the compact text alludes to marriage, immediate family, and even childbirth. These intercessory areas for St. Anne may seem odd at first when applied to a woman whose husbands perished and who was not able to raise her own children. In light of Margaret's (or La Rue's) choice of the text *Felix Anna quedam matrona*, it seems that the regent's presumed fate to remain a widow was not a foregone conclusion.

Although Margaret had been widowed twice by her mid-twenties, she remained an attractive matrimonial prize among European powers and was still well within childbearing age. Despite her outright refusal in 1506 to marry the elderly and widowed King Henry VII of England, Margaret was known to be projecting her "availability" around the time that the *St. Anne Mass* was composed. A portrait medal from around 1505 showing Margaret, victorious over Dame Fortune, as an *all'antica* nude with a low-cut garment could have marked her eligibility.¹¹⁰ And though Margaret pledged eternal loyalty to her third husband, Philibert, in the love poem known as the *Complainte* (after 1507, possibly written by Margaret herself), the regent evidently still held out hope for true love at that time, as evidenced by the initials ALCH that surface in the decorative border of the poem.¹¹¹ These initials stand for Antoine de Lalaing, Count of Hoogstraten, her finance minister and presumed suitor. Whatever their relationship, the count would receive many gifts from Margaret, including a now lost book with the intriguing title *Le secret traité de l'ard d'amour* (*The Secret Treatise of the Art of Love*).¹¹²

Love and marriage were thus realistic ideals for the regent, and the notion of a thrice-married woman did not carry the sullied connotation that it engendered a century earlier. This change in cultural attitude is thanks in part to St. Anne, who, with other "marrying" saints like Birgitta of Sweden, evinced a more accommodating view of the institution of marriage and childbearing. Through these holy women, marriage steadily accrued a positive connotation, and family life became as desirable and virtuous as the life of chastity.¹¹³ Not unlike previous works of art that reflect Margaret's emotional state, the mass for St. Anne was a vehicle that had the potential to express her marrying and family-oriented energies in the sound world.

While the regent's love interests did not immediately materialize, her desire for children remained very much alive, and her case was made known in public and private spaces. The governing antiphon of La Rue's *St. Anne Mass* (*Felix Anna quedam matrona*) may be a window into the regent's sentiments. The suggestive phrase *quedam matrona legitima* ("one certain chosen mother") within the antiphon points to the idea of motherhood and the privilege to bear children. This idea could be as much an aspiration of Margaret's as it was a character trait of St. Anne. The regent only briefly tasted the joy of motherhood as her only child with Juan of Castile did not survive long after birth.

The naming of Joachim in the antiphon *Felix Anna quedam matrona* is also instructive. While it is not unusual to see Anne's husband in the texts of the office, especially in the scene where he reunites with Anne at the Golden Gate, Joachim is rarely considered a "father" to the Virgin Mary, as intimated in the ablative *beato Ioachim* from the antiphon. As the legend goes, Mary's parents were said to be separated at the moment of the angel Gabriel's announcement of the miraculous conception to Anne. Joachim was merely informed of her conception by the angel thereafter and reunited later with Anne at the Golden Gate in Jerusalem for an innocent embrace and kiss, a common subject in the visual arts. The text of this antiphon, in contrast, makes the conception of the Virgin seem more natural and biological than was otherwise propagated in the traditional story of Mary's nativity. Recall the antiphon's verb-plus-infinitive *promeruit generare* ("deserved to produce"). This moment in the antiphon not only underscores the uncommon worthiness of the hitherto barren mother Anne but also receives artistic embellishment with the rapid accession of the range of a ninth in the single musical phrase. It is not difficult to imagine that the antiphon *Felix Anna quedam matrona* embedded in the *St. Anne Mass* was a clue to Margaret's availability and her yearning for children. Should Margaret have borne a child who came of age, she too could have claimed "blessed" offspring as the antiphon advertises for St. Anne. It is indeed fascinating to see how a composer can respond to his patroness's needs and conditions with a multilayered musical experience tailor made for her circumstances.

Aside from the antiphon on which *St. Anne Mass* is based, La Rue's elevation motet, which has received comparatively more attention in the scholarly literature, deserves comment. The setting of *O salutaris hostia*, which replaced the first Hosanna in the context of the *St. Anne Mass*, is the only motet of its kind in the composer's *oeuvre*. It fulfills the conventions of the genre as a controlled homophonic setting with minimal decoration. As such, La Rue's motet shined a light on the most poignant moment of the mass – that of the transubstantiation of the host. As the priest raises his hands with the communion wafer and with the words "Hoc est [enim] corpus meum," Christ takes flesh; his humanity is revealed, as the choirs of heaven and earth are joined. Musicologists in particular have been attuned to the emerging role of the elevation motet and other polyphonic adornments of the moment when Christ becomes visible.[114] In the present case, the fact that the motet expressly accompanies the *St. Anne Mass* in three manuscripts suggests a connection with the mass framed by the aura of the grandmother saint, even though she is not explicitly mentioned in the text of the motet. In short, it is St. Anne's generative role in the "enfleshing" of Jesus through Mary that brings the Christocentric motet into dialogue with the larger mass for Mary's mother. Again, the maternal impulse that Margaret expressed through St. Anne would seem to loom large, even in the absence of text for the *Mater matris* at the elevation.

Margaret's much-anticipated progeny represented noble reinforcements to the Habsburg-Burgundian realm. Her hopes for children and the joy of motherhood were made known in more than music: they were echoed in her most private devotions. In Margaret's innermost bedchamber hung a painting (ca. 1510–13) by Marco D'Oggiono (d. 1530) of Christ and John the Baptist explicitly as babies, embracing and kissing.[115] Further, a prayer book she took with her from Savoy contained a parturition aid with an image of the side wound of Christ, an icon commonly used by noblewomen in labor. The sacred gash, which was often inscribed on birthing amulets because it was said to ease the pain of labor, can strike one as vaginal in its appearance. The illustration of the side wound that Margaret owned carried both a description of the laceration's size and a rhymed Latin poem in praise of it.[116] Although the idea of privacy is very different from the modern conception of concealed solitude, Margaret seems to have drawn on a variety of symbols to advance her desire for children in spaces that were probably not accessible to many at the Mechelen court.

By 1507, one may suspect that Margaret's hope for maternity was fulfilled not through traditional marriage and childbirth but through her role as guardian of her nephew Charles and even other children. Despite the intracourt factions against the regent for speeding up Charles's majority, Margaret was to care not only for her nephew, but also for three of her nieces following the death of her brother Philip (Eleanor [b. 1498], Isabella [b. 1501], and Mary [b. 1505]), presumably because their widowed mother,

Juana, suffered from a mental illness.[117] For these children, Margaret held the responsibility for providing education as much as mere custody. As a foster mother of four, she was charged with raising the next generation of the Habsburg-Burgundian house. Her duties were critical, as she knew that these children would eventually claim some of the most important crowns across Europe.[118]

As mentioned earlier, La Rue's *St. Anne Mass* appears in two manuscripts that were held only at the Mechelen court (MontsM 773 and VienNB Mus. 15496). Though probably requested by the regent, the former source was presumably intended for Margaret herself, the latter for her nephew, Charles V, perhaps upon his coming of age in 1515 and subsequent rule of the Netherlands. The "internal" destination of both manuscripts allows the personal nature of the tenor's hidden sentiment to resonate at a personal level between Margaret and her nephew. The emphasis on maternity and progeny in the melody *Felix Anna quedam matrona* reflects personal and domestic concerns in an ex-voto to St. Anne. Charles was likely familiar with the iconography of the *Mater matris* and could have further understood the dynastic implications of invoking the potent grandmother of Christ. In the third source of the *St. Anne Mass* (JenaU 7), other meanings would have resonated with its recipient, Frederick the Wise, Elector of Saxony, the implications of which will surface in the next chapter.

Of all her "children," Margaret cared most deeply for Charles and placed great hope in the promise of Charles's election to Holy Roman Emperor. Her personal aspirations for her nephew were captured most vividly in her collection of eleven genealogies. These "family trees" represented not only the lineage of various houses across Europe (Burgundy, Savoy, England), but also the ancestry of another royal house – the house of David, which culminated in the birth of Christ.[119] Although it was not an uncommon practice to trace noble descent through biblical genealogies (such as the "Table of Nations" from Genesis), the most striking of the genealogies that Margaret kept was the *Genealogie abrégée* for Charles V (ca. 1527), in which her nephew's ancient and royal descent consumes some three volumes of relatives dating back some two thousand years. The author names Charles, by then the king of Spain, as the "sacred, imperial, and Catholic majesty."[120] The extensive genealogy confirms not just his royalty but his sanctity.

It is not hard to see how St. Anne, a holy figure likewise of great royal lineage, would hold symbolic value for the future Holy Roman Emperor, if not quite to the extent of his aunt Margaret. La Rue's mass for the *Mater matris* might have responded to the regent's biographical connection but also seems to have captured her private maternal aspirations. The paraphrased melody *Felix Anna quedam matrona* reflects these fervent hopes. Although suggested only in short but clear fragments, the melody repeats at every turn in the mass, rewarding the careful listener with an encoded message about the virtues of maternity and the great promise of progeny offered by the intercession of Mary's mother. For Charles, the malleable grandmother saint could reinforce his own glorious heritage symbolically rooted in biblical history. The next chapter investigates further meanings of this mass and related music for St. Anne in the context of Frederick the Wise. As with so many other Mechelen court manuscripts, the manuscript JenaU 7, which Frederick obtained, in part showcased the opulence of the Habsburg-Burgundian realm, whether it was a gift to the Elector of Saxony or requested by him. But La Rue's *St. Anne Mass* in JenaU 7 likely had different nuanced meanings for the Elector, which, together with other music from Wittenberg for St. Anne, represent yet another intriguing case of personal attachment to the legend of the Mary's mother. As part of Frederick's milieu in the time of the simmering Reformation, the controversial question of the Immaculate Conception as it relates to St. Anne will also come into view.

4 | Devotion and Letters: St. Anne in Pre-Reformation Wittenberg

As a constructed saint whose life was narrated in biblical apocrypha, St. Anne bore a wide range of attributes and intercessory capabilities, thus giving Christians an array of possibilities for targeted devotion. Although the *Mater matris* held special meaning for women, her political usefulness was a nongendered asset available to all. In the case at hand, St. Anne is found to be overrepresented in an environment in which she was valued for her wisdom in addition to her associative role in one of the more controversial doctrines of the faith in the early sixteenth century, the Immaculate Conception.

JenaU 7, Maximilian, and *Hausmacht*

The last of the three manuscripts containing La Rue's *St. Anne Mass* – JenaU 7 – was a product of the esteemed Alamire workshop and suffered a familiar fate seen with many manuscripts in the Habsburg-Burgundian complex of sources: its illuminated miniatures sadly have been subject to vandalism. The *St. Anne Mass* appears first in JenaU 7, but the initial folio of the manuscript, which no doubt contained an artistic illumination, was removed at some point. The altus and bassus of the mass are thus the first parts encountered in the source. This resultant opening folio bears the imperial double-headed eagle in the upper escutcheon and the arms of Austria in the lower escutcheon (Figure 4.1), strongly heralding Emperor Maximilian I, the father of Margaret of Austria. Emblazoned across the top of the manuscript page, the imposing motto *Halt Mas* (roughly, "Moderation in all things") points to another one of Maximilian's aphorisms. Whether Maximilian requested the manuscript or someone compiled it as a gift to him is not known, but the presence of the Holy Roman Emperor is unmistakable in this initial mass of the collection. Absent other folios that no doubt contained telling illuminations, and in spite of only a few painted and inked initials, JenaU 7 remains an impressive presentation-type manuscript with its signature Ghent-Bruges-style borders. While Herbert Kellman dated

Figure 4.1 Jena, Universitätsbibliothek, MS 7, fol. 1r.
Source: Thüringer Universitäts- und Landesbibliothek Jena (ThULB).

the manuscript between 1508 and 1519 (perhaps around 1516), Flynn Warmington has narrowed the compilation of the source from July 1515 to 1516 through more extensive study of scribal hands.[1]

The contents of JenaU 7 do not assist in settling the question of the identity of the manuscript's original recipient. As shown in Table 3.1, the choirbook contains seven masses, three by La Rue (*Missa de Sancta Anna*, *Missa Inviolata*, and *Missa de Sancto Job*), all of which were evidently "house favorites" of Margaret, considering that they were available in more than one manuscript held internally at court (MontsM 773 and VienNB Mus. 15496). Unlike these sources, however, JenaU 7 features masses by other composers, some with connections to the French court (Févin, Prioris, and Divitis). Josquin's *Missa de Nostra domina* (i.e., *Missa de beata Virgine*) completes the offerings in this manuscript.

It is not difficult to imagine Maximilian holding a cosmopolitan collection like JenaU 7, no matter if he were the commissioner or dedicatee of the manuscript. Further, the particular choice to have a mass for Mary's mother at the head of the choirbook could have symbolic implications and might constitute more than simply the first of "seven standard masses," as Eric Jas has described the contents of the manuscript.[2] The emperor was no stranger indeed to the powerful associations that St. Anne could bestow, especially the unique capability of her Holy Kinship to confer the spirit of glorious progeny and strong dynastic potential on its patrons.[3] If the juxtaposition of the imperial illuminations with the Kyrie for St. Anne does not convincingly confirm this association, Margaret's father surely reaped the outstanding benefits of St. Anne and the Holy Kinship in the visual culture of the Habsburg court. Recall Maximilian's commissioning of a family portrait (between 1515 and 1520) in which court painter Bernhard Strigel alluded to various Holy Kinship personages in his rendering of the emperor's family. Despite a minor bungling of the allegorical names, the political force of the image was clear, even in the absence of the grandmother saint. Devotion to St. Anne and her offspring – to the point of outright identification with members of the Holy Kinship – was neither an arbitrary act nor an isolated incident. The highest powers of Western Europe admired the Holy Kinship as a model of a noble family, one that fruitfully produced impressive progeny to guarantee family influence in the generations to come.

The emperor's support of Anne's trinubium and magnificent offspring is further echoed in his desire to live out the marriage-first mantra encountered earlier with his daughter Margaret (*Bella gerant alii, tu felix Austria, nube*). The impulse to use nuptials to extend empires was nothing new, and Maximilian looked no further than his own father, Holy Roman Emperor Frederick III, as a model for this strategy. Frederick did not desire the imperial role, but once elected in 1452, his reign began a virtually uninterrupted succession of Habsburg emperors that lasted until the early nineteenth century.[4] In some forty years at the helm of the empire, he wisely shored up dynastic power (*Hausmacht*) through a key marriage with the House of Burgundy. Well aware of the emerging status of Burgundian rule, Frederick astutely arranged the 1477 wedding of his son to Mary of Burgundy. Following Mary's untimely death from a horse-riding incident, Maximilian arranged a marriage by proxy to Anne of Brittany in 1490, a contract renounced when French forces led by Charles VIII invaded the Duchy of Brittany (Chapter 3). Maximilian proceeded to marry Bianca Maria Sforza, niece of the Duke of Milan, in 1494. The annulled marriage to Anne of Brittany notwithstanding, the Holy Roman Emperor had greatly strengthened Habsburg holdings in the Low Countries and Italy by these matrimonial alliances. To combat a growing threat from the French, Maximilian continued to pursue the path of *Hausmacht* by arranging the aforementioned double alliance with the Spanish House of Castile through the institution of marriage. In both words and actions, Maximilian affirmed that strategic nuptial arrangements could establish the foundation for powerful dynasties. St. Anne – increasingly viewed as an important "marrying saint" – was a natural fit for the King of the Romans and future Holy Roman Emperor.

And yet, despite the coats of arms and the symbolic connections to Maximilian, one cannot travel too far down the road with JenaU 7 and the Holy Roman Emperor. By virtue of its survival among other choirbooks at the university library in Jena, this manuscript – with La Rue's richly symbolic *St. Anne Mass* at the front – was ultimately destined for Frederick the Wise, the Elector of Saxony. The book would have arrived between 1517 and 1518 and probably functioned as mass music in the Castle Church in Wittenberg, the institution that most strongly reflected the great vision of Frederick.[5] In pre-Reformation Wittenberg, St. Anne received pride of place at the church. Illustrative of the elector's quest for spiritual fulfillment, intellectual enrichment, and sage diplomacy, Mary's mother and her pliable intercessory capabilities were well suited for both the elector and the city of Wittenberg, even as the city became an incubator for Reformation theology.

The King and the Elector

Although no document survives to explain how JenaU 7 and its Habsburg emblems entered the collection of Frederick the Wise, Maximilian and the elector had ample opportunity to facilitate such an exchange in their service to the empire. Despite the power accumulated by each man, the relationship between the two was quite close. In addition to having a blood relationship (they were cousins), Maximilian and Frederick had a vested interest in securing a strong central empire, and they were evidently in frequent contact across the decades. From 1486 and onward into the first two decades of the sixteenth century, Frederick gradually entered Maximilian's innermost circle of political consultants, often serving as the voice of caution and peace among the empire's estates. With the mutual goal of ensuring power and tranquility across the vast territories, the soon-to-be emperor and his key elector had good reason to call on St. Anne, the potent protectress of great dynasties. In fact, their shared interest in Mary's mother can be formally marked by their membership in the St. Anne confraternity in Worms, founded in 1496.[6]

Descending from the Ernestine line of the illustrious House of Wettin in (now) east central Germany, Frederick not only wielded significant power within the large duchy of Saxony, but also held great sway in the Holy Roman Empire, achieving a second-in-command status once Maximilian ascended to the imperial office in 1508.[7] It is easy to lose sight of Frederick's political authority at the dawn of the sixteenth century, especially because his notorious protection of Martin Luther and the early reform movement in Wittenberg has commanded significantly more historiographical attention. Some background on the elector's relationship with Maximilian and the Habsburg-Burgundian court will help establish a context for the presence of JenaU 7 in Frederick's musical collection and point to further connections with Mary's mother, whose intercession was widely sought even in the face of the Reformation in Wittenberg.

Frederick took an early interest in assisting with the governance of the empire, holding a number of influential offices during his life. When Maximilian was named King of the Romans in 1486, he appointed Frederick as his imperial advisor.[8] In his first year of service, Frederick was able to travel with Maximilian to celebrate the investiture of Philip the Fair as ruler of the Low Countries. It was on this particular trip that Frederick heard a mass in Mechelen and came into contact with the outstanding music cultivated in the Habsburg-Burgundian chapel.[9] But for all of his early support of Maximilian's imperial authority, the elector had competing loyalties that complicated their relationship. As the king engaged in *Hausmacht*, built an army, and set his sights on extending the perimeter of his rule, the elector was concerned about internal peace within the German estates. To this end, Frederick helped champion an imperial reform movement that won great favor among the estates, despite opposition by Maximilian. Judicial reform stumbled among the estates and was eventually taken under Maximilian's wing as the Imperial Council (*Reichshofrat*). Frederick was appointed the head (*Hofratstatthalter*) of this body, bringing him yet closer to the king in terms of power and prestige in the empire.[10] The prudent elector would go on to serve the administration in even higher ranks, culminating in his appointment to the role of *Reichsgeneralstatthalter* with the duty of ruling the empire during Maximilian's sojourn to Rome to receive the imperial crown in 1507.[11] Although Maximilian never made it to Rome and curiously declared himself the Roman emperor upon his return, he allowed Frederick to maintain the prestigious appointment indefinitely.[12] Despite his disagreements with many aspects of the imperial crown, Frederick the Wise served it nobly and carefully controlled his sympathies as elector. In turn, he was admired by Maximilian, who understood the power of the elector and kept his cousin under close watch throughout his life, rewarding him with offices through the first two decades of the sixteenth century. The opportunities for JenaU 7 to come into Frederick's fold of manuscripts were many during this period, especially in light of the elector's role as *Reichsgeneralstatthalter*. In 1518, Maximilian in fact promised to send Frederick three choirbooks, and it seems highly likely, as Karl Roediger has suggested, that JenaU 7 might have been among those manuscripts.[13] A possible conduit for the transfer of repertory could have been singer-composer Adam Rener, who was a member of Maximilian's chapel until 1503 and then appeared in Frederick's court at Torgau beginning in 1507, serving the elector for at least a decade.[14]

The political stakes between the Habsburg-Burgundian house and the elector were high. Ultimately, Frederick would help choose Maximilian's successor, and the emperor lobbied tirelessly for his grandson, Archduke Charles, to be the next Holy Roman Emperor. With no small help from Margaret and the Alamire workshop, Maximilian did everything in his power to muscle the elector into a secure vote for Charles. Among the lavish Habsburg-Burgundian manuscripts that survive in Frederick's collection, seven likely appeared between the time when Charles came of age (1514) and the death of Maximilian in 1519 – in other words, during the run-up to the imperial election.[15] When the electors convened on June 27, 1519, the chief candidates for Holy Roman Emperor were Charles V and Frederick himself. With three electors supporting Charles and three supporting the elector, Frederick became the deciding vote. In the end, the savvy elector denied himself the imperial office and opted for Charles, no doubt to ensure that his efforts toward limiting imperial authority would not go to waste.[16] The aims of the Habsburgs succeeded, and the presentation manuscripts – JenaU 7 probably among them – appeared to have done their job in helping influence the election. Even more manuscripts could have arrived in Frederick's domain as a gesture of gratitude following the all-important election of the new Holy Roman Emperor.[17] The opportunities to receive a presentation manuscript like JenaU 7 were thus ample, and La Rue's mass for Mary's mother would have been particularly welcome in the city that Frederick rebuilt. By following the *St. Anne Mass* into the milieu of the elector and pre-Reformation Wittenberg, one discovers both a culture of intense devotion and one of academic pursuit, a place in which the *Mater matris* had already won great favor and was celebrated with remarkable pomp.

The Castle Church, St. Anne, and the Holy Kinship

History remembers Frederick the Wise as the protector of Martin Luther, but Luther would not have achieved his fame were it not for two key institutions in the city of Wittenberg – the Castle Church and the University of Wittenberg. Luther was a professor of theology at the university, famously nailing the *Ninety-five Theses* to the door of the Castle Church on October 31, 1517. While these sites became emblematic of Luther's reformed theology, the church and the university together established Wittenberg as both an intellectual and a spiritual capital of Europe. The idea for these institutions was hatched by Frederick, who in 1486 set out to upgrade the academic and religious establishments that he inherited as part of electoral Saxony. As a destination for thousands of students and pilgrims, Wittenberg – the birthplace of the Reformation – began as a reflection of the values and pursuits of the sage elector himself.

As one of the last electoral territories not to have a university, Saxony finally offered an opportunity for higher learning in 1502 with the founding of the University of Wittenberg. Committed to the principles of humanism, the university became a reflection of its founder, who received a liberal arts education and was well versed in classical literature (rare for a German prince).[18] Housing some of the most forward-thinking philosophers in Europe and embracing a bold agenda rooted in humanistic study, the University of Wittenberg could soon boast the highest enrollment of any German university. But it was the All Saints Collegiate Church (*Allerheiligenkapelle*), the so-called Castle Church (*Schlosskirche*), that received considerable attention from the elector, and the institution would eventually attract thousands of devotees from great distances.[19] More so than the university, the church mirrored the elector's values and aesthetics; in this case, though, it was not his humanistic impulse, but rather his intense personal devotion to his faith and in particular the penitential system. Built over the former Ascanian castle and serving as an extension to the university, the Castle Church – burnt down in 1760 during the Seven Years' War and since rebuilt – offered an unparalleled experience for the eye and the ear for those who entered its portals. This house of worship more broadly reflected the majesty of the elector, who carefully orchestrated the intersection of faith and intellectual pursuits in his magnificent city. In the early sixteenth century, the glorious Castle Church became the site for an outpouring of ritual, visual, and aural devotion to St. Anne.

No discussion of the Castle Church can begin without mention of the vast collection of relics that it housed, rivaling those of the greatest churches in Europe. The culture of adoration for these relics was reflected in the church's liturgical year with two major feasts – All Saints Day (the church's namesake) celebrated on November 1 and the Display of Relics, a movable feast commemorated on the second Sunday after Easter. Among the most noteworthy relics at the Castle Church were the arm bone of Frederick's patron namesake and a thorn from Christ's Crown of Thorns. The story behind Frederick's amassed collection, however, begins with St. Anne. In 1493, just three years after ground broke on the construction of the Castle Church, the elector made a pilgrimage to the Holy Land and brought back a "thumb" of St. Anne, as well as an expensive gold reliquary to house the relic.[20] The acquisition of relics did not accelerate until 1507 when Pope Julius II issued a letter urging German prelates to encourage visitation of the church's collection. By 1509, Frederick's court painter Lucas Cranach the Elder developed an illustrated catalog (*Wittenberger Heiligtumsbuch*), which documented more than five thousand relics held at the Castle Church. Cranach's woodcut renderings of the St. Anne reliquaries (Figure 4.2) feature clear representations of the popular St. Anne Trinitarian image, with the characteristic miniaturized depictions of the Virgin and Christ Child in the arms of the grandmother saint.

Ten years later, the collection of relics had grown to historic proportions, reaching more than nineteen thousand articles organized into ten galleries. The sprawling collection had both practical and spiritual benefits. As a massive house of relics, the Castle Church emerged as a tourist destination for pious Christians seeking epic sums of indulgences, a practice that boosted an already healthy economy in Wittenberg.[21] In his effort to spur thousands of residents and pilgrims to private devotion, Frederick the Wise no doubt believed that his collection had spiritual carryover for him. Through the aggressive acquisition of the relics, the elector established a body of "good works" and the hope of divine favor as a result.[22]

Figure 4.2 Lucas Cranach the Elder, Relics of Saint Anne, woodcut from the Wittenberger Heiligtumsbuch. Buch 581/82. S. 69 Kupferstichkabinett, Staatliche Museen, Berlin, Germany. 1509. Photo: Bildarchiv Preußischer Kulturbesitz, Berlin / Art Resource, NY.

The Castle Church was bedecked with more than relics. With lavish visual art adorning the sanctuary's altars, the interior was a feast for gazing eyes. Visual culture was central to the remaking of Wittenberg under Frederick's watch, and the elector earned a strong reputation for supporting artists of all stripes, including painters, architects, engravers, woodcutters, and sculptors. The artists from whom Frederick generously commissioned or purchased works constitute a "who's who" of early sixteenth-century art, including Lucas Cranach the Elder, Hans Burgkmair, Albrecht Dürer,

Conrad Meit, Hans Schäufelein, Tilman Riemenschneider, and Peter Vischer the Elder.[23] During the church's construction, twenty-four altars were installed, though only thirteen dedicatees are known. Not surprisingly, one of the altars commemorates St. Anne. Unfortunately, it cannot be definitively determined whether artwork accompanied the St. Anne altar. But given that Frederick obtained a relic of the saint early in the history of the institution, many familiar with the Castle Church and its liturgical interior are convinced that some elaborate painting must have ornamented the St. Anne altar.[24]

Evidence suggests that an altarpiece by Cranach might well have served as a decorative program for the St. Anne altar in the Castle Church. Dated 1509, the work of art is known as the *Altarpiece of the Holy Kinship* (Figure 4.3), and it currently resides in Frankfurt at the Städel Museum. Cranach's triptych has also been called the "Torgau Altarpiece," because it was traditionally thought to have been located in the Marian church in Torgau. The painting became linked with the Castle Church in the mid-nineteenth century when art historian Christian Schuchardt described a painting identical to Cranach's Holy Kinship altarpiece, but assigned it to the Castle Church instead of Torgau. Whether Schuchardt was detailing the 1509 Torgau Altarpiece is not known, but his description further drove suspicions that a Holy Kinship altarpiece very similar to this (if not precisely this altarpiece) must have adorned the St. Anne altar in Frederick's church.[25]

Cranach's inspiration for the impressive Holy Kinship altarpiece might have come from Margaret of Austria, whose court the painter visited a year before this work was illustrated. No matter the influence, Cranach's triptych unleashes the full force of the Holy Kinship, with St. Anne and the Virgin Mary as the central subjects, the former holding the Christ Child, and the families of Anne's daughters occupying the wings of the altarpiece. The left panel shows Mary Cleophas (seated), and Mary Salome is on the right. Their respective husbands, Alphaeus and Zebedee, are conspicuously replaced by Frederick the Wise and his brother Duke John the Steadfast, the successor to the electorship of Saxony and frequent cosponsor of such works with Frederick. In the gallery behind Mary and her mother stand Anne's three husbands, ostensibly in proper nuptial succession from left to right. Some have noted the resemblance not only of the bearded Joachim (gallery, left) to Cranach himself, but also of Anne's second husband, Cleophas, to Maximilian (gallery, center).[26]

Cranach's *Altarpiece of the Holy Kinship* may reveal a specific benefit that Frederick harvested from devotion to St. Anne and her progeny.

Figure 4.3 Lucas Cranach, *Altarpiece of the Holy Kinship*. Städel Museum, Frankfurt, 1398. Credit: Städel Museum/ARTOTHEK.

Scholarship, however, has yet to reach a consensus on a clear message radiating from this elaborate triptych. Bridget Heal has noted the "touchingly maternal" and domestic quality of the overall image, in light of the fact that Mary Cleophas is nursing her baby on the left panel, while her sister Mary Salome fixes her son's hair on the right.[27] But the presence of Frederick and his brother amidst the Holy Kinship has also produced political interpretations of the altarpiece – a reasonable avenue of pursuit given the recent literature on such appropriations of St. Anne and her extended family by the aristocracy. Consistent with other uses of St. Anne encountered to this point, James Snyder has suggested that the elector's presence highlights his noble ancestry by blurring it with the dignity of the Holy Kinship, while Pamela Sheingorn views Frederick's presence and the other male self-portraits therein as a suppression of maternity and the cognatic (female) line intimated by the subject of St. Anne and her daughters.[28] Others have sought to account not only for the elector and his brother, but also the political implications of including what appears to be Emperor Maximilian in the gallery. Carl Christensen sees the triptych as a projection of healthy relations between the House of Wettin and Maximilian's Habsburg court.[29] Noting the presumed presence of Maximilian just above the Saxon coats of arms that adorn the frieze of the balcony, Bodo Brinkmann contends that there is a more nuanced political message at stake. According to Brinkmann, the altarpiece hints at the struggles between the princes and the imperial court, ultimately indicating the fidelity of the Saxons toward the emperor to ensure peace in Saxony and the empire at large.[30]

Obviously, the potential meanings for Cranach's *Altarpiece of the Holy Kinship* are manifold, and further observations can be made. The literature on this altarpiece has yet to mention that the elector's interest in Mary's mother could have been quite personal. St. Anne – the figure at the center of the Holy Kinship – was the patron name of the elector's longtime mistress, Anna Weller von Molsdorf. Little is known about this "Anna," as Frederick remained officially unmarried throughout his life. This woman did bear him at least two sons, and papal dispensation was given to the boys in late 1518 as a reprieve from their illegitimate status.[31] It is difficult to speculate what meaning Frederick harvested from St. Anne when viewed in the light of his relationship with Anna, but the elector's outward gaze in the altarpiece in the role of "Alphaeus" seems indifferent at best. With his hands together at his chest, the elector might have been preoccupied with the future of his "family" and claims to legitimate progeny. For all of the human interaction in the triptych, Frederick's brother also appears aloof. However, the life of the younger brother John had taken a more traditional course around the time of this altarpiece. Married with a son (John Frederick), the duke, entrenched in a book, shows none of the worry of his brother. One might detect a hint of sibling rivalry in Cranach's elaborate *Altarpiece of the Holy Kinship*.

Other interpretations may still be proffered. Just as the values of intense devotion and intellectual inquiry for Frederick the Wise materialized in the form of a splendid Castle Church and an unparalleled place of higher learning (University of Wittenberg), so too are these values captured in miniature by the triptych. By invoking the family of St. Anne in the first place, Frederick unveils his fervor for praising the full life of Mary. As Cranach's altarpiece demonstrates, the Holy Kinship has three essential characters apart from the Virgin: St. Anne, Mary Cleophas, and Mary Salome. These three figures within the triptych illuminate the circumstances surrounding the life of Mary, about which little was known from canonical sources.

At the same time, there is a subtle overlay of the elector's great passion for wisdom. Although John the Steadfast is privately engaged with a book (one sign of knowledge acquisition), it has gone unnoticed that when the altarpiece is closed, the exterior wings suggest a subtext of literacy and the pursuit of knowledge within the representation of St. Anne's family. In the closed position, the altarpiece transforms into a diptych (Figure 4.4), with Mary holding the Christ Child on the left and St. Anne alone on the right. Significantly, Anne's gaze is directed toward the book she holds, not the baby Jesus. While it would be radical to envision Anne reading anything other than the book of Psalms (a book she was said to teach to her daughter), the scene highlights a thirst for letters and reason through Mary's mother, carefully balanced with both political and spiritual implications in the triptych.

It is almost certain that Cranach's *Altarpiece of the Holy Kinship*, or a very similar work, adorned the St. Anne altar in the Castle Church. Such a glorious illustration reveals not only Frederick's taste for the finest in visual culture, but also his fondness for Mary's mother and the full kinship. In this and other altarpieces that decorated the Castle Church, Frederick displayed indelible images from the collective treasury of the faith for believers, driving them to devotion through these objects and potentially accruing divine benefits for them in the process. Visual art, however, did not operate in a vacuum at the church. For the clergy, faculty, students, townspeople, and thousands of Christian pilgrims who visited the Castle Church, the program of devotion at the institution featured ritual action and music to

Figure 4.4 Lucas Cranach, *Altarpiece of the Holy Kinship* (wings in closed position). Städel Museum, Frankfurt, 1398. Credit: Städel Museum/ARTOTHEK.

complement the visual experience, whether in the nave or in side chapels. It is not difficult to imagine La Rue's *St. Anne Mass* performed in the side chapel dedicated to Mary's mother at the Castle Church, but even more music in honor of the grandmother saint survives for consideration. This music has the potential to refine the understanding of St. Anne as projected in Wittenberg under the sponsorship of Frederick the Wise.

Office and Mass Music for St. Anne

Nearly a decade before the arrival of La Rue's mass for Mary's mother in JenaU 7, other sources of music for St. Anne, more closely tied to the Castle Church, were cultivated in Wittenberg. While JenaU 7 served as a presentation-style manuscript from the illustrious Alamire scriptorium, two modest paper manuscripts (JenaU 34 and JenaU 30) – part of a collection of eight sources known as the "Jena choirbooks" – offer music aplenty that was likely sung at the St. Anne altar.[32] In each of these manuscripts, I will show that St. Anne was overrepresented as a saint. Already one of Frederick's favored saints, Mary's mother received peculiar and noteworthy exposure in these unassuming paper books, the musical contents of which adorned liturgies for annual feasts.

The manuscript JenaU 34 contains music for Vespers, the most musically elaborate service of the liturgical day, outside of Mass. The aforementioned Adam Rener may have composed or edited the largely anonymous music of the Jena choirbooks.[33] Like all of the eight choirbooks, JenaU 34 is large (273 fols., with dimensions 475 x 310 mm) yet nondescript in its paper form: it was music for use.[34] It is reasonable to think that this music was performed at the Castle Church, because the contents of JenaU 34 reveal office music for fifteen major festivals of the liturgical year at that particular institution, beginning with Christmas and continuing through the Feast of All Saints, the namesake of the church. Eight of the fifteen feasts – the Nativity of Mary among them – held especially high rank and, as such, composers produced polyphony for both First and Second Vespers.[35] A typical Vespers service in JenaU 34 featured all five required psalm settings composed in polyphony, but could also have included additional polyphony for the hymn, responsory, suffrage, and Magnificat antiphon. This last item – the antiphon for the Magnificat – would presumably be paired with a modally concordant setting of the eight polyphonic Magnificats found in the back of the manuscript, arranged in modal order.[36]

The polyphony allotted to saints in JenaU 34 is noticeably limited, with most of the musical attention rightfully directed toward Christ and his mother. A service of First Vespers is provided for St. Stephen and St. John the Evangelist, an obvious extension of celebrations within the Christmas octave.[37] Other saints, occurring in proper liturgical order throughout the year, have an occasional polyphonic item. A suffrage for St. Blaise (*Qui pro Christe nomine*) appears in a small gathering, preceded by a complete First Vespers service for the Purification of the Virgin, a feast that falls the day before the commemoration of St. Blaise, the patron saint of throat ailments.[38] Another suffrage (*Operati sunt iusticiam*) for two lesser known saints, Gorgonio and Kunigunde, is situated between the elaborate Vespers offerings for the Nativity of Mary (September 8) and the illustrious celebration of All Saints (November 1). The polyphony for All Saints properly marks the end of the calendar of major celebrations before the large section of Magnificats, which occupies some twenty-seven folios.[39]

Between the music for All Saints and the ordered Magnificats lies a small gathering of eight folios where office music for two more saints – St. Anne and St. James – is added.[40] Interestingly, these two saints are celebrated on consecutive feast days in the liturgical year (July 26 and July 25, respectively), their placement not only liturgically out of order but physically outside the boundary of saints' feasts in the manuscript. The Vespers music is incomplete for each saint, neither offering the five psalm settings present in other major offices. In the case of St. James, only a setting of a suffrage appears (*Ante reges et presides*); whereas with St. Anne, a polyphonic hymn and responsory are included (*Lucis huius festa* and *Celebramus devotissime*, respectively). The JenaU 34 scribe often copied a suffrage into his choirbook either detached from the other Vespers music for that feast (i.e., the five psalm settings) or as a stand-alone devotional work,[41] but never did he dedicate a full gathering to these additions, as in the case of the works for St. Anne and St. James. St. Anne in particular is the only case in the manuscript that presents a hymn and responsory as stand-alone items for a feast. The question of why these office items for St. Anne were added with a suffrage for St. James in such an anomalous position in the source will have to remain unsolved. But more evidence exists to suggest that St. Anne was a crucial saint amidst the office music of JenaU 34.

Following the brief polyphonic items for St. Anne and St. James, the eight Magnificats organized by mode in JenaU 34 ostensibly represented the end of the JenaU 34 manuscript as originally conceived, serving as a kind of appendix from which one could select a musically agreeable polyphonic setting of Mary's canticle to pair with the antiphon that preceded it at Vespers. As an obvious afterthought, a partial set of Mass Propers was bound into the manuscript in a separate fascicle following the catalog of Magnificats.[42] Of all possible feasts, it turns out that these propers are in honor of St. Anne, thereby raising her profile in JenaU 34, a book otherwise devoted to office music for Vespers. Extending some seven folios, this appended polyphony for Mary's mother consists of an Introit (*Gaudeamus omnes in Domino*), Alleluia (*Alleluia. O Maria dei genetrix*), and a sequence (*Gaude mater anna gaude*). No Communion is included here, making it an incomplete cycle when viewed against other settings in the Jena choirbooks.

Kathryn Duffy has convincingly shown that the music of the Castle Church does not follow a single diocesan usage, but rather exhibits an eclectic mixture of rites to form its own liturgical usage and sometimes arranges new texts and music, a fact that harmonizes well with Frederick's bold vision for the church. The appended Mass Propers for St. Anne in JenaU 34 are no exception to these observed phenomena. For example, while the Introit for St. Anne is based on a well-circulated melody from local dioceses, the sequence *Gaude mater anna gaude* appears only in the local usages of Würzburg and Augsburg, although it was known elsewhere.[43] Tellingly, the Alleluia with verse *O Maria dei genetrix* cannot be readily associated with any of the surrounding dioceses, consistent with the notion that the Castle Church was not afraid to forge new paths for a given feast.[44]

The verse incipit of *Alleluia. O Maria dei genetrix* may strike one as lacking a connection to St. Anne, but the full text of the Alleluia verse shows Mary's mother to be the object of praise: "O Mary Mother of God, blessed be your mother Saint Anne, from whom your virginal flesh proceeds without the stain of sin" (*O Maria dei genetrix benedicta sit mater tua sancta Anna ex qua sine peccati macula processit caro tua virginea*). Notably, the emphasis on Mary's freedom from sin in this brief Alleluia seems to call attention to the controversial issue of the Immaculate Conception. The verse in fact bears some resemblance to a fourteenth-century Marian prayer known in England that includes the adjective "immaculate" to modify the word "flesh."[45] St. Anne's connection to the Conception doctrine will be examined in detail later. For now, note that the Alleluia itself comes at a comparatively high liturgical moment, as the gospel reading approached. And even though a short Alleluia verse is no place to hash out the particulars of a complex doctrine, it is noteworthy that this compact musical setting uses St. Anne – an established and stalwart saint at the Castle Church – as a platform for an apparent reference to the contentious teachings of the Immaculate Conception.

In JenaU 34, the sequence *Gaude mater anna gaude* reveals only the verses that receive polyphonic treatment. These verses, which represent the most discursive of the Proper texts, are marked with an asterisk below and presumably alternated with those sung in plainchant melodies, obtained either from memory or from another liturgical book that does not survive.

1. Gaude mater anna gaude Mater omni digna laude Mater tante filie:	Rejoice, O mother Anne, Rejoice, O worthy mother, with every glory, mother of so great a daughter:
2. *Anna recte nuncuparis Quasi graciosa paris Matris omnis gracie.	O gracious Anne, may you rightly be called the equal of the mother of all grace.
3. Anna parit tres marias Quarum primam ysaias Praedixit divinitus.	Anne brings forth three Marys of which the first Isaiah predicted would be from heaven,
4. *Virgam florem producturam Virginemque parituram Dono sancti spiritus.	A branch-flower to be produced, and a virgin to be born by the gift of the Holy Spirit.
5. Hec est radix anna pia Virga florens est maria Christus flos est inclitus.	Holy Anne is the root, Mary the blossoming branch, Christ the glorious flower.
6. *Digna radix est honore Cuius virga tali flore Fecundatur celitus.	The root is worthy with honor whose branch is divinely made fertile by so great a flower.
7. Anna stellam matutinam Stellam maris et reginam Peperit clementie,	Anne bore the morning star, the star of the sea and queen of mercy,
8. *Cum qua vere iam letatur Quia deum contemplatur Revelata facie.	With whom she now rejoices, for she notices God with a revealed face.
9. Salve mater matris Christi Que iam felix conscendisti Iubilans ad ethera.	Hail mother of Christ's mother! You, holy one, now ascended, rejoicing to heaven.
10. *Iter nobis para tutum Ut in domini virtutum Collocemur gloria.	Make a safe journey for us, so that we might be gathered in the glory of the Lord of hosts.

Among the familiar associative possibilities for St. Anne witnessed thus far, the second strophe of this sequence recalls the connection of Anne's name to "grace" (also a metonym for Mary), while the third verse makes a passing reference to the legend of the Three Marys. Allusions to the root-branch-flower metaphor (as Anne-Mary-Christ) occupy the three succeeding versicles of *Gaude mater anna gaude* (verses 4–6), a frequent analogy in the versified offices for St. Anne, briefly encountered in Chapter 2 in connection with the office for the saint in the Turin Codex. For nobility like Frederick, this kind of emphasis on heritage – verses 4 and 6 in particular augmented with polyphony – could have signaled the precious stock of the elector himself as much as his devotion to Mary and her mother.

References to the "stellar" qualities of Mary in the seventh stanza (*stellam matutinam* and *stellam maris*) may delicately hint at the doctrine of the Immaculate Conception. While the Virgin was often titled the "Star of the Sea" and "Queen of Heaven," she was also increasingly associated as the Woman of the Apocalypse, the lady who stands on the crescent moon with a crown of a dozen stars.[46] The latter understanding of Mary was quite prevalent, it turns out, in iconography associated with the Immaculate Conception. More on this soon; in the meantime, keep an eye out for suggestions of the doctrine across this musical repertory.

The manuscript JenaU 34 (together with the polyphonic Mass Propers for major Christological feasts found in JenaU 35) appears to have been completed early among the collection of Jena choirbooks, perhaps by 1507 or 1508, by a single text and music scribe (whose hand has been labeled as "Q9a9b") and with a paper containing a single, rose-shaped watermark.[47] Yet the compiler of JenaU 34 was also an amateur of sorts, arranging small gatherings to create the manuscript as a whole, effectively contrasting with the other well-planned and continuous choirbooks for the Castle Church. This fact is most visible in the music for St. Anne, who, in JenaU 34, comes off as a late addition, wedged into the manuscript with music for St. James in a fascicle before the Magnificat index, only to be appended again to the end of the manuscript in another separate gathering, now of liturgically distinct Mass Propers. These facts do not necessarily alter the date of the manuscript, because it appears to have been completed in short order by the single scribe, as mentioned. At minimum, one discovers an idiosyncratic treatment of the saint in this particular source and a fair amount of polyphony that could be used in celebration of Mary's mother at the prominent St. Anne altar of the Castle Church. This music was likely compiled and sung considerably earlier than the arrival of La Rue's mass for St. Anne in JenaU 7, which presumably appeared between 1517 and 1518.

Supplementary Proper Cycles and Their Sequences

The special status accorded to St. Anne at Frederick's esteemed church is confirmed with yet more music for the saint in a manuscript related to JenaU 34 – JenaU 30. This book of polyphony from around 1509 seems to have appeared shortly after the compilation of JenaU 34 and, more importantly, populates the major festivals with Mass Propers for the highest-ranking saints' feasts at the Castle Church. Like all of the paper choirbooks that survive for the Castle Church, the featured saints and Mass Propers in JenaU 30 cannot be linked to one specific usage in or around Wittenberg, further underscoring the independent liturgical identity sought by Frederick's impressive institution.

The collection of sanctoral polyphony in JenaU 30 begins with the feast of St. Andrew (November 30) and progresses in an orderly way through the liturgical year until the commemoration of St. Katherine (November 25).[48] Some sixteen individual saints in addition to various Marian feasts are celebrated in a span of nearly one hundred forty folios. Unsurprisingly, St. Anne is among those saints who receive polyphonic adornment in this large section. Unlike the partial cycle for St. Anne appended to JenaU 34, however, the music for Mary's mother in JenaU 30 is complete with the four Propers typically set by early sixteenth-century composers.

Introit	Gaudeamus omnes in Domino	fols. 81v–83r
Alleluia	Alleluia. Diffusa est gratia	fols. 83v–84r
Sequence	Sancte anne devotus	fols. 84v–87r
Communion	Diffusa est gratia	fols. 87v–88r

The text of the Introit *Gaudeamus omnes in Domino* is identical to that of JenaU 34, but evidently occasioned an additional polyphonic setting as part of the present cycle. Further, the Introit, Alleluia, and Communion of this cycle contain texts drawn from the commemoration of any virgin saint (ironic, considering that the legend of the Three Marys implies anything but a virgin saint!). This leaves the sequence *Sancte anne devotus* as the only truly Proper item in the mass cycle for St. Anne.

While it maintains the liturgical pastiche achieved in the Castle Church liturgy, *Sancte anne devotus* is no Wittenberg *unicum*. As Duffy has shown, it was used specifically in the liturgy of Meissen.[49] Moreover, the music of this sequence is a contrafactum of the Christmas sequence *Letabundus exsultet fidelis chorus*, a melody that inspired numerous contrafacta of both the sacred and secular variety.[50] The poet of *Sancte anne devotus* secured the connection to *Letabundus* not only through clear musical citation of the parent melody in both tenor and discantus, but also through the co-opting of the final four-syllable line of each versicle of *Letabundus* (*Alleluia*; *Res miranda*; *Sol de stella*, etc.), the text of which is by no means inappropriate for use with the new subject of Mary's mother. The lengthiest of the four Proper texts in this (or any) cycle, the sequence bears a closer look for any clues as to how St. Anne was received by early sixteenth-century Wittenberg in general and perhaps in accordance with the view of Frederick the Wise in particular. Like all sequences at the Castle Church, this music would have been performed by alternating chant and polyphony (the latter again denoted by asterisk). In this setting, however, the first two verses receive polyphonic adornment to the same music, with the second of the two verses (*Cuius partus* ...) simply placed beneath the text of the first, as one might find in a strophic song. With its double-versicle structure, the sequence is designed in such a way as to accommodate this repetition as a matter of course. The polyphony for the first verse can easily host the text of the sequence's second verse, especially because it mirrors the syllable count of the former.[51]

1. *Sancte anne devotus
decantet chorus
Alleluia.

Let the faithful chorus
sing to Saint Anne
Alleluia,

2. *Cuius partus salutem
produxit mundo,
Res miranda.

Whose offspring produced
salvation for the world,
a marvelous event.

3. *De cuius prole casta
Aeterna lux est orta
Sol de stella.

From whose pure stock
The eternal light arose,
The sun from the star.

4. Anna ex prosapia
Aaron est genita
Semper clara.

From Aaron's lineage,
Anne was begotten,
always bright.

5. Quae ut iubar fulgidum
Decoravit saeculum
Pari forma.

She is like a gleaming brightness,
adorned forever,
alike in nature.

6. *Amans Deum toto corde
nulla letali sorde
Fit corrupta.

Loving God with full heart
she is not made corrupt
by mortal stain.

7. Gignens salutis fructum
obtulit omne luctum
Valle nostra.

Bringing forth the fruit of salvation,
she bore every grief
in this valley of our world.

8. *Ex prole quam genuit
Sol verus emicuit
Carne sumpta.

Out of the stock which the true sun brought forth,
he sprang forth,
having taken up flesh.

9. Sol Christe irradia
nostra corda gracia
ne sine labe noxia
Esse ceca;

O Christ, the Sun, beam forth
our hearts with grace
lest this harm be blinded
without fault.

10. *Quem nec Judea natum credit nec immolatum Cum sint per scripta vatum Hec predicta.	The Jews believe he was neither born nor sacrificed, although these things were foretold in the writings of the prophets.
11. Nunc hora ut pia mater Et filia succurrat tibi Gens misera.	Now is the hour that the dear mother and daughter might give aid to you, miserable nation!
12. *Et te post tristia Ducat ad gaudia Hic, quem genuit Puerpera Maria.	Then may he, the one whom the childbearing Mary bore, lead you out of your sorrows toward everlasting joys.

While the first stanza clearly points to St. Anne, the sequence subtly shifts the focus to the Virgin and Christ as her crucial descendants. The sixth stanza of this sequence – notably, one of the verses set in polyphony – declares Mary to have remained uncorrupted "by mortal stain" (*nulla letali sorde / Fit corrupta*).[52] Here is another cue for the doctrine of the Immaculate Conception, a topic potentially suggested in the Alleluia verse and perhaps the sequence *Gaude mater anna gaude* from JenaU 34. Despite its length relative to an Alleluia verse, the sequence is still no forum for detailing immaculist or maculist ideologies. *Sancte anne devotus* only seems to provide a few passing indications of the divisive Immaculate Conception teaching, a subject that rarely emerges in music honoring St. Anne. The critical sixth stanza that refers to the "mortal stain" may however be bolstered by an image from the third stanza (also set in polyphony) – that of the *sol de stella* ("sun from the star"). This analogy may stand for more than "Jesus from Mary": as with the sequence *Gaude mater anna gaude*, the connection between the Virgin and the star could indirectly point yet again to an immaculist understanding of Mary.

After this Proper cycle, even more mass music for St. Anne was likely performed at her side altar. No more than fifty folios after the cycle just mentioned sits yet another set of Mass Propers for Mary's mother in JenaU 30. Conspicuously, this new cycle for St. Anne is the first one entered in a new scribal hand for a saint after the sanctoral calendar was formally completed in the annual cycle with music for the feast of St. Katherine.[53] St. Anne is not the only saint for whom music was provided twice in the manuscript, but she was the one who far and away received the most polyphony among the saints "repeated" in the appendix to this manuscript.[54] The rubric at the outset of the St. Anne cycle specifies that the singers should turn back to the Introit of the mass for St. Anne found earlier in the manuscript to sing

Gaudeamus omnes in Domino (fols. 81v–83r). But after this instruction, three new Proper settings follow in earnest for St. Anne.

Alleluia	Alleluia. Dulcis mater	fols. 138v–140r
Sequence	Alma parens anna gaude	fols. 140v–146r
Communion	Diffusa est gratia	fols. 146v–147r

While the Communion *Diffusa est gratia* constitutes an alternative setting of the common text seen in the earlier mass cycle for St. Anne in JenaU 30, the Alleluia and sequence are both unique to the Jena choirbooks and not found paired together in any surrounding diocese.[55] The amalgam of texts in this cycle of Propers again underscores the penchant of Frederick's manuscript compilers for forging an autonomous liturgical identity in Saxony through handpicked texts from various proximate locales. As with *Sancte anne devotus*, it is again the sequence (here, *Alma parens anna gaude*) that was the most provocative of the Proper texts and deserves scrutiny, because it was chosen among numerous available sequences for St. Anne.

The text of *Alma parens anna gaude* draws on the same ten-stanza poem as does the sequence *Gaude mater anna gaude* from JenaU 34, the only textual variant found in the first two words. There are two major formal differences between these sequences, however. First, while the polyphony in JenaU 34 sequence was set for the even-numbered verses, *Alma parens anna gaude* has polyphony set for the odd-numbered verses. The consequence is that the two versions could be used in an interlocking fashion to create a setting of this sequence with all verses in polyphony. JenaU 30 and 34 were roughly contemporaneous, and thus a concurrent usage of the books for a "hand-in-glove" polyphonic performance can be reasonably imagined. Such a proposal seems even more likely in light of the fact that most of the verses begin and end with F sonorities, making potential transitions between the versions seamless, if possibly monotonous (Table 4.1).[56] One can almost imagine alternating choirs ringing out these verses to achieve a constant pouring forth of richly woven sounds into the Castle Church. Because the polyphonic verses unfold more slowly than the chant does, one of the obvious results of such an arrangement would be more time consumed trumpeting the merits of St. Anne in the liturgy.

Another striking distinction between these polyphonic sequences is a special devotion to St. Anne at the conclusion of *Alma parens anna gaude*. Though a seemingly generic entreaty, the plea to St. Anne in this sequence was an unconventional appeal to Mary's mother, starkly set in polyphony (*Miserere nobis pie / Mater sancte Marie* ["Have mercy on us, O mother of

Table 4.1 Tonal transitions between *Gaude mater anna gaude* (JenaU 34) and *Alma parens anna gaude* (JenaU 30)

Verse	Text incipit	Opening sonority	Closing sonority
1	Alma parens[a]	D	F
2	Anna nuncuparis	D	F
3	Anna parit	F	F
4	Virgam florem	F	F
5	Hec est radix	C	F
6	Digna radix	F	F
7	Anna stellam	F	F
8	Cum qua vere	F	F
9	Salve mater matris	C	F
10	Iter nobis para	C	F
11	Miserere[b]	F	F

[a] *Alma parens* contains the odd-numbered verses in polyphony; the polyphonic verses of *Gaude mater* are even-numbered.
[b] This is not properly a verse of the sequence *Alma parens anna gaude*; it has been added as a petition.

blessed and devout Mary"]). Anyone familiar with the sequence in general will know that an asymmetrical rhymed couplet of this nature falls outside the norms of the genre. Indeed, this aparallel poetic appendage represents a departure from this sequence text known in other sources. The decision to include the couplet not only highlights the independence of the Castle Church liturgy, but also encapsulates the high institutional reverence for Mary's mother. The music of the supplementary *Miserere* text further participates in marking the devotional moment. Of the six voices prescribed for *Alma parens anna gaude* on the whole, the composer usually taps four at a time in varying combinations. The part labeled *vagans* (a fifth "wandering" part) is used only sparingly, as is another auxiliary voice called the *discantus primus*, the highest ranging of the six voices. In the ten or so minutes that the sequence might have taken to perform in full (polyphony plus plainchant, in this case), the polyphonic texture expands just three times to a five-voice texture, never to six voices, despite the forces to do so. The first two deployments of five voices appear subtly and arbitrarily *in medias res* (first in the middle of the third verse and again toward the end of the ninth verse). The third engagement of the five voices is a more deliberate occasion, however, as this texture occurs precisely at the beginning of the added *Miserere*. The passage is cast solemnly with a calculated, harmonically static delivery of the initial word *Miserere*. The gravity of the five voices dissipates briefly with a thinning of the texture to four voices and added rhythmic vitality, only to return to sustained declamation of *Marie* at the conclusion (Example 4.1). Despite some contrapuntal errors in the last verse, those who sang and experienced this music would likely have sensed the import of this final entreaty.[57]

It is worthwhile to take stock of the musical resources outlined to this point for the celebration of St. Anne at Frederick's esteemed Castle Church. In addition to La Rue's *St. Anne Mass*, which supplies music for the ordinary, three polyphonic cycles of Mass Propers (one incomplete) between JenaU 34 and 30 from a decade earlier can now be counted, as well as office music in the form of a polyphonic hymn and a responsory in the former manuscript. While plainchant does not survive from the church, it must have existed in full force for St. Anne and can be intuited, for example, in the unfolding of the sequence *Alma parens anna gaude*, if the latter was not used in polyphonic alternation with *Gaude mater anna gaude*. With *Alma parens anna gaude* from JenaU 30, the composer created new texts and music (the final *Miserere* entreaty) – a kind of late blooming "logogenic" troping phenomenon – within a liturgical host genre to augment the service in which it would have been used.

The evidence surviving in the manuscripts for the church reveals without question copious polyphonic settings that could be inserted into the mass and office commemorations for the *Mater matris* at her side altar from about 1507 through the entire second decade of the sixteenth century. The question of when this music might be performed is one further area to probe that holds promise not just for establishing a context for this music, but also for gaining a deeper understanding of how St. Anne's powerful sponsorship could leverage Frederick's elaborate vision for the Castle Church and indeed Saxony at large.

Tuesdays at the Castle Church

Under the watch of Frederick the Wise in the early sixteenth century, the Castle Church brimmed with new liturgical services, numbering ten thousand per year by some estimates. Most of them centered on the Virgin Mary; others stemmed from endowments to the church. In 1506, not accidentally in conjunction with the upsurge in the acquisition of relics and the probable compilation of the first Jena choirbooks, the elector founded a special chapel at the west end of the church to be used almost exclusively for Marian services.[58] Lavish in conception, this chapel received funding for

Example 4.1 *Alma parens anna gaude* in JenaU 30 (mm. 149–end).

Example 4.1 (*continued*)

Example 4.1 (*continued*)

its own personnel, who were strictly charged with providing music for the services at that station. A provision dated November 11, 1506 specified that the choir should consist of four boys and four priests, one of whom would also serve as an organist.[59]

The Hours of the Virgin would have been sung daily at the newly constructed west altar, according to a prescription that varied by liturgical season. But daily votive masses were also to be said at the Castle Church's west end, as specified in the 1506 document detailing Frederick's endowments. All votive masses except the one on Sunday celebrated some aspect of the life of the Virgin Mary.

SUNDAY: Holy Trinity
MONDAY: Assumption
TUESDAY: Conception of Mary
WEDNESDAY: Annunciation
THURSDAY: Nativity of the Virgin
FRIDAY: Compassion of the Virgin
SATURDAY: Commemoration of the Virgin

While St. Anne is often mentioned in texts surrounding the nativity of Mary, it is the Tuesday service commemorating the conception of her daughter that is of interest here. Immediately following the Propers for the weekly mass celebrating the Conception, several activities pertaining directly to St. Anne were to take place in the church. The 1506 endowment for the new services and choir makes this provision:

Und so das ambt volbracht soll von stund an der ander priester, der die woche zceyttung in kleyn khor anhebt. Das wirdig heylthumb Sancte Anne auf yren altar mit procession der Chorschuler dicz stiffts erlich tragen, und das ambt Sancte Anne halten und singen. Darzcu auch allemahl zu ordenlicher Zceyt, soll auf der orgel geslagen werden, so das beslossen, das heylthumb widerumb in den grossen khor mit procession wieuor singend die Antiphona Celebremus memoriam Sancte Anne, erlich brengen.[60]	At the conclusion of that [Tuesday] Mass [for the Conception], another priest, whose turn it is to lead the Offices that week in the Small Choir, shall carry the worthy relic of St. Anne honorably to her altar with a procession of choirboys of this endowment, and hold and sing the Office for St. Anne. Here also, the organ shall be played at the appointed time. When that is concluded, the relic shall be returned to the Large Choir with a procession as before, singing the antiphon *Celebremus memoriam Sancte Anne*.

Yet again, St. Anne is the recipient of special treatment at the Castle Church. Amid the outpouring of commemorations of the life of Mary, the compilers of the institution's liturgies made room for her mother and not without full spectacle. After the Conception Mass, a select priest processed from the west end to the altar of the saint with a relic or reliquary of St. Anne, presumably with her precious thumb, the founding relic of the church. Here, a special office (*Ambt*) for the saint was sung, notably with organ accompaniment. Upon completion of this exceptional supplementary service, as the St. Anne relic was returned to the Large Choir, the 1506 document stipulates that the antiphon *Celebremus memoriam Sancte Anne* be chanted in this concluding procession. The ritual actions even had a spiritual value: anyone who attended the procession of Anne's holy relics received an indulgence of three hundred days.[61]

Frederick created further endowments to enrich the already remarkable Tuesday rituals at the Castle Church involving this special saint. In payments dated 1514, the elector secured four additional vicars not only to augment the forces accompanying the elaborate procession for St. Anne on Tuesdays, but also to read four masses in honor of St. Anne following that procession.[62] Typically, the reading of four low masses at the Castle Church took place during a sung votive mass on the same theme, which is exactly what happened, according to a similar provision from 1511 for the weekly celebration of the Holy Cross. It is reasonably certain, then, that a full votive mass was sung for St. Anne every Tuesday as the vicars read the low masses.

Further, these expenditures for the saint in 1514 could have been describing a tradition in place since around the time of the Holy Cross provision of 1511.[63] Whatever the precise date of the vicariate's specifications, the menu of musical options for these offices indicates that musical repertory to augment the weekly procession and votive mass for St. Anne would not have been lacking.

In at least two of the liturgical items surveyed (*Alleluia. O Maria dei genetrix* from JenaU 34 and the sequence *Sancte anne devotus* from JenaU 30), there have been a few textual cues in support of the doctrine of the Immaculate Conception. One might wonder if it could be by chance that the extended rituals for St. Anne at the Castle Church fell on a day that expressly commemorated the Conception of the Virgin in the weekly cycle of Marian celebrations. While the extant documents do not expressly connect the two celebrations that took place on Tuesdays at the Castle Church, the procession for St. Anne explicitly followed the votive Conception Mass, as if a thematically related devotional series. Indeed, it would be hard to separate this string of events in situ. More evidence from music manuscripts suggests that perhaps in the mind of the elector, St. Anne was not only a strong matriarch over a powerful family, but also part of a larger devotional apparatus allied with the cause of immaculism in the debate about the nature of Mary's conception.

St. Anne and Immaculism

This chapter began with a polyphonic mass for St. Anne by La Rue, which presumably originated in the milieu of Margaret of Austria and could have passed through the court of her father before reaching Frederick the Wise after 1516. It continues by examining the content and circumstances of another mass by La Rue known to Frederick, this time on the subject of the conception of the Virgin, a commemoration that has some resonance with Mary's mother. The composer's *Missa Conceptio tua* for five voices survives in seven manuscripts, all creations of the Alamire scriptorium at the Habsburg-Burgundian court.[64] That this mass appears in so many sources is a testament either to its demand among noble circles or (more likely) to the eagerness of the Mechelen court to supply it as gifts. Two of these seven manuscripts (JenaU 4 and JenaU 5) landed in Frederick's court. Unlike the plainchant *Felix Anna* proposed as the basis of La Rue's mass for St. Anne, the antiphon on which the *Missa Conceptio tua* is based has long been identified. It is the Vespers Magnificat antiphon *Conceptio tua* (CAO 3851) from the Feast of Mary's Conception on December 8.⁶⁵

Conceptio tua,	Your conception,
Dei Genitrix Virgo,	O Virgin Mother of God,
gaudium annuntiavit	announces joy to the whole world;
universo mundo;	out of you has arisen indeed
Ex te enim ortus est sol justitiae,	the sun of justice,
Christus Deus noster.	Christ our God.

La Rue went to great lengths to emphasize the incipit of the plainchant (D D C f, and its transpositions) in the polyphonic fabric both at the head of each movement and at the major subsections of the mass, not unlike the referenced model in the composer's mass in honor of St. Anne. But even greater awareness is placed on the parent chant *Conceptio tua* in the mass setting. In contrast to the paraphrased model of the *St. Anne Mass*, La Rue set the first half of the Credo of his Conception Mass with a long-note cantus firmus in the (first) tenor voice, which divulges an unobscured version of the preexistent melody. In both JenaU 4 and JenaU 5, the tenor retains the words of the antiphon throughout much of the mass. Sometimes this text is placed beneath the words of the Ordinary. In JenaU 4, the tenor is not the only voice that bears the cantus firmus rubric for the antiphon *Conceptio tua*; in fact, all five voices on the first opening of La Rue's mass have this inscription – a rarity among cantus firmus masses.⁶⁶ The tenor drops the text of *Conceptio tua* only at the Agnus Dei III, at which point the soprano sings the antiphon's words in long notes. At every turn it seems, the composer reminds the informed listener to remain attuned to the plainchant *Conceptio tua* from the Feast of the Conception.⁶⁷

For all of its musical emphasis, the governing antiphon of La Rue's *Missa Conceptio tua* says nothing about the exact nature of the Virgin's conception in Anne's womb (the root of the doctrinal polemic). Instead, extramusical factors reorient La Rue's Conception Mass toward an immaculist ideological position. Remember that Margaret of Austria, the likely sponsor of this mass, was a vigorous supporter of the Franciscans, the most ardent defenders of the Immaculate Conception doctrine. But far more important is the program of illuminations accompanying the mass in JenaU 4, which provides an unambiguous apology for the Immaculate Conception. While most manuscripts in which La Rue's *Missa Conceptio tua* mass survives appear to have contained miniatures (including JenaU 5), only three sources remain intact (BrusBR 15075, JenaU 4, and MechAS s.s.). Significantly, each reveals an explicit immaculist agenda. Bonnie Blackburn's important study of these and other immaculist miniatures emanating from the Alamire workshop demonstrates that the doctrine was by no means settled in the early decades of the sixteenth century. Two of the three manuscripts (JenaU 4 and MechAS s.s.) that join immaculist imagery with La Rue's Conception Mass deserve comment here.[68]

Like JenaU 7, JenaU 4 was compiled after March 1516 in the Habsburg-Burgundian scriptorium and arrived at the court of Frederick the Wise.[69] The visual program that adorned La Rue's *Conceptio tua* mass in this manuscript is most striking for its theological advocacy of the Immaculate Conception doctrine, which taught that Mary was uniquely and miraculously conceived in sinlessness and not sanctified in utero, in the way of John the Baptist. Specifically, four banderoles around the border of the *Conceptio tua* mass in JenaU 4 beseech the viewer to behold the Virgin as having been purely conceived (Figure 4.5). The central miniature reinforces the immaculist ideology, as the Virgin (with child in arms) stands beneath the Tree of Good and Evil crushing the head of the serpent.[70] The intimation is that Mary blocked the flow of original sin at the moment of her conception, the essence of the doctrine.[71] If there were any doubt as to the meaning of the large illumination, five additional miniatures featuring individual defenders of the doctrine – each accompanied by a hearty theological quotation for emphasis – occupy the left and top margins of the full opening (fols. 29v–30r) of the Kyrie of La Rue's Mass for the Conception.[72] This mass (or a copy of it) could have been the one sung on Tuesdays at the Castle Church, preceding the St. Anne procession and office with organ accompaniment.

The manuscript MechAS s.s., though not intended for Frederick, provides a useful link between La Rue's *Missa Conceptio tua* and the place of St. Anne in the conception debate. Compiled between July 1515 and March 1516, this source appears to connect St. Anne with the doctrine. Like Monts773 mentioned in Chapter 3, MechAS s.s. seems to have also served as a book of "house favorites" held internally at the court of Margaret of Austria. Possibly a gift for Charles V, the manuscript bears the Habsburg and Burgundian coats of arms as well as clear Franciscan influence.[73] Similar to the *Missa Conceptio tua* found in JenaU 4, the mass in MechAS s.s. is accompanied by a slew of the doctrine's advocates including Sixtus IV, who approved the Feast of the Immaculate Conception in 1477 (Figure 4.6).[74] The central miniature at the opening of La Rue's Conception Mass is neither a theologian nor a pope: here, it is St. Anne who occupies the chief illumination of the work, with the Virgin Mary depicted as a tiny baby in her womb. Inscribed atop the canopy containing the grandmother saint is the litaneutical text *Sancta Anna ora pro* [*nobis*]. David and Solomon flank St. Anne, a familiar gesture both to the noble lineage of the Virgin and, by association, the esteemed heritage of the widowed regent Margaret who held the manuscript.

Figure 4.5 La Rue, *Missa Conceptio tua*. Jena, Universitätsbibliothek, MS 4, fols. 29v–30r.
Source: Thüringer Universitäts- und Landesbibliothek Jena (ThULB).

Figure 4.5 (*continued*)

Figure 4.6 La Rue, *Missa Conceptio tua*. Mechelen, Stadsarchief van Mechelen, MS s.s., fol. 34v. © Stadsarchief Mechelen.

That St. Anne sits in such a prominent position in a musical work centered on the Conception of the Virgin – a doctrine concerned with her daughter – seems striking. Of course, Anne's womb is the vessel in which the conception takes place, but to what extent does Anne's appearance argue for one position or another in the conception dispute? According to Virginia Nixon, Mary's mother did not become associated with one particular side of the debate; Anne was beloved and appropriated (even misunderstood) by maculists and immaculists alike.[75] Because it would seem impossible to illustrate the abstract idea of an expressly *immaculate* conception, the iconography for the doctrine was unstable in its early stages. Paintings and illuminations of the event drew heavily on scenes from other celebrations of the Virgin (e.g., Nativity and Assumption). One of the widespread depictions of the doctrine did involve the Virgin in the womb of St. Anne. Maculists originally advanced this iconography to indicate sanctification in the womb, not at the moment of conception as held by immaculists. However, Mirella Levi D'Ancona, who has produced the most definitive study of conception iconography, has convincingly shown a turning point for the use of the Virgin/St. Anne image by the end of the fifteenth century. At this time, the kind of depiction found in MechAS s.s almost exclusively marked the immaculist position, especially when the Virgin is adorned with a halo, as shown here.[76] Any vagueness in the image of the Virgin and St. Anne still benefited from other means of identification, such as auxiliary inscriptions from the various doctrinal proponents, to clarify the immaculate position. Surrounded by defenders of the doctrine, both St. Anne and La Rue's composition for the Conception Mass were pulled into the immaculist side of the debate, at least in the eyes of the influential Margaret of Austria and through the medium of manuscripts compiled at the Alamire workshop.

The Netherlandish court emphasized the conception doctrine to the court of Frederick the Wise in other ways. The elector not only received the conspicuously decorated *Conceptio tua* mass in JenaU 4, but he also encountered it again in JenaU 5, a manuscript in which the mass has a missing attribution page and might well have displayed an illumination with the usual champions of the Immaculate Conception. Both JenaU 4 and JenaU 5 also contain La Rue's *Missa Ave sanctissima Maria*.[77] Based on La Rue's motet of the same name, this parody mass uses a devotional prayer as its inspiration, penned by none other than the passionate advocate of the Immaculate Conception doctrine, Pope Sixtus IV.[78] La Rue's setting in polyphony of the *Missa Ave sanctissima Maria* was accompanied with more immaculist imagery in JenaU 5 (the Virgin with Christ Child *in sole*), as well as in other manuscripts in which it appeared. La Rue's mass for St. Anne in JenaU 7, which now may also be seen to connect indirectly to the conception (following the connection in MechAS s.s), seems to be further evidence that Margaret of Austria inundated Frederick with gifts bearing immaculist propaganda in both music and visual image. As a likely vehicle displaying the status of the Habsburg-Burgundian realm with hopes of influencing the imperial election, these manuscripts also could serve a practical purpose. As settings of the Mass Ordinary, the music sent from Margaret's court could be sung with the Proper settings in the Jena choirbooks from the previous decade.[79] With the establishment of the extensive Tuesday services for the Immaculate Conception and for St. Anne at the Castle Church, there was a time and place for all of this music: it need not have rested on shelves.

Luther, St. Anne, and Marian Devotion in Wittenberg

At the forefront of Reformation theology, the city of Wittenberg curiously tolerated immaculist imagery and music in honor of the conception, to say nothing of far-reaching saints' feasts. How Frederick could champion the Immaculate Conception doctrine and eventually defend Martin Luther is equally perplexing. One is reduced to conjecture on the elector's own attraction to the teaching of the Immaculate Conception, but the propagation of the doctrine can also be viewed from the perspective of the academic culture of Western Europe. Frederick's pursuit of humanistic and spiritual ideals drove the construction of the University of Wittenberg and the Castle Church, respectively. The church of course offered an outlet for support of this Marian celebration in its Tuesday commemorations. And while the university's official position on the Immaculate Conception is not known, other major universities rallied around the doctrine. In 1507, Anthonius Cucharus noted in his *Elucidarius* that the universities of Paris, Oxford, Cambridge, Toulouse, and Bologna advocated the Immaculate Conception. Some German universities also required a vow from students to uphold the teaching upon the receipt of their degrees.[80] Perhaps the university that Frederick founded in Wittenberg (along with the church to which it was connected) was merely following suit.

Of course, looming in the university culture at Wittenberg was Martin Luther, the professor of theology who, among other things, would become a vociferous opponent against commemorations not described in Scripture, such as the Immaculate Conception. As in the case of Frederick's ambitious acquisition of relics, Luther's story begins with St. Anne. In fact, it was to Mary's mother that Luther turned after being caught in a raging thunderstorm on his way to Erfurt in 1505. The young man cried out to St. Anne that if she saved him in this storm, he would enter monastic life and take his vow to her, which he did after being "delivered." Luther often reflected on his fascination with St. Anne as a youth, but, as his theology developed, he would point to the cult of St. Anne and its confraternities as decadent pursuits.[81] In his *Admonition to the Clergy* of 1530, the reformer denounced the excessive veneration of saints in general and of Mary's mother in particular.[82] For Luther, sanctoral veneration – particularly in the form of relics and pilgrimages, in addition to the culture of indulgences that flowed from these objects and ventures – was an egregious form of idolatry.[83]

It is not clear when Frederick became fully sympathetic to Luther's principles, but it cannot have been when the Castle Church instituted such elaborate rituals in the first two decades of the sixteenth century. Eventually, Frederick would heed Luther's criticism of the countless votive masses and ostentatious display of relics. By 1523, the elector no longer displayed the massive relic collection, and by the end of the following year, all weekday masses went by the wayside.[84] The musical establishment that Frederick had built – in particular the extensive repertory and roster of singers at the church (many university students) and at his court in Torgau – was at risk. It was not the leaders of reform who were having their way. In fact, Luther fought to keep music in a central role at the university (and the Castle Church, by association); at the same time, he advocated a new musical style with help from the composer of Frederick's *Hofkapelle*, Johann Walther.[85] But after Frederick's death in 1525, the elector's brother (John the Steadfast) determined that the size of the choirs, both at the university's chapel and at the court, were too much of a financial burden on the duchy. These institutions were out of commission by 1526, and Luther in turn pressed for musical reform in the schools of Wittenberg and Torgau, as his colleagues published textbooks and anthologies to keep sacred music a viable enterprise.[86]

As it concerns the Immaculate Conception doctrine, Luther's views on the subject were never explicit during the time in question, as his sermons on the nature of Mary's sinlessness were worked out long after Frederick's death. For the reformer, it was Christ who was sinless, a fact that did not depend on the nature of Anne's conception of Mary.[87] In Lutheran theology, Mary's humanity instead became the center of attention. The mother of Christ was neither the gateway to heaven nor the supreme mediatrix of the late Middle Ages, but rather a humble virgin who accepted her call to bear the Savior and was saved by the grace of God. Pointing to the Magnificat as the telltale sign of Mary's humility, Luther removed the Virgin from the lofty pedestal she had occupied in previous centuries and proceeded to emphasize her lowliness, meekness, and domestic virtues as "maidservant" of the Lord.[88]

The reformer's repudiation of the veneration of saints, whose rituals and intercessory specialties were deeply entrenched in quotidian life, caused an equally seismic shift of paradigm for Christians.[89] Because she was connected to Mary's humanity, St. Anne was not immediately relegated to ordinary status in the advent of the Reformation. If the new image of Mary was to be a diligent housewife and caring mother, the grandmother saint could still remain a useful auxiliary figure with unparalleled "family values." Distinct from her daughter, St. Anne might also be admired as a model for Christian marriage with her husband Joachim. A few decades into the sixteenth century, the exalted position of Mary's mother in Holy Kinship iconography would give way to a more focused image of the Holy Family, with Mary's husband, Joseph (well documented in the New Testament), effectively supplanting St. Anne in a different kind of "earthly Trinity."[90] The emerging cult of St. Joseph and the suspicion surrounding Anne's three unlikely marriages implied in the Holy Kinship slowed the flood of devotion to Mary's mother, without officially eradicating it. As attention was brought back to Jesus' nuclear family, the grandmother saint necessarily receded to some degree in cultures where Reformation ideals were taking root.

As *Mater matris*, St. Anne continued to remind Christians of the corporeality of Mary and Jesus in the context of the Holy Kinship and was a means of explaining Christ's brothers in the New Testament. Adherents of Lutheran theology in Wittenberg could thus reinterpret traditional imagery in less elevated terms. For example, in Lucas Cranach's 1509 woodcut of the Holy Kinship now with interposed text by Luther's university colleague and fellow reformer Philip Melanchthon, the interlocutor redirects the viewer toward themes of a strong Christian education.[91] Variable meanings were attached to Mary's mother in this period, from the all-purpose female advocate to the figure encouraging powerful progeny for political gain. Frederick for one seems to have understood the advantages of exhibiting St. Anne so prominently in the Castle Church, particularly in the ritual and musical culture of the institution. She appealed to almost any human condition and yet wielded great power as the matron of the Holy Kinship. At times entangled with the Immaculate Conception, St. Anne could also be dispatched more generally as a model for wisdom – fitting for the "wise" elector, who time and again kept a cool head in the throes of political unrest, even during his famous abduction of Martin Luther in 1521.[92] Historians have struggled with many contradictions in the life of the elector, but the compatibility of faith and wisdom – or spirituality and intellect – that Frederick digested in his early years as elector was never in doubt, as he founded the illustrious church and university as part of his unifying vision for the city of Wittenberg. With the strains of St. Anne echoing in the city's musical landscape in the first two decades of the sixteenth century, the wise elector was on sure footing to satisfy his own desire to become a supreme "Christian prince."[93]

5 | A "Divine Favor" at the French Court: In Pursuit of a Motet for St. Anne

Having demonstrated the variable functions and a doctrinal matter associated with St. Anne in Wittenberg, this study now shifts attention back to the French court, not for a new theological dustup (awaiting in Chapter 7), but instead for a sonic plea to Mary's mother issued by Anne of Brittany and Louis XII, a petition as political as it was devotional. The place of St. Anne in French court culture has already been discussed in the case of Margaret of Austria (Chapter 3), who spent her formative years under the tutelage of the regent Anne of France. Besides exposure to models of female empowerment like Christine de Pizan, Margaret likely encountered Mary's mother as a symbol of feminine strength, in addition to her more traditional role as an advocate for marriage, maternity, and education. The Breton duchess named Anne has likewise received mention already. As heiress to the duchy of Brittany and a perceived threat to the kingdom of France, Anne of Brittany married Margaret's father, Maximilian I, by proxy in 1490, but this short-lived political union was turned on its head when French forces overtook the vulnerable Brittany. Having come of age, Charles VIII led a siege that brought this major enemy of the French into the royal fold. Anne ended up marrying Charles and was crowned queen of France by the end of 1491, the first of her two marriages to French monarchs.

Revisiting French court life, this chapter examines a single motet for St. Anne – *Celeste beneficium* – by well-known court composer Jean Mouton. A signature work of Mouton's probably composed between 1508 and 1511, *Celeste beneficium* received widespread transmission across two decades of the early sixteenth century and must be counted as one of the more heavily circulated motets in the composer's oeuvre. While this motet has received a fair amount of scholarly attention, the sources and conditions that gave rise to this work and the larger context of devotion to St. Anne at the French court have remained unsettled. An occasional work illustrative of the monarch's plight, *Celeste beneficium* demands closer scrutiny for the values that St. Anne modeled for the queen and their political implications. Subtly blending the political and devotional possibilities of sacred music, this motet unsurprisingly reappeared in some of the major courts of

Table 5.1 Sources of the motet *Celeste beneficium* by Jean Mouton

Source	Composer Attribution	Notes
LonBLR 8 G.vii	–	2p. *Adjutorium nostrum*
RISM 1514[1]	Mouton	2p. *Adjutorium nostrum*
RISM 1526[1]	Mouton	2p. *Adjutorium nostrum*
VienNB Mus. 15941	Mouton	–
VatP 1976–9	–	*Adjutorium nostrum* as separate motet (no attr.)[a]

[a] In addition to its appearance in the Palatini partbooks (VatP 1976–9), *Adjutorium nostrum* circulated independently as a motet in Cambridge, Magdalene College, Pepys Libary, MS 1760 (CambriP 1760); Oxford, Bodleian Library, MS lat.liturg.a.8 (OxfBLL a.8); and London, Royal College of Music, MS 1070 (LonRC 1070). It is attributed to Antoine de Févin in the first two of these sources. There is no composer attribution in LonRC 1070.

Western Europe in the early sixteenth century. The circulation and impact of *Celeste beneficium* will be followed to the end of the 1520s in Chapter 6, well after the death of Anne of Brittany and Louis XII. In tracing this motet through its extant sources, a small stash of unexamined motets for St. Anne will be unveiled in a collection compiled by the Alamire scriptorium and repurposed for the Austrian branch of the Habsburg court, the archenemy of the French.

Mouton's *Celeste beneficium*, composed for four voices, survives in two prints and three manuscripts. As Table 5.1 indicates, only three of the five sources credit Mouton as the composer. Notably, a second part entitled "Adjutorium nostrum" sometimes accompanied *Celeste beneficium*.

Some key relationships emerge among the sources of Mouton's motet. The prints from 1514 and 1526 are identical in content. The 1514 print was published by Ottaviano Petrucci as *Motetti de la corona* (*Motets of the Crown*), a collection of twenty-five motets written by no fewer than ten composers (nearly all of them Franco-Flemish contemporaries).[1] The 1526 edition is simply a reissue of *Motetti de la corona* by Roman publisher Valerio Dorico and printer Giovanni Giacomo Pasoti of Parma. Reflecting the predilection for French music especially in Leonine Rome, these prints were primarily aimed at Italian buyers, but also found a market for international circulation. Several of the motets in the collection celebrate the French monarch in particular. Antoine de Févin's *Gaude francorum regia* honors Louis XII, and Antonius Divitis's *Desolatorum consolator* is a tribute to the firstborn daughter of the king and Anne of Brittany (Claude of France).[2] Further, Mouton's motet *Quis dabit oculis nostris* is a poignant lament on the death of Anne of Brittany in January 1514, the same year as the release of Petrucci's collection for the French crown. The 1514 and 1526 prints were thus fitting hosts for *Celeste beneficium*, a product of the royal court's well-known and gifted composer.

The three remaining sources of Mouton's *Celeste beneficium* were manuscript creations of the Alamire workshop in the service of the Habsburgs, the great adversary of the French. Quite possibly predating the prints that carried *Celeste beneficium* was London, British Library, MS Royal 8 G.vii (LonBLR 8 G.vii).[3] This manuscript was prepared for Henry VIII of England and Catherine of Aragon and holds special distinction among the Habsburg court compilations. Not only is this source the lone volume to reach the English royal court from the Alamire workshop, but it is also the scriptorium's only manuscript in choirbook format devoted entirely to motets (twenty-eight in total, all for four voices). While Mouton's *Celeste beneficium* is the only work in honor of St. Anne in LonBLR 8 G.vii, it is conspicuously given pride of place as the first motet in the manuscript (fols. 2v–4r).[4]

Another Alamire collection, Vienna, Österreichische Nationalbibliothek, Musiksammlung, MS Mus. 15941 (VienNB Mus. 15941), comprises three of four surviving partbooks prepared for Raimund Fugger the Elder (1489–1535), a businessman and an art collector from Augsburg's wealthy banking family. Like the manuscript intended for the English monarch, these partbooks exclusively contain motets. The collection is dominated by works of Mouton, ten in total out of the thirty-two motets in the manuscript. *Celeste beneficium* is the first motet by Mouton encountered in the partbooks (fols. 32r–33r), though this work is preceded by a handful of consecutive motets by Josquin, evidently a favorite of Raimund.[5] In 1509, Raimund's uncle Jakob Fugger, perhaps the wealthiest man of his day, financed the construction of a chapel for his family in the Carmelite church of St. Anne in Augsburg. Devotion to St. Anne in that city experienced a high point around the turn of the sixteenth century with the establishment of a confraternity to Mary's mother in 1494, whose function was to help raise funds to rebuild the church.[6]

The Fugger partbooks share a dozen concordances with the final Alamire product to contain *Celeste beneficium*, the so-called Palatini partbooks (Vatican City, Biblioteca Apostolica Vaticana, MSS Palatini Latini 1976–9). These partbooks reveal another motet-only collection from the Alamire workshop, now destined for Anna of Bohemia and Hungary and Ferdinand I, brother of Charles V.[7] These partbooks – as well as those for Raimund Fugger – date from between 1528 and 1534, more than a decade later than the original appearance of *Celeste beneficium* in LonBLR 8 G.vii.[8]

Despite a lack of composer attributions, at least seven (and possibly nine) of the thirty-eight motets belong to Mouton (the most of any composer in the partbooks), with the first securely attributed motet being *Celeste beneficium* (fols. 15v–16v).[9] Even more striking in the context of this study, Mouton's motet is just one of several in honor of St. Anne that are grouped at the outset of the Palatini partbooks. This handful of works celebrating Mary's mother and the circumstances of their reception will form the basis for discussion in Chapter 6. *Celeste beneficium* was evidently valued as one of Mouton's most important works by the Habsburg scriptorium, always appearing as the first (identifiable) motet by the composer in all three Alamire sources. Mouton's only motet on a text for Mary's mother, in short, was a "must-have" work of the international repertoire among the noblest European households.

Table 5.1 indicates that a *secunda pars* beginning "Adjutorium nostrum" follows *Celeste beneficium* in the first three of its five sources (the 1514 and 1526 prints and LonBLR 8 G.vii).[10] In the prints, the entire work is attributed to Mouton without a page turn, whereas the manuscript for the English monarch bears no composer attributions and contains a large illuminated initial for *Adjutorium nostrum* following a page turn. The evidence from these early sources could suggest that these works were conceived together, ostensibly by Mouton. *Adjutorium nostrum* does not appear in the partbooks prepared between 1528 and 1534 for Raimund Fugger. However, in the Palatini partbooks, *Adjutorium nostrum* is found as a stand-alone composition, separated from *Celeste beneficium* by some eighty folios and lacking a composer attribution (as with nearly all of the motets in that source). To complicate matters further, *Adjutorium nostrum* again occurs by itself in three additional manuscripts, two of which attribute the motet to Antoine de Févin, Mouton's colleague at the French court.[11] The dates of the two manuscripts that list Févin as composer of *Adjutorium nostrum* are not precisely known, but one or both could possibly predate the first appearance of *Adjutorium nostrum* with *Celeste beneficium*. The fact that the attribution to Févin is not late seems to favor him as the composer of *Adjutorium nostrum*.[12] Problems of conflicting attributions in fact would befall both Févin and Mouton in early sixteenth-century manuscript culture, particularly with their motets. But the question of authorship is not at the core of this investigation of musical material for St. Anne. A strategic, "topical" reason exists for an alliance between *Celeste beneficium* and *Adjutorium nostrum*, independent of the composer/s who crafted these motets at the French court.

Mouton and the Music of *Celeste beneficium*

Though much attention has been paid to the impressive state of music at the court of Francis I (r. 1515–47), the preceding monarchs also invested heavily in the arts. Anne of Brittany was a generous patroness of visual and sonic culture, sponsoring countless artists and musicians during her time at the French court. Although Anne no doubt hosted itinerant singers and instrumentalists, the French court's in-house assembly of instrumentalists and chapel singers easily rivaled those of the major European courts. The second decade of the sixteenth century in particular saw an explosion of personnel added to the rolls of the French court chapel, as the membership tripled from 1509 to 1517 into the early years of Francis's reign. By 1510, the *chapelle de la reine* could boast Jean Mouton as *magister*, and by 1513, it grew to include as many as sixteen singers, among them Antonius Divitis, Jean Richafort, and Claudin de Sermisy.[13] The significant increase in the court's musical staffing represented a marked investment by the monarch to enhance the liturgies with florid music; it was also a signal to other courts of the splendor of the French crown in its travels. Defying the trends of itinerancy that dominated musical life in the Italian courts, the French musical contingent was remarkably stable. There is little or no evidence, for instance, that Mouton or his colleagues ever sought employment outside of the French court.[14] The "Most Christian King" (*Rex christianissmus*), as the French monarch was called since the time of Clovis, deserved nothing less than for his court to be associated with the best performers and composers of the early sixteenth century.

Mouton began his service to the French court no earlier than the middle of 1502. The composer was probably handpicked by Louis XII and Anne of Brittany, who, in June of that year, visited Grenoble in the southeast of France, the city in which the composer had worked for only a year as music director and teacher of choirboys at the collegiate church of St. André. Mouton would serve as *magister* in the chapel of Anne of Brittany until the queen's death in 1514.[15] A prolific composer of about 100 motets (to say nothing of his masses and Magnificats), Mouton wrote music that was copied some two generations after his death in 1522. His highly crafted and eclectic musical style was sometimes confused with that of Josquin for its technical luster, although Josquin's music is more likely to display contrapuntal *tours de force*.[16] Music theorist Heinrich Glarean, who was acquainted with Mouton and spent time in Paris between 1517 and 1522, noted the compositional smoothness and flowing melody of his style (*facili fluentem filo cantum*).[17]

Mouton's *Celeste beneficium* is indeed characteristic of the composer's fluid manner that Glarean described, exemplifying a genre that Joshua Rifkin has called the "classic French-court motet." In this new style known for its clarity, paired imitative duos are deployed with some regularity and culminate in four-voice cadences, while homophonic passages (whether for two voices or four) may enter the texture toward the end of the motet.[18] Mouton segments *Celeste beneficium* into two musical parts of fifty-eight and thirty-four breves (not including *Adjutorium nostrum* for the moment), approaching the ratio of the Golden Section that is sometimes noted for late medieval and Renaissance musical works.[19] The strength and formality of the caesura separating the sections is articulated by a long note, sometimes with a fermata or line of division, but no change of mensuration. The musical partition in *Celeste beneficium* occurs precisely at an intense moment of supplication and is presented austerely. Despite the bipartite musical organization of *Celeste beneficium*, the text on the whole falls into three sections. The liturgical prose of the first two lines contrasts with the internally rhymed poetry of the next two lines, the latter featuring epithets set in trochaic tetrameter. The phrase *O beata Deo grata* could be said of any female saint, while the following rhymed description *Mater matris nati patris* is specific to Anne. These two middle lines have unknown origin and could very well have been developed for this motet. The third division of text at the words *Anna nos cum filia*, which begins the second section of the motet, presents a direct petition to the mother of the Virgin in rhymed heptasyllabic lines, asking St. Anne, with the help of her blessed daughter, to intercede with her grandson on behalf of the faithful one.

Celeste beneficium introivit in Annam,	A divine favor entered into Anne,
Per quam nobis nata est Maria virgo.	through whom the Virgin Mary was born to us.
O beata Deo grata,	O blessed one, pleasing to God,
Mater matris nati patris.	the mother's mother of the one born of the Father.
Anna nos cum filia,	Anne, reconcile us to Christ
Christo reconcilia.	with your daughter.

The imitative duo between superius and altus opens *Celeste beneficium* with two distinct melodic motives initiated by the altus (c-d-c-f and d-d-e-f) in m. 1–2 and mm. 7–8, respectively (Example 5.1). As this duet progresses toward a cadence in m. 13, the bassus enters in m. 11 with the principal motive already heard at the outset of the piece. The bassus

Example 5.1 Mouton, *Celeste beneficium* (opening).

continues with the tenor to form a thirteen-measure statement identical to that of the superius and altus. The two gestures are not simply contiguous but cleverly intertwined. It would have been easy to begin the bassus/tenor restatement at m. 13, but Mouton's anticipation of the head motives in the lower voices before the upper voices draw to a close shows a glimpse of his compositional command and some of the processes by which he achieves fluidity in his motets. As the bassus and tenor proceed with what would appear to be a redundant statement of mm. 1–13 (though down an octave), the composer again thwarts expectations by having the two upper voices complete the contrapuntal fabric at mm. 18–19. Mouton has done much to realize the full potential of the pitch material in this exordium, whether it is recognizing that the very grain of his opening motive could serve as cadential material (mm. 11–14) or that the duos had ample room for contrapuntal overlay (mm. 18–23).

Amid the polished contrapuntal tapestry of *Celeste beneficium*, the most striking musical moments of this short motet occur in the second section with several echoed calls to Mary's mother, which would have acted simultaneously as reinforcement to the queen's noble self-identity. The vocative *Anna* in particular receives marked homophonic treatment in this section of the motet; its simplicity and summoning quality must have arrested the sixteenth-century listener. This supplication in music, shown in Example 5.2, begins at m. 59 with the superius and altus dramatically converging to produce an unadorned appeal to St. Anne. The altus sustains f'-f' on the saint's name, while the superius issues the forthright plea with a summoning motive (a'-c'), reaching upward but evoking somberness by resting on the open fifth with the altus to form an f'-c' dyad. The tenor and bassus repeat the fervent request in their appropriate ranges. The supplication to Anne receives a final iteration in the upper voices, which this time contains a completion of the entreaty in a more elaborate imitative duet. Less than ten measures after the initial call to St. Anne, the threefold plea is delivered again but inverted, starting with the bassus and tenor and immediately repeated by the upper voices. Following a cadence in m. 75, the listener is prepared for perhaps a third appeal to St. Anne issued in the upper voices, but instead hears all four voices join in rich homophony and dissolve into an imitative texture that will drive toward a cadence in F. In this brief second section, Mouton demands attention from his audience (his patroness, for one) with lucid calls to St. Anne, while also revealing his mark as an accomplished composer with intricately woven polyphony to cap each statement. The clear style of this "classic French-court motet" would reverberate in the works of Sermisy, Certon, and Janequin.[20] And while the association of a musical trait with a court (or nation) runs the risk of essentializing the phenomenon, it is still worthwhile to keep these stylistic features in mind in the exploration of some anonymous repertory associated with *Celeste beneficium* in Chapter 6. The paired imitative duets and declamatory sections also play a role in the companion motet *Adjutorium nostrum*.

Example 5.2 Mouton, *Celeste beneficium*, mm. 59–82.

Adjutorium nostrum begins quite unassumingly with generic devotional text. It opens with a universal supplication that may allude to a text often connected with the gesture of the Sign of the Cross at Mass, directly preceding the recitation of the Confiteor. God is affirmed as a source of help, an idea quite far removed from the specific sanctoral plea issued at the end of *Celeste beneficium*. This collective supplication then devolves into a pastiche of texts, similar to *Celeste beneficium*, though with some tortured syntax.

Adjutorium nostrum in nomine Domini,	Our help is in the name of the Lord;
Quis non confitebitur tibi?	who will not be confessed to you?
Orat, plorat, et exorat Anna sibi;	Anne prays, weeps, and pleads for herself;
Te orantes deprecamur;	praying, we beseech you,
Fac ut cito adiuvemur	act that we might quickly be helped
Per tuam clementiam.	by your clemency.
O Renate tam beate	O René so blessed,
Ludovicus clamat ad te;	Louis cries out to you;
Audi queso vocem nostrum.	I beg you: hear our call.

An active subject emerges in connection with a petition by a certain "Anne" and filters through the poetry until its end. Revealed in the third person, this "Anne" weeps and implores God to lend urgent attention to her trying circumstances. This cannot be St. Anne. A two-tiered interpretation suggested in Mouton's motet is thus confirmed in *Adjutorium nostrum*, as the narrator departs from devotion to St. Anne of *Celeste beneficium* and describes the ostensible actions of Anne of Brittany, even concluding with the use of the first person in the final line (*Audi queso vocem nostrum*). As the queen becomes an active participant and narrator in the companion motet to *Celeste beneficium*, any sanctoral devotion is curiously redirected from St. Anne to St. René, the patron of male offspring. In the 1514 and 1526 prints, *Adjutorium nostrum* emphasizes that Louis (*Ludovicus*) begs for the intercession of the latter saint. More will be said in Chapter 6 on the treatment of Louis in the other sources.

If the texts stray from St. Anne toward the queen's personal experience in *Adjutorium nostrum*, musical evidence strengthens the connection between this motet and *Celeste beneficium* when they were juxtaposed.[21] For starters, both are centered on an F tonality, returning to F often at cadence points.[22] Moreover, *Adjutorium nostrum* begins with a simple head motive outlining a triad built on F (f'-a'-c'), recalling the stark plea to St. Anne issued in *Celeste beneficium* (Example 5.2), a gesture also limited to these fundamental notes. Both motets further share textures dominated by numerous points of imitation, including paired duets. Distinctions exist, to be sure, between these motets. *Adjutorium nostrum* shifts to triple mensuration at *O Renate tam beate*, a compositional decision possibly owing as much to the trochaic meter of the text as to the abrupt change of devotional subject to St. René.

As the composer restores a governing duple meter for the remainder of the motet (a cut signature, as at the outset), he sets the highly personalized plea of the king (*Ludovicus clamat ad te*) in blunt and undecorated homophony around the central tonality of F (Example 5.3). The composer's setting of the king's supplication to St. René is perhaps the most obvious piece of

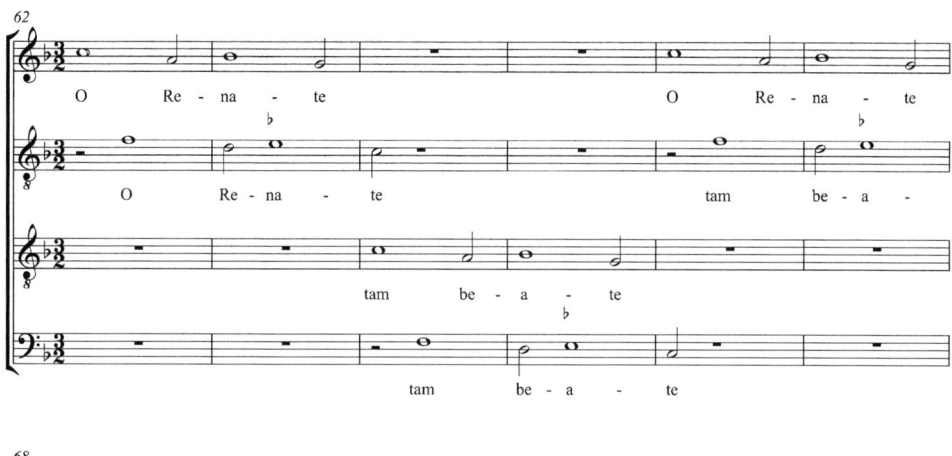

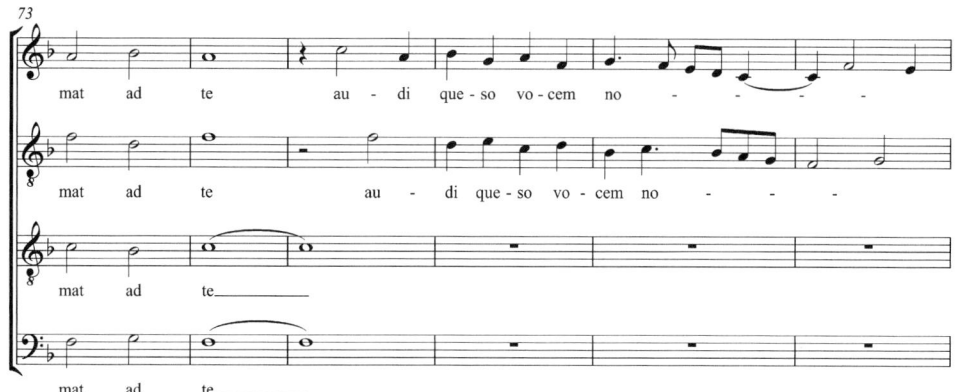

Example 5.3 Févin (or Mouton), *Adjutorium nostrum*, mm. 62–78.

musical material linking *Adjutorium nostrum* to Mouton's *Celeste beneficium* in honor of St. Anne. In both cases, this solemn moment stands apart from the unfolding of the respective motets, as the composer temporarily sacrifices his characteristic craft of intricately woven imitative polyphony to achieve a more comprehensible declaration, a quality of the early sixteenth-century French motet that John Brobeck has described as the "syntactic" style.[23] Both the call of *Anna* in Mouton's motet and the *Ludovicus* passage in *Adjutorium nostrum* are plainly set in F, though the former entreaty is restated for effect and somewhat more ambitiously conceived. Specifically, Mouton multiplies the calls to Mary's mother throughout the texture homophonically, resonating in different voice parts and creating a kind of symmetry in the aural landscape. Both motets, however, generate great clarity that results from these unadorned petitions. Some suggestions about the possible musical underpinning of *Celeste beneficium* will pave the way for a wider investigation of how St. Anne was projected at the French court and how Anne of Brittany positioned herself as a reflection of her patron namesake.

Sources of *Celeste beneficium*

Because *Celeste beneficium* has been well studied, a deep investigation into its textual and musical origins would not normally present a new avenue of inquiry. But with no surviving liturgical books that can be traced to the French court during the period in question, scholars have unsuccessfully attempted to show the basis of this motet, some of which is likely rooted in plainchant, as in the case of La Rue's *Missa de Sancta Anna* in Chapter 3. The question of the motet's underpinning thus deserves fuller treatment here.

In her 1953 dissertation on the composer's motets, Josephine Shine claimed that the basis – evidently just the textual basis – of the motet was a sequence for Mary's mother with the identical title *Celeste beneficium*, consistent through the final word *reconcilia*. (Recall the hybrid nature of the text, the latter two-thirds of *Celeste beneficium* being rhymed and metrical, unlike the first two lines.) Shine cited *Analecta hymnica* and elsewhere for verification of the sequence.[24] Her assertion would remain either unchecked or neglected in future scholarship. For instance, in his 1975 archival study of music and musicians in the retinue of Anne of Brittany, Stephen Bonime independently declared that Mouton's motet text was taken "from the sequence for the feast of St. Anne – mother of the Virgin Mary and patroness of motherhood – celebrated July 26."[25] He did not cite Shine, nor did he direct the reader to a source to verify this claim. That Bonime referred to "*the* sequence" (emphasis mine) for St. Anne should also raise suspicion. Knowing that dozens of sequences were scattered around Western Europe in honor of Mary's mother, one is compelled to investigate this sequence (if it indeed exists). The most recent mention of *Celeste beneficium* in John Brobeck's magisterial dissertation on the early sixteenth-century French motet adds to the mystery surrounding its melodic inspiration. In his extensive table outlining the sources and structures of Mouton's motets, Brobeck listed neither a known textual source nor a source melody for Mouton's motet for St. Anne, possibly out of caution.[26] The inconsistent background research on *Celeste beneficium* demands further inquiry into the motet's foundation, a rather unexpected task in the pursuit of a richer context for this well-known work.

Sequences of the later Middle Ages, especially during the time when St. Anne's cult developed in the fourteenth and fifteenth centuries, were predictably rhymed and rhythmical when compared to Notker's proses of the ninth century. Rhythm and meter do, in fact, appear in *Celeste beneficium*, as outlined earlier, but these poetic features do not occur at the outset of the text. The text later in the motet seems to borrow the kind of language seen in generic devotional texts. Consultation with *Analecta hymnica* reveals that *Celeste beneficium* was not known as a sequence, but only as an antiphon.[27] This antiphon offers the following text and is fairly consistent with the first two lines of the motet: "Caeleste beneficium introivit in Annam, *de qua* nata est nobis *pia* virgo Maria." The italicized texts differ only slightly from those found at the beginning of Mouton's motet, and other words are arranged in a different order from the motet, hardly altering the meaning of the short text.[28] This antiphon appears in First Vespers with a Magnificat – notably the liturgical, musical, and theological apogee of the service – in the pervasive office AH 25.18.[29] Recall from Chapter 3 that AH 25.18 contained another Magnificat antiphon, *Felix Anna quedam matrona* (from Second Vespers), which likely served as the foundation of La Rue's *Missa de Sancta Anna*. The generic devotional texts that follow in the motet do not seem to have concordances with the office or other repertory.[30]

With *Celeste beneficium* textually linked with an antiphon that framed the recitation of the Magnificat at Vespers for the feast of St. Anne, one is encouraged to track down a melody for this plainchant in liturgical books of the period to see if there is any musical resemblance with the material of Mouton's motet. The earliest occurrences of this antiphon can be found in two eleventh-century sources.[31] Both manuscripts represent the earliest layer of neumed antiphoners – liturgical books containing notated antiphons for use in the Divine Office. The notation in these manuscripts

Table 5.2 Select sources of the antiphon *Celeste beneficium*

Source (siglum, fol.)	Source type	Date	Feast	Geography	Genre	Mode
F-VAL 114 (149r)	Antiphoner	12th c.	Nat. Mary	France (St. Amand)	VA	D-1
I-MZ 15/79 (240v)	Antiphoner	12th c.	Nat. Mary	Pavia (St. Mayeul)	MA	D-1
I-Far (171v)	Antiphoner	12th c.	Nat. Mary	Florence	MA	D-1
GB-Wo F.160 (248r, 234v)	Antiphoner	ca. 1230	Nat. Mary	England (Worcester)	MA/MR	D-1
F-Pn lat. 10482 (466r)	Breviary	early 14th c.	Anne	Paris	VA	D-1
F-Pn lat. 15182 (269r)	Breviary	early 14th c.	Anne	Paris (Notre Dame)	LA	D-1
D-MZb C (226r)	Antiphoner	1430s	Anne	Mainz	VA	D-1
SI-Lna 19 (olim 18) (105v)	Antiphoner	1491–2	Anne	Slovenia (Krainburg)	VA	F-5
D-W 31 (156v, 161r)	Antiphoner	1507	Anne	Lower Saxony	CA	D-1

reveals staffless neume-shapes *in campo aperto* ("in the open field"), which, though doubtless full of rich gestural or performative cues, do not permit a precise retrieval of pitch. These antiphoners containing *Celeste beneficium* predate the earliest known offices of the feast of St. Anne by about three centuries, so it is not surprising to find the antiphons placed within the feast of the Nativity of Mary, a more stable liturgical feast at this time and one that had long housed references to Anne and Joachim amid the story of the Virgin's birth and early childhood.

Other sources of the antiphon *Celeste beneficium* surface in later manuscripts, from which melodies can be ascertained. Table 5.2 reveals a selection of eight sources of the antiphon from which melodies are readily accessible.[32] These manuscripts from a variety of locations around Europe are listed from earliest to latest.

The table reveals finer details about the nature of *Celeste beneficium* than those that can be gained from the office prototype in AH 25.18. First, it can be confirmed that the early instances of this melody (i.e., the twelfth- and thirteenth-century sources) were situated within offices for the Nativity of Mary and later found their way into a distinct office for Mary's mother by the fourteenth century. Indeed, a separate study would likely show a large set of plainchants from the feast of St. Anne with connections to versified offices celebrating Mary's birth on September 8, a symbolic date nine months after the feast of the Immaculate Conception. One also learns from Table 5.2 that *Celeste beneficium* was an antiphon that often occurred in the office of Matins or Vespers and was almost always set in the first melodic mode (D-1).

A synoptic transcription of these selected sources of the antiphon in Example 5.4 demonstrates the relative stability of the melody across both time and geography. The fifth-mode melody from the Slovenian antiphoner (SI-Lna 19) – the only F-5 melody of the collected chants and potentially a candidate for the basis of the motet – is clearly an anomaly. The remaining melodies present nearly identical opening gestures. In all likelihood, Mouton and his fellow musicians in the chapels of Anne of Brittany and Louis XII were acquainted with a similar first-mode *Celeste beneficium* for the feast of St. Anne. As so often occurs, the chants are most stable at the outset and show greater variance toward the middle of the four-phrase melody.

The generally consistent melodic profile across these sources is of course no guarantee that the musical substance of the motet *Celeste beneficium* derives from this first-mode chant model. It is clear by now that both *Celeste* and *Adjutorium* unambiguously center on an F tonality.[33] The opening gesture in the altus of *Celeste beneficium* (Example 5.1) serves as anacrusis to f′ (c-d-c-f′), and the interior and final cadences leave little question that F is the governing tonality in the motet. Even the multiple calls to "Anna," the most striking moment in the final section, are iterations of a chord built on F. There is no suggestion of the first mode or even a single cadence on D within either motet setting to match the plainchants above. But closer examination of these plainchants reveals first that the common opening gesture of these melodies (D-D-D-C-f) is not so far removed from the first few notes of the altus (c-d-c-f′), leaping from C (or c) to f (or f′) as a goal. The superius and tenor transpose the motivic kernel, but then ascend by step to the mediant a (or a′) at the word *beneficium* (f-g-a), similar to most untransposed versions of the D-1 chant (f-g-a-a). Mouton's setting of the word *introivit* with ascent by step in m. 8 (d-d-e-f′) and its echo in the bassus at m. 17 may be an oblique reference to the stepwise ascent of the widespread antiphon at that same word (f-g-a), but the altus precisely mirrors these notes from the plainchant in mm. 19–20.

These resemblances are of course insufficient proof of a direct association between the motet *Celeste beneficium* on the whole and the prevalent antiphon of the same name. But here it is crucial to note that Mouton, like his contemporary La Rue (Chapter 3), notoriously disguised his models. Even when scholars have uncovered preexistent melodies, it is clear that Mouton

Example 5.4 Synoptic transcription of select versions of *Celeste beneficium*.

freely paraphrased these tunes, cloaking them heavily in his smooth melodic idiom.[34] It is true that dozens of plainchants begin D-D-C-f or C-D-C-f, but it so happens that one of them happens to be the well-established Vespers antiphon for the feast of St. Anne. With his proclivity for paraphrase and modification, Mouton was likely referring to the *Celeste beneficium* antiphon in a roundabout way at the outset of his F-mode motet. At minimum, the suggestion of this parent antiphon is certainly an improvement over the early untenable suggestions of a sequence as the basis for this motet.

Adjutorium nostrum has received nothing near the attention given to Mouton's *Celeste beneficium*. If it too is based on plainchant, the evidence on which such a claim would rest is weak. Both an antiphon (CAO 1279) and a responsory (CAO 6039) begin with the text *Adjutorium nostrum in nomine domini*, but neither proceeds to the text *Quis non confitebitur tibi?* or any other text found in the motet. The antiphon and the responsory that match the title of the motet *Adjutorium nostrum* survive in numerous sources and in the first and sixth melodic modes, respectively. Both are sung in the office of Second Vespers from the generic ferial offices. Most important, neither antiphon nor responsory has a musical connection to the triadic (f'-a'-c') gesture that infuses the opening of the motet *Adjutorium nostrum*.[35] This need not derail hopes to contextualize *Adjutorium nostrum*, given the relatively firm handle on the textual and likely musical basis for Mouton's *Celeste beneficium*, the most direct link to the saint on behalf of the queen. It is now time to proceed to the larger questions of reception and meaning surrounding Mouton's motet and its affiliate composition at the end of the first decade of the sixteenth century and beyond.

Anne of Brittany and the Hope for a Son

It is nearly impossible that Mouton's *Celeste beneficium/Adjutorium nostrum* was intended for someone other than Anne of Brittany (1477–1514), the twice-crowned queen of France, who reigned for nearly a quarter of a century beginning in 1491. In the first decade of the sixteenth century, one would be hard-pressed to find a woman with more authority in all of Europe.[36] Precisely how Anne of Brittany arrived in this powerful position was less than glamorous; the inner workings of her nuptial arrangements and her lifelong struggles to produce a healthy male heir for the French throne must have weighed heavily on the queen. A thorough examination of key events in her biography will go far toward situating the ardent supplication to St. Anne that reverberated in the queen's sound world.

The annulment of Anne of Brittany's marriage by proxy to Maximilian, mentioned in Chapter 3, was triggered by force. Feeling the encroachment of the Habsburgs from a new front, Charles VIII of France surrounded the Breton city of Rennes (and ultimately Anne herself) with some fifteen thousand troops in June 1491. Duchess Anne was held captive and given the option by the crown either to enter into exile or to wed a French noble.[37] Ever politically minded, Anne of Brittany insisted on marrying a king or dauphin, but at the urging of the Breton aristocracy, she reluctantly acquiesced to nuptials with the reigning French king himself. This new marriage, which took place on December 6, 1491, necessarily dissolved Margaret of Austria's unconsummated marriage to Charles VIII and sent the young princess back to her father, Maximilian. The kingdom of France had effectively absorbed the duchy of Brittany, finally locking down one of its pesky enemies.

The termination of two political marriages (Charles VIII and Margaret of Austria; Anne of Brittany and Maximilian) to form a new alliance between the French crown and the Breton duchess did not come without a price. Phillippe de Commynes, an Italian envoy for the French court and important informant on the state of affairs in the government, cited these dissolved marriages as a possible reason behind the childbearing problems of both Margaret of Austria and Anne of Brittany. Chapter 3 explained the fate of Margaret, who saw the death of two husbands and no surviving progeny. Phillippe was quick to point out that the hasty annulments and remarriage of the French monarch violated ecclesiastical law and that the actions of these nobles might portend ill consequences when it came to producing offspring.[38] That Phillippe's sentiment was truly a concern in the innermost chambers of the French court can be seen in the resources and works that the royal court received (or requested) to combat the perceived fertility jinx. Mouton's motet *Celeste beneficium* for St. Anne should certainly be considered as part of this effort.

Across more than two decades at the French court, Queen Anne of Brittany did not produce a son who would survive long enough to ascend the throne. Her heightened devotion to saints like Anne during this time in particular exemplifies the struggle not just to bear children for the crown, but also to ensure the survival of infants past the fragile stages of early childhood. During her seven-year marriage to Charles VIII (1491–8), the queen carried as many as six children to term (at least three sons), but all died early, the most notable being Charles-Orland, who lived to see his third birthday before dying from an outbreak of measles in December 1495. The king, already in a precarious state of health at that time, died in 1498 in the aftermath of a riding accident at the royal château at Amboise that same year. The marriage contract between Charles VIII and Anne specified that the duchy of Brittany would be restored to its independence if the king preceded her in death; however, it also stipulated that Anne should marry the French king's successor if she did not have a son when Charles VIII died.[39] With the future uncertain, Anne took up the Spanish motto *Non mudera* (loosely, "I won't budge"). It was a show of strength as she again faced the possibility of "losing" the Breton estates.

In January 1499, Anne married Charles's cousin Louis d'Orléans (crowned Louis XII), which kept the duchy of Brittany folded into the kingdom of France.[40] But the new political marriage between Anne and Louis was considered as "stained" as the queen's first marriage. Although Anne was widowed, Louis was already married to Jeanne de France, the older sister of Charles VIII, at the time of the king's death. In another bold act of tampering with matrimonial contracts to gain the political upper hand, Louis sought an annulment of his present marriage in order to wed his cousin's widow and ascend the vacant throne. The proceedings were contentious, Louis maintaining that his marriage to Jeanne could not be consummated, on account of the latter's deformity. In effect, the sexual act could not be completed, according to the duke. Jeanne disputed these charges vigorously, but to no avail.[41] As Elizabeth L'Estrange has recently argued, the annulment between the couple and the prompt nuptials with Anne were almost certainly interpreted as a religious and ethical violation, one thought to compromise the fertility of the new royal couple. The notion that God determined fertility and granted it only for the righteous was nothing new and was wholly in the spirit of the biblical and apocryphal stories of holy women's conceptions that seemed to defy nature (Sarah, Hannah, Elizabeth, and Anne). Bretons especially understood the gravity of this premise. The mother of Anne of Brittany, Margaret de Foix, held a book of hours that explicitly gave thanks to God for removing her sterility, which some thought would be a permanent punishment as a result of an extramarital affair committed by her husband (Anne's father, François II, Duke of Brittany).[42]

The prayer book Chicago, Newberry Library, MS 83 reflects the doubts that Queen Anne must have had toward the new king's self-serving tactics and their potentially harmful implications for yielding offspring. The book is a collection of psalms, prayers, and indulgences, compiled around 1499 and tailored to the needs of the queen. The overwhelming emphasis is on spiritual penitence and prayers for the conception of a male heir, two related areas of intercession given the queen's plight.[43] St. Margaret and St. Anne both feature prominently in the prayer book as female mediators to achieve these ends. The name of Mary's mother is not only rubricated in both the litany and the suffrages (fols. 15v and 55v), but a prayer for the conception of the Virgin Mary *contra pestem* (fols. 49r–v) points to the queen's allegorical embodiment of the saint. The legend of St. Anne of course centers on the conception of Mary at a very old age and thus against trying circumstances. After the death of her first husband, the widowed Queen Anne was "aging" by early modern standards. She seems to have imagined herself in the role of her namesake patron: conceiving a child must have begun to feel like an unlikely achievement against the odds. Additional prayers in the Newberry manuscript to St. Leonard and St. Margaret (both saints to aid with women in labor) as well as to Abraham and Sarah (the latter, as mentioned, being a prototypical barren mother) underscore the high stakes and urgency of the questions plaguing Anne of Brittany. Would the queen ultimately be denied a son as retribution for her husband's morally objectionable annulment?

Despite many attempts, the hopes of the monarchy for a male heir under Louis XII and Anne of Brittany were dashed, as with the queen's marriage to Charles. The years 1499 through 1514 did, however, see the birth of two daughters to the royal couple, and both offspring would emerge as impressive nobles in the first half of the sixteenth century. Claude (b. 1499) and Renée (b. 1510) would rise to the title of Queen of France and Duchess of Ferrara, respectively. Other children were stillborn during this period, though the precise dates can be difficult to trace. Through no fault of trying, Anne of Brittany was ultimately unable to carry a son to term. The results of her known pregnancies are shown in Table 5.3.

In later 1507, Louis XII returned from Genoa, where he fought against a popular uprising that opposed French rule. The clash resulted in a relatively easy victory for the French forces.[44] Upon the king's arrival at the court's principal residence at Blois, Louis and Anne conceived a child, but one that presumably did not survive the complete gestation, as the king's principal biographer, Jean d'Auton (normally attuned to every move of the king), is silent about the results of this pregnancy. What is known is that the royal couple traveled to the church of St. Maurice in Angers in August 1508, likely as a response to this pregnancy and quite possibly as a vow made to the saint. Angers was a city whose cult of St. René, patron saint of those seeking male offspring (René means "reborn"), was especially well known.[45] Apparently, the two had conceived a male, but this fetus, like that of 1503, would not see the light of day. There could have been more stillbirths, of course, and there were probably more trips to Angers. Even in the absence of burial records or other informants, the trip of 1508 must have further augmented the urgent hope for a dauphin. Another stillborn son in January

Table 5.3 Children of Anne of Brittany between 1492 and 1512

Child	Date of birth	Result
With Charles VIII (d. 1498)		
Charles-Orland, dauphin of Viennois	October 10, 1492	d. December 16, 1495. Buried at St-Martin of Tours.
Unnamed	August 1493	Buried at Notre-Dame of Cléry.
Unnamed	March 1495	Not known.
Charles, dauphin of Viennois	1497	Buried at St-Martin of Tours.
François, dauphin of Viennois	1497	Buried at St-Martin of Tours.
Anne	March 20, 1498	Buried at St-Martin of Tours.
With Louis XII (d. 1515)		
Claude, duchess of Brittany, countess of Blois	October 13, 1499	Married the future King Francis I in 1514. Queen of France in 1517. d. 1524. Buried at Saint-Denis.
Unnamed	January 21, 1503	Buried at Blois?
Unnamed son	1508?	Not known.
Renée, duchess of Chartres, countess of Gisors	October 25, 1510	Married Hercule d'Este, Duke of Ferrara in 1528. d. 1575. Buried at Montargis.
Unnamed son	January 21, 1512	Buried at Blois?

Source: Adapted from Van Kerrebrouck, *Les Valois*, 157–9, 166–7 and Le Roux de Lincy, *Vie de la reine Anne de Bretagne*, I:192–3.

1512 seemed to seal the fate of the monarch and foretell the crown's passing to Francis, count of Angoulême.[46]

The precise circumstances that spurred the composition of Mouton's *Celeste beneficium* are not known, but several factors suggest its impetus between 1508 and 1511. The stillborn son in 1508 could have motivated the queen to request a piece of music to honor her sanctoral namesake and patroness of maternity. With the memory of her own mother's childbearing strife and the future of Brittany weighing on her, together with the psychological burdens of both husbands' past deeds to enter into marriage, Anne must have recognized that her hopes for male posterity might remain unfulfilled. Furthermore, it was arranged just after Claude's birth that she would marry her cousin Francis (the future Francis I). Anne fought vigorously against this proposal but could not sway her husband. Besides a blow to the potential autonomy of Brittany, the pending nuptials would also mean a political victory for the queen's archenemy Louise of Savoy, the highly influential mother of Francis, both examined in Chapter 7. Louise coldly delighted in Anne's miscarriages, knowing that each failed pregnancy was a step closer to her son's ascent to the throne. In fact, she once wrote, "Anne, queen of France … had a son, but he could not retard the exaltation of my Caesar [Francis] because he was lacking in life."[47] With such callous sentiments like this swirling around a woman twice married under sullied circumstances, it seems likely that Anne became increasingly desperate for a "divine favor."

St. Anne in Court Visual Culture

Just as *Celeste beneficium* performed a certain amount of devotional "work" for Anne of Brittany in her struggle to produce a male heir around 1508 and thereafter, visual culture honoring St. Anne likewise reflected the queen's fervent wishes and provided a graphic counterpoint to the aural and ephemeral strains found in Mouton's motet. In contrast to the music for St. Anne, which appeared in both print and manuscript and circulated around the continent (as well as in her own domain), depictions of Mary's mother survive in personal items, such as books of hours and prayer books like Chicago, Newberry Library, MS 83.[48] Although the French monarchy was quick to spread its musical splendor to other courts (creating new meanings for the works in their disparate contexts), miniatures and illuminations found in devotional items – though artistically as impressive as the music – were most effectively experienced in private quarters. These kinds of materials would tend to lose meaning if distributed beyond the court, although a hermetically sealed private audience cannot be guaranteed for even the most personal items.[49] Art of this nature reveals the most intimate points of resonance between the work and its recipient, and the particular representation of St. Anne in the court's visual culture, especially when intended for Anne of Brittany herself, can refine the image of the grandmother saint beyond the lone motet that survives in her honor.

One cannot broach the topic of art in the court of Louis XII and Anne of Brittany without mention of the lavish books of hours (Paris, Bibliothèque nationale, MS lat. 9474) completed by 1508 expressly for the queen by Jean Bourdichon (d. 1521), the longtime court painter who served four French monarchs over nearly forty years.[50] In this extraordinary manuscript, St. Anne can be found in three different illuminations, making the queen's patron namesake one of the most frequently depicted subjects in the book, exceeded only by members of the Holy Family (Jesus, Mary and Joseph). Of the nearly fifty saints illustrated in the queen's *Grandes heures*, no figure except St. Anne is portrayed more than twice. Neither Anne of Brittany nor the king receives more iconographic attention than does Mary's mother. This luxurious books of hours, notably in Anne's possession at the time of the motet for St. Anne *Celeste beneficium*, was probably guarded closely by the queen and no doubt held personal meaning for her.

Two miniatures featuring St. Anne involve traditional imagery and harvest the rich meanings associated with the *Mater matris*. The first (fol. 197v) is an image of the Education of the Virgin, the icon found mainly in England that strikingly omits Christ from a traditional St. Anne Trinitarian arrangement and instead appears to celebrate femininity and possibly literacy.[51] This subject had the most resonance over time in the case of Anne of Brittany. It seems that Anne sought to model the caring mother as instructor of the next generation. In another miniature from the *Grandes heures* (fol. 218v), St. Anne stands among members of the Holy Family, though not the Holy Kinship.[52] This kind of image occurs at a moment of transition from the Holy Kinship iconography and its genesis through the female line to Jesus' nuclear family, a representation that will be glimpsed in Chapter 7 and one that would dominate Christ's family portraiture in the second half of the sixteenth century in the wake of the Protestant Reformation. In both of Bourdichon's miniatures, it is probable that St. Anne is a stand-in for the queen herself, a point to be raised shortly in *Celeste beneficium* and other works of art. Thus in the present books of hours, the English-inspired imagery around education and literacy may correspond to Anne of Brittany's teaching and guidance of her daughter Claude, who would have been about nine years old at the time. Likewise, one could imagine the queen amidst the company of the Holy Family, as she sought a noble son, who would effectively "save" France while preserving the Breton duchy.

Most notable in the extravagant *Grandes heures* is the rendering of Anne of Brittany herself in the manuscript (fol. 3r, shown in Figure 5.1), which also features her sanctoral patroness Anne. In this image, St. Anne stands behind the kneeling queen in the company of two other female saints (Helena and Ursula). In front of the queen on a draped table lies an illuminated manuscript (likely a book of hours), which reinforces the act of supplication. The attendant saints not only bolster the queen's prayers but also help construct an image of Anne of Brittany. Outside of the queen's patron namesake Anne, Saints Helena and Ursula at first glance do not seem to be strong models for the queen, except that they are themselves crowned. Some might cautiously point to attributes of piety and feminine strength to explain the trio of saints in this famous miniature from the *Grandes heures*; others may highlight the maternal force of this scene with the mother of

Figure 5.1 Anne of Brittany with St. Anne, St. Ursula, and St. Helena. Jean Bourdichon, *Grandes Heures of Anne of Brittany*. Paris, Bibliothèque nationale de France, MS lat. 9474, fol. 3r. Photo: Bibliothèque nationale de France.

the Virgin Mary joined by the mother of Emperor Constantine, who holds a cross (having "discovered" it, according to the legend). But a motherly theme fails in the case of Ursula, who was a virgin saint and the fabled leader of the voyage of eleven thousand martyred virgins.[53] The chastity of Anne of Brittany is hardly at issue either, particularly after her two marriages and numerous pregnancies.

More incisive in the illumination of the quartet, however, is the dynastic overtone, rather than merely a feminine or maternal one. This idea of generational continuity better accounts for the collective sponsorship of the queen by the three saints Anne, Helena, and Ursula. The *Mater matris* of course holds dominion over the Holy Kinship as its genetrix; more elusive for scholars has been the fact that the two other saints have more direct connections to Breton heritage, which Anne so fiercely championed. Constantine's mother, Helena, it so happens, was often conflated with Helen, the wife of Maximus, the fourth-century emperor of Brittania and Gaul. A poem about Anne of Brittany's genealogy, read at her funeral, traces her blood heritage not only to illustrious kings "too numerous to mention" but also to St. Helena.[54] Ursula also holds an oblique connection to the founding of the duchy of Brittany. Similarly during the rule of Maximus in Gaul, the emperor appointed Conan Meriadoc (cousin of his wife Helen) king of the province of Armorica (present-day Brittany). According to an English legend, Ursula and numerous women were sent on a voyage to this new province to form a colony. On the journey, the ship encountered a storm and veered off course toward the Rhineland, where the Ursula legend resumes. More than her leadership in this voyage of countless virgins, Ursula's connection with Breton heritage – however implausible it may be – goes far toward accounting for her representation in the company of the last and greatest duchess of Brittany.[55]

Other images of St. Anne surface in the remnants of visual culture from the queen's two decades at the French court.[56] But it is the Education of the Virgin theme that has survived with some regularity. During the short life of the dauphin Charles-Orland (1492–5), the queen commissioned a stylishly illuminated prayer book by artist Jean Poyer from Tours for her son's future education and catechesis (New York, Pierpont Morgan Library, MS M.50).[57] Following an elaborate opening section containing, among other things, scenes pairing the apostles with Old Testament prophets, the book continues with a section of suffrages. The first saint honored in this section is St. Anne, shown in the act of instruction of Mary. Anne's daughter appears as a teenager and holds a rather large, oblong volume (fol. 13r, shown in Figure 5.2). That Anne of Brittany and her name saint were central figures

Figure 5.2 *Education of the Three Marys* in the Prayer Book of Anne de Bretagne. New York, Pierpont Morgan Library, MS M.50, fol. 13r. Photo credit: The Pierpont Morgan Library, New York. MS M.50. Purchased by J. Pierpont Morgan (1837–1913) in 1905.

in the context of this devotional aid is confirmed by the letters A, N, and E (the three letters that form the name "Anne"), which decorate the borders of this and the thirty-three other illuminations in the prayer book.

Striking details appear in this particular scene of the Education of the Virgin. On one hand, Anne is holding a stylus and writing in the book, though the text is deliberately illegible. But even more exceptional, the duo in the foreground is matched by a pair of women in the background waiting to receive instruction with their own books. These surrounding women can be securely identified as the daughters of St. Anne (Mary Cleophas and Mary Salome), two women whose very existence would be challenged by French biblical humanists (discussed in Chapter 7). Though curiously seeming a bit older than Mary, her sisters can be safely distinguished because of the text beneath the scene, which continues onto the next folio. This text reveals a kind of mnemonic for remembering the offspring of the Holy Kinship (*ex tribus alma viris peperit tres anna marias*) and is comparable with the better known *aide-mémoire* circulated in Voragine's *Golden Legend*.[58] This scene importantly combines two aspects of St. Anne iconography that are rarely conjoined – her instruction of the Virgin and the first "layer" of Holy Kinship progeny in the Three Marys. These topics attach importance to the value of the female line in the monarchy, charged with both producing the next generation of noble offspring (a major priority of any kingdom) and instilling wisdom in it. It is not difficult to imagine that the queen would be expected to play the kind of role that St. Anne is playing for the Virgin in this image. Considering that her firstborn son was of a tender age and that the manuscript presents textual abbreviations and a *bâtarde* script, it can be inferred that Anne of Brittany read the texts to Charles-Orland while he gazed at the images.[59]

Carefully cultivated devotion to St. Anne continued into Claude's formative years (ca. 1505–10) and was registered in an illuminated primer commissioned by Anne for her daughter (Cambridge, Fitzwilliam Museum, MS 159). Like all primers, this book was intended to teach children to read by exposing them to short prayers in both Latin and French. As a characteristically wise mother and teacher of the Virgin Mary, St. Anne unsurprisingly plays an important role in the manuscript's iconographic program. The first folio of the book (Figure 5.3, left) features Mary's mother presenting both a girl (either Anne of Brittany or Claude) and the Virgin Mary to St. Claudius of Besançon, the patron saint of Claude of France.[60] The girl kneels and rests her hands on a closed book. The primer's final illumination (Figure 5.3, right) is closely modeled on – and further dramatizes – the opening image, as it is transformed to show St. Claudius presenting Claude

Figure 5.3 (a) *A Girl Kneels at a Desk with the Virgin and Saints*, from a Primer, c.1500-10 (ink & gold ink on parchment), Master of Antoine de Roche / Fitzwilliam Museum, MS 159, p. 1. University of Cambridge, UK and (b) *St. Claude Presents a Kneeling Girl to St. Anne and the Virgin*, c.1500-10 (vellum), French School, (16th century) / Fitzwilliam Museum, MS 159, p. 14, University of Cambridge, UK. Photos: The Bridgeman Art Library.

of France to St. Anne and the Virgin Mary. Claude kneels in this miniature with the book open on the prie-dieu. Another book has entered the scene, as St. Anne and Mary peer at a slightly larger volume, the mother instructing the daughter. Claude's open book almost certainly symbolizes her accomplishment for having completed the prayer book and may offer hope for future engagement with literature gained by experience with the elementary volume. A close look at the young Claude in the final illumination reveals her looking past the miniaturized Virgin Mary and instead gazing at St. Anne. One would only do this if there were an especially strong relationship to the grandmother saint. The illuminator (or commissioner) might have intended for Claude to recognize her mother in the figure of St. Anne, even while the daughter achieves a level of independence from her mother by learning to read and pray with the help of her own personal intercessor. Anne of Brittany was patterned after her name saint, here as a sage teacher of her children.[61]

The Education of the Virgin iconography persisted at the French court, even after Anne's death in 1514. In a very small prayer book prepared expressly for Queen Claude (New York, Pierpont Morgan Library, MS M.1166), St. Anne is again commemorated as a teacher. Compiled after Claude's marriage to Francis I around the time of the 1517 coronation, the prayer book is the work of an artist from Tours known only as the Master of Claude of France, a likely protégé of the illuminator Jean Poyer mentioned earlier in connection with the primer for Charles-Orland.[62] After a series of scenes and texts of the Passion and standard prayers to the Virgin comes a large section of some twenty-eight folios with prayers to saints. In the spirit of a book of hours, each suffrage begins with an "antiphon" (*antiphona*) followed by a versicle (or response) and a prayer (*oratio*).

The prayers to St. Anne do not fall at the beginning of this section, unlike in Pierpont Morgan Library, MS M.50. This honor belongs to the Holy Trinity (fols. 24v–25r), an image that was connected with the royal family, a point explored in Chapter 7. Despite the relatively unassuming location of St. Anne tucked in the middle of the suffrages on fol. 42r (Figure 5.4), the confluence of images and text on this single folio provides unexpected clues to understanding Mary's mother to an extent not seen in the artifacts surviving from the time of Anne of Brittany. The depiction of St. Anne instructing her daughter appears inset with the prayers to St. Anne on the left center of the folio. Her hands together in prayer, the young Virgin Mary poses reverently, but at the same time is actively engaged with her mother, who holds an open book for study. The border of the folio features an illustration of the Annunciation to St. Anne described in apocryphal literature, a highly

Figure 5.4 St. Anne teaching the Virgin Mary to read and the Annunciation to St. Anne. Master of Claude of France, Prayer Book of Queen Claude of France, ca. 1517. Photo credit: The Pierpont Morgan Library, New York. MS M.1166, fol. 42r. Gift of Mrs. Alexandre P. Rosenberg in memory of her husband, Alexandre Paul Rosenberg, 2008.

infrequent subject in visual art for St. Anne.[63] The combination of these two images delivers a strong emphasis on maternity, from the moment of conception through the bonds formed by spirited interaction around learning. But there is more to the picture.

The few who have pored over this tiny manuscript have generally gravitated toward providing remarks on the fine program of illuminations by the Master of Claude of France. With respect to the St. Anne suffrage, nothing has been said about the inset prayer that occupies the majority of the folio. As can be seen in Figure 5.4, the antiphon is none other than *Celeste beneficium*, evoking not only the title of Mouton's motet, but also that of the widespread antiphon of the same name surveyed earlier. With the simple reversal of the words *Maria* and *virgo*, the antiphon in this prayer book in fact more closely matches the opening text of Mouton's motet than the variants in the antiphons found in the liturgical books (Example 5.4).[64] It hardly seems out of place to see the amplified aural-visual devotion to St. Anne prompted in the prayer book as closely allied with the dynamic aural strains of well-woven polyphony heard at the French court.

With the appearance of this text in Claude's prayer book, the significance of Mouton's *Celeste beneficium* may also begin to be narrowed. Claude of France would be expected to hold the prayer book and physically utter the antiphon text, which speaks of the "divine favor" that entered into Anne. While she spoke this antiphon, her eye would be drawn to the two rarely juxtaposed scenes from the life of St. Anne. The antiphon relates squarely to the elegant illumination on the margins of the folio, the moment of annunciation. The other depiction – the Education of the Virgin – is not echoed in the text and was not typically a subject of the office antiphons and responsories. Despite their uncommon juxtaposition, the two tableaux of the annunciation and education become thematic complements, together suggesting the full sweep of motherhood, from the moment of conception to a tutorial scene involving the mother and considerably mature offspring. The text and images of this single canvas take a powerful theme of maternity and multiply it graphically. The education scene, though seemingly discordant with the antiphon, is also tinged with political value and was evidently the queen's preferred portrayal of St. Anne. Education (literacy in particular) was a form of power, especially for early modern women. Anne of Brittany no doubt wished for Claude to have several healthy progeny that could both provide joy to her daughter and much-needed political insurance for the duchy of Brittany. In the education of the Virgin imagery, the queen developed her own identity while finding subtle ways to endow her offspring with the kind of authority that she had at the French court. Mouton's *Celeste beneficium* from nearly a decade earlier bears similar political overtones through a conscious blending of devotion to St. Anne with the aspirations of the French crown.

The Politics of Association: A Motet Intensified

The motets written at the French court during the time of Queen Anne's reign served multiple functions. They were sometimes expressions of devotion, but it was also not uncommon for motets to build or reinforce an image of the monarch, whether publicly for state occasions or privately among courtiers. Mouton directed the chapel of Anne of Brittany until the queen's death and transferred to the chapel of Louis XII (though he did not ascend to the position of *magister* in the latter placement). In both roles, he was the de facto court composer and produced commemorative works for both the queen and king. Some of Mouton's custom-tailored motets brought diverse texts together into musical settings. His motet *Quis dabit oculis*, for example, laments Anne's death in 1514, incorporating texts used from the sermon delivered at her funeral. The composer's *Non nobis Domine* celebrated the 1510 birth of Renée, the second of the surviving daughters of Anne and Louis. This motet cites the king, queen, and daughter by name, but also offers a biblical frame, citing verses from Psalm 113. Mouton's routine juxtaposition of sacred and political texts in his motets can also be found in his setting of *O Christe redemptor*, which bids happiness to the king and fertility to the queen (*fit regi felicitas, reginae fecunditas*), as well as in the Christmas motet *Puer natus est nobis*, a work punctuated with the royal acclamation *Vivat rex in aeternum*.[65]

Celeste beneficium contains no obvious intermingling of secular or political texts with the core devotional text, except that Anne of Brittany would have easily identified with a motet's subject and the vivid calls to *Anna*. However, the companion motet *Adjutorium nostrum* – paired with *Celeste beneficium* in more than half of the sources of the latter (Table 5.1) – takes a more overt tack, suggesting the very fragile circumstances surrounding the monarch. Far more intriguing to the historian than questions of attribution are the occasions when these works were set contiguously. The effect of this coupling throws a more patent political and personalized hue on the untainted (strictly speaking) devotional text in honor of St. Anne presented in *Celeste beneficium*.

While the text of *Celeste beneficium* does not seamlessly flow into that of *Adjutorium nostrum*, the musical points of connection outlined earlier produce a viable association between the two settings. The homophonic supplications around a clear F tonality – the plea to *Anna* in *Celeste beneficium* and the *Ludovicus* petition in *Adjutorium nostrum* – are the most discernible of musical events binding the two motets, frozen in time with a calculated entreaty in the "syntactic" style. These poignant moments suggest the important cultural work these politico-devotional compositions accomplished on the monarch's behalf. The pieces give voice to the wishes of the crown, with texts that penetrated the listening experience, highly contrasting with the scattered delivery of words in the general contrapuntal tapestry of the respective works. In the cases where *Celeste* and *Adjutorium* were positioned as *prima* and *secunda pars* respectively, one can picture a united plea emanating from both Anne and the king. Moreover, by fastening *Adjutorium* to *Celeste*, scribes and publishers clarified and intensified the devotion to St. Anne in Mouton's motet setting, which by itself only implicitly captures the ardent hopes, even desperation, of the French court between 1508 and 1511. The construction of the queen's identity in the image of St. Anne and her reliance on her namesake to intervene in all aspects of maternal life are confirmed in the court's visual artifacts.

The transmission history of *Celeste beneficium*, as detailed in Table 5.1, merits further study, transporting the discussion beyond French court circles and toward new aristocratic contexts into which this music would hold meaningful symbolism for its recipients. A fascinating detour for the motet occurred when it fell into the hands of the archrival of the French court – the Habsburgs. Not only did *Celeste beneficium* remain in dialogue with other works to magnify devotion to St. Anne, but the conditions surrounding devotion to Mary's mother would shift yet again. Far beyond her intercession on behalf of mothers, the figure of St. Anne crept into humanist and reformationist polemics of the early sixteenth century, last seen in the German north in the milieu of Frederick the Wise.

6 | Devotion without Borders: The Afterlife of *Celeste beneficium*

This study of music for Mary's mother has been anchored by repertory prepared for some of the major courts in fifteenth- and sixteenth-century Europe. In the present case, the transmission history of *Celeste beneficium* leads to a small treasure trove of musical works for St. Anne delivered to the Austrian branch of Habsburgs, led by the future Holy Roman Emperor Ferdinand, the younger brother of Charles V, and his wife, Anna (queen of Bohemia and Hungary). This collection of pieces contributes additional modes of understanding the political usefulness of the saint, a topic at the heart of this investigation. In the process, one witnesses how French court music for the grandmother saint transcended imperial boundaries and functioned in another elite environment.

Of the sources for *Celeste beneficium* mentioned in the previous chapter, only in the 1514 and 1526 prints does *Adjutorium nostrum* expressly name Louis XII in a personal plea to St. René for intercession. What of the other manuscripts in which the motet occurs? The king and queen of France are in fact named in *Adjutorium nostrum* in two additional manuscripts (CambriP 1760 and LonRC 1070), but these sources do not contain Mouton's *Celeste beneficium* in connection with the companion motet. In other manuscripts, the names were altered or omitted. The Palatini partbooks, for example, do not link *Adjutorium nostrum* with *Celeste beneficium*; eighty-one folios separate the two works. *Adjutorium nostrum* retains all of the "Anna" references but omits mention of "Ludovicus," a point examined later.

Another possibility for the arrangement of these motets comes from one of the earlier (if not the earliest) sources for *Adjutorium nostrum*, LonBLR 8 G.vii, a manuscript from the Alamire workshop prepared for Henry VIII of England and Catherine of Aragon. Here, *Celeste beneficium* and *Adjutorium nostrum* are set as *prima* and *secunda partes* and without composer attribution. In *Adjutorium nostrum*, the names of the English monarch "Henricus rex" and "Katherina," rather than those of the French crown, are employed. Notably, a plea to St. George ("Georgi") is found in place of the appeal to St. René, to cater to the English court audience (Figure 6.1). While George was a patron saint of England in general and the royal family in particular, he is

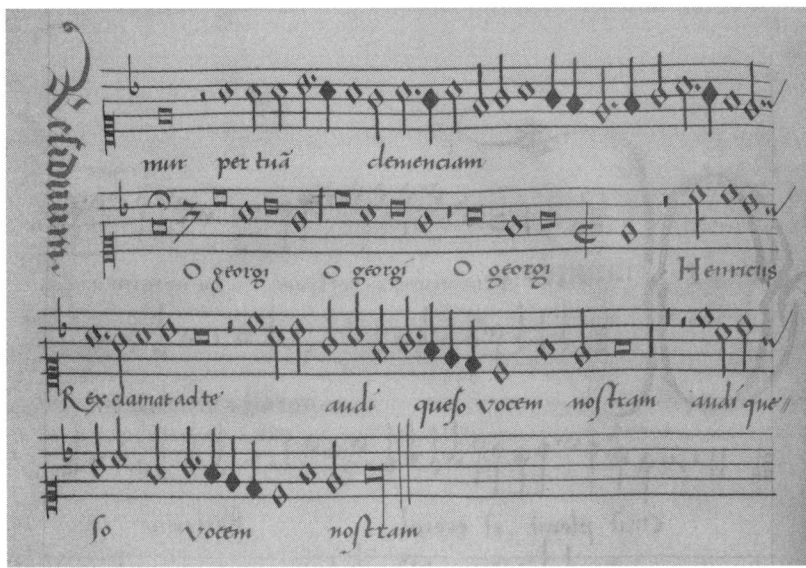

Figure 6.1 *Adjutorium nostrum*, superius part. © The British Library Board. London, British Library, MS Royal 8.G.VII, fol. 5v, upper half. All Rights Reserved 24/04/2013.

hardly recognized as an intercessor for those wishing to conceive offspring. The substitution was therefore purely a gesture toward the English monarch and quite dismissive of the meaning attached to the motet in the context of the French court.

The alteration of the subject of a composition to suit the recipient of a manuscript was nothing new in the early sixteenth century. Consider Josquin's mass for Hercules, the Duke of Ferrara, whose elemental musical material was derived from the vowels of the duke's name, using a technique known as the *soggetto cavato dalle vocali* ("subject drawn from the vowels"). Josquin's mass for the duke was repurposed for both Philip the Fair (king of Castile, brother of Margaret of Austria) in 1505 and Frederick the Wise around 1518–20 with the titles *Missa Philippus rex Castiliae* and *Missa Fredericus dux Saxoniae*, respectively.[1] The biographical circumstances of the king and the elector are difficult to compare with those of the Duke of Ferrara, which suggests that the mass was chiefly regarded as distinguished music, recyclable for notable figures. It did not require a fundamental change in the musical substance of these new works, as the technique might otherwise dictate. But there seems to be a richer story behind the appearance of *Celeste beneficium/Adjutorium* in LonBLR 8 G.vii involving Margaret of Austria – the likely commissioner of the manuscript – and the English royal couple.

Petrus Alamire, the compiler of LonBLR 8 G.vii, not only positioned *Celeste beneficium* and *Adjutorium nostrum* contiguously in the manuscript, but he also placed the works at the head of this all-motet collection, no doubt a signal to the historian of their central meaning for the recipient. Some have noted that the following anonymous motet *Nesciens mater* in LonBLR 8 G.vii further sustains the momentum of the dynastic plea for offspring, with its mention of Christ's birth and his suckling of the Virgin Mary.[2] As Jennifer Thomas has convincingly proposed, the Habsburg-Burgundian manuscript probably represents a profound expression of sympathy for Catherine of Aragon from Margaret of Austria.[3] The two became sisters-in-law during Margaret's residency at the Spanish court with her marriage to Catherine's brother, Juan of Castile. For a time, Margaret and Catherine must have been close, the former teaching the latter how to speak French. Their lives intertwined even after Juan's passing in 1497. Both women became aunts to the future Emperor Charles V and were in regular communication.

Above all, each woman had experienced widowhood and the grief of unsuccessful pregnancies. Margaret of course was widowed twice and prematurely bore a daughter who did not survive. Meanwhile, Catherine of Aragon witnessed the death of the heir apparent to the English throne (Arthur, Prince of Wales) in 1502 and suffered no fewer than five fruitless pregnancies as queen consort to Henry VIII. While Thomas acknowledged the desperate circumstances of both women, she only attributed to St. Anne a measure of Catholic solidarity between Margaret and Catherine.[4] But the placement of *Celeste beneficium* and its companion motet at the front of this manuscript would seem to impel a stronger reading. The invocation of St. Anne at the outset of LonBLR 8 G.vii specifically unites the plight of both women around Mary's mother, offering the comfort of St. Anne as both mother and potent stewardess of political dynasties. The urgency of a male heir is clarified in *Adjutorium nostrum* and troped again in *Nesciens mater*.

There is no more intriguing occasion in the transmission history of *Celeste beneficium*, however, than its appearance in another Alamire creation, now prepared for the Austrian Habsburgs. Dating between 1528 and 1534, the Palatini partbooks were expressly dedicated to Anna, Queen of Bohemia and Hungary. Critical to this entire study of Renaissance music for Mary's mother, the Palatini partbooks open with a substantial outpouring of polyphonic music for St. Anne (Table 6.1). This subsection of motets can be considered a well-planned "Anne group," though it properly ends with Mathieu Gascongne's *Christus vincit*, if judged from the illumination program (discussed later).[5]

Table 6.1 Opening group of motets in Vatican City, Biblioteca Apostolica Vaticana, MSS Palatini Latini 1976–9

Motet	Composer	Fols.
Pater noster	[Willaert]	2v–4v
Anna matrona nobilis	anon.	5v–8v
Transit Anna timor	Agricola	8v–11r
Theodoce matrem	anon.	11v–14r
Ave mater matris Dei	anon.	14r–15r
Celeste beneficium	[Mouton]	15v–16v
Christus vincit	[Gascongne]	17r–20r

Adrian Willaert's *Pater noster* christens the entire collection, not an unreasonable selection for the Central European monarch given the composer's service to Cardinal Ippolito I d'Este when the latter departed for a stint in Hungary from October 1517 until August 1519.[6] Herbert Kellman, who has done the most codicological work on the Palatini partbooks, was the first to note that the introductory *Pater noster* is contained in a detachable four-folio gathering and might have been a late addition to the compilation.[7] That Willaert's motet seems to stand apart from the other motets in the collection is also evidenced by its rubrication in the table of contents at the front of the manuscript, as well as its missing *secunda pars* "Ave Maria gratia plena," which paraphrases the popular Marian antiphon.[8] The implications of the "missing" Ave Maria are addressed later in this chapter. In the meantime, these facts would seem to elevate even further the high status of the five contiguous motets that follow Willaert's motet, constituting the "Anne group." Four of the five members of the group are directly in honor of St. Anne, while one motet (Agricola's *Transit Anna timor*) is an occasional work, originally for Anne of Brittany and Louis XII, similar to *Adjutorium nostrum*. The heading of the table of contents in each book (*Registrum dive regine hungarie*) indicates that the partbooks were prepared expressly for Anna, Queen of Bohemia and Hungary, and sporadic references to Ferdinand and Anna in a few motets, including *Adjutorium nostrum*, leave no question as to the recipient of the partbooks.[9]

The proposed dating of the Palatini partbooks between 1528 and 1534 stands on firm ground. Anna and Ferdinand were not officially monarchs until 1528, and thus could not have been called queen and king in the manuscript before this date. Furthermore, Petrus Alamire, supervisor and/or compiler of the manuscripts, retired in 1534 and died in 1536, providing a *terminus ante quem* for the partbooks. Kellman's suggestion of 1531–2 for the arrival of the Palatini partbooks can be better evaluated with a wide view of the situation in the eastern half of the Habsburg Empire along with close examination of several motets in the collection.[10] That the group of five "Anne" motets has received scant attention should come as no surprise because three of the five are anonymous works. The other two (*Transit Anna timor* and *Celeste beneficium*) have securable ties to the French court. Although this is no forum for editions and full commentaries on the individual motets of the "Anne group" (to say nothing of the partbooks on the whole), they most certainly warrant a hearty description and thorough assessment. Of the handful of "Anne" motets in the Palatini partbooks, *Celeste beneficium* is more than familiar by now, even in the absence of its "other half," *Adjutorium nostrum*. Mouton's well-circulated piece, however, is positioned as the last of the group and will be briefly reconsidered after a review of the other motets.

Anna matrona nobilis

The compiler of the partbooks began the "Anne group" with the largest motet of the set, the anonymous *Anna matrona nobilis* (fols. 5v–8v). Because this motet has never been studied, it must be said that its text derives from the sequence *Testamento veteri* for St. Anne, the second stanza of which typically begins *Haec matrona nobilis* …, obviously making *Anna matrona nobilis* a significant textual variant, one more immediately symbolic of the queen. All four voices of the motet *Anna matrona nobilis* appear freely composed, none resembling the first-mode sequence melody associated with this text.[11] The most discursive of the texts used in the liturgy, the sequence as a genre offers an excellent opportunity for commentary on the significance of St. Anne at the outset of this carefully arranged "Anne group." (Remember from Chapter 4 that themes of the Immaculate Conception were unveiled in connection with sequences.) A rhymed and rhythmical text characteristic of the later sequence, the poetry of *Anna matrona nobilis* makes reference to the extended period of infertility for Mary's mother before she conceived the Virgin, an event predicted by the ancients. Further, clear Marian epithets are repurposed for St. Anne in the sixth stanza (*Rubens rosa speciosa, Florens inter lilia*), and a whiff of Immaculist ideology is applied to Mary's mother in this same versicle, as she is characterized as "free of blemish" (*labe carens*). In the concluding strophes, the supplicants plead directly with Anne for intercession, that she may protect these sinners from harm and campaign for them before God.

Anna matrona nobilis	The noble matron Anne
Diu fuerat sterilis	had long been sterile
In magna tristitia.	and in great sadness.
Cui fructum contulit	She bore fruit
Et sic luctura abstulit	and thus her grief was taken away
Divina clementia.	with divine clemency.
Patriarchis edita,	Foretold by the fathers,
Anna luce predita	Anne was gifted with the light
In perenni gloria.	in everlasting glory.
Testamento veteri	From the Old Testament
Anna fuit genita	and the royal lineage,
Et de stirpe regia.	Anne was to give birth.
Deprecamur, inclita,	We pray you, illustrious one,
Ut per tua merita	that through your merits
Nobis donetur gratia.	grace might be given to us.
Anna parens, labe carens,	O mother Anne, free of blemish,
Rubens rosa speciosa,	beautiful rose, growing red and
Florens inter lilia,	flowering among the lilies,
Matrem Christi genuisti;	You bore the mother of Christ;
Tua prece	may you protect us from a harmful death
nos a nece Tuearis noxia.	with your prayer.
Testamento veteri …	From the Old Testament …
Ecce lucis officina	Behold, the workshop of light,
Egris spes et medicina;	the hope and remedy for the sick;
Tua proles est regina	your offspring is Queen
In celesti patria.	in the kingdom of heaven.
Ipsa cunctis jam praelata	Now preferred by all,
Per te sumens hec precata	through you, accepting these prayers,
Nostra [fiat] advocata,	may you become our advocate
In Dei presentia.	in the presence of God.
Testamento veteri …	From the Old Testament …

Anna matrona nobilis contains all of the musical hallmarks of the streamlined French motet that flourished in the time of Francis I, the groundwork of which was laid by Mouton. The anonymous motet, which could well be the work of Mouton, begins homophonically in the "syntactic" style mentioned in Chapter 5, an ideal setting for communicating lucidly with the listener. Sections of limited musical decoration return often, but the motet also includes numerous points of imitation and abundant duets. Set in rhythmically energetic counterpoint, this motet draws out an already

Example 6.1 Anonymous, *Anna matrona nobilis*, mm. 55–69.

lengthy sequence text. Further augmenting the dimensions of this motet – and most striking about *Anna matrona nobilis* overall – is the unusual return of the fourth stanza (*Testamento veteri, Anna fuit genita et de stirpe regia*) once after the seventh stanza and again as the work's final musical gesture. With each iteration of this twelve-measure mantra (Example 6.1, mm. 55–66 are identical to mm. 132–43 and 204–15), the music accompanying the stanza remains constant, thus establishing these three crucial poetic lines as a kind of musical refrain for the piece. Composed with minimal adornment and halting rests (plus a fermata in m. 66), the recurrent motto is the most communicative gesture in the motet. The three phrases of starkly set homophony each have cadences prepared by a suspension, the most incisive of which occurs with the 9–8 suspension on the word *genita*.

The reorganization of the text in the motet relative to the conventional sequence is both curious and telling. The typical beginning of the sequence

Testamento veteri was jettisoned at the outset in favor of *Anna matrona*, itself altered from *haec matrona*, likely to emphasize the name of the motet's dedicatee. The versicle beginning *Testamento veteri*, seemingly demoted to the fourth stanza, is then amplified in the anonymous *Anna matrona nobilis* through repetition. In short space, this recurring versicle impresses on its listeners the two-pronged notion that St. Anne's conception and birth of the Virgin was not only an event long foretold in the Old Testament, but also one traceable through the stock of ancient kings (*stirpe regia*). These ideas of royal and ancient lineage, sonically projected as the mantra of the motet, have political force, as observed in Chapter 2 and elsewhere in this study. If not written explicitly for the queen of Bohemia and Hungary, the work still would have resonated well with the imperial circumstances around the end of the 1520s.

Transit Anna timor

Approaching the sheer size of *Anna matrona nobilis*, the ensuing motet in the "Anne group" of the Palatini partbooks, *Transit Anna timor*, is the only motet out of the thirty-eight in the collection with a composer attribution. In the tenor partbook only, it is credited to the itinerant South Netherlandish composer Alexander Agricola (MS: *Allexander Agricola*). The motet has attracted some notice in the musicological literature in studies of Agricola's biography, but its survival only in the Palatini partbooks demands more focused attention. *Transit Anna timor* is Agricola's only attempt at an "occasional" motet; at the same time, it constitutes the only motet of the "Anne group" that does not speak explicitly of St. Anne. It is the sole reason that this chapter speaks of an "Anne group" instead of a "St. Anne group." Although the Palatini partbooks are the only source of *Transit Anna timor*, its secular text clearly points to French court culture during the reign of Anne of Brittany and Louis XII. Agricola seems to have served the French crown between 1486 and 1491, just before Anne's arrival at the royal court.[12] However, *Transit Anna timor* dates from a considerably later period, as it is written in thanksgiving of the recovery of Louis XII from one of his bouts with illness, likely between the years 1503 and 1505. The poetry is ascribed to Claude de Chanvreux, a counselor to the king, though Agricola's text contains significant variants, amounting to nonsense in some places. The text, articulated in two parts in the music, begins by lauding Anne of Brittany for her support of Louis during the time of his near-death malady and concludes with praises for the king's convalescence.

Transit Anna timor niveos regina per artus asscripta est cordis dira favilla tui, marcida dum regis prospectas hora mariti, vitae interstitio mortis, et haesit amor gallica [hungarica] neu remis variis pertusa fatiscat viribus et remis rex redivive vales. Que distinxti labiis perplexa voluntans vota Deo superum solve benigna tibi.	Fear passed, Queen Anne, through your white limbs, the dreadful embers of your heart were extinguished; as you gazed on the countenance of your husband the king, Love stopped on the boundary of life and death, lest France [Hungary] gape open, pierced by various fissures. King, who has come back to life, you are vigorous in strength and wealth. The vows that you (the Queen) formed with your lips wavering in perplexity, fulfill to the God of heaven, well disposed to you.
Regia sed soboles Francae spes Claudia gentis, Fortunae refugas disce puella vices. Auspice qui Christo censeris, nomine Christo, numine sub trino rex Ludovice [Ferdinande] vale. Sospite te, salva est respublica, maxime regum, justitiae robur et religionis honos.	But, royal offspring, Claude, hope of the French race, learn, maiden, the fleeting vicissitudes of Fortune. You who are enrolled with Christ taking the auspices, in Christ's name, under threefold Godhead, King Louis [Ferdinand], be well. While you are preserved, the State is safe, greatest of kings, mainstay of justice, honor of religion.[13]

The conditions that prompted Agricola's setting of this occasional text can be narrowed but not precisely determined. While Louis's health was ailing between 1503 and 1505, Agricola was a member of the Habsburg chapel under Philip the Fair. A few opportunities would have brought the two courts together, facilitating an occasion for the motet's composition. The most attractive context would seem to be around the Treaty of Blois (signed September 22, 1504), which proposed the marriage of Claude of France to the future Charles V, an offer that never came to fruition.[14] The signing of the treaty would have convened Louis XII, Philip the Fair, Maximilian, and likely their musical contingents. Although Louis's illness of 1505 was particularly severe, he had also spent the summer of 1504 at Blois battling sickness. After 1505, all bets were off on a marriage between the French and the Habsburgs, as Francis of Angoulême was quietly being told to prepare for accession to the throne.

The style of *Transit Anna timor* echoes that of the previous French motets.[15] Agricola constantly refreshes the texture with numerous points of imitation and playful (and sometimes long-winded) duets. To this, the composer adds a handful of arresting phrases in "syntactic" choral homophony (*et haesit gallica, Rex redivive vales, vota Deo, numine sub trino,* and *Rex Ludovice*). These moments of ostensible clarity are in fact clouded by further scribal inconsistency in the assembly of this motet in the Palatini partbooks. Of the five phrases just mentioned, two are particularly striking because their texts have been altered in certain partbooks. In the altus partbook, *et haesit gallica* appears as *et haesit hungarica,* and similarly in both bassus and altus books, *Rex Ludovice* is changed to *Rex Ferdinande,* obviously in recognition of the new imperial milieu for the Palatini partbooks.[16]

These partial emendations raise important questions about the function of this occasional motet and its "mixed message." There was clearly an attempt to repurpose the music for Ferdinand and Anna, and indeed the name "Anna" did not need to be changed in the opening text of this motet, as Christopher Reynolds has noticed.[17] But the firstborn of the French royal court (Claude) remains unaltered in the text, to say nothing of the narrative of the motet, which is quite specific to Louis's circumstances a generation earlier. Nothing is known about how the singers at Ferdinand's court might have executed this motet, nor how it was received in performance, but the work hardly applies to the Habsburg recipients. Even if the homophonic moments were coordinated among the voices for the sake of textual lucidity, the retelling of a French triumph would not serve any useful political end for Habsburg ears around 1530. Claude of France died well before the partbooks appeared, and the interpolation of Ferdinand and Anna into the French chronicle would spark confusion at best. At this moment in history, the French became allied with the Ottoman Empire, uniting against Habsburg interests in Central Europe. Human error is the only reasonable explanation for the Alamire workshop's bungling of this partial diplomatic retooling of the motet.

Theodoce matrem

The third motet that one encounters in the "Anne group" is the anonymous *Theodoce matrem/Firma fide fidens,* another *unicum* in the subsection of motets in the Palatini partbooks. Like *Celeste beneficium,* this four-voice work paraphrases an office plainchant for the feast of St. Anne in the tenor. In contrast to Mouton's motet, the foundational chant is cited (*Firma fide fidens*) and underlaid throughout the motet. The three surrounding voice parts (superius, altus, and bassus) sing the text of

Theodoce matrem, a text not known from liturgical or paraliturgical sources. The motet is arranged in two parts, shifting from a perfect mensuration (three subdivisions of the measure) to a faster duple division in a "cut" signature. A full transcription of *Theodoce matrem/Firma fide fidens* appears in Appendix A.

Beyond the playful textual alliteration at the outset, the tenor *Firma fide fidens* issues a general plea to Christians to have faith in God, pointing to the evidence of St. Anne's miraculous conception of the Virgin Mary at an old age as proof of the power of faith. The more substantive commentary in the other voice parts, not easily discerned in the Latin, reveals two ideas redolent of the versified office explored in Chapter 2, namely the assertion of ancient biblical heritage and the analogy involving the image of the organic root-branch-flower. These images testify to the notions of lineage and progeny, respectively, while also offering political utility.

Theodoce matrem	Let us celebrate in Bethlehem
celebremus bethlemitam	the God-bearing mother,
Que duxit celibem Joachim	who led a celibate life
cum coniuge vitam	with her husband Joachim.
Anna sacerdos tuum series	Anne is your priestess, line
et filia regum	and daughter of kings.
prole carens gratis	Freely lacking offspring,
yzacar coniunctia	joined with Isaac,
vatis accepit	she received the sacred hands of the prophet,
sacras manus spernentis adorat	and honors the secrets
tristis secreta	of the scorned and the sad.
representes penetralia sancta.	May you reveal the sacred innermost places.
Anna dei matrem	Anne shows us
generalis plantula	the mother of God
virgam rore rigata	with a natural shoot of her nature,
poli que florem	a stem moistened
prefert orbi	with the dew of heaven.
flos Christus	She presents a flower to the world;
virga dice	the flower is Christ,
virgo Maria	the stem is the Virgin Mary.
Anna tuorum	O Anne, ask the accused
jam famulorum	for courage
post resolutum	to be loosened
mente reatum	with the joys
cum gaudia posce. Amen.	of your servants. Amen.

Tenor

Firma fide	Trusting with firm faith, believe
fidens crede	and do not be beyond doubt,
nec [sis] ultra dubius	since the womb
cum presertim Anne annus	of the aged woman, Anne,
dum tumescit uterus.	now swells.
Quia deus	Because of this, your loving God
vestros pius	Listened to my cry,
exaudivit me gemitus,	since the womb
cum presertim Anne annus	of the aged woman, Anne,
iam tumescit uterus.	now swells.

Akin to the motets in the Palatini partbooks mentioned earlier, *Theodoce matrem/Firma fide fidens* blends contrapuntal duets with thicker four-voice textures to declaim the words commemorating Mary's mother. Stylistically, however, the anonymous motet does not achieve the balance, concision, and technical polish of the previous works in the group. Its peculiarities can be found at the outset with two duets consuming the first twenty-four measures. The length of the duet would not attract so much attention were it not for the lack of imitation between the parts, a property that one comes to expect from the elite style of sixteenth-century polyphony, indeed a technique that propels this kind of music forward. Further slowing the momentum is a protracted trio in the lower three voices at the beginning of the motet's *secunda pars* (Appendix A, m. 66). The work plods along for an uncomfortable period of time (twenty measures) and in the muddied lower register, even when the faster "cut" signature is taken into account. A few amateurish errors in voice leading and unmotivated dissonances (not attributable to scribal error) further diminish the stature of *Theodoce matrem* and may explain its absence from other sources.[18]

Firma fide fidens, the name of the tenor in *Theodoce matrem*, is the most curious aspect of this four-voice motet and has hitherto received no attention in the scholarly literature. The general shape of the melody somewhat resembles a third-mode Matins responsory *Firma fide fidens*, which is found in the same office for St. Anne (AH 25.18) that brought to light the antiphons *Celeste beneficium* and *Felix Anna quedam matrona*. Because the tenor only paraphrases the chant, the references to the E-mode chant melody are unsurprisingly weak.[19] While it was not inconceivable to present a cantus firmus in the tenor of a motet in the early sixteenth century, it was hardly the stylistic norm of the generation leading up to the compilation of the Palatini partbooks around 1530. Dating back to the works of Johannes Regis in the mid-to-late fifteenth century, the motet built on a cantus firmus generally waned during the sixteenth century. The technique, when used, has tended to involve more than four voices or was often employed for ceremonial occasions. While one witnesses polytextual cantus firmus motets into the mid-century with Cristóbal de Morales, composers at the French court have not usually been associated with this style. Only a small fraction of Mouton's motets were polytextual works on tenor cantus firmi, and none were set for less than five voices.[20] Neither Févin nor Sermisy – both active in the French court – composed a motet of this nature. It is certainly possible that *Theodoce matrem/ Firma fide fidens* preceded the other motets in the "Anne group" by a generation or more, which would make its appearance in a set of partbooks from around 1530 quite remarkable.

The long-winded setting of the tenor *Firma fide fidens* suggests that the composer freely transformed the chant model in the motet. The threefold repetition of the word *uterus* (mm. 51–64) is also uncharacteristic of an office plainchant and does not concord with known versions of *Firma fide fidens*. Even though the composer is not strictly setting a chant melody in this paraphrase, he interestingly observes the *repetendum* (structural repeat) of the responsory text following the declamation of the verse beginning *Quia deus*. For all of the attention given to lucid "call-out" moments in the earlier "Anne" motets of the Palatini partbooks, one hesitates to point to anything in a polytextual motet that would project words with any force. Not atypical of late fifteenth-century motets, the plentiful duets that thin the texture surprisingly do not deploy syllables in a concerted way as one might expect. The scribe in fact was quite aware of how the words were to be set across the voice parts (observing rests, omitting texts for reasons of pacing, etc.), but the result of the double texts and the offsetting of harmonious syllables produces a stream of discordant vowel sounds on the sonic surface of the anonymous motet. The separate declamations of the name *Anna* (and forms thereof) in the work – normally an opportunity for a composer to announce the dedicatee in homophony – are each buried in the motet by either the intervening tenor or the scattered positioning of syllables (Appendix A, mm. 33–6 and mm. 66–87).

Music historians have traditionally pointed to sensitive text setting as a hallmark of Renaissance music, a commonly "essentialized" attribute rehearsed in textbooks. Recent work, however, has suggested that the idea may be an anachronism, or perhaps a trait that should be applied to vernacular texts in a different literary register.[21] Although several clarion "syntactic" moments for St. Anne emerge, in which a composer obviously intends to have the listener take note of the text, this technique was by no means a universal urge among composers, especially those of the later fifteenth century (if *Theodoce matrem/Firma fide fidens* indeed dates from that time). Surviving in singers' partbooks, the music's functional nature is evident; it was to be heard at a court chapel and (lacking a deluxe format) was probably not seen in score by patrons. All the more demands for text comprehensibility in performance, it would seem. Unless somehow rigorously studied by its dedicatee, the richness of the texts for St. Anne, from her illustrious lineage to her unlikely maternity wrought by faith, would be lost to the ephemeral soundscape. Though topically concordant with the motet politicking already seen, this unpolished creation is the most likely of the "Anne group" to have the thrust of its text go unnoticed when realized in performance.

Ave mater matris Dei

The fourth member of the "Anne group" is *Ave mater matris Dei*, the shortest of the five Anne motets in the Palatini partbooks. Another overlooked motet suffering from anonymity, it has gone unrecognized that the work also appears in a 1534 print of four- and five-voice motets published by illustrious French printer Pierre Attaingnant, where it is one of eight anonymous motets in the collection.[22] The text of *Ave mater matris Dei* was set by at least four other composers of the sixteenth century, including Nicolas Gombert and Orlande de Lassus.[23] Peter Bergquist, the editor of Lassus's setting of this text, has speculated that the rhymed poetry appears to derive from a stanza of an unidentified hymn or sequence melody for St. Anne.[24] It turns out that the complete text of the motet *Ave mater matris Dei* instead can be traced to a first-mode office antiphon for St. Anne, though no known melodies associated with this antiphon resemble the motet's tenor.[25] Set in trochaic tetrameter, the rhymed poetry reveals little about Mary's mother beyond her role as a faithful intermediary between the sinner and God or Christ. Silent on the saint's decades of infertility or magnificent ancestry, the text of the motet attributes one key trait to the *Mater matris*: she is "fertile with offspring" (*prole fecundata*), a point addressed later.

Ave mater matris Dei	Hail, mother of the mother of God,
Per quam salvi fiunt rei.	through whom sinners are saved.
Ave prole fecundata	Hail, fertile with offspring,
Anna Deo dedicata	Anne dedicated to God
Pro fideli plebe tota	for the faithful people, may you be
Apud Christum sis devota.	fully devoted before Christ.
Amen.	Amen.

The musical setting of this antiphon text in the F-mode presents a more compressed range than that seen in the forgoing "Anne" motets. The highest-sounding voice (superius) of *Ave mater matris Dei* uses the C4 clef, which puts the compass of this part squarely in the "tenor" range and permits it to intermingle freely with the other voices (altus and tenor) also set in the vocal compass of a modern-day tenor.[26] The motet begins in sprightly imitative counterpoint with a motivic outline (f-g-f...b♭-a) quite similar to that of Mouton's *Celeste beneficium* (c-d-c-f'), which is incidentally the motet that follows it in the Palatini partbooks. The former motet ends in imitative contrapuntal fashion with all parts declaiming the text *apud Christum sis devota*, sonically multiplying the supplicant's plea to St. Anne.

Not unlike other motets in the "Anne group," the unnamed composer draws particular attention to certain words through deliberately homophonic presentation, accompanied by a change of mensuration (Example 6.2). The harmonious declamation of text, reflective of the "syntactic" style, comes into view just before the change of meter at the word *fecundata* (mm. 36–8). Immediately following this plainly set word, the name *Anna* is further marked for aural attention: the bassus descends to its lowest note of the motet (E♭), and the stark phrase is repeated for emphasis, separated by rests. The composer's sleight of hand artificially joins the words *fecundata* and *Anna* ("fertile Anne") for the listener, as the former duple meter winds down (mm. 36–42). This juxtaposition seems to call attention to the saint's direct association with the production of flesh. The name *Anna* technically occurs only once in the text of the antiphon, but the anonymous composer delivers it four times – twice in arresting isolation between mm. 39–42 and then twice again, as part of the phrase *Anna deo dedicata* in m. 43 and m. 47.

The similarity of the opening motive between *Ave mater* and *Celeste beneficium* has already been mentioned, but the twin pronouncements of the name *Anna* in mm. 39–42 likewise have a striking relationship to the triple calls to St. Anne in Mouton's motet, the next and final member of the "Anne group" in the partbooks. Yet more evidence links the two contiguous motets. Both operate within an F tonality, and the supplications issued in the top voices remarkably mirror one another (c-a in *Ave mater* [mm. 39–40] and a'-c' in *Celeste beneficium* [mm. 59–61]). When one considers the fact that both motets also paraphrase an office antiphon for the feast of St. Anne, it is no stretch to say that these two contiguous motets in the Palatini partbooks may be in dialogue with each other. Indeed, they could be heard in succession without an interruption in tonality and may be considered to some extent a scribal or compositional "pair." These points of musical correlation between *Ave mater* and *Celeste beneficium* are striking and provide an additional unifying element within the already cohesive "Anne group."

Example 6.2 Anonymous, *Ave mater matris Dei*, mm. 36–57.

With an unusually high level of agreement between these two motets, one is tempted to connect *Ave mater matris Dei* – and possibly more anonymous motets of the "Anne group" – to the French court culture of the first or second decade of the sixteenth century, during Mouton's tenure. The rather pedestrian treatment of the four-voice polyphonic texture overall would seem to discourage ascription of *Ave mater* directly to Mouton, better known for his technical skill with the polyphonic style. The triple-metered section shown earlier, however, might give some pause whether to discard Mouton so quickly as a possible composer. One might expect that this brief homophonic section would create syntactic clarity in polyphonic form; instead, the composer of *Ave mater matris Dei* offers an awkward pattern of accentuation. The declamatory distortion again raises the question of whether text expressivity is a viable compositional end in early sixteenth-century polyphony. Interestingly, however, this kind of clumsy word declamation has been noticed in several of Mouton's motets, though not in *Celeste beneficium*.[27] Could Mouton have written this motet? While it is probably wise to avoid any firm attribution by style alone, further codicological evidence suggests that the first member of the "Anne group" (*Anna matrona nobilis*) might also be the work of Mouton.

It was mentioned in the discussion of *Anna matrona nobilis* that the clarion homophonic sections, copious duets, and points of imitation were properties of the motet cultivated at the French court during the time of Mouton and his immediate successors. A cursory survey of the partbooks' organization reveals that Mouton should receive additional consideration as the author of *Anna matrona nobilis* because of the conspicuous position of this motet in the manuscript. As Kellman noted, the manuscript falls into four major sections, which together may have symbolic meaning in light of St. Anne at the head of the partbooks, a point examined later.[28] As if to emphasize the sectionalization of the manuscript, the compiler or owner tabbed each section with a colored bead that protrudes from the book's' edge. The motet at the beginning of each marked section of the partbooks contains an intricate and magnificently colored border in Ghent-Bruges style (Figure 6.2). Outside of a coat of arms located on fol. 2v of each partbook and occasional red calligraphic initials, no other decorations exist in the manuscript.[29] Therefore, only four of the thirty-eight motets receive this kind of visual enhancement in the partbooks: *Anna matrona nobilis*, *Ave fuit prima salus*, *Delicta iuventutis*, and *Non nobis Domine*. All except *Anna matrona nobilis* are securely attributed to Jean Mouton. It seems quite possible that Petrus Alamire could have inaugurated each section opening with a motet by Mouton. After all, he is the composer who already dominates the motet collection with at least seven firmly attributed works. Given the stylistic connections to the French chapel circles in the early sixteenth century, a tentative ascription of *Anna matrona nobilis* (and potentially *Ave mater matris Dei*) to Mouton is not an unreasonable proposal.

The motets in the "Anne group" and their collective vestiges of French musical style having been scrutinized, the lens can now be widened with regard to these works, and the issues of audience and agency with the Palatini partbooks

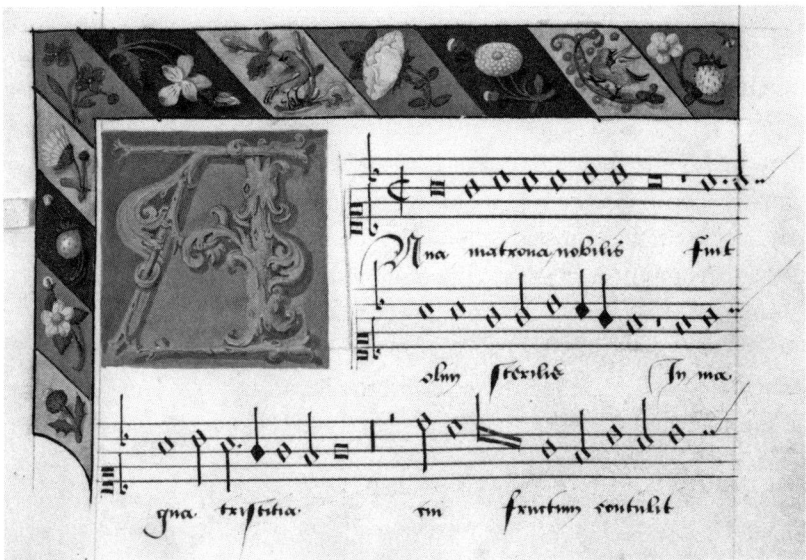

Figure 6.2 Anonymous, *Anna matrona nobilis*, opening of superius partbook. Vatican City, Biblioteca Apostolica Vaticana, MSS Palatini Latini 1976, fol. 5v. © 2013 Biblioteca Apostolica Vaticana.

can be broached. As noted, the "Anne" motets constitute the first major section of the manuscript and range from occasional music (i.e., *Transit Anna timor*, adjusted for a new recipient) to works containing special pleas to the saint and hailing the value of maternity (*Anna matrona nobilis*, *Ave mater matris Dei*, and *Celeste beneficium*). Even the most stylistically dissimilar and likely the most chronologically removed member of the group (*Theodoce matrem/Firma fide*) has a message for the careful listener, one that endows Mary's mother with royal heritage and celebrates the improbability of an elderly woman's womb swelling "with excitement." In search of a context for these motets, it is now time to take stock of the political environment into which these works for Anne were received, as well as other events concurrent with the arrival of the Palatini partbooks at the Austrian Habsburg court in Vienna.

"Let Others Wage War … " Revisited

As revealed in the table of contents and in emendations to various motets, the Palatini partbooks were expressly prepared for Anna, Queen of Bohemia and Hungary and, by association, her husband, Ferdinand I. Though it is possible that these Central European monarchs requested the books from the Alamire workshop, it is more likely that a Habsburg sent them to the royal couple as a gift. Little has been written about the situation "on the ground" in Central Europe in conjunction with the arrival of the partbooks between 1528 and 1534, a time in which Ferdinand had been invested with full control of the kingdoms of Bohemia and Hungary to add to the Austrian hereditary lands that he had acquired earlier. It is amidst these conditions that a context for emphasis on Mary's mother can be proposed, one that reaches beyond the name of the queen. The story begins as many Habsburg ventures do – in a strategically arranged dynastic marriage alliance, an area in which St. Anne had great oversight.

The union of the Castilian-born Habsburg Ferdinand and Anna Jagiellon was part of a double marriage agreement struck by none other than Maximilian I, who embodied the house motto "Let others wage war, but you, O blessed Austria, marry!" As with all of his dealings and arrangements, Maximilian aggressively sought to perpetuate the sovereignty of the House of Austria. At the first Vienna Congress of 1515, he concluded his final set of constructive marriage compacts with the Jagiellonian King Vladislaus II of Hungary and Bohemia (r. 1490–1516), with the hope of establishing firm control on the eastern reaches of the empire, a crucial territory for the Holy Roman Empire over the next four centuries. Maximilian was deeply concerned with the westward ambitions of the Jagiellonian kingdom of Poland. Moreover, French negotiations to form an alliance with Poland drove the emperor to explore an association with the rather weak king of Bohemia and Hungary. A coalition between the Jagiellonians and the Habsburgs would halt the much-despised French from surrounding them on all sides in Danubian Europe.[30]

In an effort to protect the core territory of Central Europe, Maximilian arranged for two of his grandchildren, Archduchess Marie and the Habsburg prince Ferdinand, to marry the two children of Vladislaus II – Louis and Anna Jagiellon, respectively. Despite the assumed political advantages of the double alliance for the Austrian monarchy, the agreement was also something of a gamble on the part of the Habsburg and Jagiellonian houses. In effect, the dynasty that survived would inherit the patrimony of the other. Vladislaus II died in 1516, and Louis ascended the throne of Bohemia and Hungary at age ten, the upper hand seeming to favor the Jagiellonian house. By 1522, both couples were formally married, and, in that same year, Charles V assigned his brother the hereditary lands, which included Austria, the Tyrol (and its mines), and modern-day Slovenia, via the Treaty of Brussels. Ferdinand and Anna – shown in Figure 6.3 in a portrait by Jan Cornelisz Vermeyen – were designated Archduke and Archduchess of

Figure 6.3 Jan Cornelisz Vermeyen, Emperor Ferdinand I and Anna of Hungary, after 1531. Innsbruck, Tyrolean State Museum Ferdinandeum, inv. no. Gem 114 and Gem 115; © Tyrolean States Museums, Innsbruck.

Austria.³¹ Within a few years, the Habsburgs would gain more ground in Central Europe, as a fluid series of events changed the political landscape in 1526. In late August of that year, Ottoman sultan Suleiman the Magnificent launched a major offensive into the region. Louis's forces of some twenty thousand were no match for the sultan's army, which penetrated the southwest Hungarian border and advanced into the area of Transdanubia. A major battle was fought on the marshy lands of Mohács, on the right bank of the Danube; Louis's forces were crushed in a matter of hours. As the king fled the battlefield, his horse toppled and the king drowned on the spot.³²

Louis having died without children, questions about his successor in Bohemia and Hungary temporarily hung in the balance. In the Bohemian estates, Ferdinand was perceived as faithful to the Jagiellonian dynasty, given his status as brother in-law and son-in-law of two Jagiellonian kings. This was enough to win unanimous election by the estates just two months after the fateful Battle of Mohács. He was subsequently crowned king of Bohemia in February 1527. Ascending the throne of Hungary required more effort, however. Though Ferdinand and Anna could claim the throne by reason of birthright of the latter and support from the Treaty of Brussels, a select diet of nobles conferred the Hungarian crown on John Zapolya in November 1526. Zapolya was a wealthy governor (*voivode*) of the eastern region of Transylvania and would be a constant thorn in the side of the Austrian Habsburgs for the next decade. Within a few weeks of the voivode's coronation, Louis's widow (and Ferdinand's sister), Marie, hastily convened another diet of nobles in Pozsony, now representing western portions of Hungary. This diet proclaimed Ferdinand king of Hungary, which put the two claimants to the throne on a crash course.

In August 1527, one of Ferdinand's commanders drove Zapolya back in northeast Hungary at Tokaj. Ferdinand was again declared the kingdom's monarch, and the Habsburg victor was crowned in November 1527 in the city of Székesfehérvár. The king's sister Marie remained with the new king and queen for a few years, but was then assigned a position as regent of the Netherlands in 1531, following the death of Margaret of Austria. That same year, Ferdinand was elected King of the Romans, making him the putative successor to his brother Charles (the Holy Roman Emperor). The emperorship would indeed materialize for Ferdinand, though more than a generation later (1558). Nevertheless, Ferdinand was in a position before 1530 to become one of the most influential of the Habsburgs and a critical figure in the Reformation politics of Central Europe.

Like so many manuscripts from the Alamire workshop, the Palatini partbooks leave no trace of the circumstances of their compilation and delivery to the court of Anna and Ferdinand. No records survive from either the Vienna court chapel of the Austrian Habsburgs or the Stephansdom (St. Stephen's Cathedral, Vienna's principal landmark) during the years in which the Palatini partbooks arrived. What is known is that Arnold von Bruck held the position of court Kapellmeister beginning in mid-1527. He succeeded Heinrich Finck, who, at age eighty-two, died just six months into his appointment by Ferdinand. Employed as a boy chorister in the Habsburg chapel of Charles V until 1519, Bruck was given charge of Ferdinand's chapel until his retirement at the end of 1545.[33] While he is best known for his sacred and secular German lieder, he would have been well acquainted with the polyphonic style of the "Josquin generation." His reworking of a four-voice motet by Antoine de Févin (*Sancta Trinitas*) for six voices marks Bruck's direct interaction with the French court repertory, the very repertory that dominates the Palatini partbooks.[34]

Additional considerations can improve the current understanding of these partbooks received after Ferdinand secured the Bohemian and Hungarian monarchies (late 1527) but before the year of Petrus Alamire's retirement (1534). The sociocultural conditions of the court can help establish a context for the reception of the partbooks in general and the St. Anne music in particular. As in the cases of Anne of Cyprus and Anne of Brittany, there is almost certainly more to the picture than viewing the preponderance of music for St. Anne as a reflection of the name of the queen. Habsburg historians will be quick to note the "problem" of the Turks and the spread of Reformation thought in Central Europe as key issues during the time in question; a closer analysis of the inner circle at the sovereign court, however, suggests an appropriate and familiar place for Mary's mother as a symbolic custodian of Habsburg posterity, especially of the children born to Anna and Ferdinand by the end of the third decade of the sixteenth century. Light will also be thrown on St. Anne's connection to Erasmus, the Christian humanist philosopher highly esteemed by the Austrian Habsburgs.

A Biography in Music?

Herbert Kellman proposed the arrival of the Palatini partbooks between the years 1531 and 1532. This hypothesis is based on a close reading of select motet texts, which represent, in his words, a "little chronicle of significant events in the lives of Anna and Ferdinand in the years 1526–31." Kellman traced the posited biography with clues from the texts of six motets scattered across the partbooks. The works that Kellman found most telling have received little or no attention on the whole and deserve scrutiny here. For Kellman, a subgroup of three motets potentially revealing clues to the impetus for the partbooks revolves around the subject of war, particularly the anxiety that surrounds it and the dire outcomes it produces. Pierre de La Rue's *Delicta iuventutis* (fols. 44v–47v, the fourteenth motet in the Palatini partbooks), originally marking the untimely death of Philip the Fair, may be understood, according to Kellman, as a commemoration of Louis II, who died on the Mohács battlefield in 1526. In an oblique way, Agricola's *Transit Anna timor*, together with Jean Richafort's *Exaudiat te dominus* (fols. 53v–57v, the seventeenth motet of the Palatini partbooks), may also register a plea for Ferdinand's safety as he waged war with the Ottoman sultan.[35]

Considering that the Ottoman attack of 1526 predated the partbooks, the concerns about war expressed in the two motets might have centered on the movement of the Turks through Hungary, culminating in the Siege of Vienna of 1529. John Zapolya, the aforementioned claimant to the Hungarian throne, continued to threaten annexation of parts of the kingdom based on a treatise signed in the late fifteenth century.[36] In January 1528, Zapolya entered into an alliance with the feared sultan Suleiman and was actively conspiring with the French monarch Francis I. Ferdinand quickly organized a delegation to meet with Ottoman representatives, but his weak efforts toward a diplomatic solution failed. The Habsburg king pleaded with several allies for troops, as his Hungarian kingdom braced for an imminent attack. Charles V and Margaret of Austria were not first in line to pledge support, as they regarded the anti-Turk strategy as a nuisance on the periphery of the empire. Suleiman's forces advanced in 1529, and Ferdinand brought the urgency of the matter to the Diet of Speier, a meeting of Catholic and Protestant princes and dignitaries in that same year. Representatives of the diet heeded the pressing call for action and promised some sixteen thousand troops to Ferdinand. Casting the impending battle as a defense of "Jerusalem," the king issued a special appeal to Pope Clement VII for support. Ottoman forces moved into Budapest by July 1529 and had penetrated Vienna two months later. By that time, however, Suleiman's army was depleted and supplies were running short. The sultan's military was further unprepared for the harsh weather conditions in the north. Suleiman ordered a retreat by October 1529.[37] By no means a decisive defeat by the imperial forces, the small victory was a credit to Ferdinand, though he and his commanders had every reason to think that future battles were in the kingdom's future. If one is to read the "war" motets closely, the explicit plea of the "Hungarians" (named in *Transit Anna timor*) in particular could call attention to a time around the middle of 1529, when that territory was under attack and Ferdinand rushed for a solution. Of course, Agricola's motet was written for very different circumstances and the text of *Transit Anna timor* was also copied in a slipshod manner.

Kellman's appraisal of key motets in the Palatini partbooks with an eye toward biography continues with French composer Mathieu Gascongne's *Christus vincit, Christus regnat, Christus imperat*, the motet that directly follows the "Anne group." It is a rare polyphonic setting of the opening of the royal acclamations known as the *laudes regiae*, a tradition used for more than five centuries at French coronations.[38] The praises issued in Gascongne's motet, including a small litany to select saints (though not Anne), might have originally been composed for the crowning of Francis I, whom the composer probably served around 1515.[39] Gascongne's motet in the Palatini partbooks, according to Kellman, signals Ferdinand's acquisition of three prestigious crowns between 1527 and 1531.[40] While the monarchies in Bohemia and Hungary were important achievements for the archduke, the election to the title of King of the Romans in 1531 was indeed far more impressive from the larger Habsburg perspective, effectively making Ferdinand the heir apparent to the Holy Roman Emperor.

Ferdinand's election to rule over the German estates could not have happened until his brother was crowned Holy Roman Emperor at the hands of Clement VII, an event which did not take place until 1530 in Bologna, following the Habsburg victory over the French in Italy. Charles's coronation was a necessary but insufficient step toward Ferdinand's appointment to imperial successor by the German electors, who were skeptical, at least in the mid-1520s, of setting a precedent for what appeared to be imperial dynastic succession. By 1530, however, Ferdinand's handling of the Turkish threat along with his acquisition of the crowns of Hungary and Bohemia began to sway the regional princes toward his goal of securing the role of imperial heir apparent.[41] The Lutheran electors – Elector John of Saxony, Landgrave Philip of Hesse, and Duke Ernst of Lüneberg – would prove the most difficult to persuade, but Charles, more actively campaigning for his brother's candidacy, successfully made the case for Ferdinand's deserved promotion at the Diet of Augsburg in mid-1530.[42]

The September recess of the otherwise disastrous Augsburg diet united Protestants, but the sweeping religious reform movement oddly could not stand in the way of the German electors, whom Charles called to Cologne in January 1531 to approve the election of his brother to the role of second in command. The elector of Saxony and successor to Frederick the Wise, John the Constant, along with the dukes of Bavaria, avoided the summons to Cologne in protest of Ferdinand's proposed election, but the attending college unanimously authorized the appointment, citing the precedent of Frederick III's promotion of Maximilian to this same position. With no small hint of corruption in the lobbying process, the Habsburgs borrowed in excess of three hundred fifty thousand *gulden* from the Fuggers in Augsburg (themselves recipients of Alamire partbooks) to line the pockets and secure the votes of any waffling electors. With the exception of John of Saxony, all electors would come to support Ferdinand's candidacy.[43] Ferdinand was crowned in Aachen – the last coronation in that city – just six days after the election. In many Protestant municipalities (and even some Catholic ones), the swift act of the electoral college gave the appearance of the imperial throne as hereditary and was treated with suspicion. Within a month, a half dozen Protestant princes and ten cities established the Schmalkaldic League (*Schmalkaldischer Bund*) to counter the Habsburg efforts to consolidate power.

To return to Gascongne's *Christus vincit*, it is certainly possible that this motet was recycled to commemorate the "triple crown" honors that Ferdinand achieved by 1531, but it is also conceivable that the motet could have simply celebrated the acquisition of the first two crowns (Bohemia and Hungary), which Ferdinand had won by the end of 1527. If Gascongne's motet was originally written and performed in the context of the French monarch's (single) coronation, then a third crown for Ferdinand was obviously not an essential condition for this piece to be placed in the Palatini partbooks. In the latter scenario, one might expect the words *Rex romanorum* ("King of the Romans") to be interpolated somewhere in the motet or elsewhere in the partbooks. To be sure, there is direct mention of Francis I in Gascongne's original motet, ripe for alteration in the Palatini partbooks, as in *Transit Anna*. The scribes did not enter the name "Francisco" where it fell in the motet but simply left the word out, disrupting the syntax and meaning of the sentence that begins to deify the king (*Exaudi Christe,* [*ut clero Francisco*] *serenissimo et a deo coronato …*). The effect instead produces an awkward moment of wordless music in the motet.[44]

The royal acclamation inherent within *Christus vincit* unquestionably lends a majestic air to the opening thrust of the collection, but the impact of the preceding "Anne group" deserves at least as much attention. While it is true that dynastic succession was in the purview of St. Anne's intercessory capabilities, it is unclear nevertheless whether *Christus vincit* implied (1) Ferdinand's 1531 election to the role of heir apparent, (2) the "promise" of Ferdinand's election to King of the Romans (pre-1531), or merely (3) the acquisition of the Bohemian and Hungarian crowns of 1527. When one considers the Palatini partbooks through the lens of the "Anne group," new considerations emerge that may narrow the circumstances of the reception of the musical collection.

A Place for St. Anne

A final "biographical" observation Kellman made concerning the partbooks has gone unchecked and needs revision. Not unrelated to the notion of dynastic succession, it concerns the hope of offspring and therefore impinges on territory closer to St. Anne. Kellman points out that Jean Mouton's *Non nobis Domine* – the twenty-fourth motet in the partbooks (fols. 75v–78r) – directly suggests the hope for a son with its ending *da filium nobilem* ("grant a noble son"). This motet was mentioned in Chapter 5 in the context of the French court of Anne of Brittany and Louis XII as a commemorative work for the 1510 birth of Renée, the second of the surviving daughters of Anne of Brittany and Louis XII. While one reference to St. René (French patron saint of male offspring) is maintained in *Non nobis Domine* in the Palatini partbooks, another potential allusion is altered to avoid mention of that saint: *O regnate* [formerly *Renate*], *parens regni* ("Rule [?], parent of the kingdom"). Louis's name does not appear in the supplication *Audi preces* [*Ludovici*], nor do the names of Ferdinand and Anna. This is a clue to the nonparallel circumstances of the Habsburg monarch compared to those of the French from two decades earlier. The omissions and attempted revisions also foreground the presence of the Alamire workshop in the assembly process, an operation that occasionally took diplomatic missteps as seen earlier in *Transit Anna timor*.

Kellman further notes that the presence of *Adjutorium nostrum*, though separated from its erstwhile *prima pars*, may also hint at Anna and Ferdinand's hope for a male successor. It has been overlooked, however, that the words "Renate" and "Ludovicus" in *Adjutorium nostrum* were eliminated in all voice parts, producing the following: *Tam beate, tam beate, clamat ad te* (formerly: *O Renate, tam beate, Ludovicus clamat ad te*). This revision borders on nonsense with the removal of the subject "Ludovicus" (and no Habsburg replacement), similar to Mouton's *Non nobis Domine*. The gaping untexted space, occupying the place of "Ludovicus," produces an unusual musical effect in context. The scribe was clearly attuned to the text of *Adjutorium nostrum* and evidently went to some length in the motet to avoid the citation of St. René as well as mention of the French king. It was not unconventional to alter the personages named in political motets, but the scribe's unwillingness to supplant the name of Louis XII with references to Ferdinand and Anna further shines a light on the partial bungling of the compilation at the scriptorium.

In his argument concerning the impetus for the "biographical" motets in the partbooks, Kellman notes that the birth of a second daughter to Anna and Ferdinand in 1528 may mirror the French court's commemoration of Renée's birth, the second daughter of Anne of Brittany, as communicated in *Non nobis Domine*. Queen Anna of Bohemia and Hungary had two daughters, and each extended the family's dominion through matrimonial alliances. The queen bore her first daughter, Elizabeth, in July 1526 (who would eventually marry the king of Poland, Sigismund II Augustus). The queen's namesake and second born, Anna of Austria (b. July 1528), was engaged several times, finally wedding Duke Albert V of Bavaria in 1546. But Kellman's observations omit a critical detail: Anna had given birth to two sons by 1529, in addition to the two daughters he mentions. The Austrian Habsburgs in fact would produce fifteen children in total. Their first son, Maximilian II, came in 1527. He would marry his cousin Maria (Charles's daughter) and would rise to the Holy Roman emperorship in 1564. The birth of another son in 1529 (Ferdinand II) was further "insurance" for the Austrian branch, and this boy would assume only some of his father's titles.[45] In any event, fertility was hardly a problem for the Austrian Habsburgs in the late 1520s and onward.

Alluring as it is to witness biography in a half dozen motets scattered around the Palatini partbooks, the results generate confusion for the analyst in search of a date for this collection of motets. If Gascongne's *Christus vincit* marks Ferdinand's promotion to King of the Romans, this would put the arrival of the partbooks somewhere in the middle of 1531 or later, as Kellman has suggested. However, if the hope for a son (prompted by the recycled French motets) were the concern of the Austrian Habsburgs, one would have to place the date *before* the birth of Maximilian II in July 1527. The latter scenario is not tenable because Anna and Ferdinand are named as queen and king respectively in the Palatini partbooks, and this could not be said of them before the end of 1527. Looming combats or the consequences of war may also be suggested in the motets of La Rue (*Delicta iuventutis*) and Richafort (*Exaudiat te dominus*), but it is difficult to whittle down a period when the Ottoman Empire did not pose a threat to the Austrian Habsburgs.

The obvious lesson here is that not every motet in the Palatini partbooks can be read (and heard) as "topical," that is, with allegorical reference to the biography of the royal couple. Some of the evidence must weigh more heavily on the case than other potential clues. It remains possible, for instance, that Gascongne's *Christus vincit* motet did not refer to the election of Ferdinand as King of the Romans, thus allowing the partbooks to be dated earlier than 1531. Kellman's claim of a "little chronicle of significant events" therefore becomes problematic when the analysis privileges certain motets. Even with an allegorical eye toward selected motets, one is no closer to determining the dates of the partbooks; they must be after 1527 for the king and queen to be named and before the retirement of Petrus Alamire in 1534. Kellman's inclination to date the partbooks between 1531–2 favors the evidence of Gascongne's motet in the aftermath of Ferdinand's 1531 election and forces the author to posit the idea of a biographical summary for the other motets that may point to an earlier period.

As seen in Table 6.1, *Christus vincit* is the seventh motet of the collection, preceded by the handful of motets constituting the "Anne group." Addressing these five motets as a whole would seem the most logical step in assessing the repertory presented in the partbooks. But how can this motet grouping be understood? Not unlike Kellman's six selected "biographical" motets, the motets of the "Anne group" can be cryptic when viewed individually, with no clear allusions to the biography of either Anna or Ferdinand. One might start with Agricola's *Transit Anna timor*, because it is both one of Kellman's biographical motets and a member of the "Anne group." Kellman pegged this motet to a time of war, but the Habsburgs fought major battles in 1527, 1529, and 1533, in no way restricting the possibilities for understanding this motet as topically motivated. The retention of the text concerning Claude of France and the illness of the monarch in the music further clouds any biographical connection. As mentioned earlier, Agricola's motet is the outlier of the "Anne group" for not treating St. Anne directly. The original "Anne" clearly referenced Anne of Brittany and was evidently meant to stand for Anna Jagiellon in this case. Still, analysis of the contiguously assembled "Anne group" requires a less selective approach than Kellman's methodology, and the texts may combine to offer a message for the Austrian Habsburgs.

If producing offspring (even a son) was not an issue for Anna and Ferdinand by 1528, it is likely that the "Anne group" stood for something quite beyond a prayer to Mary's mother for fertility intervention. The year 1528 was when Anna bore her second daughter, Anna of Austria, thereby highlighting the importance of the name at the outset of the partbooks.[46] But the naming of Anna is just one of many details transmitted in the group of motets for St. Anne. In the absence of a smoking gun to explain the appearance of these partbooks and repertory as a whole, at least one can still ask what other biographical or allegorical messages are suggested in the "Anne group" of motets. Who is sending such messages and why did the donor or compiler of the partbooks open with this set of motets, mainly for Mary's mother? And how might the "Anne group" have been understood by Anna Jagiellon (or Ferdinand) at court? Apart from the oddity of Agricola's motet, a synthesized view of the "Anne group" may offer some insight on these pressing questions.

Recall that *Anna matrona nobilis*, at one time the opening motet of the entire partbook collection, altered the title of a sequence to project the name "Anna" at the outset as an expressly noble mother. The anonymous composer also took the unusual step of emphasizing a threefold declamation of the fourth stanza (*Testamento veteri, Anna fuit genita et de stirpe regia*), which functions as a mantra highlighting at once the ancient and royal heritage of the mother. It is hard not to hear this refrain as an allegory for the Habsburg matron Anna and (if after 1528) her daughter of the same name. Three of the four voices of *Theodoce matrem* likewise connect St. Anne with precious regal and biblical roots (*sacerdos tuum series et filia regum*).

The tenor of the anonymous *Theodoce matrem*, however, presents the notion that "the womb of the aged Anne now swells" (*cum presertim Anne annus iam tumescit uterus*). The use of the tenor cantus firmus in *Theodoce matrem* has already been noted for its rarity in a four-voice setting, but the present tense of this governing idea ("now swells") is further striking in the motet. Of course, there is no sense in understanding Anna Jagiellon as "aged," but the fruitful one-per-year rate at which she bore children between 1526 and 1529 suggests that her womb was consistently "swollen." Similarly, the following motet *Ave mater matris Dei* says nothing about the infertility from the legend of St. Anne, but rather focuses on Mary's mother as "fertile with offspring" (*fecundata prole*). The text of the final member of the "Anne group" – Mouton's *Celeste beneficium* – puts the suggestion of childbirth in the past tense; the "divine favor" had already "entered into Anne" (*Celeste beneficium introivit in Annam*). In short, the "present-ness" – and "past-ness" – of these sentiments may hint at the successful maternity of Queen Anna of Bohemia and Hungary, even though it would have acted as a wish for Anne of Brittany.

If a biography was couched in these devotional works, it was not the biography of a woman who needed help conceiving children. If not reflective of Anna's own prayers to St. Anne, the hope of the patron of the Palatini partbooks – no doubt a Habsburg – would have been for the health of the children born to the queen after 1526 and the potential for more heirs in the years ahead. As is apparent throughout this study, such aspirations have a political hue as well: healthy and copious progeny were means to an end, especially for a ruling house that let others wage war while its leaders arranged matrimonial pacts for the family's offspring. Just as St. Anne was chosen to bear the magnificent Virgin, who in turn splendidly gave birth to Christ, so one can understand the "Anne group" as bolstering the case for Anna Jagiellon as "chosen" to perpetuate the illustrious stock of the Austrian Habsburgs. With the music for St. Anne assuming pride of place in the Palatini partbooks, these works might be viewed as a kind of affirmation, even a gesture of thanksgiving, for the progeny of Anna and Ferdinand. It would be perfectly reasonable to place these manuscripts not long after the 1527 coronation, perhaps after the birth of Anna of Austria (July 1528) or following the Ottoman retreat of October 1529. The latter date in particular was a time when momentum was turning toward Ferdinand and the Habsburgs on the whole. The king's temporary suppression of the Turkish threat and his acquisition of two crowns were key steps that paved the way to the role of imperial heir apparent. If Gascongne's "coronation" motet is not to be read as applying to three crowns, there is no reason to push the arrival of the manuscripts toward 1532 to accommodate the extent of the biography that might have been projected in the array of motets.

As with so many manuscripts from the Alamire workshop, it is unclear who was behind the request to compile these works into a musical collection. The culture of gift giving in premodern times that Rob Wegman has outlined might suggest that the requisition for these books was probably not made by Ferdinand and Anna but possibly another Habsburg, one with interest in the welfare of the Austrian branch of the dynasty.[47] Kellman has suggested that Ferdinand's sister Marie of Hungary might have requested the partbooks as a gift. Before she assumed the regency of the Netherlands in 1531 following the death of her aunt Margaret of Austria, Marie lived with her brother and Anna after her husband Louis's death in 1526. In July 1542, she was tapped by Ferdinand to recommend a qualified individual to assist Arnold von Bruck with his duties in the Viennese court chapel.[48] Though there is little circumstantial evidence other than this to advance Marie's potential sponsorship of the Palatini partbooks, she would have had the unique vantage point to call for an arrangement of pieces fit for her sister-in-law Anna Jagiellon, with whom she shared the title "Queen of Hungary," precisely the title inscribed on the partbooks' register of pieces (*Registrum dive regine hungarie*).[49]

Marie's predecessor, Margaret of Austria, must also be strongly considered as a potential commissioner of the partbooks. This other regent of the Netherlands was quite close to the culture of manuscript production in connection with the Alamire scriptorium, and of course was well aware of the multivalent meanings that could be harvested from St. Anne. If Margaret supported the creation of the Palatini partbooks, her death in December 1530 provides a *terminus ante quem* for the request, a point consistent with the revised chronology suggested previously. What may tilt the scales in favor of Margaret-as-commissioner are her other artistic commissions directly involving the Austrian Habsburg branch just before her death. As will be remembered from Chapter 3, Margaret was keenly interested in promoting her Burgundian ducal heritage with selected portraits displayed in the *première chambre* of her Mechelen court. Probably following the death of her father and the election of Charles as Holy Roman Emperor in 1519, the regent seems to have warmed up to the value of her Habsburg lineage. Toward the end of her life, Margaret was quite insistent on collecting portraiture of the imperial family, especially the members of Anna and Ferdinand's house. In the middle of 1530, she sent painter Jan Cornelisz Vermeyen to the Diet of Augsburg, asking him to produce at least nineteen portraits, many of which were made of Ferdinand, Anna, and their four children (few survive, unfortunately).[50] Perhaps it was the ever-savvy regent of the Netherlands who, around the same time or even earlier, desired a set of partbooks for the queen of Bohemia and Hungary highlighting works for St. Anne, custodian of royal families.

A broader question Kellman posed may be addressed briefly: What of the prevalence of somewhat outdated French repertory in the Palatini partbooks? There is no question that Ferdinand and Charles had no greater enemy than the French monarch Francis I. This fact was especially true in light of the discussions in 1528 concerning a French alliance with the Hungarian archrival John Zapolya. How could repertory of this nature be tolerated? First, it should be said that works by composers who operated in France (many in the royal chapel) were very much viable candidates for inclusion in Alamire manuscripts. Mouton was foremost among a half dozen composers who have multiple works in the various creations of the Habsburg scriptorium.[51] Indeed, this influx of French composers supplemented the exclusively Netherlandish works that characterized the beginning stages of Alamire output.[52] The scribe's atelier was a major contributor to the spread of an elite musical repertory; its activities helped transform the landscape of the literate musical culture of Renaissance Europe. *Theodoce matrem* aside, the French style of the motet was no doubt en vogue, and the "Anne group" on the whole demonstrates the value of this style dominated by contrapuntal duets and "block" homophonic writing. Consider also that Alamire's dossier for "royal" motets in the early sixteenth century would almost exclusively point to the French monarch, the only "king" with a substantial stable of motet composers.

Even if Mouton and other French composers did not offend Habsburg sensibilities in principle, *Transit Anna timor* from the "Anne group" would seem to exceed the boundaries of acceptable music to be heard in a rival court. It is likely, however, that the garbled Latin in this motet, some of which was adjusted expressly for Ferdinand, might have been too much for a listener to unscramble. One might focus instead on the conscious attribution of *Transit Anna* to Agricola – strangely the only attribution made in the manuscript. Perhaps this motet was instead part of an effort to diffuse the contradiction of a French "biographical" motet in Habsburg hands. Having spent at least five years at Philip the Fair's Burgundian court, the otherwise itinerant Agricola was probably known to Ferdinand and Marie (though not to Anna Jagiellon) as one of "their" composers, no matter the extent of his previous activities in French royal circles. With all of the other controversial texts adjusted for Anna and Ferdinand, it seems that the Austrian Habsburgs turned a blind eye toward the French-ness of these motets, with the help of composers unnamed in the manuscripts and some attempts at scribal "diplomacy." In the realm of devotional music, the rivalry between the French and the Habsburgs was quelled, even imperceptible.

A Rosary of St. Anne and Erasmian Sympathy

One final issue remains to settle concerning the "Anne group" in the Palatini partbooks. In Kellman's survey of the collection, he wondered if the five Anne-focused motets formed a discrete devotional section akin to the organization of prayers in the recitation of the Rosary. He proposed the idea that Willaert's *Pater noster* and Gascongne's *Christus vincit* effectively framed the interior works for St. Anne. Together with other themed groupings in the partbooks, Kellman posited, the motet collection as a whole imitates the Rosary, specifically in what he called the "very popular contemporary genre of pseudo-Rosaries to St. Anne."[53] The observation is perceptive and provocative, but has also gone unexamined. Especially in this study whose exclusive focus is music for the mother of Mary, Kellman's assertion involving the "pseudo-Rosary of St. Anne" deserves close scrutiny.

It is true that in the context of the Rosary – a devotional phenomenon still developing at the turn of the sixteenth century – the *Pater noster* typically initiates a chain of devotions to the Blessed Virgin. As noted earlier, Willaert's *Pater noster* is missing its *secunda pars*, "Ave Maria," which would seem to bolster the case for a substitution of St. Anne in a Rosary-like configuration. No small part of devotion to St. Anne in the fifteenth and early sixteenth centuries was accomplished through the simple substitution of Anne's name for that of her daughter.[54] But the stubborn fact is that the "pseudo-Rosary of St. Anne" was hardly the pervasive phenomenon that Kellman has described. For example, a Rosary expressly in honor of Mary's mother receives no mention in Anne Winston-Allen's study of the development of the Rosary in the late Middle Ages, nor is the topic treated at any length (if at all) in the major studies of St. Anne. To be sure, however, the idea of a Rosary of St. Anne was not unheard of, just not widespread. Allusions to the Rosary transformed to commemorate the merits of Mary's mother occur almost exclusively in humanist circles of northern Europe, particularly in the Netherlands and the Rhineland. Jodocus Beisselius penned prayers constituting a *Rosarium de sancta Anna* within a larger devotional work dedicated to St. Anne, which was one of many devotional works and lives (*vitae*) produced for the burgeoning cult of that saint in the Rhineland.[55] Further, an artist associated with a group of Netherlandish illuminators known as the Masters of the Dark Eyes illustrated a prayer book that contains weekly devotional exercises, including a Rosary of St. Anne, nestled within a series of prayers to Mary's mother, Mary herself, and Christ.[56] It is not impossible that Margaret of Austria would have gotten wind of such devotions, but given the isolated nature of Rosary-type prayers to St. Anne, the deliberate arrangement of the Palatini partbooks in a configuration inspired by the Rosary seems to require an imaginative leap, at least in the absence of further evidence.

If there were aspects of Christian humanist devotion centered around St. Anne that resonated with the Austrian Habsburgs or the commissioner of the Palatini partbooks, one might instead point to Erasmus of Rotterdam, who not only had demonstrable ties to the court of Ferdinand and Anna, but who also greatly affected the monarch's thinking with regard to religious tolerance. As is well known, the Ottoman threat on the empire's borders was matched by internal political conflict on the question of Protestantism (Lutheranism in particular). Luther's theological tracts reached Vienna as early as 1520, and his teachings were readily accepted on the whole. The kingdom of Bohemia had also taken its distance from orthodoxy, dating back to the Hussite Wars of the early fifteenth century.[57] Religious hostilities abounded on a larger scale by the early-to-mid 1520s, and a 1526 convention at Speier gave Protestant princes temporary religious freedom under a moderate policy, later formalized in the law known as *cuius regio eius religio* ("whose the region, his the religion"). The aforementioned 1529 Diet of Speier reconsidered this policy. As Ferdinand brought together princes of the Catholic estates to confer on the matter, they established a Catholic league, which effectively revoked the concessions to Protestant princes and naturally escalated the tensions between Habsburg rule and the Lutheran-dominated territories. To add insult to injury, the influence of the religious reform movement also found sympathizers within the Habsburg court itself, most notably with the king's sister and widow of Louis II, Marie of Hungary. For all of his public affirmations of Catholicism, both Ferdinand and his brother Charles V were resigned to the competing religious forces at play, and they retained a surprisingly moderate *Religionspolitik* toward governing the situation. Ever practical rulers, the imperial Habsburgs were – at least by the late 1520s – reluctant defenders of the minority religion across Hungary, Bohemia, and the Austrian hereditary lands.[58]

The moderation Ferdinand showed in particular toward a confessionally divided Central Europe may be explained in part by his advocacy of reason and the humanistic fervor that suffused early sixteenth-century intellectual culture, particularly around the time that the Palatini partbooks arrived at the Habsburg court. Despite some of his actions, Ferdinand was never fanatical about the Roman Church, and he and his advisors recognized the benefits of dialogue between Catholics and Lutherans. Ferdinand was very much a subscriber to the positions of Erasmus, one of the early voices of religious tolerance.[59] Erasmus, it should be said, was already a Habsburg favorite, having served as a tutor for Charles V at the Mechelen court of Margaret of Austria. On the heels of the acquisition of the Hungarian and Bohemian crowns, Ferdinand invited Erasmus to pursue his scholarship at the University of Vienna in 1528, promising an annual salary of four hundred *florins*; the Low Countries humanist also received letters and gifts from Ferdinand, clear evidence of his admiration for the philosopher. Though flattered by the prestigious offer, Erasmus turned down the opportunity to relocate.[60]

Erasmus's absence did not mean his presence was not felt. Undeterred by the philosopher's rejection, Ferdinand proceeded to surround himself at his Austrian court with Christian humanists in the mold of Erasmus. These men were not always nobles by birth, but more often scholars committed to the faith and to moderate policies wrought through dialogue in the spirit of the esteemed philosopher.[61] Erasmus's writings also would have remained in circulation in the Habsburg domain. The philosopher in fact penned a poem in praise of St. Anne early in his career (ca. 1490–1), and it was later published as the first poem in the *Epigrammata* of 1518 (*Rhythmus iambicus in laudem Annae, aviae Iesu Christi*). In a letter accompanying the poem sent to his former patroness Anna van Borssele, Erasmus claimed that, from his earliest years, he "burned with eager devotion to that saint [St. Anne]," an attempt to elevate the subject of the poem beyond the namesake of his sponsor.[62] Ferdinand was a voracious reader of Erasmus and almost certainly encountered the *Epigrammata* and its opening poem to St. Anne. Through its rhythmical verses, Erasmus reminds his audience of the wide-ranging benefits of venerating Mary's mother, pointedly described as "the best of mothers" (*mater optima*). In addition to unfolding an encapsulated narrative of the apocryphal *Protoevangelium of James*, the Christian humanist emphasizes figures that are directly and indirectly associated with St. Anne, connecting her not only with her daughter and grandson (filial), but also with the barren mother exemplars of Sarah and Hannah (historical/allegorical). The themes of maternity and biblical heritage are of course also revealed in the "Anne group" of motets in the Palatini partbooks. It may be the case that Ferdinand (and Anna) "burned" with the same eager devotion expressed by the monarch's most favored philosopher, Erasmus.

To return to the succession of "Anne" motets between *Pater noster* and *Christus vincit* in the Palatini partbooks (Table 6.1), one detects a majestic or royalist sweep to the opening works that include the "Anne group." Despite its physical detachment from the "Anne group," the *Pater noster* provides a suitably broad introduction – a kind of "blessing" – to a collection of motets, not unlike a Marian motet would have been placed at the head of a chansonnier. Interestingly, Willaert's *Pater noster* was first in the order of motets in two additional collections from a later period.[63] The royal acclamation given in Gascongne's *Christus vincit* deifies an unnamed king and unashamedly equates him with Christ. In terms of sheer numbers, however, the "Anne group" accounts for the initial thrust of the Palatini partbooks, leaning as heavily as ever on the plasticity of the saint's intercessory powers.

The Austrian Habsburgs were especially familiar with the meanings associated with St. Anne. More than a decade prior to the arrival of the partbooks, Ferdinand and his brother were allegorized in a painting by Strigel as grandchildren within the Holy Kinship, the family of holy men and women over which St. Anne implicitly stood. The political role of the saint as supervisor of prodigious dynasties was thus always expected in the Habsburg artistic culture that invoked her. The more common understanding of the saint as a fertility aid, though certainly appealing in the case of Anne of Brittany, cannot be reasonably posited for the queen of Bohemia and Hungary, who was blessed with four children (two of them boys) by

1529. The birth of Anna of Austria in July 1528 to a woman named Anna must figure into any assessment of the arrival of the Palatini partbooks, but the deliberate assembly of an "Anne group" at the head of the partbooks may suggest something broader in court devotional life. Masters of matchmaking in the first half of the sixteenth century, the Habsburgs looked to St. Anne ("marrying saint" herself) to steward Ferdinand's healthy children for the benefit of the house through matrimonial coalitions. The humanists' interest in the grandmother saint probably provided further assurance for the ruling house. The political utility of St. Anne, manifold as ever, will be examined as the final chapter returns to French court circles to witness more music for St. Anne now in plainchant – a genre that hardly waned in the cultural soundscape of the nobility.

7 | The French Royal Trinity, Biblical Humanism, and Chanted Mass Propers for St. Anne

By now, St. Anne has been seen in just about all of her guises, politicized to one degree or another in the context of noble life. She has played a role not only as fertility specialist and matron extraordinaire, but also as protectress of noble dynasties. As an advocate for impressive progeny, Anne was of great value to some of the dominant entities of Western Europe in the advent of the Reformation, when saints lost some, though not all, of their staying power. The narrative now resumes with a return to the French court in the years following the reign of Louis XII and Anne of Brittany. Against the background of the new regime, the grandmother saint had considerable impact on the lives of Louise of Savoy and her two children, Marguerite and Francis, the latter ascending to the French throne in 1515. Louise is familiar to the reader from Chapter 3: following the death of her mother, Margaret of Bourbon in 1483, she and her younger brother Philibert were sent by the House of Savoy to the French court to be raised by Anne of France. Louise was also the one who callously celebrated the miscarriages of Anne of Brittany (Chapter 5), in hopes that her son Francis could ascend the throne.

As noted in Chapter 3, the image of St. Anne, despite its occasional appearance at the French court, would probably not have made much of an impression upon the young Louise and her brother during the years under Anne of France's supervision at the court's Amboise château. Nevertheless, St. Anne came to play a surprisingly central role in the politics of the kingdom after Francis inherited the realm from Louis XII. Louise, Francis, and Marguerite together formed a potent trio widely recognized as a "Royal Trinity," with all of its sacred connotations intact. The female-dominated triad calls to mind the image of the "St. Anne Trinitarian" that was popular in the Low Countries and in the Rhineland. During the second decade of the sixteenth century in France, however, the figure of St. Anne became one of the subjects of a raging debate between Christian biblical humanists and conservative theologians, a quarrel that impacted the kingdom in general and the court in particular.

The reform movement of biblical humanism was encountered in Chapter 6, mentioned in connection with Erasmus's moderate attitude toward the hostilities between Lutherans and Catholics, a position the Habsburgs embraced. The Christian humanist movement sought to question Catholic practices that were not expressly derived from scriptural texts and to resolve conflicts that arose from interpreting Scripture. In its French manifestation under Jacques Lefèvre d'Etaples, biblical humanism made a significant impression on the French court, ultimately dividing family loyalties in the 1530s. The earliest manifestations of that split occurred in the late 1510s and featured a debate about how St. Anne was to be venerated. After highlighting the members of the "Royal Trinity" and explaining the core arguments of the biblical humanists, this chapter examines a monophonic mass in honor of St. Anne dedicated to Marguerite, sister of the king and advocate of reform. This plainchant mass is found in the manuscript Bibliothèque nationale de France, MS fr. 1035 and consists of six notated Propers. It has hitherto received no attention from musicologists and only sparse commentary from historians in general. Because St. Anne was a pivotal figure whose legend Christian humanists reassessed in the early reign of Francis I, a full appraisal of these unassuming chants, their sources, and meanings is in order. The Propers on the subject of St. Anne that Marguerite received, in conjunction with the multifaceted introduction to the mass, confirm that the saint was so deeply ingrained in the court culture that she could act as a gateway for all kinds of personal and political ends. The author of the plainchant mass carefully avoided the theological controversy involving St. Anne and demonstrated instead that the saint could function not only as reassurance for a barren mother, but also as the preferred intercessor to bring hope and peace to the kingdom of France.

The Noble Angoulême Family and Its Rise to Power

Louise of Savoy departed the French court in 1487 at age eleven to marry Charles, Count of Angoulême in a political union arranged by Louis XI. The count was a first cousin of the future king Louis XII (then Duke of Orléans) and was next in line to the French throne. Charles fathered two illegitimate children with one of Louise's ladies-in-waiting (Antoinette de Polignac), with whom he had an open affair, but the official marriage produced Marguerite (b. 1492) and Francis (b. 1494), who would play a guiding role in the kingdom in the years to come.[1] Charles died in 1496, putting Francis on a direct path to the throne should Louis XII and Queen Anne of Brittany fail to have a male child. After Charles's death, the king, who was the closest male kin to the children, kept close watch over the heir apparent (as well as his mother and sister), ordering them to the château at Chinon under the evidently unpleasant supervision of the royal confidante Pierre de Rohan, marshal of France and relative of Louise's deceased husband.[2] Louise was still very much in command of her children's education, but also became fixated on ensuring Francis's ascent to the throne of France. That Francis would become king was foretold to Louise by Francis of Paule (a Franciscan monk from Italy and founder of the reformed order of Minimes) before she even had children.[3] These events explain in part Louise's satisfaction with the stillbirths of Anne of Brittany. Louise's focus on the crown was captured in her journal, in which she referred to Francis well before the first year of his reign as "my king, my lord, my Caesar, and my son" (*mon roi, mon seigneur, mon César, et mon fils*).[4] As Louis XII's health diminished and the hope for a son waned, Francis was groomed to be his successor and was married in 1514 to Claude of France, the firstborn daughter of the reigning French couple. Claude of course was mentioned in Agricola's motet *Transit Anna timor* examined in Chapter 6.

The death of Louis XII on January 1, 1515 elevated his cousin (and son-in-law) Francis I to the throne with Queen Claude. The new queen being prone to illness and also relatively soft-spoken, it was the king's sister Marguerite (Figure 7.1) who took on a dynamic diplomatic role in conjunction with her mother and younger brother. Marguerite in fact attended the coronation of her brother in place of Claude in the grand ceremony at Reims, and foreign ambassadors mentioned her in official correspondence.[5] For all of her service to the court, Marguerite (queen of Navarre after her marriage to Henry II of Navarre in 1527) is best known for having written *The Heptaméron*, a collection of seventy-two provocative novellas in the French vernacular, modeled after Boccaccio's *Decameron* and published posthumously in 1558 (she died in 1549).[6] *The Heptaméron*, along with her other writings and significant areas of patronage, secured her reputation as "Mother of the Renaissance."[7] Marriage plans for Marguerite began around 1503 when she was eleven, the same age at which her mother married the count of Angoulême. Louis XII set his sights high for Marguerite, exploring marriages for her with no less than Henry VIII of England, the king of Naples (Ferdinand II "the Catholic," also king of Aragon), and even Charles V of the Habsburg house. As none of these proposals was accepted, it was

Figure 7.1 *Portrait of Marguerite of Navarre*, attributed to Jean Clouet, ca. 1527. Photo courtesy of the National Museums Liverpool, Walker Art Gallery.

decided that the young princess of the Valois-Angoulême branch could be a vehicle to ameliorate domestic territorial disputes in France rather than to foster farther-reaching international alliances. Marguerite eventually wed Charles of the French duchy of Alençon in 1509; their union settled a small land dispute over the county of Armagnac (in the southwest of France) between the houses of Angoulême and Alençon.[8]

Not atypical of arranged noble marriages, the relationship between Marguerite and the duke from Alençon was not particularly affectionate and possibly bordered on estrangement. The duke was notably absent, it should be said, because of his position as the lieutenant general of

French forces in command of Normandy and Brittany. The marriage produced no children, a significant point that greatly troubled Marguerite, as revealed in her correspondence with the Bishop of Meaux, Guillaume Briçonnet, about whom more will be said later. Charles died not long after the French defeat at the Battle of Pavia in 1525, paving the way for Marguerite's second and more fruitful marriage to Henry II of Navarre shortly thereafter.[9]

Marguerite's relationship with her brother Francis was unusually close, so much so that following his death in 1547, she noted that she and Francis had been "one body, one heart, one will, one desire."[10] Raised together by Louise, the two received the kind of quality education and undivided attention that their mother had received at Amboise less than a generation earlier.[11] Louise's care for the education of her children exemplified her motto "my books and my children" (*libris et liberis*). Although Marguerite and Francis each acquired a high level of literacy, the two assumed conventional gender roles for the period. Margaret was groomed as the more bookish of the two, absorbing much literature at Chinon (and later Blois and Amboise); her brother much preferred the thrill of hunting and sport throughout his life.[12] The conservative religious upbringing of Francis and Marguerite under Louise's tutelage – soon challenged in the advent of church reform movements – likely centered on the study of moral treatises in the vernacular and prayer books.[13] Louise did not stop requesting instructional or devotional manuscripts when the children grew into adulthood, and may indeed have been the impetus behind the monophonic mass for St. Anne prepared for Marguerite.

The tightly knit triad of Francis, Louise, and Marguerite had its hands in countless state affairs, and each member could be trusted to perform the work of another to some extent. Louise twice assumed the role of regent when Francis was on the battlefield, and Marguerite played an unusually strong role in French diplomacy, as mentioned.[14] Aside from his involvement with the Italian Wars, Francis has to be recognized as a major patron of poets and musicians at court; he acknowledged the value of a robust state of the arts in the kingdom, earning the epithet *père et restaurateur des lettres*. Similarly, Marguerite promoted humanist scholarship and the merit of the vernacular in French literature, but she further became an arbiter in the religious reform movement percolating in France. It was no accident that this dynamic, ambitious trio was dubbed the "Royal Trinity" by their contemporaries, and it is in this symbolic threefold entity that St. Anne begins to resurface at the French court.

The French Royal Trinity and a Streamlined Holy Family in Art

Since the early Middle Ages, popes wishing to align with a particular secular monarch would refer to him as a "Most Christian King" (*rex christianissimus*). By the twelfth century, papal favor rested with some consistency on French monarchs, and thereby the coveted title "Most Christian King" became the exclusive property of that nation, a point French historians and chroniclers emphasized.[15] With the epithet came responsibilities. The French sovereign was uniquely allied with the papacy and vowed to rush to its defense in territorial conflicts. Kings themselves were also transformed by the title; they not only performed the duties of a worldly ruler, but also acted as an exemplary Christian before the French people.[16] Among the monarch's most important responsibilities as a "priestly king" was to uphold the faith rigorously and even take steps if needed toward ecclesiastical reform to strengthen the Church Militant. If Francis I was the *rex christianissimus* after 1515, his mother and daughter were to share in his distinction, given their powerful roles as close confidantes of the king. The "Royal Trinity" sobriquet was thus a fitting analogy, evoking the three discrete "persons" of the monarchy – Francis, Louise, and Marguerite. Trinitarian symbolism had been associated with the French crown since the fourteenth century. The royal *fleur de lis* – the triangular arrangement of three golden lilies on a blue background – particularly lured authors to an analogy involving the Trinity and the monarchy.[17] But the Royal Trinity metaphor was explicitly invoked for the Angoulême family by Francis du Moulin de Rochefort, who served the king as his tutor and later as Grand Almoner (head of all chapel activities). Du Moulin also ministered to Louise as a spiritual advisor during the first quarter of the sixteenth century. Once the Royal Trinity moniker was posited, the royal family took up the analogy and used it in its correspondence. The allegory soon gained significant traction among those within and outside court circles.[18]

Visual culture at the French court also blurred representations of the three-person royal family with the Holy Trinity. In a book of prayers created for Louise known as the *Orationes devotissimae* (ca. 1527), one quickly sees that the illustrator of one of the opening miniatures was no stranger to the Trinitarian motif, as a depiction of the three members of the royal family is accompanied by a banderole reading "O noble trinity of the king, of the mother, and of the sister, unity is your desire" (*O nobile ternarium regis / matris/ et sororis unum est desiderium*).[19] Some better-known Italian paintings from the end of the second decade of the sixteenth century seem to transport the Trinity topos toward the realm of the Holy Family, the result of which foregrounded contemporary theological debates in France surrounding St. Anne. Andrea del Sarto's *Holy Family with Angels* and Raphael and Giulio Romano's allegorical *Holy Family of François I* are remarkably similar paintings, both on display today at the Louvre. Despite the divergent titles, both paintings feature Mary and Jesus together with an older woman (presumably Elizabeth) and another young boy (John the Baptist). These works both arrived at the French court around 1518 and would have been understood as expressions of the power of the monarchy. Important for this study, the Raphael-Romano painting was alternatively retitled *Saint Anne* in its 1537 restoration, a reference to the nucleus of the older woman, her daughter, and the grandson(s). It is possible that Sarto's painting was also known as a "Saint Anne" representation in its time.[20]

The most memorable Italian painting encountered by the French monarch, again exposing parallels with the Holy Family, was Leonardo da Vinci's *Virgin and Child with Saint Anne* (Figure 7.2), also found in the Louvre. Although the painting was developed over the course of a decade and probably completed around 1510, it was present in Leonardo's workshop when he served Francis's court and took up residence in 1517 at the Clos Lucé, steps from the château of Amboise, one of the court's key residences.[21] In this well-known work of astonishing realism, the lineage of Jesus is vividly expressed as Mary is seated on the lap of a relatively young St. Anne. Both women gaze at the Christ Child, whose hand grasps the Lamb of God. Visually interlocked with her mother, Mary attempts to restrain her son as he clutches the sacrificial Lamb. Given the early date of the work, Leonardo would not have been privy to the royal Trinitarian symbolism and thus could not have deliberately allegorized the royal trio in the original conception. The artist was also not likely acquainted with the St. Anne Trinitarian or Holy Kinship imagery, ideas propagated in northern Europe and in the Rhineland. Italians were traditionally slow to embrace the legend of Mary's mother, as she was not heavily celebrated in liturgies. What is notable, however, about all of these Italian works is the power and interconnectedness of the small (female-dominated) family nucleus, the political implications of which would have been unmistakable in the eyes of the new monarch and his loyal mother and sister, the co-custodians of the kingdom.

Louise spent much time at Amboise during Leonardo's residency. At the same time, an inchoate theological revolution was developing in France, under the aegis of the Royal Trinity. Religious reformer Jacques Lefèvre d'Etaples established a foundation for biblical humanism both by

Figure 7.2 Leonardo da Vinci (1452–1519), *Virgin and Child with Saint Anne*, ca 1510. Paris, Musée National du Louvre. © RMN-Grand Palais / Art Resource, NY.

scrutinizing traditional devotions and by encouraging reexamination of Scripture to excavate its truth. Lefèvre's journey began with the then radical suggestions that Mary Magdalene was not a single entity (but three separate persons) and that the "Three Marys" were not daughters of St. Anne. With the latter argument, Lefèvre intended to streamline devotion to the "true" members of the Holy Family (St. Anne being the preferred intercessor over Mary's husband, Joseph, who had no biological connection to

Christ). As Myra Orth has pointed out, it is not hard to imagine that the timely paintings of the condensed Holy Family under St. Anne – Leonardo's the most impressive – could be unplanned visual "proof" of the theology of the moment advanced by reformers. This theological stance emphasized devotion to known entities, most certainly not the fictitious sisters of the Virgin Mary (and the egregious claims of a massive Holy Kinship), as the activists saw it. By this time, the image of St. Anne was thoroughly embedded at court, and overzealous devotion to the legends surrounding the grandmother of Christ would be called into question. It is necessary to become further acquainted with biblical humanism and the controversy surrounding Mary's mother, as it forms an essential backdrop against which a musical artifact for St. Anne can be evaluated.

Biblical Humanism, the Magdalene Controversy, and a Treatise on St. Anne

In the second decade of the sixteenth century, Christian humanists in France quietly began to seek a purified church doctrine, and yet, like Erasmus, they did not seek to sever ties with the traditional church.[22] Their strategy was not complicated: attack unfounded popular devotional practices, rampant clerical abuses, and exegetical contradictions and focus squarely on illuminating the message of the evangelists. For these reformers, Scripture was open for all to interpret, not just to a privileged few from history. The biblical humanists also questioned the validity of the layers of patristic interpretation honored by the Church. Their nonconformist writings unsurprisingly met with much resistance by the abidingly conservative Faculty of Theology at the University of Paris, who stood by the notion that interrogation of the faith in this way would prove harmful to the foundation of the church as an institution. By 1521, prominent reformers relocated to the city of Meaux, where Bishop Guillaume Briçonnet had initiated a reform of diocesan clergy in 1518. Briçonnet welcomed the help of Lefèvre (his former teacher) and Lefèvre's disciples; in turn, Briçonnet sheltered the reformers from threats by the champions of orthodoxy. The Meaux group had temporary success in the early 1520s, producing a substantial body of literature, chiefly biblical translations, which quickly found their way into the hands of the laity.

The Meaux reformers – also known as the "Meaux Circle" (*Cercle de Meaux*) – would not have achieved their early feats without the tacit endorsement of the royal court, Marguerite in particular. Her unwavering patronage of humanist writers and other polymaths, in addition to her own literary works, have earned her high esteem among Renaissance historians. Further, Marguerite was a passionate advocate for ecclesial reform, and she encouraged the Meaux reformers to propagate their translations, treatises, and biblical commentaries. Despite her fervent wishes, Marguerite's inability to convince her brother and mother to take action and fully achieve religious reform in France is one of the great questions that scholars have consistently raised about her life.[23] Marguerite's commitment to the values of the reformers comes to light in her correspondence during the early 1520s with the host of the Meaux Circle, Guillaume Briçonnet. The Royal Trinity's strongest gesture to defend biblical humanism came in 1523, when the court exonerated one of the king's counselors, Louis de Berquin, whose possession of Lutheran treatises had infuriated the Faculty of Theology of Paris and the Parlement of Paris. Berquin was eventually burned at the stake.[24] Marguerite and Louise were subsequently accused of protecting such heretics, and the pendulum began to swing the other way. Though Marguerite was probably not deterred by the charge, her mother took decisive actions to shore up the court's orthodox reputation.[25]

St. Anne in fact became a topic associated with the struggle between orthodoxy and reform, and she obliquely was drawn into the debate through questions raised about the identity of Mary Magdalene, which were brewing in the years preceding the formation of the Meaux consortium. After Francis I had won a major victory in 1515 at the Battle of Marignano, Louise, Marguerite, and Claude traveled to meet the king in Provence. On their journey south, the women passed through towns with churches and convents that boasted the relics of Mary Magdalene and the two alleged daughters of St. Anne, Mary Iacobi and Mary Salome, all of whom, according to a popular legend, were said to have migrated to the south of France after Christ's resurrection. The members of the royal family showed great interest in the relics of these storied women and promised generous gifts to fund restoration projects at the various institutions.[26] Louise's genuine curiosity about Mary Magdalene in particular resulted in a request to her resident spiritual advisor, the aforementioned Francis du Moulin, for a *vita* of the saint. Du Moulin obliged and a life appeared around the middle of 1517, complete with no fewer than seventy miniatures of traditional scenes painted by Godefroy le Batave. Du Moulin dutifully documented the scriptural passages that involve the Magdalene, but his tract also carefully kept the legends surrounding the saint (e.g., her journey to the south of France) quarantined from the biblical references.

Throughout the *vita*, Du Moulin subtly interrogated the identity of the Magdalene, a follower of Christ whose multifaceted character is confusing even if confined to the Gospels alone.[27]

In his treatise for Louise of Savoy, Du Moulin's hesitations about the life of a single, discernible Mary Magdalene seems to have prompted another work that appeared in print later that same year (1517), one that more thoroughly and forcefully questioned the received figure of the Magdalene. Jacques Lefèvre d'Etaples, already mentioned as a crucial reformer of the period in France, published two short tracts presented together, each challenging traditional views on important subjects from the Gospels. His *De Maria magdalena, et triduo Christi disceptatio* (*Discussion of Mary Magdalene and Christ's Triduum*) on one hand tried to separate the accepted single identity of the Magdalene into three distinct personages, while also clarifying the meaning of the "three days and three nights" of Jesus' death and resurrection. It was the Magdalene argument that touched a nerve with the University of Paris's conservative Faculty of Theology, igniting what became known as the "Quarrel of the Magdalenes." Until that point, medieval commentary had combined three biblical women into the single figure of Mary Magdalene.[28] Lefèvre relied on the evangelists and select early Christian commentators such as Origen, Ambrose, and Jerome to demonstrate that these women were distinct followers of Christ. He argued that the consolidation into a single Magdalene entity was an invention of writers like Augustine and Gregory.[29]

Lefèvre's treatise on the problematic merged identity of Mary Magdalene drew several immediate and heated responses from members of the Paris theology faculty, a fact that the author acknowledged in the second edition of *De Maria magdalena*.[30] This lightly revised rerelease, also known as the *Secunda Emissio*, was issued in the summer of 1518. While the substance of the Magdalene and the Triduum sections was largely untouched, a new tract on the legend of St. Anne entitled *De una ex tribus* (*On the One [Mary] in Place of Three*) was appended to the publication. As in all of his writings, Lefèvre was not determined to eradicate devotion to these well-known saints, but rather to separate biblical authority from the accretions of legend and unfounded popular devotional practices. Small wonder that in the St. Anne treatise, Lefèvre challenged the identities of the two alleged daughters of St. Anne named Mary Iacobi and Mary Salome, who were said to be (half-) sisters of the Virgin Mary. The *De una ex tribus* treatise was dedicated to Du Moulin, a strong indication that these ideas likely found their way into the inner chambers of the French court.

In *De una ex tribus*, Lefèvre argued that Cleophas and Salome were fabricated personages and could not have been husbands of the already elderly St. Anne, who by some accounts gave birth to the first Mary (i.e., the Virgin Mary) in her eightieth year. Like other biblical humanists, he dismissed the existence of the third husband named Salome, insisting that this was the name of a woman, thus making it impossible for this person to marry St. Anne and produce another Mary. The author also goes to some length to argue that, by assigning additional husbands to St. Anne and sisters to Mary, Christian exegetes diminished the extraordinary nature of the Virgin Mary's conception and her role in salvation history, and they further defiled the "purity" of St. Anne.[31] Lefèvre had effectively reduced the size of the Holy Kinship with the elimination of the husbands and daughters of St. Anne, unintentionally complementary to what Leonardo and other Italian painters had portrayed in French visual culture. In his St. Anne essay, Lefèvre noted a kind of conceptual balance in these theological debates on sanctoral devotion: Mary Magdalene was expanded from a single entity to three discrete persons, while the "Three Marys" were pared down to the single (Virgin) Mary by purging the imagined husbands of St. Anne.[32] These treatises of course do not give direct access to the beliefs of the members of the Royal Trinity, but they do provide a sense of the theological dynamics swirling at the French court, as well as the identity crisis befalling Mary's mother in France.

The *Petit livret* and Royal Protection

Lefèvre's call for a single Magdalene and a more compact Holy Family under the matriarch St. Anne lost no steam at the end of the second decade of the sixteenth century, with new editions of his treatise released in 1519, including a *Tertia Emissio* containing the three tracts already described. Although these Latin commentaries targeted the intellectual elite, they were dedicated to Du Moulin, a friar who had nothing of the academic training of Lefèvre. What Du Moulin did have was precious access to the royal family. Having served the court for more than twenty-five years, whether as Francis's personal tutor, the regent Louise's spiritual counselor, or the king's personal chaplain, Du Moulin was like a close relative in the eyes of the Royal Trinity. He guided the family in matters transcendent, intellectual, and practical, but was also sympathetic to the nascent voices of reform – humanists like Erasmus and his friend Lefèvre. The reformers needed an advocate like

Du Moulin at the court to ensure that their voices would be heard when supporters of orthodoxy resisted their arguments.[33]

Noël Beda, a member of the prestigious Paris theology faculty, issued a scathing response to Lefèvre's St. Anne treatise in his *Apologia pro filiabus et nepotibus beatae Annae* (*Defense of the Daughters and Relatives of Blessed Anne*) from 1520.[34] Despite its title, the theologian hardly spent time protecting the popular genealogy associated with the Holy Kinship; instead, he ruminated on the damage that Lefèvre and his ilk do when they so easily discard the scholastic traditions and legends of the church in favor of new iconoclastic positions.[35] Already ruffled, the theologians on the faculty of the University of Paris did not take long to formalize their objections to the reform ideology. With regard to the Magdalene debate, they circulated a pronouncement known as the *Determinatio* in 1521, which banned any public discussion or tracts on the plural Magdalenes.[36] Again, Du Moulin's activism at the French court was an essential counterweight to the declarations against ("Lutheran") heresy disseminated by the Faculty of Theology. As a proponent of both church reform and devotional piety, the court's resident spiritual guide was perfectly positioned to advance the cause of the reformers while assuaging the concerns of an attack on orthodoxy.

Just as Lefèvre followed his Magdalene publication with a St. Anne treatise, so too did Du Moulin issue a document on St. Anne in the wake of his own Magdalene essay from 1517. Du Moulin's manuscript in honor of St. Anne (*Petit livret faict à l'honneur de Madame Sainte Anne*) drew the royal family into the thick of the debate over the Three Marys and again pushed for reform without the intent to abolish the institution or its rituals of devotion. The "little booklet" of seventy-two leaves was produced in late 1518 (or early 1519) and was dedicated to Louise of Savoy, not unusual given her interest in Mary Magdalene, St. Anne, and the grandmother saint's alleged daughters.[37] The idea for the tract, however, was not prompted by Louise but rather by her son, who, during the recitation of Jesus' lineage (presumably at Christmas Mass), apparently asked Du Moulin about the genealogy of Mary.[38] Godefroy le Batave again was tapped to decorate the manuscript and provided six miniatures drawn in a heavy grisaille. This effort paled in comparison with the artist's copious images supplied for Du Moulin's *vita* of the Magdalene.[39]

Du Moulin assumed a strategy with the *Petit livret* similar to the one he took with the Magdalene treatise: the iconography was wholly traditional, but again the text (set in the vernacular) called the legend into question and carefully pruned the extended family of Jesus. In one miniature, for example, Mary Cleophas corrals her four boys (Joseph the Just, James the

Figure 7.3 Dedication to Louise of Savoy, miniature on paper from *Petit livret faict à l'honneur de Madame Sainte Anne*. Paris, Bibliothèque de l'Arsenal, MS 4009. fol. 1v. 1518–19. Photo: Bibliothèque nationale de France.

Younger, Simon, and Jude), who are each labeled. Du Moulin's surrounding text, all the while, details how Mary Cleophas cannot be related to the Virgin Mary. Other miniatures involving the Holy Kinship are accompanied by commentary that confronts the very traditions suggested in the imagery. Not unlike his friend Lefèvre, Du Moulin interrogated the name Salome as necessarily a woman's name, never mind the nearby miniature of "Mary Salome," "Zebedee," and their two sons. He then provided extensive calculations of the purported ages of the youngest generation of the kinship to demonstrate the implausibility of the offspring of Mary's "sisters."[40]

Despite its conventional imagery of St. Anne and the Three Marys, Du Moulin's *Petit livret* was a vernacular digest of Lefèvre's *De una ex tribus*, geared for his patroness Louise. That the trusted advisor to the court was effectively endorsing Lefèvre and registering his dissent by developing a court-friendly version of the dense Latin treatise is made plain by the opening miniature, which shows Du Moulin presenting Lefèvre to Louise of Savoy, his controversial friend kneeling before the regent and offering her a book (Figure 7.3).

But the subversive treatise was more than a translation of Lefèvre: it was a bid for royal protection. If Lefèvre could also be sheltered under the wing of the monarch (or his mother), the conservative voices of the Faculty of Theology might subside because of the king's good standing with the pope. Unconcealed flattery of Louise and her family played no small role in the *Petit livret*. Du Moulin brilliantly and delicately worked his dedicatee into his treatise, likening the regent to St. Anne herself. He reminded Louise that she was married only once and had no desire to remarry, precisely parallel to the life of Mary's mother, at least as he and the reformers imagined it. St. Anne's true course of life, according to Du Moulin, echoed the long history of widows in the Old Testament. The court's devotional counselor knew his patroness well and deftly aligned her widowhood with that of (the revised) St. Anne, judging it ethically superior to the case of Louise's former rival Anne of Brittany, who married twice.[41] After rehearsing the extensive kinship (with illustrations), he clarified the argument in no uncertain terms: "This image [of the Three Marys and their progeny] is apocryphal and false although the Theologians of Paris have long approved of it. And speaking in reverence to you, MADAME, those who said so, lied. For Saint Anne, good and chaste widow, was satisfied with one husband – that is, Joachim, who was father only of the Virgin Mary."[42]

The extent to which Louise (or the king) engaged with the rebellious *Petit livret*, or whether she knew that her commissions were meant to reorient, not reinforce, her existing devotional energy toward St. Anne, is of course not known, but her sympathy for a budding French Reformation in general cannot be denied. Louise was probably not fully attuned to the biographical adjustments to the figure of St. Anne (or the Magdalene) that Du Moulin had made. So long as the king's mother could continue to venerate these saints, all was satisfactory. The dissident details of the little book were likely blunted by the personalized flattery for the regent. What is critical is that Du Moulin's tactics to garner court protection for Lefèvre's polemical voice worked like a charm. Lefèvre received royal shelter, most fanatically by Marguerite, until the time of his death in 1536.[43]

With these court undercurrents in mind, an even smaller "little book" in honor of St. Anne, now for the duchess Marguerite, can now be examined. This document contains music for the mother of Mary and surprisingly represents an orthodox position, conspicuously out of step with the aforementioned treatises of the French biblical humanists. Though it has both a personal and political agenda tailored to the sister of the king, this musical artifact defies some of the trends already seen with St. Anne by adhering to the expanded kinship model of old. Embracing the traditional notions associated with Mary's mother, the unnamed author of the document on one hand appealed to Marguerite using a familiar image of the grandmother saint, while attempting to steer the duchess's attention toward issues of greater concern to the kingdom.

The *Mass for St. Anne* – Structure, Image, and Texts

The high water mark for devotion to St. Anne at the royal court in the mid- to-late 1510s makes the discovery of special liturgical music composed in the saint's honor during this period hardly remarkable, even as the legend was coming under attack. As the seeds of biblical humanism were planted in the French court, this musical artifact noticeably maintains a sense of orthodoxy amid the clamor for reform. It is a document that deployed St. Anne to promote both grand and timely ideas, some personally directed to Marguerite and others more broadly aimed at court diplomacy of the time, which the king's sister could potentially affect.

The anonymous *Mass for St. Anne* (henceforth the name of this document) survives in good condition with its original blue silk binding. It is a medium-sized (237 x 173 mm) handheld booklet of just sixteen folios with an extensive preface followed by a set of six plainchants for the Proper of the Mass. The *Mass for St. Anne* has received little comment from art historians, and it has also escaped the attention of musicologists, likely because it does not feature polyphonic music, the major attraction of sixteenth-century studies. With the impetus for this manuscript and the meaning for its recipient not immediately evident, the contents of the *Mass for St. Anne* demand investigation.

The modest book containing this mass divides precisely into two halves. The first half consists of a long-winded introduction with illustrations and the texts of the Mass Propers (fols. 1v–8v); the second half features notated music for these Propers (fols. 9r–16r). Fol. 16v has staffs drawn, but no music, an indication that the notating scribe had more room if needed to enter the mass chants. The *Mass for St. Anne* begins with a large dedication miniature featuring an enthroned Marguerite attended by nine women, with two men kneeling before her (Figure 7.4). A monk – probably a Franciscan and presumably the author of the manuscript – hands Marguerite the *Mass for St. Anne*, a blue book as it survives today.[44] The author in turn is presented to the duchess by an unidentified noble, who is wearing a *collier* of the Order of St. Michael, a chivalric order for French knights formed under Louis XI in 1469. The man's *collier* partially encircles the arms of France, which

Figure 7.4 Dedication of the *Mass for St. Anne*. Paris, Bibliothèque nationale de France, MS fr. 1035, fol. 1v. Photo: Bibliothèque nationale de France.

caused Myra Orth to presume that this man was Francis I. But the king was not the only one to don the collar with the kingdom's arms; indeed, more than thirty "companions" of the Order of St. Michael wore the same collar.[45]

The coat of arms located at the foot of Marguerite's throne juxtaposes the royal crest with that of the Alençon duchy. The inscription below the image of Marguerite addresses her as both MADAME and the Duchesse Dallençon et de Berry. This particular formulation helps narrow the date of the manuscript to some degree. Marguerite acquired the first title (Duchess of Alençon) upon her marriage to Charles of Alençon in 1509, but the king exclusively endowed his sister with the duchy of Berry in October 1517. This title was no small gift, as it designated a ducal peerage for Marguerite (and not her husband), effectively granting the duchess all rights that would normally be held by a male duke.[46] The more familiar title "Queen of Navarre" would have been inscribed in any depiction of Marguerite after 1527 in recognition of her second marriage to Henry II of Navarre in that year. The inscription thus places the manuscript between late 1517 and 1526, coincident with this volatile period in French religious reform.

The texts of the *Mass for St. Anne* are transcribed in full in Appendix B. The document begins with a short dedication to the duchess, but quickly develops into an unusually discursive preface in the vernacular that far exceeds the conventions of a foreword. Nothing obvious in the passage can further constrict the date or circumstances surrounding the modest book. The first few folios of the introduction speak of Abraham's great faith and lineage that formed the church under Christ. The author then folds in St. Anne as descended from the holy lineage of Abraham and therefore most worthy of honor. The preface on the whole suggests that Mary's mother and her precious lineage are, above all, symbols of a stable and unified church. The writer's expressly conservative position toward St. Anne is revealed in his references to her as "rightfully married" (*legitimement mariee*) to three husbands and as the "mother of the three noble Marys" (*mere des troyes nobles maries*). The anonymous author importantly contends that the broken Church Militant can benefit from collective veneration of St. Anne, because it was her magnificent family – specifically her seven grandsons – who established a firm foundation of the church in a time when "universal peace reigned" (*paix universelle regnoit*).[47] A miniature demonstrating the writer's wish for church unification under Jesus the shepherd is supplemented by marginalia containing biblical excerpts. The annotations curiously cite passages involving the number seven, ostensibly an allusion to Anne's seven grandchildren.[48] The references to an extended family for St. Anne almost certainly eliminate the document as the work of a biblical humanist.

The remaining vernacular portion of the introduction is addressed to four discrete groups and set in rhymed verse. The author directed (1) the pope and all clergymen to seek peace through patience, avoiding ambition at all turns. (2) To the kings and princes of Europe, the author urges the pursuit of devotion to St. Anne to find peace and achieve a "prompt victory against the Turks" (*victoire promptement des turcs*). (3) The noblewomen of France are given the greatest attention. The author advises them that their authentic rank can be maintained through devotion to St. Anne, herself descended from the most precious stock of Jewish kings (familiar political territory), and that prayers to Mary's mother can avoid disastrous wars. Finally, (4) the French people at large are encouraged to pray for peace, so that France may be restored as a leader (*chevetaine*) among the nations.[49] The obvious concern about the threat of war and the need for Christian unity is enhanced with another half-page illustration featuring the battling front lines of the French (signaled by the arms) and the enemy.[50] This search for a restoration of national peace cannot, however, be used to definitively date the source. In one sense, the idea of a grand crusade was a widespread topic in Western Europe during the late fifteenth century. Note that relations between the French and the Ottoman Empire were not entirely adversarial after Francis took the throne in 1515.[51] More will be said on the topic of a crusade later. That the document was meant for an audience broader than its initial dedicatee is made clear in the author's charge to Marguerite to make sure that his *Mass for St. Anne* circulates well among French churches.[52] For the moment, the urgent plea of the author was only registered with the politically powerful duchess; the extent of the mass's transmission beyond her is not known.

The document says next to nothing about Anne's traditional domain of maternity and makes only passing reference to her legend; rather, the author explains how devotion to her can produce unity among Christians. Throughout the introduction, he uses the phrase "firm faith" (*ferme foy*) with some frequency, but this cannot be viewed as an allusion to the doctrine of *sola fide* embraced by reformers.[53] The preamble concludes with a fully rubricated paragraph in Latin, the author reiterating that St. Anne's sterile-turned-fecund experience is a prefiguration of the "peace of the universal church and unity from the omnipotent God" (*universalis ecclesie pacem et unitatem ab omnipotenti deo*).[54] Immediately following the rubricated passage are the complete texts of the Propers to be set to music later in the manuscript. This apparent redundancy might suggest that the mass was to be used with some regularity (perhaps weekly), whether recited or sung, depending on circumstances. The incipits and biblical sources of the texts that constitute the Proper of the Mass are provided in Table 7.1.

Texts from the Old Testament, particularly those from the prophet Isaiah, dominate the Proper settings. The Introit of the Mass, however, presents select verses from 2 Esdras, a composite of Christian apocryphal texts dating from between the late first century and the third century.[55] Both features are hardly the norm for Proper texts, which tend to be drawn from the book of Psalms and the New Testament. No text concords with the settings

Table 7.1 Proper texts in the *Mass for St. Anne*

Proper	Incipit	Textual Source
Introit	*Noli timere mater filiorum* V. *Mater amplectere*	2 Esdras 2:17, 19; 15[b]
Collect[a]	*Deus qui in utero virginis*	–
Epistle[a]	*Letare sterilis que non paris*	Isaiah 54:1–6
Gradual[c]	*Exsurge iherusalem* V. *Ponam omnes terminos tuos*	Baruch 5:5; Isaiah 54:12–13
Alleluia	*Alleluia* V. *Multiplicabitur que derelicta fuerat*	Isaiah 6:12–13
Tract	*Commovebo celum*	Haggai 2:7–8
Gospel reading[a]	*Nemo potest vasa fortis ingressus*	Mark 3:27–35
Offertory	*Luce splendida fulgebis*	Tobias 13:17–18
Secret[a]	*Sacramentis tuis*	–
Communion	*Gaudium et leticia invenietur*	Isaiah 51:3; 65:23; 66:12
Post-communion[a]	*Ora quos opus deus*	–

[a] intoned [b] apocryphal [c] called "Responsorium"

typically found in masses for St. Anne in late medieval France. This is especially unusual for mass texts, which are considerably more uniform in their transmission than those of the Divine Office for a given feast.[56] That the compiler selected these uncommon texts for a "St. Anne" mass is a clue that it was probably tailor made for Marguerite.

Two distinct themes emerge from the Proper texts obliquely in honor of Mary's mother. On one hand, the notion of fertility undeniably permeates the items of this mass. The texts collectively reassure the reader or listener that a sterile mother will eventually exult with gladness in her precious children. The Epistle from Isaiah urges "you who are barren" to "rejoice" and "sing out praise" (*Letare sterilis que non paris; decanta laudem* …), while the Offertory from Tobias similarly encourages the listener to "rejoice in your children" (*letaberis in filiis tuis*). The Alleluia suggests that a "seed of peace" (*semen pacis*) awaits "she who was left forsaken" (*derelicta fuerat*), a fertility plea encountered previously in noble courts. The apocryphal Introit from 2 Esdras opening the *Mass for St. Anne* is equally heartening as a "maternity" text. With allegorical verses reflecting God's instruction to the church on how to care for her people, the text reminds the matron church that she was specially chosen to bear children and that these children will be filled with joy (again, see Appendix B for the complete texts).

On the other hand, the compiler of these Proper texts in the *Mass for St. Anne* placed noticeable emphasis on national deliverance and the restoration of peace, a reprise of ideas offered in the preface and a further politicization of the liturgy nominally in celebration of Mary's mother. The Tract, a mass chant typically sung in penitential seasons in place of the Alleluia, sets verses from the book of Haggai, in which the Lord promises to move all nations and instill peace, so that the desired one may come forth. Just as the foreword addressed the sovereigns of Christian nations, the intoned prose of the Collect directly asks God to bless the "Christian kings and princes" to unite the nation, so that the lives of the faithful can advance.[57] The Communion chant remarkably integrates the theme of peace and unity on earth with that of esteemed maternal offspring. The text is excerpted from Isaiah and concerns the renewal of the people of Israel (though it can be understood as being directed to a mother). The chant reminds the reader-listener that "my elect shall not produce in trouble: they are the seed of the Lord's blessed" and that they will be brought "a river of peace."[58] In sum, the collage of Old Testament texts that dominate the Propers provides encouragement for a barren mother, but the political thrust of the document centers on national tranquility, the implications of which will be discussed shortly. Although no Mass Proper text mentions Mary's mother, the select Old Testament verses could reasonably be applied to St. Anne, the holy woman who fulfilled the role of matron and stewardess of prosperous dynasties.

The *Mass for St. Anne* – Music

Of course, the *Mass for St. Anne* is not simply a succession of liturgical texts. These suggestive biblical and apocryphal texts, along with the Proper recitations, are each declaimed through the medium of plainsong, six of which are set in square notation and consume the latter half of the manuscript. It was of course unnecessary to notate all of the Propers, as some of these items (Collect, Gospel, Secret, and Postcommunion) would have been intoned to the simplest of melodic formulas. Regarding the formal section of notated music, each folio is generously spaced, containing five staves of four lines (most with C4 and C3 clefs) on either side of an opening.[59] Each notated plainchant begins with some kind of unassuming illustration, ranging from a calligraphic initial to a simple coat of arms in the case of the Introit *Noli timere mater filiorum*. The heraldic emblem here reveals the merged arms of the French crown and the duchy of Alençon (Figure 7.5), first seen in the dedicatory miniature.[60]

Some global comments about the Propers can be made, along with brief observations on the individual settings in the *Mass for St. Anne*. In another sign that the mass was likely compiled ad hoc, the Proper chants lack firm

Figure 7.5 The Introit *Noli timere mater filiorum* (opening) from the *Mass for St. Anne*. Paris, Bibliothèque nationale de France, MS fr. 1035, fol. 9r. Photo: Bibliothèque nationale de France.

concordances with the vast plainchant repertory that has survived. But this is not to say that the melodies themselves were freshly created for the occasion. Although the texts of the mass do not correspond to any texts or melodies associated with St. Anne, one can still account for at least one-third of the musical content that appears in the document (Table 7.2).

The Offertory *Luce splendida fulgebis* features a text that has been set as an antiphon for the Common of Kings, a responsory verse for Paschaltide, and a Gradual composed by Guillaume Du Fay for the Recollection of Feasts for the Blessed Virgin Mary (*Recollectio festorum Beatae Mariae Virginis*).[61]

Table 7.2 Melodic modes and sources of the Propers in the *Mass for St. Anne*

Proper	Incipit	Fols.	Mode	Melodic Source
Introit	*Noli timere mater filiorum*	9r–10r	E–3	–
Gradual	*Exsurge iherusalem*	10r–12r	F–5	Gr. *Specie tua*
Alleluia	*Alleluia* V. *Multiplicabitur*	12r–13r	G–7	All. V. *Dilexisti iusticiam*
Offertory	*Luce splendida fulgebis*	13r–14r	D–2	Ant. from Common of Kings?
Communion	*Gaudium et leticia invenietur*	14r–15r	D–1	–
Tract	*Commovebo celum*	15r–16r	G–8	–

However, no surviving notated source that sets this text matches the second-mode melody found in the *Mass for St. Anne*. Secure concordances, however, may be found in two Propers from the *Mass for St. Anne*, which are identifiably contrafacta of preexistent mass chants. It is clear, for example, that the fifth-mode Gradual *Exsurge iherusalem* sets the words of Baruch and Isaiah to the melody of the Gradual *Specie tua et pulchritudine tua* from the Common of a Virgin.[62] Also, the Alleluia from the *Mass for St. Anne* with the verse *Multiplicabitur que derelicta fuerat* is nearly identical to a seventh-mode Alleluia (V. *Dilexisti iusticiam et odisti iniquitatem*) from the mass for the virgin martyr Lucy. The latter Alleluia is known only from two northern French sources and perhaps others known to the court that do not survive.[63] In a notable compositional turn, the compiler or scribe of the *Mass for St. Anne* elected to rewrite the ending of the Alleluia verse. (It is also possible that he was faithfully copying another version.) This variant eliminated the soloist's spectacular climb to g' – the octave above the expected final – that concludes the version known from the concordant sources (Example 7.1). The respond and the first part of the verse of *Alleluia* V. *Multiplicabitur*, however, are in lockstep with that of *Alleluia* V. *Dilexisti*.

The emendation to the known melody for the mass of St. Lucy obviously renders the *Alleluia* V. *Multiplicabitur* a considerably more modest Alleluia than if the compiler had followed the melody from northern French sources that ascends to the octave above the final. As the synoptic transcription reveals beginning at the words *erit id*, the scribe maintains the basic contour of the related Alleluia, but at a fourth or fifth lower than the "parent" chant. The effect of course flattens the range of the Alleluia at hand. As a chant directly preceding the reading of the Gospel, the Alleluia traditionally commands an expansive and virtuosic setting fit for a soloist. And indeed, *Alleluia* V. *Multiplicabitur* is recognizably the shapeliest of the melodies in the *Mass for St. Anne*. As it stands, though, the Alleluia inhabits a rather

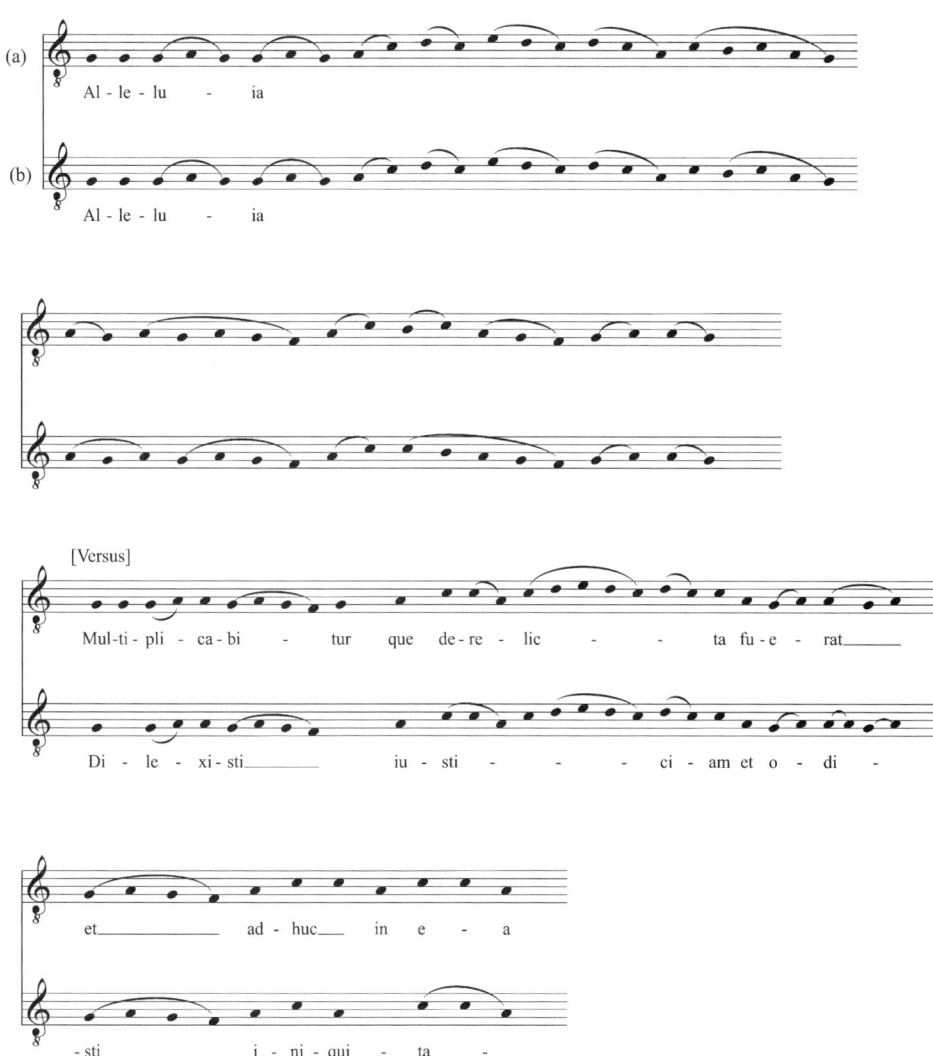

Example 7.1 (a) *Alleluia* V. *Multiplicabitur* from the *Mass for St. Anne* (fols. 12r–13r), compared with (b) *Alleluia* V. *Dilexisti iusticiam et odisti iniquitatem*.

confined musical space and minimizes melodic leaps. The chant does not approach the range of the octave, a property that one might anticipate in a seventh-mode Alleluia. The compression of the musical range in the present Alleluia could be evidence that performability of the music was a concern of the compiler. Recall that the author of the *Mass for St. Anne* wished his mass to fall into the hands of many French churches in an effort to distribute his message. Perhaps removing some of the virtuosic elements from the Alleluia verse was one step toward a larger institutional acceptance. There

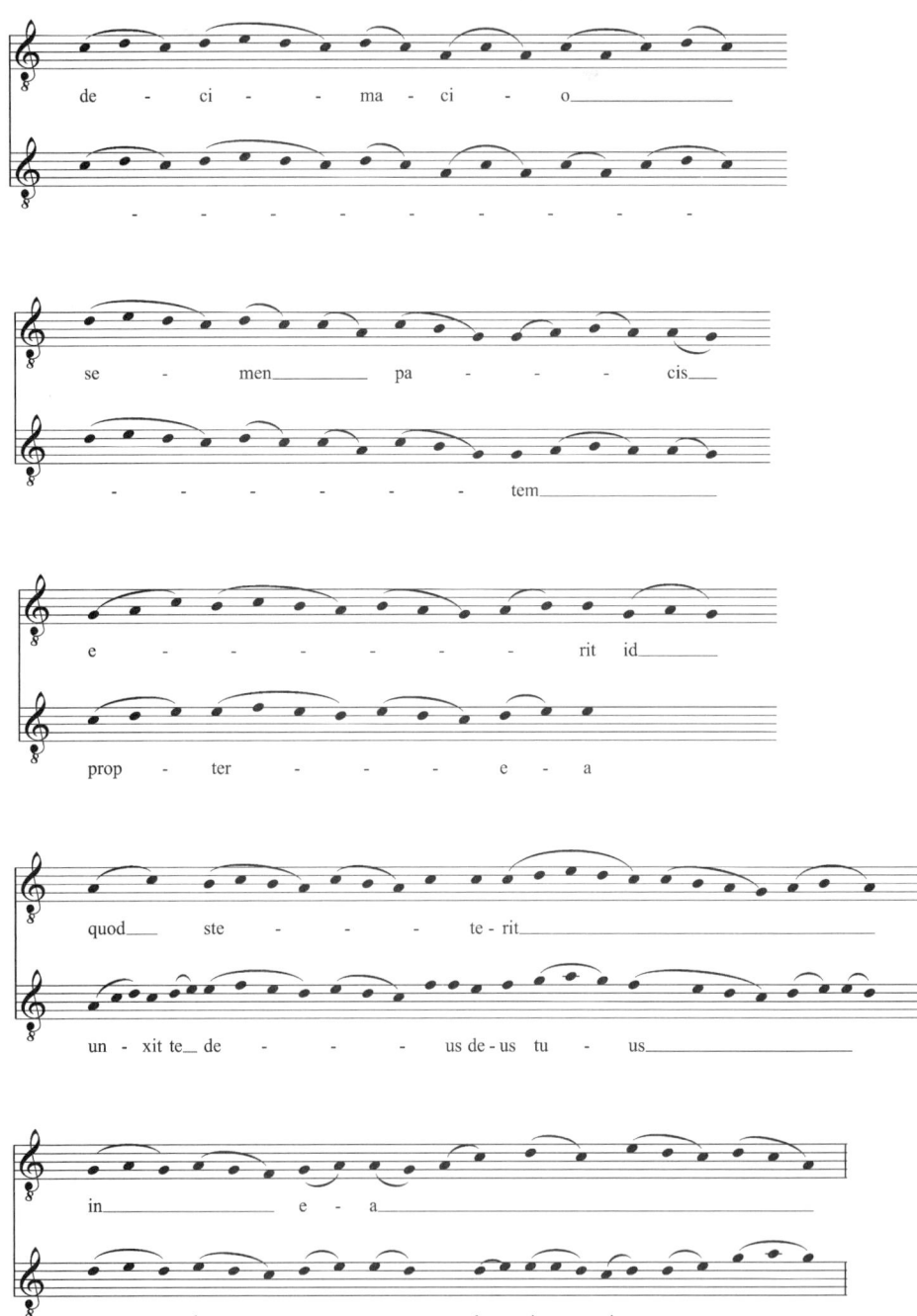

Example 7.1 (*continued*)

is more support for this claim in the aforementioned Offertory *Luce splendida fulgebis*, which likewise reveals a rather timid setting relative to the norms of the genre. Nowhere in this Offertory does one find the expansive melismas nor repeated pitches associated with Offertories. There is also no confusion about the mode of *Luce splendida fulgebis* (as sometimes befalls Offertories), as the register stays relatively compact in the second mode.

The three remaining notated plainchants in the *Mass for St. Anne* (Introit, Tract, and Communion) are only remarkable for their strong links to the conventions of traditional plainchant. The Tract *Commovebo celum* is cast in the eighth mode, one of the two modes in which tracts were set. Dominated by cadences on f and g and bordering on recitation at times, the melody strongly hews to the line of the medieval tract.[64] Separate from the issue of style, note that *Commovebo celum* appears at the end of the notated section of mass music, as Table 7.2 indicates. This contrasts with the placement of the tract after the Alleluia, as it was presented in the full text of the mass given at the end of the preface. (Being a chant used in place of the Alleluia during penitential seasons, the tract would never occur alongside the Alleluia in practice.) Although apparently not a mistake in the copying plan of the manuscript, the placement of *Commovebo celum* at the end of the *Mass for St. Anne* gives it a feeling of being optional, perhaps according to liturgical season.[65] Given that St. Anne's July 26 feast day has no chance of falling within a penitential season, the author evidently had high hopes for the recitation or performance of this mass throughout the year. Whether read or sung, in the mind or out loud, in public or private, the *Mass for St. Anne* was almost certainly not bound to her feast day. The "topical" texts of the Propers (lacking any specific reference to Mary's mother) and the aspirational thrust of the preface suggest that this music could be experienced at any time.

Like the tract, the mass's Introit *Noli timere mater filiorum* clings to the conventions of its genre. The third-mode melody is a typical mode for the Introit, and some of its internal characteristics (such as a recitation on c and a prominent g-a-c motive) are commonly found in E-mode Introits. The opening exhortation of *Noli timere mater filiorum* is an inelegant gesture that might at first appear uncharacteristic of any chant (Example 7.2). Of the twelve notes assigned to the first two words (*Noli timere*), five intervals are accomplished by a leap, and two of these intervals are ascending fourths. Spanning an octave in this twelve-note incipit, the opening line alternates two- and three-note groupings and comes to rest on an unstable b♮. The gesture, however, is surprisingly typical among third-mode Introits, except that the end of the line usually ends on c, the reciting tone of the mode.[66]

As for the Communion of the *Mass for St. Anne* (*Gaudium et leticia invenietur*), it too fulfills the general expectations of a Communion setting

Example 7.2 The Introit *Noli timere mater filiorum* in Paris, Bibliothèque nationale de France, MS fr. 1035, fol. 8r (opening).

Example 7.3 The Communion *Gaudium et leticia invenietur* in Paris, Bibliothèque nationale de France, MS fr. 1035, fols. 14r–15r.

(Example 7.3). The chant is set in first mode, the D-mode being the most common mode in the Communion corpus. With a simple syllabic-neumatic style, *Gaudium et leticia invenietur* is moderate in design, again not surprising for the genre. What is outside the norm for Communions is the shape of the last line of the antiphon at the words *fluvium pacis* ("river of peace"). Clearly, the composer was aiming for a depiction of this "river of peace" in musical form by noticeably breaking with the declamatory pattern of the Communion and assigning twenty-five notes to the final two words almost completely using stepwise motion. A smoothly flowing river indeed! The brief melismatic burst at the end of the chant is uncommon for the genre, and word painting is rare in plainchant on the whole.[67] The text-music correspondence is striking, despite the awkward musical flourish on the penultimate (unaccented) syllable of *fluvium*. One can probably assume that *Gaudium et leticia invenietur* is not a contrafactum, and it is quite possible that this chant was newly composed for the duchess, although with substantial debt to the tradition of Communions.

From a musical perspective, the mass hardly departs from the traditions of plainchant in place for centuries.[68] But this quality scarcely diminishes the function and potential efficacy of the music. The unadventurous settings may even have lent a certain level of prestige to the plainchants. The transparency and compression of the melodies could further help one listening to the *Mass for St. Anne* to focus on the power of the biblical texts without the encumbrances of a stretched sonic medium. With two contrafacta and four other chants in a moderate, unobtrusive style of chant, the spotlight will now shift to the texts for closer analysis. The most meaningful stylistic observations and concordances with this music having been made, the question of the two principal – and seemingly incompatible – topics raised in the anonymous *Mass for St. Anne* will take center stage: fertility and national peace.

Maternity, Christian Unity, and a Date for the *Mass for St. Anne*

As mentioned, few have commented on the *Mass for St. Anne*, despite the fact that it is a document in the life of Marguerite of Navarre, one of the key figures of the Renaissance. The manuscript has received some attention from Myra Orth, who has pointed to the author's orthodox view on St. Anne. Unlike the reformers who railed against the saint's trinubium, the preface takes an uncritical stance toward the Three Marys tradition, as shown earlier.[69] Further, the anonymous author explains that St. Anne's seven grandsons played a foundational role in the development of the Church, implicitly reinforcing the traditional view that St. Anne's progeny stemmed from the three alleged marriages. Orth also noted that the emphasis on infertility in the manuscript is not at odds with Marguerite's lack of children (a point examined shortly). Based on this evidence, she suggested 1518 as a possible date for the manuscript.[70]

Orth's proposed date for the mass of course places it at a time when biblical humanism was beginning to filter into the French court environment, a point that Orth does not address. As discussed already, there were at least two treatises on St. Anne during the period in question – one by Lefèvre (*De una ex tribus*, attached to the reissue of his Magdalene treatise), the other by Du Moulin (*Petit livret*). The essays, which both appeared between 1518 and 1519, dismantled the traditions surrounding the legend of the Three Marys, Du Moulin's vernacular treatise being the more discreet of the two. The *Mass for St. Anne*, whether in its preface or Proper plainchants, seems strangely oblivious to these nascent revisions to Christian traditions around the Magdalene and St. Anne. But the manuscript cannot be placed earlier than 1518; it must have been compiled and delivered to Marguerite after she acquired the duchy of Berry in late 1517. If indeed this small devotional booklet emerged around 1518 (or possibly early 1519), what can be said about the dual emphases on maternity and Christian unity in the *Mass for St. Anne*? These issues raised in the mass have yet to be explored in the context of French foreign affairs in general and Marguerite's life in particular.

One may begin by reflecting on the unusual conclusion to the Communion in the *Mass for St. Anne*. Although melismatic passages are *de rigueur* for the responsorial chants in the Mass, the unexpected ornamentation of the last phrase of *Gaudium et leticia invenietur* stands out against the conventions of the musically conservative Communion genre and deserves further comment. The uncharacteristic treatment at the "river of peace" declamation seems marked for importance in the context of the anonymous mass and may open a window to aid in the interpretation of both the mass texts and the manuscript's cryptic preface. As the final non-formulaic Proper of any mass, the Communion commonly features either a psalm text or, more often, a text from the gospel of the day (or another New Testament reading), and it serves to summarize the festal theme in a concise way. *Gaudium et leticia invenietur* offers no pithy excerpt from the New Testament, but instead a pastiche from the prophet Isaiah, the dominant source of texts in the anonymous mass:

Gaudium et leticia invenietur in ea quoniam electi mei non generabunt in conturbatione quia semen benedictorum domini est. Ecce ego de-climabo super eam quasi fluvium pacis.	Joy and gladness shall be found therein, thanksgiving, and the voice of praise [Is 51:3], for my elect shall not produce in trouble: they are the seed of the Lord's blessed [Is 65:23]. Behold I will bring upon her, as it were, a river of peace [Is 66:12].

The Communion speaks to God's chosen people, assuring them that they will be kept from all harm. The excerpt from chapter 65 of Isaiah pledges to the servants of God that they will become part of a precious lineage, by now a familiar point of connection with devotion to St. Anne. The concluding selection from chapter 66, however, brings the link to Mary's mother into yet sharper focus, if the context of the biblical passage is taken into consideration. In the verses surrounding the "river of peace" (v. 12), the Lord encourages his elect to rejoice in the new Jerusalem, as a child would be delighted in a lactating mother.[71] The "her" to whom a river of peace will be brought in the Communion antiphon is not the metaphorical lactating mother but rather Jerusalem (or Zion). Therefore, in light of this passage involving a mother and a people (or nation), there is a firmer connection not only to the implicit honoree St. Anne, but to the two thematic emphases in the anonymous *Mass for St. Anne* – motherhood and peace among nations. It is worthwhile to explore further the comfort that this mass attempts to extend to a woman hopeful for progeny and a nation eager to find peace among Christian powers.

The mass's texts on the subject of fertility are well suited to Marguerite, whose anxieties about motherhood and her fruitless marriage to Duke Charles of Alençon have survived in documents. There is no direct evidence of her "domestic" frustrations around 1518; instead, her exasperation comes into view from a cache of correspondence between 1521 and 1523 with one of the key figures of Reformation theology, Guillaume Briçonnet. Briçonnet was the Bishop of Meaux and became a kind of spiritual advisor for the duchess, as 123 valuable letters between the two attest.[72] Marguerite's disappointment and perceived inadequacy from sterility was a topic raised often with Briçonnet in the letters, and her state of mind can be reasonably presumed to have been of several years standing. The two developed a close patron-client relationship, Marguerite ironically casting their rapport in terms of a mother writing to a son.[73] The duchess's signatures in her correspondence with Briçonnet capture in miniature her deflated, self-denigrating mindset. She closed her letters by calling herself "your sterile mother," or more often, "your useless mother."[74] Briçonnet encouraged Marguerite to have faith despite her lack of children, just as other barren women of the Old Testament (like Sarah) trusted in God to help them conceive against trying circumstances.[75] The allusion to the ancient sterile-women-turned-mothers resonates in the foreword of the *Mass for St. Anne*, in which the author sets the stage for her legend by noting the similar faith in God shown by Abraham and Sarah to bear a child.[76] The analogy is of course not evidence that Briçonnet had any part in the mass composed for Marguerite. Rather, it is confirmation – seen more than once throughout this study – that those who promoted St. Anne relied heavily on portraying her impressive lineage, usually by demonstrating the parallels with the barren-mother prototype of the Old Testament.

The anonymous author of the preamble to the *Mass for St. Anne* was plainly aware of the powerful hold on maternity accorded to Mary's mother, but he was also aiming for something much broader in advocating devotion to the grandmother of Christ. He boldly believed that the church could be restored and a lasting peace among Christians could be achieved with fervent prayers to Mary's mother, whose seven grandsons secured the church in a time of ecclesiastical unity.[77] The author's hope for the church's renewal exceeds what one expects in a simple orthodox treatise on St. Anne (let alone a mass), which might defend the Three Marys and the power of the Holy Kinship at more length. Instead, St. Anne seems to be a ready portal to the author's deeper political concerns. The anonymous writer invited all Christians in France to use the saint as motivation to set aside differences, band together under one church, and confront the persistent Turkish threat.

The author of the *Mass for St. Anne* appears favorable to the Holy See, his only admonition to the pope (Leo X) and his prelates being to seek "the rich and precious treasure of peace" (*le riche et precieux tresor de paix*) among Christians and to avoid excesses and corruption.[78] The generally positive outlook toward Rome supports the proposed date of 1518 for the mass. French relations with the pope were mollified after 1515 in the wake of the Battle of Marignano. The 1516 pact known as the Concordat of Bologna abolished the long-standing "Pragmatic Sanction of Bourges," a controversial decree from 1438 by the French king Charles VII requiring the pope to submit to conciliar authority every ten years. With other provisions, the Concordat brought substantial income from France to Rome, while giving the crown authority to nominate most bishops and abbots.[79] The warming relationship between Leo X and Francis I would briefly strengthen French claims in Milan and Naples.

The *Mass for St. Anne* more than once floats the idea of a crusade against the infidel. These references to a united holy war against the Turks were also likely a product of the closing years of the second decade of the sixteenth century. A fragile peace having been attained between the French and the Habsburgs in a treaty signed at Cambrai in 1517, the two sides agreed to join forces if attacked or if called to undertake a crusade against their common enemy. The promise does not appear to have been made in vain or without reason. That same year, the Ottoman Empire, then under Selim I, had made significant territorial gains in the Balkans, as well as in Syria and Egypt. Leo X took notice of these conquests, and the College of Cardinals proposed a military campaign to be led jointly by Francis I and the Holy Roman Emperor (still Maximilian). The crusade never materialized, a sign that the two parties were not quite willing to set aside all their differences for a unified Christian cause.[80] Any hope for a meaningful partnership between France, the Holy Roman Empire, and the papacy evaporated with the election of Charles V as Holy Roman Emperor in June 1519, at which point Leo X became more strongly allied with the Habsburgs. The mass's call for a unified Christian initiative against the Turks therefore seems less probable the more one moves past 1519 into the early-to-mid 1520s. By then, the French focus was squarely on the Italian Wars, which ended in the king's imprisonment in 1525.

To sum up the rationale for dating the manuscript around 1518 (or early 1519), one can start with the author's casual mention of the Three Marys and the seven grandsons of St. Anne. Few at the court would have batted an eye at the reference to the members of the Holy Kinship at this time, especially considering the travels of Louise, Claude, and Marguerite in late 1515 to the reliquary sites of Mary Iacobi and Mary Salome. The subject of Jesus' extended family, rife with the attendant political implications, was evidently en vogue for the remainder of the decade, as Sarto's *Holy Family with Angels* and Raphael and Romano's *Holy Family of François I* testify in court visual culture. The St. Anne treatises by Lefèvre and Du Moulin that revised the saint's legend were presumably known to the Royal Trinity by 1519, but Beda's *Apologia* of 1520 seems to mark the waning of the fad.

In the advent of the court's complicity with the Meaux Circle after 1520, Marguerite herself would have been increasingly unreceptive to a document in honor of Mary's mother that did not take a hard look at the legend of St. Anne. Though her core religious beliefs have been much debated, Marguerite's sympathies increasingly lay with the reformers after 1520, at least compared to her mother and brother. For the conservatively leaning *Mass for St. Anne* to have impact with the duchess of Alençon and Berry, it stands to reason that the manuscript would have to have been delivered in a time when the grandmother saint was a relevant topic at court, but no earlier than Marguerite's acquisition of the duchy of Berry. The logical deduction is that the implicit defense of St. Anne and the inflated hopes for a political reconciliation among Christian powers demonstrated in this mass must place it around 1518 or possibly early 1519. Orth's suggested date of 1518 for the *Mass for St. Anne* thus holds up to scrutiny. Furthermore, the proposed timing of the manuscript accommodates the peace that the author extends to both an infertile woman and a nation embroiled in internal struggles. What kind of person with ties to the court could have created this musico-political document?

The Problem of Authorship

With the date of the *Mass for St. Anne* reasonably confined, some final conjecture on the authorship of the document is in order. It is difficult, for starters, to opine about a composer of plainchant for the mass. Chant studies have necessarily avoided composer attributions, if only because ascriptions, especially in the earliest chants, were virtually nonexistent and inappropriate for the genre. (At least two of the Propers, to be sure, were contrafacta.) Concerning music at Francis's court, modern scholarship has exclusively devoted itself to the bounty of polyphony that survives from that time and place. It will prove most useful to focus on the Proper texts and the extensive foreword to whittle down the kind of person who might have had a hand in the mass for Marguerite.

Some biographical information about this writer can be obtained in the preface, but the clues leave many questions. The author is evidently an ardent St. Anne devotee, who casually reveals that he has already penned two treatises or books (*livres*) to the saint prior to the compilation of the *Mass for St. Anne*. He also explains that he will be undertaking a journey to visit three churches dedicated to the mother of the Virgin Mary.[81] The only two surviving treatises on St. Anne associated with the court during the period in question are familiar by now – Lefèvre's *De una ex tribus* and Du Moulin's *Petit livret*. Lefèvre's direct tone, preference for Latin, and criticism of the Three Marys would certainly eliminate him as a potential author of the *Mass for St. Anne*. Du Moulin, the more duplicitous of the two, similarly cannot be proposed as a serious candidate; frankly, there are not enough hints of reformational thinking in the introduction for it to be the work of the king's tutor and chaplain.

The two previous St. Anne treatises that the author apparently composed (presumably in the vernacular) have obviously not survived, and there is no way of knowing who took leave at the court during this time to visit churches dedicated to Mary's mother. When one considers that Francis's royal entourage alone had more than five hundred officials, it is like finding a needle in a haystack.[82] In the king's chapel alone, there was an abundance of chaplains (and singers!) who could have manufactured a document like this, though not Francis's confessor Guillaume Petit. Although Petit held conservative views, he was a Dominican and presumably would not have embraced the Three Marys legend so quickly. Any nominee put forward must be a traditional voice in the St. Anne debate with some ties to the court.

As mentioned earlier, the author, probably a Franciscan, presents the volume to the duchess in the dedicatory miniature of the mass (Figure 7.4). It is true that the opening image of the *Petit livret* showed Lefèvre presenting the work of Du Moulin while kneeling before Louise (Figure 7.3), but this is probably the author himself offering the book to the duchess in the case of the *Mass for St. Anne*. The Royal Trinity's penchant for the Franciscans is well known, as is the Franciscan order's fondness for St. Anne, seen in Chapter 3. Recall also that it was the Franciscan friar Francis of Paule who predicted to Louise that she would not only give birth to a son, but that this boy would become king, a prophecy that hardly seemed believable around 1490. The Franciscan, who specialized in asking God to help noble families produce daughters and (especially) sons, served the court of Louis XI beginning in 1482 and remained there after his death. Francis of Paule died in 1507, and therefore could not have played a role in the *Mass for St. Anne*.[83]

All three members of the Royal Trinity, especially Marguerite, were specifically interested in reform of the Franciscans and other religious orders. In the 1510s, the Franciscans had split into three suborders (Observant, Conventual, and reformed Conventual), which sparred over the proper role and responsibilities of the order, especially with regard to the vow of poverty.[84] After Francis of Paule's death, a friar by the name of Boniface de Ceva seemed to carry the torch of the Franciscans in the eyes of the French court. De Ceva, a leading minister within the reformed Conventual branch of Franciscans, arose as a favorite of the Royal Trinity. Noticed even by the pope, De Ceva preached a message of unity among the Franciscan houses. As an important gesture of support for De Ceva's goals, Louise and Marguerite invited the reformed Conventual minister to preach at court during Advent in 1515.[85] But De Ceva's death in 1516 would seem to exclude him from having a hand in the *Mass for St. Anne*, which must have been compiled after 1517.

Other clergymen at the French court during this period have received little or no study. Almost nothing is known, for instance, about Louise's confessor Bernardin, a Franciscan friar.[86] But one final nameable figure, Franciscan friar Jean Thenaud (ca. 1480–1542), does emerge in court circles as a possible contributor to the *Mass for St. Anne*.[87] Louise apparently discovered Thenaud within a Franciscan community in Angoulême, though his first known work – commissioned by Louise for Marguerite – is from 1508. Well credentialed with a master of arts and doctor of theology degree, Thenaud is better known for his literary works honoring Francis, his most famous one being the *Le Triumphe de vertuz*, which mythologizes the king as a valiant crusader and fighter of the Turks.[88] Certainly the Turkish threat is very much a concern in the preface of the *Mass for St. Anne*.

Thenaud further kept an eye on diplomatic relations on behalf of Louise, and from 1511 until 1513, he even journeyed to Jerusalem at the regent's request.[89] He also received commissions from Louise to write edifying works for both Francis and Marguerite and was a fixture at the court into the early 1530s, when he was listed as an almoner to the king. Thenaud wrote two treatises for Francis in particular on the tradition of Jewish mysticism known as cabalism, the principles of which the king had eagerly sought at court around 1518. This philosophy was one manifestation of a relatively small Christian "magical movement" (even by the late sixteenth century) that also included emphasis on astrology, numerology, and Pythagoreanism to locate esoteric truths that could unlock mysteries of the ancient past. Cabalism received attention from humanists as well, apparently for the hope it brought of revealing hidden teachings in the Old Testament.[90] Remember that the author of the *Mass for St. Anne* was obsessed with the number seven in the preface, and he indeed filled the document with more references to the Old Testament than to St. Anne herself.

Perhaps Louise tapped Thenaud for this mass. Although no record of his musical inclinations survives, there is some evidence that Thenaud might have written a "Mass for Three Marys," possibly fulfilling the requirement of having composed earlier documents on the subject of St. Anne, an important biographical point for any author-candidate. Orth at one point dismissed Thenaud as a potential author for the *Mass for St. Anne*, possibly because of a misreading of earlier scholarship, but the suggestion of Thenaud's authorship clearly has to be reentertained.[91]

There is obviously no smoking gun in the search for an agent to connect to the anonymous *Mass for St. Anne*. What is not in dispute is that the saint had become so much of an institution for the Royal Trinity that invocations for the sake of maternity were just the beginning of the usages that could be harvested from her patronage. The image of the saint had long been cultivated at the French court, but St. Anne was thrown into sharp relief in works such as Leonardo's *Virgin and Child with Saint Anne*, illustrative at once of the intimacy and potency of the nation's Royal Trinity. Amid the demands for ecclesiastical reform within the court that would come to a head in the early 1520s, a most unusual artifact appeared in the royal circle. An unassuming mass – isolated from any formal liturgical book yet containing liturgically proper utterances in song – was compiled with biblical and apocryphal texts (transferable to St. Anne) and aimed to comfort a childless duchess. But the curious introduction to these liturgical pieces, possibly written by Jean Thenaud, unveils how St. Anne was a sanctoral gateway to current pressing issues in France at the end of the 1510s. Most urgently, the anonymous writer sought a lasting peace among Christians under the auspices of St. Anne, who is treated with the utmost conservative view in the manuscript. A unified Christendom in turn could rally together against a greater enemy of the faith. The sky was truly the limit for the church's venerable grandmother saint.

Postlude

The vast utility of St. Anne in premodern devotional life stems from two broadly related circumstances. On one hand, her apocryphal legend contained plentiful details that could be amplified to suit different cultural contexts; whether as compassionate matron or royal protectress, Mary's mother could be summoned by individuals of all social stripes. At the same time, St. Anne's efficacy can be viewed as a social response to a period of dynamic cultural changes and a growing need for a meritorious woman of faith to supplement the increasing devotion to the Virgin Mary. For example, St. Anne could be invoked for the cause of female literacy or for inspiration in the path of married life, ideas that took root during the late Middle Ages. With her extensive realms of intercession, the mother of Mary predictably found her way into some of the highest courts of early modern Europe, no doubt more than this study has offered. The disproportionate level of devotion accorded to St. Anne relative to her daughter was captured by Martin Luther, who, in 1525, wrote succinctly in protest: "She [Anne] is exalted almost above the Blessed Virgin."[1]

Apart from the cultural surge in commemorations of Mary's mother, there have been some unexpected turns in this study of sovereign devotion to the apocryphal grandmother of Christ. As it concerns studies of St. Anne, Chapter 4, for instance, revealed how the doctrine of the Immaculate Conception played an integral role in the devotional program of the Castle Church in Wittenberg, a finding that runs counter to recent analyses of Mary's mother that have kept the controversial teaching at an arm's length from the veneration of St. Anne.[2] From a musicological point of view, there have also been some unpredictable discoveries. In Chapter 7, it was shown most vividly that the simplest of plainchants could function as a crucial vehicle in devotional politics, as a monophonic *Mass for St. Anne* served both as a fertility plea and as a starting point for promoting an agenda for a royal court. All too often, plainchant has been the second fiddle in Renaissance musicological scholarship. By framing this entire study with two cases of monophony for St. Anne, it is the hope that more attention will be drawn to the value of plainchant as a contributor to noble prestige and self-fashioning.

It is significant that almost all of the sources tapped for this study are well known to musicologists, thereby confirming that one does not have to go far to find music for St. Anne on rich musicological turf. Several of the surveyed manuscripts are part of the output from the Alamire scriptorium, the most prestigious workshop of the period.[3] Apart from the Alamire compilations, the early fifteenth-century Turin Codex (Chapter 2) remains one of the most significant musical sources of its time, and even the modestly compiled Jena choirbooks, associated with the Castle Church in Wittenberg (examined in Chapter 4), received a full-length study in 1995.[4] Music for St. Anne was prominently featured in all of these important sources (most notably in the Palatini partbooks in Chapter 6), which speaks to the saint's high regard and broad areas of intercession. More importantly, though, this study has explored the function and utility of this music in the lives of the nobles who received it. Without question, women have dominated the cast of characters. It is no surprise that women should be connected with the "grandmother saint," but it is instructive to see ruling women at or near the center of the reception history of these important sources of fifteenth- and early sixteenth-century music. As this study has demonstrated, the realm of music, open to both men and women as a distinguished pursuit and marker of nobility, was a particularly advantageous space for women to cultivate the dynastic ambitions of a noble house and advance political strategies.

This has not been an exhaustive study of music for St. Anne, and there is no doubt much more fertile territory to explore that commemorates Mary's mother in song. As with any saint, a full study of the versified office repertory can fill in many gaps in the portrayal of a saint across the late Middle Ages. As mentioned in Chapter 2, more than twenty versified offices survive for St. Anne, representing a flurry of new musical activity reflective of the saint's outstanding reputation and no doubt intercessory flexibility. Although not all pieces in honor of St. Anne will prove to have a discernible political motive, opportunities also abound to contextualize polyphonic works for St. Anne, perhaps beginning with John Dunstaple's polytextual motet *Gaude felix mater Anna / Gaude mater / Anna parens*.[5] Other polyphonic works for the grandmother saint in the sixteenth century and beyond also await study. Jacquet of Mantua's motet *Ave mater matris Dei* is especially intriguing for being modeled on the well-known melody "Fortuna desperata."[6] Particular geographical locations devoted to St. Anne could be probed for extant musical sources. As Virginia Nixon's study has revealed, the Rhineland was a major center of veneration of Mary's mother, St. Anne, yet the region did not emerge in this study of musical artifacts, admittedly focused on patronage from major European courts. The cities of

Aachen, Trier, and Cologne were all notable places of pilgrimage to visit the *Mater matris*, and churches in this region almost invariably possessed some image or relic of St. Anne; surely, music was one of the cultural products that helped people honor their patroness.[7]

As St. Bonaventure once declared, "Those things which are only heard fall into oblivion more easily than those things which are seen."[8] This idea captures the state of scholarship on St. Anne for the past century. Art historical studies have held court among those in pursuit of the various meanings behind Mary's mother in the late Middle Ages and the Renaissance. Only now is the discipline of musicology joining the scholarly conversation. Naturally, investigations of visual art and music (as well as literature) can help provide a more balanced picture in studies of the grandmother saint. Especially in this case of a figure with mutable areas of intercession, it makes sense to account for all areas of cultural production to form a picture of St. Anne's unusually strong impact on devotional and political life in the advent of the Reformation. In this survey of music for Mary's mother, significant substance has been put to the idea that St. Anne was more than a preferred mother: her illustrious heritage and eminent progeny were assets that had great appeal to those who wielded political power in Western Europe.

Appendix A

251

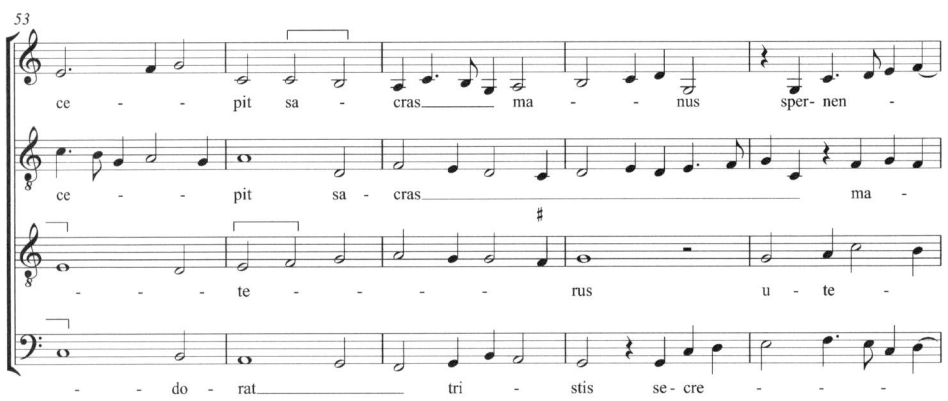

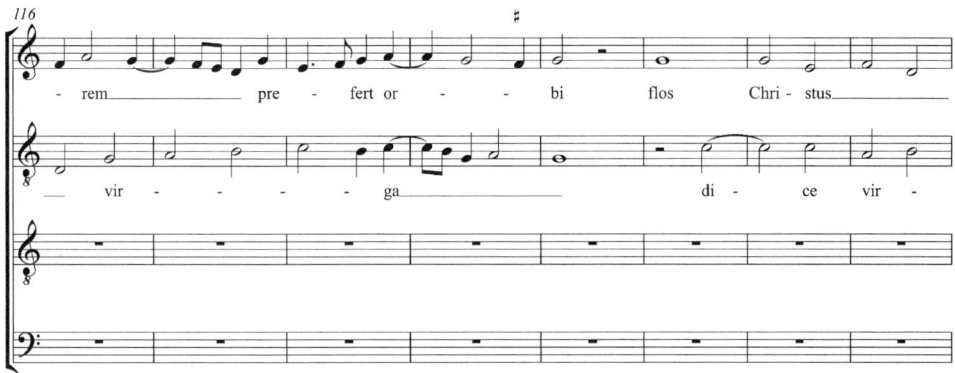

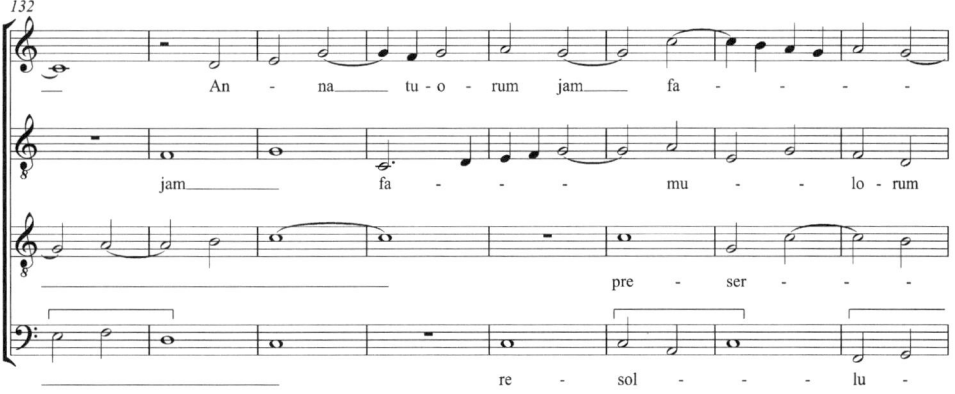

258   *Appendix A*

Appendix B: Complete Text of the *Mass for St. Anne* (Paris, Bibliothèque nationale de France, MS fr. 1035)

- The use of italics indicates that the text is rubricated in the manuscript.
- Underlined text indicates that these words were written in the preface but were not set to music in the manuscript.
- Full translation available at www.esm.rochester.edu/andersonbook/.

[1r] *De S^e Anne mere des trois maries une messe*

[1v] Marguerite de France
Duchesse d'Allencon et de Berry
Jay souvent medite ma dame que ferme foy est
actente certaine de tout bien qui par provi-
dence de dieu doit advenir a ceulx qui per fidelite

[2r] *et bones operations le meriteront envers luy. En cest espoir*
ie ay escript ce que s'en sust. et le vous presente ma dame vous suppliant
tres humblement qu'il vous plaise de vostre grace le prendre en gre.
Celluy qui desire ediffier quelque bonne
oeuvre permanente a perpetuite doit
prendre fondamente si ferme que la
sollidite d'icelluy puisse porter et soustenir la perfection de l'ediffice. A l'example de ihesu crist
qui ediffice son eglise dessus luy mesmes qui est
le vray et ferme fondement dessus lequel le bon
patriarche abraham fonda sa foy quant la re-
promission divine luy fut faicte que toutes
nations heriteroyent en sa semence. Et iacoisse
qu'il fust nonagenaire invetere. Et aussi que sa
femme eust desia dessiste d'avoir les signes na-
turelz d'aptitude de conceptuoir il eut creance
en dieu. Et telle creance comme dit le scripture. Luy fut reputee a iustice dont merita
davoir lignee. Ce qui tousiours il avoit desire sur toutes choses. Parce susdit apert
assez que ferme foy est de merite si excellent

et si subtil en bien que par vertu d'icelle
tout ce quon scait iustement desirer et sou-
haiter facillement vient a perfection de bon effect.
Meu de telle consideration iay visite les
escriptures sainctes ou iay comprins que la

[2v] fidelle propagation d'abraham a este tellement
continuee que dicelle est procedee une tres
vertueuse dame. Laquelle fut legitimement
mariee a troys marys. Et d'un chascun
diceulx eut une fille. Et les troyes filles
eurent sept filz. Et quant iay eu bien
souvent medite ce que dit est iay con-
temple que saincte eglise millitante nous
fut directement prefiguree en icelle saincte
lignee. au temps de la nativitate de ihsus
crist qui en est procede quant a l'huma-
nite miraculeusement unie a sa divinite
tres excellente pour subvenir misericordiai-
sement a noz fragillitez humaines. Cest
ce qui me donne esperance et ferme foy que
quelque chose que nous humains puiss-
ions et doyvons iustement desirer et sou-
haiter pourra estre par ferme foy impe-
tree et obtenue par ceulx ou celles qui de-
votament requerront ladicte tres saincte
lignee et reverence de laquelle(.) La messe
qui s'ensuit a este composee et ordonne et
tres bien experimentee en ce que toutes choses
a l'intention desquelles obtenir a este celebree devotement sont advenues au profit
et plaisir de ceulx qui de bon cueur ont

[3r] adresse leur devotion a ladicte saincte lignee
par l'intercession de laquelle nous verrons
l'eglise millitante pasciffiee les Roys et princes de la xpiante unys et assemblez pour
soustenir nostre saincte foy catholique
dessoubs l'obeissance de la tres saincte et sacree Romanie eglise mere et maistresse

de toutes autres eglises. Dont a bon droit
elle nous a este presignee et prefiguree per
ladicte saincte anne mere des troyes nobles
maries signifiantes les troyes partyes du
monde esquelles toutes eglises signiffies
par les sept filz sont construistes et ediffices.
Puis doncques que du temps quilz estoient vivans au monde paix universelle regnoit. Et aussi que l'universite de
l'eglise nous a este prefiguree comme
dit est en icelle saincte cognation. Nous
pouons devenient esperer que par l'intercession dicelle apres ce que les tres nobles roys
et princes de la xpinante par une tres bonne
union auront destruictez et desconfis les
infidelles. Nous verrons de rechief paix
universelle regner selon les vrayes propheties declairees au sainct apocalipse.
Et celles qui sont contenues icy apres

[3v] et ordonnees en la composition dicelle messe
lesquelles vous seront exposees en langaige
francoys par ung petit traicte que iay ia
commence a composer. Et l'auray acheve
bientost apres que seray revenu du voyaige que ie propose faire quant a visiter
troyes devotes eglises ediffiees construie-
tes en l'honneur de dieu et fondees ou nom
de ladicte saincte anne. Et espere vous pre-
senter ma dame moy revenu le dicte traicte
pour vous deduire et recreer en le lisant
quant aurez apperceu que dieu vous aura
visitee de sa grace ainsi quil visita icelle
glorieuse saincte par l'intercession laquelle
il a lmparti plusieurs graces depuis qua-
tre ans en ca a maintes dames. Et de ce
vous ma dame pourrez estre acertenee quant
vous laurez experimente par effect. Et combien que mon frere qui pour honneur
de vous ma dame m'a bien souvent sol-

icite d'entreprendre ledict voyaige vous
ait presente ladicte messe laquelle depuis
a este notee et myse en forme comienent
pour estre celebree a autre voix en saincte eglise. Je vous supplie tres humblement ma dame qu'il vous plaise prier

[4r] monseigneur reverendissime mon seigneur le legat que son plaisir soit de
aproner ladicte messe d'auctre apostolicque. Affin que plus devotement et
affectueusement elle puisse estre celebree
en toute la crestiante. Et au moyen de
ce par les prieres et intercessions des
saincts et sainctes dicelle tres sacree lignee et noble generation. Vous ma dame puissies obtenir voz nobles et iu-
stes desirs. Et paix universelle nous
puisse estre octroyee de dieu en toute
la crestiante ainsi que doibuons esperer selon l'intelligence spirituelle des
sainctes propheties specifiees en icelle
comme desia nous en avons bonne et
certaine experience. Car par la bonne a-
liance de paix qui doibt estre main-
tenant confermee entre les deux nobles et puissans roys tous aultres
roys et princes pourront estre au moy-
en diceulx alies et unis dessoubs l'o
beissance de la tres saincte et sacree
Romaine eglise pour la deffence de
la foy catholique comme dit est.
Et pour les inciter soustisamment a ce

[4v] grant bien soustiroit qu'il leur pleust
devmnt contemplee la devote hystoire presente figuree en deux sep-
tennaires significantes les deux peuples
iuifz et gentiles qui doibuent estre une
fois assemblez en simple et seul nombre de sept dans ung parc soubz ung
seul pasteur.

ILLUSTRATION
Marginalia (counterclockwise from top left, corresponding to pictures of commentary on the text):
de animantibus mundis tolles
septena et septena
Sumite tauros septem et ari-
etes septem.
Letamini gentes cum
plebe eius.
Et erit unum oville et unus pastor.
Isti sunt septem oculi
domini qui discurunt
super universam fa-
ctem terre.
Benedicat vos altis-
simus et sitis sicut
columne [recte: columbe] septem civitatis refugii
Anna in sterili-
tate synagogam
in fecunditate uni-
versalem ecclesiam
militate persignavit.

[5r] *A nostre tressaincte pere le pape*
et messeigneurs le prelatz de saincte eglise.
Meilleur moyen ny a dessoubz les cieulz
pour obtenir le riche et precieux
tresor de paix. Et eviter l'oultrance
de mars pervers cruel ambitieux
que contempler de cueur devocieux
le script present. lhystoire. et la substance
Ne cuidez pas que dieu de l'assustance
Veu quil monstre estieue et qui sustante
ce beau signe misericordieux.
Regardez le. de misericors veulx
Vous messieurs procurans pacience.
Aux tres illustres et puissans roys
et princes de la crestiante.
Tres nobles roys advisez aussi en ce.
princes vsez de devote science

Et pour avoir victoire promptement
des turcs suyvez le train de sapience
et poursuyvez d'acquerir l'aliance
de saincte anne. Car anne proprement
est nom propre/ tres apropriement
dit fondement de grace qui soustient.
parquoy certes pourrez tresaisement
a son moyen vivre paisiblement
selon le sens que l'hystoire contient.

[5v] *A la royne ma souvevaine dame*
et mes dames du royal sang de France.
Nobles dames a vous bien appartient
tenir propoz de celle qui maintient
le vostre estat en ranc tres augtenticque
le royal sang. de france elle entretient
pour ce quil est ainsi que chascun tient
le plus ferme en la foy catholicque.
Considerez que la plus pacificque
magnificque dame qui ait este
en la lignee royalle iudaicque
tresanticque nacion hebraicque
marie excluse. Cest Anne en verite.
Pour ce que par experienc on a veu au
moyen dicelle maintes graces advenir ie dis.
En partie ay escript et recite
sa sainctete, ses vertus, sa bonte
en deux livres. Et comme pourrez veoir
par le dernier proesme du traicte
ie prove a plain par mainte auctorite
que envers dieu a tressouveraine povoir
de nous aider si nous faisons debuoir
de la servir honnorer et requerrer
Lescript present le vous fait assavoir
Vous plaise donc y entendre et provoir
Et vous verrez roys et princes sans guerre.

[6r] *Les propheties et sainctes escriptures*
tesmoignent que ceste figure est veritable.
Ja ne convient laide daultres saincts querre

pour impetrer. obtenir. et acquerre
joye. sante. et generation.
Croyez de vray si lescripture ne erre
mars viydera aussi tost que tonnerre
sans excerse extermination.
sauf sus la faulce extere nation.
signifiee par ung monstre infesste
qui sera mis en conculcation
a tresbon droit par sa malle action.
com lhystoire presente manifeste.

ILLUSTRATION
Nunquid tu percusisti superbum vulneristi draconem. PSA C° LI°
dictum est de dyabolo quia leo et draco est.
Leo propter impetum. Draco propter insidias. AUGUSTI

[6v] *Au devot et catholicque*
peuple de France.
Peuple francoys chascun de vous sapreste
de prier dieu qui nous donne et nous preste
le don de paix. dont il monstre leseigne
Et informez a la myenne requeste
Voz esperitz visitans par enqueste
la cronicque du grant roy charlemaigne
qui declaire nous aprent et enseigne
que lydolle salacandis lairra
tumber sa clef. par indice certaine
quem france aura une fois chevetaine
qui les ydolles du monde deservira.
Officium misse ad honorem sanctissime
generationis dive anne in qua sancta millitans
ecclesia prefigurata fuit tempore regis pa-
cifici christi pace universaliter regnante
Et quem predicta sancta anna prius sterilis
postmodum fecunda fuit merito credendum
est fecunditatis aptitudinem universalis
ecclesie pacem et unitatem ab omnipotenti deo ob-
tineri posce intercessionem sanctorum et sanctarum
sacratissime generationis predicte iuxta sub
sequentium prophetiarum spiritualem intelligen-

tiam [Nam iiii° esdre. c° ii°] *scriptum est.*

Officium.
[7r] Noli timere mater
filiorum quoniam te elegi
et paravi tibi montes inmen-
sos septem habentes rosam et lilium in
quibus implebo filios tuos pace et
gaudio *Versus* [Psalmus in music]. Mater amplectere filios tuos. *Responsorem.* Educa illos in leticia.
[Collect]
Deus qui in utero virginis de
sacerdotali et regali progenie
preelecte cooperante gratia spiritussancti
unigenitum tuum pro reconsiliatione
humam generis concipi huicque mundo salubriter oriri sanxisti. Omnibus
sanctis nobilissime generationis in qua hu-
manitatem assumere dignatus est intercedentibus. ecclesiam militantem. reges et principes christiani nobis unire et pascificare eiusque
generosam prolem ad tue sacre fidei augmentum concedere digneris. Per eundem…
Epistola Lectio ysaye prophete
Letare sterilis que non paris. decanta laudem et hymni que non
pariebas. Quoniam multi filii deserte
magis quam eius que habebat virum
dicit dominus dilata locum tentorii

[7v] tui et pelles tabernaculorum tuorum exten-
de. Ne parcas. Longos fac funiculos
tuos et clavos tuos consolida. Ad dex-
teram enim et ad levam penetrabis
et semen tuum gentes hereditabit et
civitates desertas in habitabit. Noli
timere quia non confunderis neque eru-
besces. Non enim te pudebit. Quia con-
fusionis adolescentie tue oblivisceris
et opprobrii viduitatis tue non recor-

daberis amplius. Quia donabitur
tui qui fecit te. Dominus exercituum nomen
eius et redemptor tuus sanctus israel
deus omnis terre vocabitur. Quia ut
mulierem derelictam et merentem spiritu
vocavit te dominus et uxorem ab adolescen-
tia abiectam dixit deus tuus dominus.
Exsurge iherusalem et sta in. *Responsorem.*
excelso et vide collectos filios ab
oriente sole usque ad occidentem in ver-
bo sancti gaudentes dei memoria. *Versus.*
Ponam omnes terminos tuos in lapides

[8r] desiderabiles universos filios tuos doc-
tos a domino et multitudinem pacis filiis tuis.
Alleluia. *Versus.* Multiplicabitur que
derelicta fuerat et aduc in ea deci-
macio. semen pacis erit id quod steterit
in ea.
Tractus.
Commovebo celum et terram et ma-
re et aridam. *Versus.* Et movebo omnes
gentes et veniet desideratus cunctis gen-
tibus. *Versus.* Et in loco ista [music: isto] dabo pacem genti-
bus dixit [music: dicit] dominus.
Evangelium secundum marcum. [3:28]
In illo tempore dixit iesus discipulis suis. Nemo
potest vasa fortis ingressus in
domum dirripere nisi prius fortem alli-
get et tunc domum eius dirripiet. Amen
dico vobis quoniam omnia dimittentur filiis
hominum peccata et blaphemie quibus blaphe-
marverunt. Qui autem blaphemave-
rit in spiritum sanctum non habebit remissio-
nem in eternum sed reus erit eterni delicit
quem dicebant spem in mundum habet.
Et veniunt mater eius et fratres et foris
stantes miserunt ad eum vocantes eum.
Et sedebat circa eum turba et dicunt ei.

[8v] Ecce mater tua et fratres tui foris que-
runt te. Et responderis eis ait. Que est
mater mea et qui sunt fratres mei?
Et circunspiciens eos qui in circuitu eius
sedebant ait. Ecce mater mea et fratres
mei. Qui enim fecerit voluntatem dei
ipse meus frater soror mea et mater mea est.
Offertorium.
Luce splendida fulgebis et
omnes fines terre adorabunt te. Tu
autem letaberis in filiis tuis beati omnes
qui diligunt te et qui gaudent super
pace tua.
Secreta.
Sacramentis tuis quis domine intende
placatus et intercedentibus omnibus
sanctis nobilissime generationis beatissime
anne devotioni nostre proficiant et
saluti, per domini.
Communio.
Gaudium et leticia invenietur in ea
<u>gratiarum actio et vox laudis</u> quoniam
electi mei non generabunt in conturbatione
quia semen benedictorum domini est. Ecce ego de-
climabo super eam quasi fluvium pacis.
Postcommunio.
Ora quos opus deus ut quorum memoriam sacramen-
ti participatione recolimus eorum intercessionem que
ore contingimus pura mente capiamus. p.d. [per dominum]

Notes

1 Mary's Mother

1. The work of Jennifer Bloxam in particular has been valuable. See her "In Praise of Spurious Saints" and "Sacred Polyphony and Local Traditions of Liturgy and Plainsong."
2. A classic article on music and the anxiety regarding salvation around the turn of the sixteenth century remains Howard Mayer Brown, "The Mirror of Man's Salvation."
3. Bonnie Blackburn has demonstrated a flurry of polyphonic composition in connection with the rise of the Immaculate Conception teaching in her "Virgin in the Sun." More recently, Anne Robertson has shown the Marian resonance in the Caput masses in "The Savior, the Woman, and the Head of the Dragon." For a set of chants composed for a new feast of the Virgin Mary, written by no less than Guillaume Du Fay, see Haggh, "The Celebration of the 'Recollectio Festorum Beatae Mariae Virginis.'"
4. The German rendering of "Holy Kinship" (*Heilige Sippe*) is often encountered in the scholarly literature, much less so the Latin terms *Sancta parentela* and *Mariae cognatio*. See Esser, "Die Heilige Sippe," 8.
5. Huizinga, *The Autumn of the Middle Ages*, esp. 294–328.
6. Two recent studies that spring to mind in this regard are Robertson, "The Man with the Pale Face" and Rothenberg, "The Most Prudent Virgin and the Wise King."
7. More generally, studies of music and politics of the fifteenth and sixteenth centuries are plentiful. See, for example, Kellman, ed., *The Treasury of Petrus Alamire*; Strohm, "European Politics and the Distribution of Music"; and Wright, "Musicology and the Fifteenth Century."
8. Hankeln, *Political Plainchant?*, 3–4.
9. Byrd's recusant lifestyle and his musical output based on the politics of the English monarch are described in Kerman, *The Masses and Motets of William Byrd*, and more recently, Monson, "Byrd, the Catholics, and the Motet" and McCarthy, *Liturgy and Contemplation in Byrd's* Gradualia.
10. Andrew Kirkman has produced excellent studies of the development of the polyphonic mass and its cultural meaning. See his *The Cultural Life of the Early Polyphonic Mass* and "The Invention of the Cyclic Mass."
11. I am not aware of a study that addresses the broader phenomenon of music for patrons' namesake saints. For a close study of music for Obrecht's mass for John

the Baptist and its connection to Leo X (himself a "John," *Giovanni de' Medici*), see Anderson, "'His Name Will Be Called John.'" On patron dedications in prints (though without mention of namesake saints), see the essays in Bossuyt et al., eds., *Cui dono lepidum novum libellum?*.

12 In Eastern Christendom, the *Protoevangelium* was considered an authoritative source, and Greeks, Syrians, and Copts sometimes read parts of it during Marian feasts. The survival of numerous manuscripts not only in Greek but also in Coptic (Sahidic), Syriac, Armenian, Georgian, Ethiopic, Old Church Slavonic, and Arabic translations testifies to the high status of the *Protoevangelium* in the Eastern Church. See Ashley and Sheingorn, eds., *Interpreting Cultural Symbols*, 6–10.

13 For an English translation, see Elliott, ed., *Apocryphal New Testament*, 57–9.

14 Anne even asks God to help her conceive in the manner of Sarah (ibid., 58). The name Hannah, from which Anne (*Anna*) is derived, means "grace" in Hebrew. Many versified offices for St. Anne use this etymology to connect St. Anne with her daughter Mary ("full of grace").

15 Luke 1:11–20.

16 Its accounts deemed unreliable in the fourth and fifth centuries by Jerome and others, the *Protoevangelium* was later revived during the Carolingian era, and a family of texts dubbed *Pseudo-Matthew* transmitted the most popular parts of St. Anne's legend within the infancy narrative of the Virgin Mary. See Reames, ed., *Middle English Legends of Women Saints*, 249. For the development of the *Pseudo-Matthew* texts in particular, see Gijsel, *Die unmittelbare Textüberlieferung*. On the revival of the *Protoevangelium* during Carolingian times, see Amann, *Le Protevangile de Jacques*, 138–76.

17 Mark 6:3 and Matthew 12:47, 13:55.

18 The commentary is found in Jerome, "De perpetua virginitate, adversus Helvidium," in PL 23:193–216.

19 Haymo [of Halberstadt], "Historiae sacrae epitome," in PL 118:823–4. The various Marys, the subject of vigorous debate in early sixteenth-century France, can be found in Matthew 27:56, 61; Mark 15:40, 16:1; Luke 24:10; and John 19:25.

20 Sheingorn, "Appropriating the Holy Kinship," 185.

21 For the diffusion of the concept of the trinubium and the response of theologians, see Esser, "Die Heilige Sippe," 17–24. Theologians such as Peter Lombard and Petrus Comestor continued to propagate the details of the triple marriage. See Petrus Lombardus, "Collectanea in Epistolas Pauli. In Epistolam ad Galatas," in PL 192: 101ff. and Petrus Comestor, "Historia Scholastica. In Actus Apostolorum," in PL 198: 1563ff.

22 Voragine, *The Golden Legend*, 2:150. The Latin is additionally provided in this English translation.

23 The genealogy of Jesus is given in Matthew 1:1–17 and Luke 3:23–38. Voragine's rebuke of the evangelists runs counter to the prevailing trends of the thirteenth

century. Filial relationships were normally traced through the male and female lines (bilineal or cognatic kin) until the eleventh century, when patrilineage ("agnation") rose in prominence in literature and the visual arts. The agnatic line was especially important among the aristocracy, for whom ancestry was a crucial claim to nobility. See, for example, Herlihy, *Medieval Households*, vi.

24 To this twenty-two-person assembly was sometimes added St. Servatius – a fourth-century bishop from Maastricht said to descend from Anne's sister, Esmeria. Depictions of the extended Holy Kinship peaked in Germany and the Netherlands around 1500. See, for example, Kleinschmidt, *Die heilige Anna*, 263–81 and Esser, "Die Heilige Sippe," 42, 108–9. For a summary of the legend of Anne's mother, Emerentia, see Brandenbarg, "St. Anne and Her Family," 101.

25 The English were the first to recognize the universal feast day for Anne in the West (July 26). See Pfaff, *New Liturgical Feasts in Later Medieval England*, 2. The date of November 21 may also hold significance as the feast of the Presentation of Mary in the temple, a feast that traditionally includes mention of her parents, Anne and Joachim.

26 See, for example, Nixon, *Mary's Mother*, 73.

27 Steinberg, *The Sexuality of Christ*, 9.

28 The Dutch rendering *Anna-te-Drieen* also connotes the subsidiary role for Mary's mother.

29 For a history of the St. Anne Trinitarian in art, see, for example, Kleinschmidt, *Die heilige Anna*, 217–51; for the multiple meanings attached to this theme, see Nixon, *Mary's Mother*, 2–4 and passim.

30 Infant mortality was a serious concern of late medieval society, with as many as 30 percent of babies failing to make it through their first year. See Ward, *Women in Medieval Europe*, 51.

31 Terris, *Sainte Anne d'Apt*, 33 and Wilson, *The Magical Universe*, 136. Devotion to St. Anne in the south of France grew from a late medieval legend, which claimed that Anne's two daughters (Mary Cleophas and Mary Salome) and Mary Magdalene journeyed to that area following the Resurrection.

32 Brandenbarg, "Saint Anne: A Holy Grandmother and Her Children," 56. On similar devotional objects thought to aid the birthing process in the early modern period, see Gélis, *History of Childbirth*, 147–9.

33 For women and their newborns, the saint's patronage extended to the act of breastfeeding in some locales. In Normandy, for instance, women could bathe in the "wells of St. Anne" to create the flow of breast milk for their young. See Wilson, *The Magical Universe*, 266.

34 Gill, "Female Piety and Impiety" and Sheingorn, " 'The Wise Mother.' " See also Sanders, *Gender and Literacy*, 9–12.

35 Exclusive studies of St. Anne confraternities include Dörfler-Diercken, *Vorreformation Bruderschaften* and Dörfler-Diercken, *Die Verehrung der heiligen Anna*. Confraternities have also formed parts of studies by Brandenbarg, "Saint Anne: A Holy Grandmother and Her Children," 31–6 and Nixon, *Mary's Mother*,

esp. 67–9. On the general reception of St. Anne in northern humanist circles, see Tilmans, "Sancta Mater versus Sanctus Doctus," 336–49.

36 On the changing view of marriage, the value of sacramental marriage, and alternatives to the life of virginity, see Atkinson, *The Oldest Vocation*; Kamerick, *Popular Piety and Art in the Late Middle Ages*, 91; and Lipton, *Affections of the Mind*, 1–2. For contemporaneous evidence of the congruence of marriage and holy life, particularly with regard to St. Anne, see Denemarken, *Die Historie*.

37 Fleming, *Family and Household*, 84–9.

38 Dörfler-Diercken, *Vorreformation Bruderschaften*.

39 Nixon, *Mary's Mother*, esp. 42, 58. The author has drawn special attention to the expressly salvific power of St. Anne trumpeted in the imagery of the *Anna Selbdritt* and in *vitae* of the period.

40 Martin Luther, amid his criticism of invoking saints for trivial matters, mentions St. Anne not as a protector of women or the family, but as an advocate for those in search of earthly riches. See Luther, *Kritischer Gesammtausgabe*, II: 69ff. On St. Anne's oversight of the economic status of the faithful in the Rhineland, see Nixon, *Mary's Mother*, 76–9.

41 On the full range of Anne's intercessory capabilities arranged in alphabetical order (in German), see Gatz, "Zur Geschichte der Annaverehrungen," 155–6.

42 Walker and Luyster, *Negotiating Secular and Sacred in Medieval Art*, 1–8, and Cutler, "Sacred and Profane," 317.

43 The classic study on the *laudes* is Kantorowicz, *Laudes Regiae*. For a particularly vivid description of the use of the *laudes regiae* at Reims Cathedral, see Robertson, *Guillaume de Machaut and Reims*, 63–8.

44 Villani, *Cronica di Giovanni Villani*, IV:37. The missal Biblioteca Medicea Laurenziana, Florence, MS Edili 106 (from after 1427) confirms the liturgical presence of the feast of St. Anne at Santa Maria del Fiore in Florence. See Tacconi, *Cathedral and Civic Ritual in Late Medieval and Renaissance Florence*, 76. St. Anne was a popular subject in Florentine visual arts during this time, reflecting not her typical maternal qualities, but instead evoking an expressly republican spirit. See Crum and Wilkins, "In the Defense of Florentine Republicanism," 131–68.

45 See, for example, Nixon, *Mary's Mother*, 28, 52–3.

46 Philip I of Castile, son of Maximilian and Mary of Burgundy, is labeled as James the Less, while Charles V, the grandson of Maximilian (and future Holy Roman Emperor), is compared to Simon. Charles's brother, Ferdinand I (another future Holy Roman Emperor), receives an inscription identifying him as Joseph the Just.

47 Bloch, *Etymologies and Genealogies*, 70–81.

48 On the institution and customs of Western Christian marriage in the Middle Ages, see Goody, *The Development of the Family and Marriage in Europe*; Duby, *The Knight, the Lady, and the Priest*; Duby, *Love and Marriage in the Middle Ages*; and Lynch, *The Medieval Church*, 289–93.

49 See Fassler, "Mary's Nativity, Fulbert of Chartres, and the *Stirps Jesse*," esp. 411–12.
50 Nixon, *Mary's Mother*, 53. For the office references to the Jesse heritage, see *Virga Iesse protulit* (VA5, AH 5.34); *Inclita stirps Iesse* (VR, AH 25.18); and *Anna Iesse plantula* (VE, AH 5.35). Also, see *Gloriosa de te dicta* (MR3, AH 17.11) for specific use of the title *radix Iesse*.
51 Charland, *Madame saincte Anne*. Other brief mentions of music in the literature for St. Anne include Masseron, *Sainte Anne*, 46 and Dörfler-Dierken, *Die Verehrung der heiligen Anna*, 33.
52 Bonime, "Anne de Bretagne (1477–1514) and Music," 75.
53 Anna de' Medici (1616–76) was the archduchess of the Tyrolean branch of the Habsburgs, wife of Archduke Ferdinand Karl. On Barbara Strozzi's collection of solo pieces for Anna de' Medici entitled *Sacri musicali affetti*, see Kendrick, "Intent and Intertextuality."
54 The misperceptions about the waning of St. Anne after the Reformation have been brought to light by Welsh, *Mother, Matron, Matriarch*. Welsh disputes the notion that the cult rose and faded between the years 1480 and 1550, as many studies have assumed.

2 Heritage and Progeny in an Office for St. Anne

1 Throughout this chapter, I will forgo the abbreviation TurBN I.II.9 given for the Turin Codex in the *Census-Catalogue of Manuscript Sources of Polyphonic Music 1400–1550*.
2 Four of the five major sections feature a range of complex mensural polyphony. The second section contains seven paired settings of the Gloria and Credo from the Mass Ordinary, while the third section comprises forty-one polytextual motets commemorating a wide set of liturgical occasions. French ballades, virelais, and rondeaux populate the fourth and fifth fascicles.
3 This bull is one of several issued on November 23, 1413 to benefit Janus I of Cyprus. See Rome, Archivio Segreto Vaticano, Reg. Lat. 172, fol. 138.
4 The office for St. Anne is found on fols. 14r–19r; the considerably larger liturgy for Hilarion occurs on fols. 1r–13r. Six plainchant mass cycles are also contained in the first fascicle. Of interest to scholars has also been one of the earlier examples of a polyphonic mass to be based on a single melody, which is inserted later into the manuscript at fols. 139v–141v.
5 The red color of the saints' books matches – and thus may cross-reference – the color of the manuscript's coat of arms to be discussed shortly.
6 Data and Kügle, eds., *The Codex J.II.9, Torino, Biblioteca Nazionale Universitaria*, 25.
7 For his initial study, see Hoppin, "The Cypriot-French Repertory of the Manuscript Turin, Bibliotheca Nazionale, J.II.9." For editions of the polyphony, see Hoppin, ed., *The Cypriot-French Repertory of the Manuscript Torino, Biblioteca Nazionale, J.II.9*. For the plainchant, see Hoppin, ed., *Cypriot Plainchant of the Manuscript Torino, Biblioteca nazionale J.II.9*.

8 The proceedings of this congress are published in Günther and Finscher, eds., *The Cypriot-French Repertory of the Manuscript Turin J.II.9*.
9 Data and Kügle, eds., *The Codex J.II.9, Torino, Biblioteca Nazionale Universitaria*.
10 Kügle, "Glorious Sounds for a Holy Warrior."
11 Giaccaria, "Il codice franco-cipriota J.II.9," 12.
12 There is no medieval equivalent for the modern term "versified office." The word *historia*, first used by Amalarius of Metz, stands for a set of responsories (possibly with additional antiphons) to be sung during a specific liturgical feast day, usually following a narrative format. For the problems of classification, especially with the early versified offices, see Jonsson, *Historia*, 9–29. The tradition of composing or compiling rhymed, metrical offices is thought to have been inspired by the office for Trinity Sunday produced by or for Bishop Stephen of Liège around the year 920. See Hughes, "Late Medieval Rhymed Offices."
13 See Hiley, *Western Plainchant*, 273–4. "New" saints like St. Anne or wholly added feasts to the calendar such as the feast of Corpus Christi almost invariably spurred the creation of a versified office. For a preliminary study on the versified offices for Thomas of Canterbury, see Hughes, "Chants in the Rhymed Office of St. Thomas of Canterbury." Saints arriving late to the canon were more likely local heroes elevated to sainthood. The texts of hundreds of versified offices have been available for study in *Analecta Hymnica* for more than a century. The chief volumes for study of the versified offices in AH are 5, 13, 17, 18, 24, 25, 26, 28, and 45(a). The recent advancements in online databases and software (CANTUS, The Medieval Music Database [La Trobe University], the NEUMES Project, Cantus Planus/Regensburg, and the Global Chant Database) hold promise for those studying the late medieval office.
14 Latin language historian F. J. E. Raby (*A History of Christian-Latin Poetry*, 456) called versified office poetry "barbarous and despicable."
15 Twenty-two offices are listed in AH: 5.34, 5.35, 5.36, 5.37, 5.38, 5.39, 14b.II.4, 17.11, 25.18, 25.19, 25.20, 25.21, 25.22, 25.23, 25.24, 25.25, 25.26, 25.27, 25.28, 25.29, 25.30, 41a.II.4.
16 John Stevens (*Words and Music in the Middle Ages*, 250–3) has called versified offices "double historia" because of the reinforcing nature of lections and the surrounding antiphons and responsories.
17 See, for example, Fassler, "Mary's Nativity, Fulbert of Chartres, and the *Stirps Jesse*," 422.
18 Hughes, *Late Medieval Liturgical Offices: Resources for Electronic Research: Texts* and Hughes, *Late Medieval Liturgical Offices: Resources for Electronic Research: Sources and Chants*. There is never more than one canticle antiphon (E) in Vespers or Lauds; therefore, the use of a numeral is inessential to the designation.

19 The arrangement of the office is nearly identical between secular and monastic institutions, the essential difference being in the organization of the service of Matins. The secular cursus dictates the use of three nocturns, each of which contained three antiphons with psalms and three responsories (for a total of nine in each genre), as is the case here. The more elaborate monastic cursus, however, would call for twelve antiphons and responsories, with a canticle antiphon intervening between the eighth and ninth responsory.

20 The office for St. Anne properly begins with a chapter reading – "Mulierem fortem quis inveniet" from the Common of Virgins.

21 Tonaries may have influenced the ordering by mode (see Huglo, *Les tonaires*, 122). In the later offices, the modal category is prescriptive for the composition of a chant, whereas in tonaries, the mode is descriptive of a preexistent chant. See, for example, Haug, "Neue Ansätze im 9. Jahrhundert," 117–19.

22 For a study on modal ordering, see Andrew Hughes, "Modal Order and Disorder."

23 For modal analysis of the office for St. Hilarion, see Hoppin, *Cypriot Plainchant of the Manuscript Torino, Biblioteca nazionale J.II.9*, 27. One might also cite the systematic organization of a set of motets in the manuscript's third fascicle, which cycles through the "O Antiphons." The ordered motets (fols. 80v–88r) are cataloged as numbers 23–30 in Hoppin, *The Cypriot-French Repertory of the Manuscript Torino, Biblioteca Nazionale J.II.9*, 100–40.

24 Hoppin, *Cypriot Plainchant of the Manuscript Torino, Biblioteca nazionale J.II.9*, 27–9.

25 Ibid., 20–2.

26 Fols. 284v–287r.

27 Hoppin, *Cypriot Plainchant of the Manuscript Torino, Biblioteca nazionale J.II.9*, 23–5.

28 Cattin, "The Texts of the Offices," 265. Andrew Wathey has expressly pointed to the transmission of a motet in the Turin manuscript, evidently inspired by Philippe de Vitry's *Impudenter circuivi/Virtutis laudabilis*/TENOR, as evidence of continental influence, specifically from the Bourbon dynasty, with which the French composer and Cypriot court both had contact. See Wathey, "European Politics and Musical Culture," 35–44.

29 Reames, "Origins and Affiliations." The pre-Sarum office for St. Anne in the Stowe Breviary appears on fols. 280v–283r. The original layer of the Stowe manuscript, which contains this office, has been reliably dated between 1322 and 1325. A Sarum office for Anne (fols. 386r–388r) was added later, probably after 1400, as Reames has observed.

30 Ibid., 354–67.

31 For a simplified matrix comparing these offices, see Anderson, "Symbols of Saints," II:402–5.

32 Évreux, Bibliothèque municipale, MS lat. 89. The manuscript (29.3 x 21.4 cm) consists of 237 parchment folios with modern foliation. The music format

features square notation on red, four-line staffs. On the dating of the manuscript, see Anderson, "Symbols of Saints," II:400–11. On the history of the abbey of Lyre, see Guéry, *Histoire de l'abbaye de Lyre*.

33 Eight of the twenty-nine chants in common between the Turin Codex and the Lyre antiphoner share the same mode. For a comparison of the modes between the offices, as well as a close musical evaluation of select Lauds antiphons with the same mode, see Anderson, "Symbols of Saints," II:416–33. John Stinson's unpublished analysis of the melodies of the Turin office ("The Turin Manuscript and Late Medieval Chant Reforms") suggested a Dominican dialect for the plainchant repertory, and it is possible that the entire St. Anne office was reset with Dominican musical reforms in mind, befitting the rite used at the Lusignan court since the middle of the fourteenth century.

34 For the hymn and its sources, see AH 52.101.

35 Stäblein, *Die mittelalterlichen Hymnenmelodien des Abendlandes*, 672. Melody nos. 67, 69, 149, 200.

36 Fol. 4v. On the larger question of modal ordering in the Lyre antiphoner, a possible clue to its antiquity, the modes of the office ascend systematically through the first six antiphons of Matins and again through the first five modes in order for the antiphons at Lauds. This arrangement is difficult to compare with the Turin Codex, which as shown contains only some systematization.

37 Hoppin, *Cypriot Plainchant of the Manuscript Torino, Biblioteca nazionale J.II.9*, 45, 52.

38 The widespread dissemination of the sermon suits the reputation of Osbert as a "tireless self-promoter," according to Reames. See her "Origins and Affiliations," 363–5. This sermon from which the office for St. Anne derives can be found in Wilmart, "Les Compositions d'Osbert de Clare en l'honneur de sainte Anne."

39 *Acta Sanctorum* IX:16–59.

40 Cyprus was not known for conflicts between Latins and Greeks, especially in the fifteenth century. Historical evidence, in fact, reveals an air of peace and toleration, as well as a degree of autonomy for non-Latin Christians on the island. See Schabel, "Religion." On the weakening of the Latin Church in the fifteenth century and the atmosphere of religious syncretism between Orthodox Greeks and Catholics, see Christoforaki, "Patronage, Art, and Society," I:78–82. The presence of Greeks and Syrians in the Lusignan administration has been described by Edbury, *The Kingdom of Cyprus and the Crusades*, 180–95.

41 Schabel, "Religion," 214 and Severis, *Ladies of Medieval Cyprus and Catherine Cornaro*, 94.

42 The relics include a "large piece" of St. Anne at the Benedictine monastery of Stavrovouni and a part of the saint's head at the chapel of the commandery of the Knights Hospitallers in Nicosia. See Cobham, *Excerpta Cypria*, 27, 30.

43 Makhairas, *Recital Concerning the Sweet Land of Cyprus, entitled "Chronicle,"* I:624–5, II:213.

44 Collenberg, "Les Lusignan de Chypre," 179.

45 Evidence is lacking as to how precisely the manuscript arrived in Savoy. The orthodox view considers the Turin Codex part of the dowry brought from Anne of Cyprus to the continent. See, for instance, Data and Kügle, eds., *The Codex J.II.9, Torino, Biblioteca Nazionale Universitaria*, 67. This theory, however, rests on no firm evidence and needs to be reassessed in light of Kügle's recent discoveries on the northern Italian impetus for the manuscript.

46 Boynton, *Shaping a Monastic Identity*, 69–70.

47 The use of E♭ is especially rare and dramatic for a G-mode responsory, especially one that does not even draw on a single B♭, a note that is more likely to occur before expanding the tonal palette to include E♭.

48 Osbert's sermon to which these particular chants can be traced can be found in Wilmart, "Les Compositions d'Osbert de Clare en l'honneur de sainte Anne," 26–30. In other sources of this office, the word *tela* replaced the word *stella*. While the Turin office bears a harmless variant in this case, these other sources bolster the analogy as the linen of virginity appears "out of this loom" (*ex hac tela*) rather than "out of this star" (*ex hac stella*). See *Linea virginitatis*, for example, in the Lyre antiphoner (Évreux, Bibliothèque municipale, MS lat. 89) at fol. 2v, along with all of the sources studies in Reames. For the passage in the office compared with the sermon of Osbert of Clare, see Reames, "Origins and Affiliations," 364.

49 Pizan, *Le Livre des Trois Vertus*, 156.

50 Hufton, *The Prospect before Her*, 212, and Karras, "'This Skill in a Woman is By No Means to Be Despised,'" 102–4.

51 Constas, *Proclus of Constantinople*, 317. Additional evidence for this interpretation of the analogy can be found in the antiphon for St. Anne *Beatus auctor seculi* (MA1, AH 25.25), which speaks of the "white robe of the flesh" (*carnis trabeam*).

52 Elliott, *Apocryphal New Testament*, 61.

53 The royal significance of purple is most notably seen in the Passion narrative, as the soldiers dress Christ ("King of the Jews") with a purple garment before mocking him. See Matthew 27:28, Mark 15:17, and John 19:2. In the Matins responsory *Annos Anna pubertatis* from the St. Anne office composed by Christian von Lilienfeld (MA3, AH 41a.4), Mary's mother is herself described as wearing a purple garment, presumably as a testament to her own noble upbringing.

54 Hufton, *The Prospect before Her*, 399.

55 Explicit devotion to the tree of the cross developed from the Gallican feast of the Invention of the Cross (May 3) and the Roman feast of the Exaltation of the Cross (September 14), as well as legendary materials recounting the discovery of the cross in Jerusalem by St. Helena, including Cynewulf's poem "Elene." See Ritchey, "Spiritual Arborescence," 2–6.

56 For analogies drawing on the olive tree, see *Accedat reus propere* (MA5, AH 5.34), *O mater Anna nobilis* (MR8, AH 25.19), and *Radix viva* (WE, AH 25.19).

Patristic exegetes have generally understood the olive tree as an allegory for the Virgin Mary. For the relationship between the tree and Mary via Psalms 52:10, see Ritchey, "Spiritual Arborescence," 26–7. The connection is easily transferable from Mary to her mother, and the olive tree further signifies vitality at an old age, thereby strengthening the relationship to Anne as an unlikely (elderly) matron.

57 See Tertullian, *De carne Christi liber*, 215. Commentators have further noted the similarity of *virgo* and *virga* to strengthen the analogy. Early Christian commentators have likewise recognized the resemblance of "Jesus" to "Jesse" as further proof of their genealogical relationship. See Bloch, *Etymologies and Genealogies*, 87–91.

58 The root of Jesse metaphor itself was developed in plainchant, not for the feast of the Immaculate Conception, which was not formally approved until 1477 by Sixtus IV, but for the feast of Mary's nativity (September 8), as Margot Fassler has shown ("Mary's Nativity, Fulbert of Chartres, and the *Stirps Jesse*").

59 In the visual arts, some works feature Jesse by himself surrounded by the gifts of the Holy Spirit, while others provide any number of prophets through the branch that sprouted Mary and the flower of Christ. On the typology of the early trees of Jesse, see, for example, Watson, *The Early Iconography of the Tree of Jesse*, 163–71. On the *Arbor Annae* ("Tree of Anne") subject in late medieval Netherlandish art and its relationship to traditional Tree of Jesse imagery, see Esser, "Die Heilige Sippe," 111–14.

60 Kleinschmidt, *Die heilige Anna*, 236 and Sheingorn, "The Holy Kinship," 281.

61 See, for instance, Constable, "Twelfth-Century Spirituality."

62 1 Samuel 1:1–2:11.

63 The adjective *felix* holds a range of meanings – often "happy" or "fortunate," but also "holy" or "blessed" in the case of saints. That the word does not typically mean "fertile" is proven by its use in connection with virgin saints and male saints.

64 For liturgical items connecting St. Anne with Sarah, see *Tu es sara fecunda* from (MR4, AH 25.24); *Prima vestrae gentis mater* (MR9, AH 25.18); and *In exemplum statim saram* (MR4, AH 5.35). Sarah is another barren mother prototype like Hannah, not conceiving until a very old age, before God granted her offspring (i.e., Isaac). See Genesis 21:1–3. Other offices for St. Anne likewise draw on other unexpected figures of the Old Testament. Two responsories, for example, mention St. Anne in the lineage of Aaron the High Priest. See *Stirps Aaron sancta* (MR2, AH 25.19) and *Preclara mater Anna* (MR2, AH 25.24).

65 References to St. Anne's Davidic lineage also occur in the Matins hymn *O quam mirifica luce corruscat*, as well as in the first antiphon in the service of Lauds (*Ad legis metas*).

66 Psalm 44:11. "Hearken, O daughter, and see, and incline thy ear: and forget thy people and thy father's house."

67 The lection that follows this antiphon continues the arboreal and natural imagery, if not a connection to the Old Testament, by describing St. Anne as a "good tree, from which the cut-off branch blossomed from heaven through itself" (*arbor bona, de qua virga excisa per se divinitus floruit*).

68 The reign of Peter (r. 1359–69) and his father, Hugh IV (r. 1324–59), represented the height of power for the kingdom, originally claimed by Crusaders at the end of the twelfth century. See Wathey, "European Politics and Musical Culture," 33–4.

69 The matrimonial ceremony was celebrated by proxy in 1409 and consummated in 1411. For these events in Cypriot history, see Hill, *A History of Cyprus*, II:447–67. On the composers, see Wathey, "European Politics and Musical Culture," 35 and Kügle, "Glorious Sounds for a Holy Warrior," 669–79.

70 Hill, *A History of Cyprus*, II:460–6.

71 Edbury, *The Lusignan Kingdom of Cyprus*, 7–23 and Hill, *A History of Cyprus*, II:476–93.

72 The standard account on Brescian history remains Treccani degli Alfieri, *Storia di Brescia*; for the period of interest, see I:856–76, 1064–1124 and II:3–171, 397–436.

73 Kügle, "Glorious Sounds for a Holy Warrior," 655, 661.

74 Kügle, "The Repertory of the Manuscript Torino, Biblioteca Nazionale J.II.9," 170.

75 The court was ostensibly reimbursing Savoyard courtier Richard de Colombier. See Torino, Archivio di Stato, Inv. 16, n. 81 (Secundus computus nobilis Bartholomei Chabodi thesaurarii sabaudie de anno miiijcxxxvj [24.9.1435–24.9.1436]), fols. 207v–208r.

76 For Anne's journey to the mainland, see Cognasso, *Amedeo VIII*, 114–17. On the wedding and surrounding events, see Data and Kügle, eds., *The Codex J.II.9, Torino, Biblioteca Nazionale Universitaria*, 68–70 and Hill, *The History of Cyprus*, II:496–8.

77 The wedding of Anne of Cyprus and Louis of Savoy on February 1, 1434 seems to have provided the occasion for Du Fay to meet Burgundian composer Gilles de Binchois, as recorded by Martin le Franc (then poet and secretary to Amadeus VIII) in his celebrated epic poem *Le champion des dames* (ca. 1440–2). It is in this poem that mention of the infamously intractable term *contenance angloise* in the works of Du Fay and Binchois has become the subject of much debate among music historians. For recent appraisals of the musical meaning of the six stanzas of this poem, see Bent, "The Musical Stanzas"; Wegman, "New Music for a World Grown Old"; and Page, "Reading and Reminiscence," 2–4. On Du Fay's ongoing relationship with the court of Savoy even during his years with the court of Burgundy amidst the papal schism of the 1440s, see Planchart, "Connecting the Dots."

78 Archival documents reveal a significant investment in Savoyard musical life overall comparable to its competitors: musicians were compensated

higher than their were counterparts in other courts, and many books of music are mentioned, though these sources lack the specificity concerning the repertory that was heard at the court. Also, both Louis of Savoy and Anne of Cyprus played musical instruments. Records show that the former purchased a harp in 1427, and the latter received a lute and harp strings from the court in 1438. For an overview on the richness of musical life in Savoy, especially among the nobility, see Bradley, "Musical Life and Culture at Savoy," I:24–7.

79 Remember that, twenty years into her marriage to Louis of Savoy, Anne of Cyprus persuaded her husband to obtain the most important and precious piece of cloth known in the fifteenth century – the holy Shroud of Turin (*Sacra sindone*). That Anne of Cyprus or others at the court understood the full extent of the extended textile metaphor in the St. Anne office is of course not known, but the peculiar series of subtle references to the craft of weaving, cloth production, and regal vestiture could not have gone unnoticed in the performance of the service of Matins or for one casually browsing the folios of the office.

80 For a color reproduction of the illuminations in this manuscript, see *Le Livre d'heures du duc Louis de Savoie*.

81 Taverna, *Anna di Cipro*, 119–27. The most famous of these offspring is Amadeus IX, the couple's firstborn child, who would marry Yolande of France, daughter of Charles VII.

82 Cognasso, *I Savoia*, 275. While some reports attest to Anne's attractiveness and her exotic way of dressing, other descriptions have noted her supposedly mischievous nature and corrupt behavior; her Cypriot cohorts fared no better, sometimes cast as scandalous and morally depraved. These tales are likely exaggerated or outright fictional. The unnecessarily exoticized image is perpetuated, for example, in Hill, *A History of Cyprus*, II:494–5 and Taverna, *Anna di Cipro*, 8–15.

83 The motet *Magni patris magna mira/Ovent cyprus palestina* (fols. 74v–75r) details the life of St. Hilarion with reference to King Janus. The cantus II of the motet *Gemma florens militia/Hec est dies gloriosa* (fols. 65v–66r) aligns Janus with John the Baptist.

84 On the library of Amadeus VIII, see Edmunds, "The Medieval Library of Savoy," 321.

85 Kügle, "Glorious Sounds for a Holy Warrior," 678.

86 Bradley, "Musical Life and Culture at Savoy," I:73.

87 Duby, "Structures de parenté et noblesse," 283.

88 Hoppin, *Cypriot Plainchant of the Manuscript Torino, Biblioteca nazionale J.II.9*, 43–54.

89 On the layering of temporalities in the liturgical offices, see Boynton, *Shaping a Monastic Identity*, 36.

3 Of Widowhood and Maternity

1. For the most recent biography of La Rue, with analysis of style and reception of his works, see Meconi, *Pierre de la Rue and Musical Life*.
2. Vienna, Österreichische Nationalbibliothek, MS Supplementum Musica 15496, fols. 18v–35r (hereafter, VienNB Mus. 15496); Montserrat, Biblioteca del Monestir, MS 773, fols. 1v–14r (hereafter, MontsM 773); Jena, Universitätsbibliothek, MS 7, fols. 1v–16r (hereafter, JenaU 7). On the importance of Alamire as a music scribe in the courts of Margaret of Austria and Charles V, see Kellman, ed., *The Treasury of Petrus Alamire*, esp. 7–38; Heide, "Polytekstuele religieuze muziek"; Kellman, "The Origins of the Chigi Codex"; Picker, *The Chanson Albums of Margaret of Austria*, 32–5; Kellman, "Josquin and the Courts of the Netherlands and France"; and Howard Mayer Brown, "In Alamire's Workshop."
3. In JenaU 7, the initial folio, which might have contained a composer attribution, title, and tenor rubric, was pilfered. Small passages in the Agnus Dei have also been removed in this source. In MontsM 773, only the Credo survives in its entirety. The vandalism of this manuscript has resulted in neither a title nor an attribution in this manuscript. On the dating of these masses by La Rue, see Meconi, *Pierre de la Rue and Musical Life*, 98, 185, and 270. VienNB Mus. 15496, for instance, falls in Meconi's "second group" of works from sources dating between 1506 and March 1516.
4. Two sources, not properly part of the stemma for the mass, transmit only the motet *O salutaris hostia*, both with no composer attribution: (1) Brussels, Bibliothèque royale de Belgique, MS IV.922 ("Occo Codex"), fols. 4v–5r and (2) Uppsala, Universitets-Biblioteket, Vokalmusik I Handskrift 76b, fols. 63v–64r. If the motet is by La Rue (and there is no attribution to him in any source of this particular motet), it would be his shortest motet (34 breves). The idea for the elevation motet was probably taken from Gaspar van Weerbeke and his use of *motetti missales* (a Milanese practice). See Meconi, *Pierre de la Rue and Musical Life*, 65, 175 and Meconi, "La Rue, Pierre de." For a discussion of the elevation motet, see Long, "Symbol and Ritual in Josquin's *Missa di Dadi*," 12.
5. This rubric appears in only one source of the mass (VienNB Mus. 15496). None of the three modern editions of the *St. Anne Mass* has launched any special inquiry into its context or origin.
6. On the history of the court chapel from 1508 to 1516, see Meconi, *Pierre de la Rue and Musical Life*, 41–3.
7. Ibid., 83–8, 185, 270.
8. Ibid., 130.
9. La Rue, *Opera Omnia*, II:lxix–lxx.
10. For studies on paraphrase technique, see Boyd, "The Development of Paraphrase Technique"; Reynolds, "The Counterpoint of Allusion"; and Godt, "Renaissance Paraphrase Technique." One is hesitant to call La Rue's *St. Anne*

Mass a parody mass without knowing the exact source. The strict definition of parody technique, so popular in the early sixteenth century, includes an infusion of the complete substance of the model into the new piece. A parody work takes not just a melody or theme, but also emblematic progressions and chords and subjects them to variation. See Tilmouth and Sherr, "Parody (i)." On the rhetorical basis for the unifying and varied gestures in fifteenth-century masses, see Luko, "Unification and Varietas."

11 Other internal statements of the paraphrased melody occur at the "Christe," "In nomine," and the "Dona nobis"; partial (or modified) statements can be found at the "Et resurrexit," "Et vitam venturi," "Hosanna" (II), and "Agnus" (II).

12 See Meconi, Review of Pierre de la Rue, *Opera Omnia*, 291.

13 On the uncertainty surrounding La Rue's borrowing procedures, see Meconi, *Pierre de la Rue and Musical Life*, 115–27.

14 Robyns, *Pierre de la Rue (circa 1460–1518)*, 87.

15 Picker, Review of *Drie Missen van Pierre de la Rue*, 263. Picker directs attention to a particular section of the Credo (mm. 20–63), but never shows a formal comparison with the traditional Marian antiphon, which naturally has numerous variants.

16 The *Missa Alma Redemptoris mater* by Leonel Power was one of the earliest masses known to employ a unifying cantus firmus across its sections of the mass. Other noteworthy settings of the melody have been composed by Du Fay, Ockeghem, Obrecht, Josquin, Gombert, Mouton, Palestrina, and Victoria.

17 La Rue, *Opera Omnia*, II:lxviii.

18 Meconi, "Habsburg-Burgundian Manuscripts."

19 For short discussions of the symbolic potential of cantus firmi, see Wright, *The Maze and the Warrior*, 163–4 and Bloxam, "Cantus Firmus."

20 Meconi, "La Rue, Pierre de," XIV:286.

21 In contrast, the other known *Felix Anna* liturgical items turn up only sporadically, none in more than a handful of manuscripts. For a more thorough analysis of these texts and melodies, see Anderson, "Symbols of Saints," III:510–14.

22 Hughes, "Rhymed Offices."

23 Hughes's catalog of melodies from the late versified office was an important first step in electronic cataloging (*Late Medieval Liturgical Offices: Resources for Electronic Research: Sources and Chants*). The new CANTUS database (http://cantusdatabase.org) and the collected information of the IMS Study Group Cantus Planus (www.cantusplanus.org) are other important electronic resources for the study of plainchant. Connections between the CANTUS database and the Global Chant Database (www.globalchant.org) have also facilitated chant research. The indices Bryden and Hughes compiled (*An Index of Gregorian chant*) cannot be consulted for this study because, like many collections such as Hesbert's CAO, this catalog surveys only the early layers of plainchant, of which the St. Anne melodies are not a part.

24 Anderson, "Symbols of Saints," III:512–13.

25 See, for instance, Copenhagen, Det kongelige Bibliotek Slotsholmen, Gl. Kgl. S. 3449, 8o X, fol. 66r–v.

26 In a set of detailed chapel regulations from 1469, Charles the Bold specified that the Parisian rite should be used for the celebration of the Mass and Office by the court's *grande chapelle*. However, as Meconi has shown, the statutes were not all necessarily followed during the time when La Rue was employed at the court chapel. To complicate matters further, multiple "uses" were associated with Paris, and the Burgundian court was known to draw from different liturgies and add feasts to forge its own usage. See Meconi, *Pierre de la Rue and Musical Life*, 53–63 and Haggh, "Binchois and Sacred Music," 11–17.

27 Paris, Bibliothèque nationale de France, MS lat. 15182 (fol. 269v) is a late thirteenth-century summer breviary, and Paris, Bibliothèque nationale de France, MS lat. 10482 (fol. 466r) dates from the early fourteenth century.

28 Bloxam, Review of *Opera Omnia*, 409. She referred expressly to the manuscript Paris, Bibliothèque nationale de France, MS lat. 10482.

29 Graz, Universitätsbibliothek MS 30 (olim 38/9), fol. 200r, 201v; Ljubljana, Nadškofijski arhiv (Archiepiscopal Archives), MS 19 (olim 18), fol. 108v.

30 Mainz, Bischöfliches Dom- und Diözesanmuseum, Codex C, fol. 226v. For a transcription of the St. Anne office in this antiphoner, see Boyce, "Cantica Carmelitana," II:126–53.

31 Carmelites trace their devotion to the thirteenth century, certainly making them the first among the religious orders to celebrate the feast. See Jotischky, *The Carmelites and Antiquity*, 226–7.

32 Although scholarship on plainchant usually downplays word painting, it is not inconceivable that the text at this moment could have inspired this expansive gesture spanning a ninth (C-d) in the fifth line of the example. In this musical phrase, the text *promeruit generare* ("deserved to produce") might have "produced" or "generated" the extra invocation of the motive *ut-mi-fa-sol* in the new hexachord.

33 The spanning of the C-c octave and avoidance of the tetrachord beneath the C final encourage a categorization as either a fifth mode (if B♮ dominates) or a seventh mode (if B♭ dominates) antiphon, each transposed to a C final.

34 I can find no musical connection between La Rue's mass and the following three motets: *Gaude felix Anna/Gaude mater matris/Anna parens* (Dunstaple), *O felix Anna* (Gombert), and *Gaude felix Anna* (Clemens non Papa).

35 An incomplete set of partbooks (altus part only) indicates that *Felix Anna quedam matrona* was included in a print from 1521 by Antico (RISM 1521[4]). The manuscript Padua, Biblioteca Capitolare del Duomo, A.17 (fols. 19v–20r) was compiled at a similar time (1522), while Bergamo, Archivio della Cappella di S. Maria Maggiore, 1209D (fols. 12v–13r) was copied around 1541 or later. For the dating of these manuscripts, see Festa, *Opera omnia*, V:x–xi.

36 This example is largely based on the transcription in ibid., V:63–5, although editorial revisions appear in the use of *musica ficta* compared to the critical

edition. Seay's edition does not incorporate information from the 1521 printed source, because of the survival of only one partbook.

37 For a description of Cambrai, Mediathèque Municipale, MSS 125–8, see the *Census-Catalogue of Manuscript Sources of Polyphonic Music 1400–1550*, I:125. A full study of the partbooks can be found in Diehl, *The Partbooks of a Renaissance Merchant*. For an edition of the anonymous *Felix Anna quedam matrona*, see Maldeghem, ed., *Trésor musical*, V:XX:10. Special thanks to Aaron James for alerting me to this anonymous motet.

38 AH lists numerous sources from a wide geography for office 25.18, though the editors were notoriously imprecise with bibliographic citations of their sources.

39 In the critical edition of this motet (Festa, *Opera omnia*, V:xvii), the editor does not make it explicit that the plainchant basis for the motet is the antiphon *Felix Anna quedam matrona*. Seay only states, "The text is in honor of St. Anne, Mother of the Blessed Virgin Mary, presumably to be used on July 26." Therefore, this study brings more light to the information known about the basis of this motet.

40 For recent biographical literature on Margaret of Austria, see Soisson, *Margaret* and Tamussino, *Margarete von Österreich*. For a biography in English, in need of updating, see Iongh, *Margaret of Austria*.

41 Blockmans, "The Devotion of a Lonely Duchess," 38.

42 These female representatives of the Burgundian claims to Ghent were copied into the registers of the Guild in 1473 and 1476, respectively. See Rudy, "Women's Devotions at Court," 232.

43 Blockmans, "The Devotion of a Lonely Duchess," 38. The St. Anne altar in Ghent, which contained an ancient relic of the saint, had been in the St. Nicolas church since the beginning of the fourteenth century. For additional discussion and a color reproduction, see Kren and McKendrick, eds. *Illuminating the Renaissance: The Triumph of Flemish Manuscript Painting in Europe*, 126–8, 150 (no. 23). For Margaret of York's devotion to St. Anne and other select female saints, see Warren, *Women of God and Arms*, 39–45.

44 Colette's *vita* was compiled by her confessor and biographer Pierre de Vaux ("*Vita* of Colette of Corbie," *Acta Sanctorum*, March 6, 539–89). For analysis of the relevant passages, see Ashley, "Image and Ideology," 117–18.

45 Two "visions" of St. Anne are captured together in a multipanel altarpiece dedicated to the saint, made for a Carmelite church in Frankfurt (*Saint Anne Altarpiece*, Frankfurt am Main, Historisches Museum [end of fifteenth century]). The first vision has already been described, but a second vision features Colette kneeling before an altarpiece featuring the St. Anne Trinitarian image. In the background, St. Anne is pictured in heaven, gathering prayers for Colette from the company of saints. For a description of each panel of this extraordinary multipanel work along with a photograph of the image, see Ashley and Sheingorn, eds., *Interpreting Cultural Symbols*, 27–43.

46 Ghent, Poor Clares, MS 8, fol. 40v. Reproductions of this illumination can be seen in Blockmans, "The Devotion of a Lonely Duchess," 37, figure 6 and Pierre de Vaux, *Vita Sanctae Coletae* (1381–1447), 218–19.

47 On Colette's strong political influence, particularly with the House of Burgundy, see Warren, *Women of God and Arms*, 11–35 and Sheingorn, "The Holy Kinship," 280, 283–4.

48 In this manuscript, the vision of St. Colette is inscribed with Margaret's motto and coat of arms, quite rare across Margaret's collection. See *Vie abregée de Sainte Colette* (Arras, Bibliothèque municipale, MS 461, South Netherlandish, 1510) and Debae, *La bibliothèque de Margaret d'Autriche*, 472–3, no. 338.

49 Viollet, "Comment les femmes," 5–58.

50 Iongh, *Margaret of Austria*, 33–5.

51 On the delicate claims of Maximilian and his conflicts with local territories, see Wiesflecker, *Maximilian I*, 365–75.

52 For an excellent biography of Louise of Savoy, see Matarasso, *Queen's Mate*, 9–48.

53 On Anne of France's identification with Mary's mother, see L'Estrange, *Holy Motherhood*, 53, 113. For the regent's patronage of St. Anne for political symbolism, particularly in relation to her daughter Suzanne and Bourbon dynastic goals, see L'Estrange, "Sainte Anne et le mécénat d'Anne de France."

54 Iongh, *Margaret of Austria*, 49–53.

55 For critical editions, see Curnow, "The *Livre de la Cité des Dames* of Christine de Pisan" and Pizan, *Le Livre des Trois Vertus*.

56 Margaret owned a large tapestry depicting the "City of Ladies," given to her as a gift from the Flemish town of Tournai. See Bell, *The Lost Tapestries of the City of Ladies*, 167–8, 175.

57 Anne of France also penned her own handbook for Suzanne. For a translation with commentary, see Jansen, ed., *Anne of France*.

58 Brussels, Bibliothèque royale de Belgique, MS 9551 (from Paris, 1415–20), MS 9236 (from Mons, 1460–70), MS 10974 (ca. 1470). See Debae, *La bibliothèque de Margaret d'Autriche*, 184–6 and 247–51.

59 See this sculpture in Joan Evans, *Art in Medieval France*, fig. 279 and Muller, *Sculpture in the Netherlands /Germany /France /Spain*, 189–93, figure A.

60 The image can be found in Tolley, "Monarchy and Prestige in France," 153, plate 4.18. For more discussion of this work, see Matarasso, *Queen's Mate*, 108–9 and Ring, *A Century of French Painting*, 236.

61 Iongh, *Margaret of Austria*, 56–62.

62 Molinet, *Chroniques*, II:441.

63 Picker, *The Chanson Albums of Margaret of Austria*, 13.

64 Pizan, *The Book of the City of Ladies*, xxiv. For a later treatise on widows by a Christian writer who was close to Margaret of Austria, see Erasmus, "De Vidua Christiana," 177–331.

65 Willard, "Margaret of Austria," 352.

66 Eichberger, "Margaret of Austria," 50.
67 In the *Book of the City of Ladies*, wives are obliged to manage their family's estate, advise their husbands, and save them from death and misfortune. See Pizan, *The Book of the City of Ladies*, xxi.
68 Iongh, *Margaret of Austria*, 97.
69 Levy, "Widow's Peek," 1–2; Welzel, "Princeps Vidua, Mater Castrorum."
70 Pizan, *A Medieval Woman's Mirror of Honor*, 201.
71 Pizan, *The Book of the City of Ladies*, 256.
72 Welzel, "Widowhood," 108.
73 The city of Bruges rebelled against taxes by Maximilian and went so far as to take him captive for four months in 1488. See Wellens, "La revolte brugeoise de 1488."
74 Castiglione, *The Book of the Courtier*, 236.
75 This portrait by Margaret's court painter Bernard van Orley was completed more than a decade after she became Regent of the Netherlands.
76 Margaret apparently recruited Erasmus to tutor her nephew, Charles. He became one of Charles's advisors in 1519 and dedicated his 1516 treatise, *The Education of a Christian Prince*, to Charles. See Tremayne, *The First Governess of the Netherlands*, 111.
77 On Margaret's patronage of the arts, see Eichberger, *Leben mit Kunst, Wirken durch Kunst* and Picker, *The Chanson Albums of Margaret of Austria*, 9–31. For Margaret's extensive library, see Debae, *La Bibliothèque de Marguerite d'Autriche* and Debae, *La Librairie de Marguerite d'Autriche*. On the regent's contact with the Savoyard library, see Debae, "La Bibliothèque de Marguerite d'Autriche."
78 Gelfand, "Regency, Power, and Dynastic Visual Memory." On the political threats to Margaret at the beginning of her regency, see Haliczer, *The Comuneros of Castile*, 138 and Pérez, *La révolution des 'Comunidades' de Castille (1520–1521)*, 120.
79 Eichberger, "Margaret of Austria's Portrait Collection," 261.
80 Eichberger and Beaven, "Family Members and Political Allies," 230.
81 Pearson, *Envisioning Gender in Burgundian Devotional Art, 1350–1530*, 4, 39 and Gelfand, "Regency, Power, and Dynastic Visual Memory," 210. The earliest diptych features Margaret (just three years old) with her brother Philip. For a reproduction of Margaret's half (found in the Musée nationale du Château de Versailles), see Eichberger, ed., *Women of Distinction*, 120, figure 22.
82 On the retrospective art and architecture of the Royal Monastery of Brou, as well as the tomb for Philibert, see Gelfand, "Margaret of Austria and the Encoding of Power in Patronage," 153–6 and Gelfand, "Regency, Power, and Dynastic Visual Memory," 209–18.
83 On the political value of a strong commitment to faith through visual art in the case of Burgundian court culture, see Pearson, *Envisioning Gender in Burgundian Devotional Art*, 182–91; on Christine de Pizan's advocacy of feminine political authority, see Delogu, "Advocate et moyenne."

84 Pizan, *The Book of the City of Ladies*, 143–7.
85 The statue was crafted ca. 1526–8 and is housed in Bayerisches Nationalmuseum in Munich. For discussion of this work and a color reproduction, see Welzel, "Widowhood," 105–8.
86 Men also invoked Judith in visual culture. For instance, Philip the Good of Burgundy owned a tapestry of the Jewish heroine. See Franke, *Assuerus und Esther am Burgunderhof*, 109.
87 Works honoring St. Margaret were seen in the life of Margaret of Austria as early as 1493, in a portable altar which bore an image of the saint. A description of this artifact is found in Vienna, Austrian State Archive, Haus-, Hof-, und Staatsarchiv, Habsburgisch-Lothringisches Familienarchiv, Familienjunde n. 827, fol. 7r.
88 For devotion to Saints Clare and Colette by Isabella of Portugal (Duchess of Burgundy, mother of Charles the Bold), see LeMaire, *Isabelle de Portugal*, 69–70. On the veneration of these saints by Margaret of York, see Blockmans, "The Devotion of a Lonely Duchess," 36; Morgan, "Texts of Devotion and Religious Instruction"; and Pearson, "Margaret of Austria's Devotional Portrait Diptychs," 23.
89 Warren, "Colette of Corbie"; Warren, "Monastic Politics"; Legaré, "'La librairye de Madame,'" 207–8. For Pierre de Vaux's biography in translation, see Lopez, *Vie de soeur Colette*.
90 Rudy, "Women's Devotions at Court," 232.
91 Warren, "Monastic Politics," 227.
92 Corblet, *Hagiographie du Diocèse d'Amiens*, I:413–14.
93 Schnitker, "Margaret of York on Pilgrimage," 88–9.
94 In 1508, she called on Bernardin du Pré, Minister General of the Franciscans, for Colette's canonization, ultimately lobbying Leo X for support. See Bruchet, *Marguerite d'Autriche duchesse de Savoie*, 353–4 and Boom, *Marguerite d'Autriche-Savoie et la Pré-Renaissance*, 114.
95 For a description of this embroidered work of art, see Michelant, *Inventaire des vaisselles, joyaux, peintures, manuscrits, etc.*, 88.
96 For commentary on this manuscript and its connection to Margaret's life, see Picker, *The Chanson Albums of Marguerite of Austria* and Picker, ed. *Album de Marguerite d'Autriche*.
97 On the dating of BrusBR 228, see Warmington, "A Survey of Scribal Hands in the Manuscripts" and Warmington, "A Master Calligrapher in Alamire's Workshop."
98 The Marian motet *Ave sanctissima Maria* (fols. 1v–2) is now firmly attributed to La Rue.
99 Marvin, "*Regret* Chansons for Marguerite d'Autriche by Octovien de Saint-Gelais."
100 *Ce n'est pas jeu d'estre sy fortunée, /Qu'eslonger fault ce que l'on aime bien/ Et sy suis sceure que pas de luy ne vient, /Mais me procede de ma grant destinée.*

("It is not pleasant to be so unlucky, /As to have to send away what one loves so much, /And thus I am certain it isn't his fault, / Instead a result of my great destiny.")

101 Meconi, *Pierre de la Rue and Musical Life*, 86.
102 Meconi, "Margaret of Austria, Visual Representation, and Brussels, Royal Library, Ms. 228."
103 The mass for St. Job falls as the fifth of seven masses in VienNB Mus. 15496 (fols. 67v–81); the seventh of nine masses in MontsM 773 (fols. 85v–98); and the sixth of seven masses in JenaU 7 (fols. 78v–91). For an edition, see La Rue, *Opera omnia*, III:97–136, with commentary at xxxviii–xlv. For the literature on this mass and its relationship to Pipelare's *Missa Floruit egregiis*, see Pipelare, *Opera Omnia*, I:ix–x and Bloxam, "In Praise of Spurious Saints."
104 On the Job appearances in the Office of the Dead and books of hours, see Sargent-Baur, *Brothers of Dragons*, 38–53. On the evolution of the legend of St. Job, see Datz, *Die Gestalt Hiobs in der Kirchlichen Exegese*, 95–177. St. Job is commemorated on May 10 in Venice, Bologna, and Antwerp. On the Eastern veneration of Job and his steady adoption into the Western calendar, see Besserman, *The Legend of Job in the Middle Ages*, 57–64.
105 In addition to his role as just sufferer, Job was known in the Low Countries as a patron of musicians and was the dedicatee of several musicians' guilds in Antwerp and Brussels. See Denis, "Saint Job, patron des musiciens" and Meyer, "St. Job as a Patron of Music." On the musicians' guild for St. Job in Antwerp and La Rue's mass for St. Job, see Bloxam, "In Praise of Spurious Saints," 198–212.
106 For a discussion of this altarpiece, see Wauters, *Bernard van Orley*, 34–8, 41–5.
107 A mass for St. Margaret (*Missa O gloriosa* [*domina*] *Margareta*) occurs in MontsM 773 (fols. 45v–60r), but this work is clearly pointing to Margaret herself.
108 In the Mechelen church of St. Katelijne, a votive service (*lof*) for St. Anne was established in the fifteenth century. Confraternities devoted to St. Anne have been documented in nearby Brussels (at St. Goedele) and Antwerp (Church of Our Lady). See Haggh, "Music, Liturgy, and Ceremony in Brussels," 106, 421, 701–2 and Forney, "Music, Ritual and Patronage," 25.
109 Blackburn, "Messages in Miniature," 165.
110 Crafted around 1505, the portrait medal shows Margaret (recto) and Fortuna (verso). It is housed in Vienna at the Kunsthistorisches Museum (Münzkabinett). The luxurious dress of the regent in a 1510 painting has invited comparisons with Mary Magdalene. See London, The National Gallery, inv. no. NG 2614. For a more compelling depiction of Margaret as Mary Magdalene, see the undated painting by Bernard van Orley in the Bayerische Staatsgemäldesammlungen (Munich); reproduced as plate 1 in Tamussino, *Margarete von Österreich*.

111 The *Complainte de Marguerite d'Autriche* is catalogued as Vienna, Österreichische Nationalbibliothek, MS 2584. For a discussion and a color illustration of the miniature in question, see Eichberger, "The Culture of Gifts," 293.

112 On Margaret's relationship with Lalaing, see Michelant, *Inventaire des vaisselles, joyaux, peintures, manuscrits, etc.*, 102 and Eichberger, *Leben mit Kunst, Wirken durch Kunst*, 408. For a reproduction of a folio from the *Complainte* with the count's initials, see Eichberger, ed., *Women of Distinction*, 249. Another love interest of Margaret's, though likely later than the time of La Rue's *St. Anne Mass*, was Lord Charles Brandon. On the nature of this relationship, see Rawdon Brown, ed., *Calendar of State Papers and Manuscripts*, 157–8 (item 371). For the mixed messages that Margaret was sending in visual culture during the last two decades of her life, see Meconi, "Margaret of Austria, Visual Representation, and Brussels, Royal Library, Ms. 228," 30.

113 On the value of married life (related to the larger idea of the "feminization of sanctity") in the late Middle Ages, see Sheingorn, "The Holy Kinship," 270–2; Herlihy, *Medieval Households*, 129; and Brandenbarg, "Saint Anne: A Holy Grandmother and Her Children," 48.

114 For a recent evaluation of the climatic role of the Sanctus (and its parts) at the moment of transubstantiation, see Kirkman, *The Cultural Life of the Early Polyphonic Mass*, 192–201. For a related discussion on the Elevation, see Long, "Symbol and Ritual in Josquin's *Missa di Dadi*," 4–7. On the use of the *O salutaris hostia* at the Cathedral of Notre Dame in Paris in the early sixteenth century, see Wright, *Music and Ceremony*, 220–1.

115 This Italian motif could have spurred the increase in popularity among Netherlandish painters. See Eichberger, *Leben mit Kunst, Wirken durch Kunst*, 307–9. For a color reproduction of the panel (found in Windsor, The Royal Collection), see Eichberger, ed., *Women of Distinction*, 261. A later painting by Bernard van Orley features a devotional diptych with the Madonna with Child occupying the left side and the widow Margaret on the right. The image of the Virgin is that of the *Maria lactans*, an obvious symbol of life-sustaining motherhood. On the Orley diptych, see Laskin and Pantazzi, *European and American Painting, Sculpture, and Decorative Arts*, 210–13 and Ainsworth, "Bernaert van Orley. Virgin with Child."

116 The prayer book is Brussels, Bibliothèque royale de Belgique, MS 10389. The sacred wound is surrounded by the emblems of the four evangelists, who each hold banners collectively reading *O bone* [held by Matthew] *Jhesu* [held by John] *exaudi* [held by Luke] *me* [held by Mark] ("O good Jesus, hear me"). Running along the four sides of the diamond-shaped wound in Margaret's prayer book is the text *Hec est mensura plage lateris Domini Nostri Jhesu Christi secundum quot fuit revelatum sancto Dionisio de Bartoma* ("This is the measure of our Lord Jesus Christ's side wound, following the one that was revealed to Saint Dionysius of Bartoma" [presumably the

fifteenth-century theologian Denis the Carthusian]). The full text of the rhymed prayer following the illustration can be found in Rudy, "Women's Devotions at Court," 233, fn. 12.

117 For a collection of essays on the reception history of Juana and her mental state, see Gómez, Juan-Navarro, and Zatlin, eds., *Juana of Castile: History and Myth of the Mad Queen*.

118 Willard, "Margaret of Austria," 355; Iongh, *Margaret of Austria*, 142–3. Eleanor would become queen of Portugal and then of France; Isabella would become queen of Denmark, Sweden and Norway; and Mary would briefly be queen of Hungary, eventually succeeding Margaret as governess of the Netherlands. Margaret also had Anne Boleyn in her entourage (one of her *filles d'honneur*). Anne would be the queen of England and the second wife of Henry VIII. On Anne Boleyn's stay at the Mechelen court, see Ives, *The Life and Death of Anne Boleyn*, 18–26.

119 Eichberger and Beaven, "Family Members and Political Allies," 244–6. On the practice of linking noble lineage with biblical lineage via the tenth chapter of Genesis, see Thornton, "Genealogies, Royal."

120 Written by Jean Franco, the secretary of Charles V, and dedicated to Margaret, the *Genealogie abrégée* is catalogued as Paris, Bibliothèque nationale de France, MS fr. 5616 (fol. 48r). For a description, see Debae, *La Librairie de Marguerite d'Autriche*, 156–8.

4 Devotion and Letters

1 For an early overview of Jena U 7, see Roediger, *Die geistlichen Musikhandschriften der Universitäts-Bibliothek Jena*, I:47–8. For a more recent description, see Jas, "Jena, Thüringer Universitäts- und Landesbibliothek, MS 7," 96. Warmington's study appears in "A Survey of Scribal Hands in the Manuscripts." The dates of the manuscripts suggested by Warmington are generally accepted in Meconi, *Pierre de la Rue and Musical Life*.

2 Jas, "Jena, Thüringer Universitäts- und Landesbibliothek, MS 7," 96.

3 On the emperor's broad efforts to project his legitimacy as Holy Roman Emperor through the commissioning of genealogies, see Silver, *Marketing Maximilian*, 41–76. For his particular alignment with the notion of the "most prudent Virgin" in music as part of his campaign to improve his image, see Rothenberg, "The Most Prudent Virgin and the Wise King."

4 See, for example, Michael Hughes, *Early Modern Germany, 1477–1806*, 22–3.

5 Jas, "Jena, Thüringer Universitäts- und Landesbibliothek, MS 7," 96. For a recent summary of the unresolved debate concerning where the Alamire manuscripts were held (the Castle Church in Wittenberg or Frederick's *Hofkapelle* in Torgau), see Mowrey, "The Alamire Manuscripts of Frederick the Wise," 356–82.

6 Dörfler-Dierken, *Vorreformation Bruderschaften der hl. Anna*, 175.

7 Frederick attended every imperial diet and was charged with selecting the emperor in consultation with six other temporal and ecclesiastical electors (known as the "First Estate") – the Margrave of Brandenburg, the king of Bohemia, the Rhenish Count Palatine, and the archbishops of Cologne, Mainz, and Trier.
8 Ludolphy, *Friedrich der Weise*, 145.
9 Spalatin, *Friedrichs des Weisen*, 228.
10 Ludolphy, *Friedrich der Weise*, 157–68.
11 See, for example, Zophy, *The Holy Roman Empire*, 235.
12 Ludolphy, *Friedrich der Weise*, 195–204.
13 Roediger, *Die geistlichen Musikhandschriften*, I:11, 62. He has also proposed that JenaU 4 and 9 were also part of this gift.
14 On Rener's time in Frederick's *Hofkapelle*, see Duffy, "Netherlands Manuscripts at a Saxon Court," 221–3.
15 Meconi, "Foundation for an Empire," 32. For a close study of the eleven manuscripts Frederick acquired from the Alamire workshop, see Mowrey, "The Alamire Manuscripts of Frederick the Wise," 143–355.
16 Ludolphy, *Friedrich der Weise*, 216–19.
17 The election of Charles could have spurred the manuscripts JenaU 3, 5, and 12 as gifts of gratitude. See Mowrey, "The Alamire Manuscripts of Frederick the Wise," 387–401.
18 Junghans, *Wittenberg als Lutherstadt*, 51–9; Grossman, *Humanism in Wittenberg*, 36–75; and Ozment, *A Mighty Fortress*, 70. Frederick was especially drawn to classical texts and knew Latin well enough to collect and translate axioms from Cicero, Seneca, and other ancient Roman authors. He might have influenced the curriculum at the University of Wittenberg in the most general sense, as classes were offered in Latin, Greek, and Hebrew.
19 On the physical characteristics of the church and a catalog of its visual culture and material holdings, see Bellman, Harksen, and Werner, eds., *Die Denkmale der Lutherstadt Wittenberg*, 90–7, 239–67.
20 Ludolphy, *Friedrich der Weise*, 83, 355 and Moeller, "A Luther Relic," 51.
21 On the collection, see, for instance, Bacon, "Art Patronage and Piety in Electoral Saxony," 997; Borkowsky, *Das Leben Friedrichs des Weisen*, 56–7; and Ozment, *The Reformation in the Cities*, 139. With the issue of ecclesiastical indulgences in full swing, a comprehensive tour of the relic-filled galleries at the Castle Church could net a single pilgrim an almost two-million-year (1,902,202) reduction from a purgatory sentence.
22 Bacon, "A Mirror of a Christian Prince," 11.
23 The sponsorship of the visual arts by Frederick the Wise has been well studied. See, for example, Gurlitt, *Die Kunst unter Kurfürst Friedrich dem Weisen*; Bruck, *Friedrich der Weise als Förderer der Kunst*; and Ludolphy, *Friedrich der Weise*, 101–12.
24 Wentz, "Das Kollegiatstift Allerheiligen in Wittenberg," 150–2.

25 Schuchardt, *Lucas Cranach des Ältern*, I:45, fn. 2 and Bacon, "A Mirror of a Christian Prince," 155.

26 Swarenski, "Cranachs Altarbild von 1509 im Städelschen Kunstinstitut zu Frankfurt," 57; Friedländer and Rosenberg, eds., *The Paintings of Lucas Cranach*, 70; Grossman, *Humanism in Wittenberg*, 127; Schade, *Cranach*, 30; and Christensen, *Princes and Propaganda*, 13–19.

27 Heal, *The Cult of the Virgin Mary in Early Modern Germany*, 267–8. One could strengthen her interpretation by citing not only the central female figures of St. Anne and Mary, but also the sleeping Joseph and the young children at play in the work's foreground.

28 Snyder, *Northern Renaissance Art*, 375; Sheingorn, "Appropriating the Holy Kinship," 189.

29 Christensen, *Princes and Propaganda*, 18, fn. 7.

30 Brinkmann, ed., *Cranach*, 154.

31 Ludolphy, *Friedrich der Weise*, 47–9 and Levi, *Renaissance and Reformation*, 247. The boys were named Fritz and Bastel.

32 Jürgen Heidrich (*Die Deutschen Chorbücher aus der Hofkapelle Friedrichs des Weisen*, 256–62) has theorized that the music in JenaU 30 could have been sung at the elector's *Hofkapelle* instead of the Castle Church, but his study is based on codicological observations and not the liturgical usage of the institutions.

33 For Rener's probable authorship of much of the music in the Jena choirbooks, see Gerken, ed., *Three Mass Proper Cycles from Jena 35*, viii.

34 For the literature on JenaU 34, see Roediger, *Die geistlichen Musikhandschriften*, I:53–4 and II:113–48 and Engelbrecht, "Die Psalmsätze des Jenaer Chorbuches 34."

35 The eight feasts receiving two Vespers services are Christmas, Display of the Relics, Pentecost, Trinity, Visitation, Assumption, Nativity of Mary, and All Saints.

36 Fols. 235v–261r.

37 The office music for St. Stephen is found on fols. 30v–37r, with that of St. John the Evangelist on fols. 37v–43v.

38 Fols. 59v–60r.

39 A far more impressive manuscript devoted exclusively to polyphonic Magnificats (JenaU 20) was sent to Frederick from the Alamire scriptorium between 1515 and 1525. See Jas and Kellman, "Jena, Thüringer Universitäts- und Landesbibliothek MS 20."

40 Fols. 227v–234r.

41 For instance, a suffrage for Christmas (37v–38r) appears after music for the feast of St. Stephen; similarly, after the Second Vespers service for the Display of Relics is a suffrage for Easter (fols. 92v–93r), the full service of which occurred earlier in the manuscript. The suffrage for St. Blaise mentioned earlier (fols. 59v–60r) may serve as an example of a stand-alone devotional work, lacking a full complement of psalm settings.

42 Fols. 263r–273v.
43 Mone, *Lateinische hymnen des mittelalters*, III:184.
44 Duffy, "The Jena Choirbooks," II:394. The sequence (AH 55.61) occurs in more than two dozen sources. The Alleluia, however, is not listed in either volume of Alleluia melodies cataloged in Schlager, *Alleluia-Melodien*.
45 The Alleluia verse resembles one of the many early orally transmitted petitions attached to the "Ave Maria" in the fourteenth century, before the widespread prayer was codified in the later sixteenth century. For the similarity between this verse and one known from England, see Dugdale, *Monasticon Anglicanum*, VI:525. On the early history of the "Ave Maria" in music, see Anderson, "Enhancing the Ave Maria in the *Ars Antiqua*," esp. 45.
46 Indeed, the Virgin *in sole* (connecting her to the Woman of the Apocalypse) would become the prevailing image to symbolize the doctrine. See D'Ancona, *The Iconography of the Immaculate Conception*, 15, 24–6 and Vloberg, "The Iconography of the Immaculate Conception," 471.
47 Duffy, "The Jena Choirbooks," I:243.
48 The opening folio of the manuscript bears an illumination of St. Andrew, one of only two illuminations across the eight Jena choirbooks; the other was St. Katherine, patron saint of the University of Wittenberg, who was honored with her own side altar at the Castle Church.
49 Duffy, "The Jena Choirbooks," III:556–60, 575–6. Thirty-four sources are listed for *Sancte anne devotus* (AH 55.64).
50 Stevens, *Words and Music in the Middle Ages*, 91–3.
51 For an edition, see Gerken, "The Polyphonic Cycles of the Proper of the Mass," III:150–62.
52 The music appears to highlight this immaculist text with an archaic gesture in *fauxbourdon* style.
53 Duffy ("The Jena Choirbooks," I:225) calls the scribal hand "D3," and this hand represents one of several new scribal hands (text and music) that appear in the second half of JenaU 30.
54 There is additional music for Peter and Paul (fols. 147v–150r), St. Lawrence (199v–201r), St. Martin of Tours (202v–203r), and the Assumption (fols. 151v–158v). Two full cycles for the Dedication of a Church – a feast not properly celebrating a saint – represent the most extensive treatment of a feast in the appendix to JenaU 30.
55 Duffy, "The Jena Choirbooks," II:443–8. The Alleluia (with verse *Dulcis mater*) has been traced to liturgical sources in Mainz, whereas the sequence *Alma parens anna gaude* seems to derive from one known in the dioceses of Würzburg or Augsburg.
56 Note also that verses 1 and 2, as well as 9 and 10, match in their tonal "progressions" (from D to F and C to F, respectively), further implying the influence of one on the other.
57 These errors involve possible copying mistakes in the tenor part and improper resolution of suspensions. Emendations have been made to the tenor in mm.

162–4, 168–71. Resolution problems arise in mm. 162–3, 171, 177, and 183. The tenor part in mm. 180–3 is quite discordant. It could be misplaced rhythmically, or there could be a scribal error.

58 The construction of the chapel involved increasing the overall length of the church by one-third. See Wentz, "Das Kollegiatstift Allerheiligen in Wittenberg," 98.
59 Weimar, Ernestinesches Gesamtarchiv, Staatsarchiv Weimar, Reg. O 159 (Reg. O. pag. 90 A), fol. 2v.
60 Ibid., fol. 3v.
61 Kalkoff, *Ablaß und Reliquienverehrung*, 12 and Wentz, "Das Kollegiatstift Allerheiligen in Wittenberg," 101.
62 Israel, *Das Wittenberger Universitätsarchiv*, 80, no. 103.
63 Duffy, "The Jena Choirbooks," I:161.
64 The seven sources of the *Missa Conceptio tua* are Mechelen, Stadsarchief van Mechelen, MS s.s. ("Livre de choeur"), fols. 34v–44r; Antwerp, Musée Plantin Moretus, MS M 18.13, fols. 1r–6v; Brussels, Bibliothèque royale de Belgique, MS 6428, fols. 1v–17r; Brussels, Bibliothèque royale de Belgique, MS 15075, fols 1v–21r; JenaU 4, fols. 29v–41r; JenaU 5, fols. 11r–25r; and Vatican Library, Cappella Sistina 34, fols. 36r–50r. No mass from the Alamire scriptorium was copied more than seven times, and just three other masses in addition to the *Missa Conceptio tua* were copied seven times (*Missa de feria, Missa Ista est speciosa,* and the *Missa Ave sanctissima Maria*). For the critical edition of La Rue's *Missa Conceptio tua*, see La Rue, *Opera omnia*, II:1–50.
65 Ibid., II:XIV–XV. The editors of La Rue's mass have noted that the melody matches that of the chant *Maternitas tua* in AM 1085; however, this chant was better known as *Nativitas tua*, sung during Mary's nativity feast on September 8.
66 On the variations in rubrication in the surviving manuscripts, see Meconi, "Habsburg-Burgundian Manuscripts, Borrowed Material, and the Practice of Naming," 117.
67 Mowrey, "The Alamire Manuscripts of Frederick the Wise," 201–2.
68 For the imagery accompanying this mass in BrusBR 15075, see Blackburn, "Messages in Miniature," 173–4.
69 JenaU 4 could have originally been intended as a gift from Maximilian I to the childless Henry VIII and Catherine of Aragon, on account of the fact that these two are shown in a miniature within La Rue's *Conceptio tua* mass in this manuscript. On the complete program of miniatures in JenaU 4, see Thoss, "Flemish Miniature Painting in the Alamire Manuscripts," 53–62.
70 Eve is positioned to Mary's left beneath the same symbolic tree, while one of the banderoles within the miniature reads: "For Eve, like a deadly tree, [bears] evil fruits: concupiscence according to the original sin of flesh" (*Eva siquidem tamquam arbor letifera [fert] fructus malos concupiscentiam secundum carnis originale peccatum*).
71 The debate peaked in the mid-fifteenth century, particularly in church conclaves of the time. At the Council of Basel (1431–49), advocates of the immaculist view

affirmed their position in part by arguing that Mary, as much as Christ, was the one who crushed the dragon's head. The title of a chapter of Franciscan conciliarist John of Segovia's *Septem Allegationes* is instructive: "Testimonium Dei, quia Virgo contritura erat caput serpentis, et Diabolus insidiaturus calcaneo ejus, sed non conterens caput Virginis per peccatum" ("The Testimony of God that the Virgin will crush the head of the serpent, and the Devil will wound her in the heel without crushing the head of the Virgin through sin"). See Segovia, *Septem allegationes et totidem avisamenta pro informatione partum Concilii Basiliensis*, 260–1.

72 With the exception of the image of Innocent V, each of the miniatures contains a figure central to the promulgation of the Immaculate Conception doctrine, from Franciscan Duns Scotus (d. 1308), the greatest defender of the doctrine, to Pope Sixtus IV. See Blackburn, "Messages in Miniature," 182–3. On the tradition of including the Church Fathers, doctors, and other doctrinal advocates in Immaculate Conception art, see D'Ancona, *The Iconography of the Immaculate Conception*, 11.

73 Fols. 1v, 2v.

74 Several popes are included: Leo I, Alexander V, Gregory I, Innocent V, and Nicholas IV. See Blackburn, "Messages in Miniature," 179. On the contribution of Sixtus IV to the Immaculate Conception debate, see Laurentin, "The Role of the Papal Magisterium," 275.

75 Nixon, *Mary's Mother*, 73.

76 D'Ancona, *The Iconography of the Immaculate Conception*, 7, 15, 40, 47–8. See also the comment on the Mechelen manuscript in Vloberg, "The Iconography of the Immaculate Conception," 466.

77 The precise chronology of these manuscripts is not known. They both seem to have been received by Frederick between 1516 and 1525. See Meconi, *Pierre de la Rue and Musical Life*, 272–3 and Mowrey, "The Alamire Manuscripts of Frederick the Wise," 326–31. La Rue's *Missa Ave sanctissima Maria* leads off the manuscript in JenaU 5 (fols. 1v–10v) and appears on fols. 8v–14r in JenaU 4.

78 The prayer speaks of the spotlessness of the Virgin, and Christians who uttered it earned the sum of eleven thousand years of indulgences. The "Ave sanctissima Maria" text became the basis for some forty-five polyphonic works by numerous composers, clearly advancing the immaculist agenda in each case. See Blackburn, "The Virgin in the Sun."

79 On the simultaneous use of polyphonic Propers and polyphonic Ordinaries for a single feast, see Duffy, "The Jena Choirbooks," II:264–5.

80 Sebastian, "The Controversy after Scotus to 1900," 239. Universities at Cologne (1499), Mainz (1500), and Vienna (1501) adopted the oath. As early as 1497, the Sorbonne announced its practice of having candidates take the oath to uphold the Immaculate Conception doctrine.

81 See, for example, Brecht, *Martin Luther*, 20, 48–9.

82 Heal, *The Cult of the Virgin Mary in Early Modern Germany*, 129.

83 Luther published two tracts that particularly condemn the veneration of saints: *An den christlichen Adel deutscher Nation* and *Wider den neuen Abgott und alten Teufel, der zu Meissen soll erhoben werden.*
84 Grossman, *Humanism in Wittenberg*, 119.
85 On his defense of music as vital to the city of Wittenberg, see Luther, *Dr. Martin Luther's sämmtliche Werke*, LIII:375.
86 Music publisher Georg Rhau was central to this end. See, for instance, Leaver, *Luther's Liturgical Music*, 36–40.
87 Kreitzer, *Reforming Mary*, 123–4.
88 In his 1521 *Commentary on the Magnificat,* the reformer described Mary's domestic duties. See Luther, *Werke: Kritische Gesammtausgabe*, VII:575.
89 On songs that helped shift the paradigm, see Oettinger, *Music as Propaganda in the German Reformation*, 55.
90 Friesen, "Luther and St. Anne in the Art of the Northern Renaissance," 4 and Heal, *The Cult of the Virgin Mary in Early Modern Germany*, 31–2. For a recent view of the ways devotion to St. Anne was transformed in the wake of the Reformation until the eighteenth century, see Welsh, "Mother, Matron, Matriarch." On the rise of the cult of Joseph in the late Middle Ages, see Herlihy, *Medieval Households*, 127–30.
91 On the image, see Bott, ed., *Martin Luther und die Reformation in Deutschland*, no. 592 and Hoffman, ed., *Luther und die Folgen für die Kunst*, 118. On reinterpretations of Cranach more generally, see Andersson, "Religiöse Bilder Cranachs im Dienste der Reformation."
92 On Luther's abduction, see, for example, Holburn, *A History of Modern Germany*, I:167.
93 Bacon, "A Mirror of a Christian Prince," 1.

5 A "Divine Favor" at the French Court

1 For a survey of the contents of Petrucci's 1514 *Motetti de la corona*, a collection that itself went through three editions in the same year, see Boorman, *Ottaviano Petrucci*, 760–74. Andreas de Silva (composer of the motet *Letatus sum in his*) is the only composer not properly from the north, though he too might have spent time training at the French court. Silva was one of the favorite composers of Leo X.
2 Heartz, *Pierre Attaingnant*, 39–40.
3 The date of the choirbook LonBLR 8 G.vii has been the subject of much debate. Meconi has proposed a date of around 1513 ("Another Look at Absalon"), while a later range of dates has been suggested by Kellman, "Josquin and the Courts of the Netherlands and France," 212 and Kellman, ed., *London, British Library, MS Royal 8.G.vii*, vii–viii. For a more radical dating between 1502 and 1512, see Tirro, "Royal 8.G.vii: Strawberry Leaves, Single Arch, and Wrong-Way Lions," 6.

4 It follows *Honi soit qui mal y pense* by Morel, a canon (8 *ex* 2) that opens the collection (fol. 1v) but is not properly the beginning of the more carefully planned unfolding of motets in the manuscript. For a more general discussion of the contents of this manuscript, see Kellman, *London, British Library, MS Royal 8.G.vii*, v–viii.

5 Kellman, "Josquin and the Courts of the Netherlands and France," 201–4 and Jammers, "Vienna, Österreichische Nationalbibliothek, Musiksammlung, MS Mus. 15941."

6 Nixon, *Mary's Mother*, 85–90.

7 I will use "Palatini partbooks" rather than the abbreviation VatP 1976-9 in prose.

8 Kellman, "Vatican City, Biblioteca Apostolica Vaticana MSS Palatini Latini 1976–79."

9 The other motets by Mouton include *Ave fuit prima salus* (fols. 22v–25r), *Gratia plena ipsa* (fols. 25r–29r); *O quam fulges* (fols. 33v–36r), *Miseremini mei* (fols. 62v–64v); *Non nobis domine* (fols. 75v–78r), and *Illuminare Jerusalem* (fols. 99r–101v). *Christus resurgens* (fols. 83r–85r) is attributed to Mouton in just one of more than a dozen sources in which it appears. It is most likely the work of Jean Richafort.

10 The only notational alteration from Mouton's motet to *Adjutorium nostrum* is in the soprano part, where the clef is adjusted from C2 to C1. All other parts smoothly connect, both visually on the page and musically, as will be shown.

11 CambriP 1760, no. 15 (copied in France between 1498 and 1516); OxfBLL a.8, fols. 2r–3r (Alamire workshop; dated between 1512 and 1525); and LonRC 1070, no. 41 (copied in France; dated between 1510 and 1536). On the individual manuscripts, see *Census-Catalogue of Manuscript Sources of Polyphonic Music 1400–1550*, I:128; II:119, 283.

12 Indeed, Févin is currently credited as the composer of this motet in the *New Grove Dictionary*. See Brown and Keahey, "Févin, Antoine de."

13 Sherr, "The Membership of the Chapels of Louis XII and Anne de Bretagne," 79–80, and Brobeck, "Musical Patronage in the Royal Chapel of France," 233. For a study of the instrumental musicians of the royal *Écurie* (King's Stable), see Bonime, "The Musicians of the Royal Stable."

14 Brobeck, "The Motet at the Court of Francis I," 20, 48–9.

15 For a recent summary of Mouton's biography, see Rifkin, "A Black Hole? Problems in the Motet Around 1500," 31–4.

16 Stewart, "Jean Mouton," 155–7.

17 Glareanus, *Dodecachordon*, 464.

18 Rifkin, "A Black Hole? Problems in the Motet Around 1500," 27.

19 For a full study on this concept in music, see Madden, *Fib and Phi in Music*.

20 Brobeck, "The Motet at the Court of Francis I," 299–344 and Brobeck, "Style and Authenticity in the Motets of Claudin de Sermisy," 59.

21 For a complete edition of *Adjutorium nostrum* as the *secunda pars* to *Celeste beneficium*, see Sherr, ed. *Selections from Motetti de la corona*, 118–23.

22 The total length of each motet is also comparable (92 and 86 breves for *Celeste* and *Adjutorium* respectively, not counting final longs), and a major sectional division occurs about two-thirds of the way through each piece. Three-quarters of the cadences (12 of 16) in *Celeste beneficium* are on F, while 80 percent (12 of 15) of cadences go to F in the case of *Adjutorium nostrum*. On this kind of tonal reinforcement as a model for Claudin de Sermisy's "syntactic" pieces of the next generation, see Brobeck, "The Motet at the Court of Francis I," 206.

23 Ibid., 181–363.

24 Shine, "The Motets of Jean Mouton," III:163.

25 Bonime, "Anne de Bretagne (1477–1514) and Music," 75.

26 Table III–5A in Brobeck, "The Motet at the Court of Francis I," 302.

27 VE, AH 25.18. Shine likely consulted volume 3 of Chevalier, ed., *Repertorium Hymnologicum*, which catalogs the text as no. 24692, but does not state its genre. This source refers the reader to AH 22, [page] 55, which erroneously turns out to be a part of an abecedarian hymn for St. Benedict. Eight hymns to St. Anne are located earlier in this volume, but none comes close to matching the text found in the motet. It appears that there might have been a typographical error in *Repertorium Hymnologicum*; the text can be found in AH 25, [page] 52 (a possible misreading of AH 22, [page] 55), where it is clearly an antiphon for St. Anne, not a sequence.

28 A gloss of *Caeleste beneficium*, politically repurposed for a motet glorifying Germany and the spirit of the Lutheran Reformation, was ascribed to one "kegus" (almost certainly not Johannes Ockeghem), in a set of partbooks from after 1538 (Bischöfliche Zentralbibliothek, Proske-Musikbibliothek, B.211–15, fols. 158v–161r). For commentary and an edition among Ockeghem's *opera dubia*, see Ockeghem, *Collected Works*, III:l–li and III:26–34.

29 AH 25.18 is found in numerous sources (manuscript and print), dating from the fourteenth through the sixteenth century.

30 A fuller study of the textual sources of Mouton's motets is eagerly awaited in the release of the critical edition of the composer's works beyond his masses.

31 The antiphon is listed as no. 1832 and occurs in Ivrea, Chaiptre MS 106 with the title *Coeleste beneficium*. It is the first antiphon of the first nocturn of Matins. In Verona, Chaiptre XCVIII, the antiphon is entitled *Celestem beneficium* and is placed as the second antiphon of the first nocturn of Matins. See CAO, I:299.

32 My thanks to Debra Lacoste of the CANTUS database project for her invaluable assistance with locating these melodies.

33 For the problem of identifying mode in polyphony, the classic article on this topic remains Powers, "Is Mode Real?" For more recent literature, see Owens, "Concepts of Pitch in English Music Theory, c. 1560–1640" and Judd, "Josquin's Gospel Motets and Chant-Based Tonality."

34 See, for example, Mouton's *Noli flere, Maria* and *Regem confessorum Dominum*.

35 For a notated example of the first-mode antiphon *Adjutorium nostrum*, see Paris, Bibliothèque nationale de France, MS lat. 1090, fol. 32v; for the responsory, see

Paris, Bibliothèque nationale de France, MS lat. 12044, fol. 33r. The only chant of which I am aware that is both proper to the feast of St. Anne and reveals a triadic gesture at the outset is *Annae tres sunt filiae*, a fifth-mode antiphon from First Vespers. Outside of the rather common musical opening, there is no reason to connect this to *Adjutorium nostrum*, because the motet does not properly speak of Mary's mother (only Anne of Brittany).

36 There is no shortage of monographs on Anne of Brittany, which began as early as the mid-nineteenth century with Le Roux de Lincy, *Vie de la reine Anne de Bretagne*. Other early studies include Sanborn, *Anne of Brittany* and Gabory, *Anne de Bretagne*. For recent scholarship of note, see Matarasso, *Queen's Mate*; Brown, ed., *The Cultural and Political Legacy of Anne de Bretagne*; and Brown, *The Queen's Library*.

37 On this episode, see, for example, Knecht, *The Valois*, 111–14.

38 Commynes, *Mémoires*, 515–17.

39 Baumgartner, *Louis XII*, 71.

40 On the provisions the queen made for the distinct status of the duchy of Brittany, see Durtelle de Saint-Sauveur, *Histoire de Bretagne des origines à nos jours*, I:385–93.

41 Le Fur, *Louis XII, 1498–1515*, 39–40.

42 For Margaret de Foix's book of hours, see London, Victorian and Albert Museum, MS Salting 1222. On the implications for Margaret's sterility, see L'Estrange, *Holy Motherhood*, 217–26.

43 On this prayer book, see Saenger, *A Catalogue of the Pre-1500 Western Manuscript Books*, 155–7; Kamerick, "Patronage and Devotion"; and L'Estrange, "Penitence, Motherhood, and Passion Devotion."

44 Baumgartner, *Louis XII*, 184–7.

45 Farcy, *Monographie de la cathédrale d'Angers*, IV:172–4. St. Maurice was the seat of the confraternity of St. René, an important saint for that city. Anne similarly traveled to the town of Saint Claude in the Franche-Comté region early in 1500, following the birth of Claude of France, almost certainly to thank the patron saint Claudius of Besançon. See D'Auton, *Chroniques de Louis XII*, I:197.

46 *Lettres de Louis XII*, III:148.

47 "Anne, reine de France … eut un fils, mais il ne pouvoit retarder l'exaltation de mon Caesar, car il avoit faute de vie." See *Collections complètes des Mémoires relatifs à l'histoire de France*, XVI:390–1. On the questions of authorship in Louise's journal, see Orth, "Francis du Moulin and the Journal of Louise of Savoy."

48 For Anne's library, which contained numerous devotional materials, see Michael Jones, "Les Manuscrits d'Anne de Bretagne."

49 One can imagine, for example, that Anne of Brittany's ladies-in-waiting would have had access to her prayer books and devotional items.

50 A reproduction of the abundant illuminations in this manuscript as well as brief commentary on them is given in Omont, ed. *Heures d'Anne de Bretagne*.

51 Sheingorn, "'The Wise Mother.'"
52 For a reproduction of these two images, see Omont, *Heures d'Anne de Bretagne*, 51, 60. The editor seems to have confused St. Anne and St. Elizabeth in another illumination (21), which features the Visitation, an event that did not include Mary's mother.
53 On St. Ursula, see Kauffmann, *The Legend of Saint Ursula* and, more recently, Montgomery, *St. Ursula and the Eleven Thousand Virgins of Cologne*.
54 Sanborn, *Anne of Brittany*, 5.
55 On the connection between Ursula and the duchy, see Powell, *The History of the Ancient Britons and Their Descendants*, 147.
56 For an extant miniature of the St. Anne Trinitarian from around 1500 at the court, see Paris, Musée du Louvre, Departement des Arts graphiques RF 1699, recto; reprinted in *Anne de Bretagne: une histoire, un mythe*, cat. 110, with color photo on 62.
57 A full reproduction of the manuscript can be accessed at www.themorgan.org/exhibitions/exhibOnlineThumbs.asp?id=OnlinePoyetAB (accessed May 1, 2013). For a discussion of the manuscript, see *The Prayer Book of Anne de Bretagne*.
58 Voragine, *The Golden Legend*, II:150.
59 My thanks to Roger Wieck for reaffirming these observations in private correspondence. On the illustration from New York, Pierpont Morgan Library, MS M.50, see *The Prayer Book of Anne de Bretagne*, 139.
60 For a summary of the identity of the kneeling girls in these images, see Cynthia Jane Brown, "Like Mother, Like Daughter," 103.
61 On the parallels between the queen and St. Anne as seen in this primer, as well as the role of women's education during this period, see Sanders, *Gender and Literacy on Stage in Early Modern England*, 12–13.
62 For introduction to this manuscript and its illuminations, see www.themorgan.org/exhibitions/claude.asp (accessed May 1, 2013).
63 See the details of the Annunciation in Elliott, ed., *Apocryphal New Testament*, 57–9.
64 In a source potentially connected to the workshop of Jean Bourdichon, the creator of the visual program in Anne of Brittany's *Grand heures*, *Celeste beneficium* is found twice in Copenhagen, The Royal Library, MS Additamenta 64 8°, fols. 90v, 170v.
65 On these political and occasional motets, see Bonime, "Anne de Bretagne (1477–1514) and Music," 73; Brobeck, "The Motet at the Court of Francis I," 331; and Shine, "The Motets of Jean Mouton," III:128. Other motets such as *Inter natos mulierum* or *Regem confessorum* might have been motivated by occasional circumstances. See Brown and MacCracken, "Mouton, Jean," XVII:240.

6 Devotion without Borders

1 The *Missa Philippus rex Castiliae* is found in Brussels, Bibliothèque royale de Belgique, MS 9126, fols. 72v–82r; for the *Missa Fredericus dux Saxoniae*, see

Jena, Thüringer Universitäts- und Landesbibliothek MS 3, fols. 15v–28. For a discussion of the textual alterations, see Reynolds, "Interpreting and Dating Josquin's *Missa Hercules dux ferrarie*," 100–1.

2 Kellman, "London, British Library MS Royal 8.G.vii," 110.
3 Thomas, "Patronage and Personal Narrative in a Music Manuscript."
4 Ibid., 351.
5 Kellman, "Vatican City, Biblioteca Apostolica Vaticana, MSS Palatini Latini 1976–79," 130.
6 Lockwood, "Adrian Willaert and Cardinal Ippolito d'Este," 87–8.
7 Kellman, "Vatican City, Biblioteca Apostolica Vaticana, MSS Palatini Latini 1976–79," 130.
8 For an edition of Willaert's *Pater noster/Ave Maria* for four voices, see Willaert, *Opera omnia*, II:10–17.
9 In addition to the references to the names of Ferdinand and Anna, the words "Bohemia" and "Hungary" are planted in various texts. Bohemian and Hungarian coats of arms are also present in two of the part books. See Kellman, "Two Sixteenth-Century Palatine Manuscripts," 29.
10 Kellman, "Vatican City, Biblioteca Apostolica Vaticana, MSS Palatini Latini 1976–79," 130.
11 There are a few sources of the *Testamento veteri* melody, the most accessible being Oxford, Bodleian Library, MS Lat. liturg. b.5 (fol. 105v), the facsimile of which was published as Hiley, ed., *Oxford, Bodleian Library, MS. Lat. liturg. b. 5*. I would like to thank Calvin M. Bower for alerting me to this source. With the exception of the rearranged stanzas that have been noted, the text of the motet closely follows the sequence text provided in AH 8.125.
12 Agricola is not listed as a member of the royal chapel in 1486; however, he must have served there before 1491, as he is cited as having left without permission for positions in Mantua and Florence. See Wegman, "Agricola, Alexander."
13 I am extremely grateful to Leofranc Holford-Strevens, who has kindly and nobly attempted the translation of Agricola's text. The text by Claude de Chanvreux follows: Transiit, Anna, timor niveos, regina, per artus / Absorpta est cordis dira favilla tui, / Marcida dum regis prospectas ora mariti, / Vite intersticio mortis et hesit amor. / Gallica neu rimis navis pertusa fatiscat / Viribus et remis, rex redivive vales. / Regia sed soboles, France spes Claudia gentis, / Fortune refugas disce, puella, vices. / Auspice qui Christo censeris nomine Christi, / Numine sub trino, Rex Ludovice, vale. / Sospite te salva est respublica, maxime regna, / Iustitie robur, religionis honor. For an edition, see Tournoy-Thoen, "Le manuscrit 1010 de la Biblioteca de Cataluña," 65.
14 For additional contacts between the French and the Habsburg courts and other possible occasions for Agricola's motet, see Bonime, "Anne de Bretagne (1477–1514) and Music," 69–70.
15 For an edition of *Transit Anna timor*, see Agricola, *Opera omnia*, IV:41–6.
16 The tenor and bassus rest in the music during the time in which they might have sung *hungarica*; thus, no textual revision was required.

17 Reynolds, "Interpreting and Dating Josquin's *Missa Hercules dux ferrariae*," 109, fn. 22.

18 For example, forbidden parallel triads occur in m. 79, and an unusual leap to a dissonance can be seen in m. 116.

19 For a transcription of the third-mode plainchant responsory found in Mainz, Bischöfliches Dom- und Diözesanmuseum, Codex C (fol. 230r), see Boyce, "Cantica Carmelitana," II:135. A first-mode melody set to this text can be seen in Paris, Bibliothèque nationale de France, Département de la Musique, lat. 15182 (fol. 267v).

20 Only five motets fit this description: *Confitemini Domino/Per singulos dies benedicimus te* by Mouton has a tenor, as do *Exsultet conjubilando Deo/Sine macula beatus Romanus/Pater ecclesiae, Romane*; *Fulgebunt justi/Christus vincit, Christus regnat/Omnes sancti et sancte Dei*; *Missus est Gabriel angelus/Vera fides geniti*; and *Moriens lux amantissima/Tibi soli peccavi*. These motets represent about 5 percent of the composer's motet output.

21 See, for example, Schmidt-Beste, *Textdeklamation in der Motette des 15. Jahrhunderts* and a series of articles by Warwick Edwards (from whom I borrow the phrase "syllable deployment"), including "Alexander Agricola and Intuitive Syllable Deployment."

22 *Ave mater matris Dei* is listed as number 16 of twenty-nine motets in *Liber quartus XXIX. musicales quatuor vel quinque parium vocum modulos habet* (Paris: Attaingnant, 1534). The motet is transcribed in *Treize livres de Motets parus chez Pierre Attaingnant en 1534 et 1535*, IV:94–8. This edition is transposed up to G without explanation. The Attaingnant print contains attributions to a dozen different composers. Three composers (Verdelot, Hesdin, Consilium) have at least three entries in the 1534 print. Many of the composers listed in the volume are French natives who spent time in northern Italy.

23 A five-voice setting by Jacquet de Mantua is in third mode (an E-mode) and places the popular melody "Fortuna desperata" in the tenor. For a transcription and commentary, see Meconi, ed., *Fortuna Desperata*, 122–5, 184–5. The lesser-known French composer Jean Lhéritier, possibly active around the time of Mouton but also serving various courts in Italy, set this text with the litanical addition of *Ora pro nobis beata Anna*. This motet survives in no fewer than three sources. The melody paraphrased in Lhéritier's tenor (and superius), possibly derived from a third-mode chant, somewhat resembles Jacquet's tenor in his *Ave mater matris Dei* motet ("Fortuna," no less). For a transcription and commentary, see Lhéritier, *Opera Omnia*, pt. I: lv, 95–8. If Lassus placed a cantus firmus in the tenor of his motet for four voices, it is not concordant with the opening of the anonymous motet in the Palatini partbooks. His motet is set in a G-mode and transcribed in Lassus, *Motets for Three to Twelve Voices from Magnum opus musicum (Munich, 1604)*, 42–4. Gombert's setting of the text does not appear to reference any plainchant and is set in G with a flat in the signature. For an edition, see Gombert, *Opera omnia*, VII:184–7.

24 Lassus, *Motets for Three to Twelve Voices from Magnum opus musicum*, xvii.
25 There are other sources of the antiphon, with which I have not been able to consult or which do not contain notated melodies. Andrew Hughes generously provided me with an office melody associated with this text from Fribourg, Chapter Library, MS 7, fol. 137r. The chant in this source is a first-mode melody (with a range of an eleventh), in no way matching the gestures of the F-mode setting of the anonymous motet.
26 C1 and C2 clefs dominate the superius of the other motets of the "Anne group" in the Palatini partbooks.
27 On Mouton's frequent "indifference" to text declamation, see Brown and MacCracken, "Mouton, Jean," XVII:241.
28 Kellman, "Vatican City, Biblioteca Apostolica Vaticana, MSS Palatini Latini 1976–79," 130.
29 Each of the four partbooks received a different coat of arms: Hungary (superius), Burgundy (altus), Bohemia (tenor), and Austria (bassus).
30 Fichtner, *The Habsburg Monarchy, 1490–1848*, 6–7.
31 Vermeyen was in the service of Margaret of Austria and Charles V and was best known for his portraiture. For the most comprehensive study of Vermeyen's works, see Horn, *Jan Cornelisz Vermeyen*.
32 There are numerous accounts of these events. See, for example, Fichtner, *Ferdinand I of Austria*, 50.
33 Bruck's nearly two decades of service to Ferdinand brought a number of valuable ecclesiastical benefices. He held a canonry at Ljubljana Cathedral (from 1527) and another at Zagreb Cathedral (from 1528). The definitive study on Bruck remains Wessely, "Arnold von Bruck." On the Habsburg chapels more generally, with some attention to Ferdinand's chapel, see Seifert, "The Institution of the Imperial Court Chapel from Maximilian I to Charles VI."
34 For an edition and commentary on this *si placet* motet, see Schlagel, *Si Placet Parts for Motets by Josquin and his Contemporaries*, xii, 63–71. It has been suggested that Bruck's arrangement could have been made between 1527 and 1531.
35 Kellman, "Vatican City, Biblioteca Apostolica Vaticana, MSS Palatini Latini 1976–79," 130–2. The author notes that *Transit Anna timor* may also refer to an illness that Ferdinand developed as he was setting off to war. I am not aware of such an illness, nor is one typically mentioned in the general biographies of Ferdinand.
36 Fichtner, *Ferdinand I of Austria*, 50–7.
37 Ibid., 80–4.
38 In addition to Gascongne's *Christus vincit*, I am aware of just four other polyphonic settings from the fifteenth and sixteenth centuries that invoke this text, the earliest being that of Hugo de Lantins in Bologna, Biblioteca Universitaria, MS 2216, fols. 30v–31r. There are two settings by Mouton, possibly for the election of Leo X. One motet survives only in the alto part (1521^4), but another motet,

Fulgebunt justi/Christus vincit, Christus regnat/Omnes sancti et sancte Dei, is an eight-voice polytextual work with chant *Christus vincit* set as the cantus firmus. This motet remains unedited, surviving in Verona, Accademia Filarmonica, Biblioteca e Archivio, MS 218, fols. 19r–20r. The six-voice motet *Ecce advenit dominator* by Costanzo Festa likewise uses the *Christus vincit* intonation as a cantus firmus. For an edition, see Festa, *Opera Omnia*, IV:39–42. None of these four settings mentioned treats the larger text from the *laudes regiae* as comprehensively as Gascongne's motet.

39 Gascongne is listed prominently as a singer in the royal chapel in 1517–18. See Swing, "Gascongne, Mathieu."

40 Kellman, "Vatican City, Biblioteca Apostolica Vaticana, MSS Palatini Latini 1976–79," 132.

41 Brandi, *Die Deutsche Reformation und Gegenreformation*, I:190–1 and Fichtner, *Ferdinand I of Austria*, 86–7.

42 Charles expressed his inclination to endorse his brother's candidacy in a letter to Ferdinand on January 11, 1530 in *Die Korrespondenz Ferdinands I*, 2^2:555, 563.

43 On the financing of the election by members of the Fugger family and their reciprocal elevation to the rank of *Freiherren*, see Pölnitz, *Anton Fugger*, I:209–10.

44 Later in Gascongne's *Christus vincit* motet, a litany emerges, which asks for the help of several personages including Jesus (*Salvator mundi*); the Virgin Mary; the angels Michael and Gabriel; Saints Peter, Paul, and Martin; and Francis (namesake of the French king). As another sign of the inconsistency and attempts at diplomacy one finds in the scribal process, the partbooks do not uniformly present the litany when it comes to mention of Francis. The Superius and Bassus partbooks retain the name *sancte Francisce* in the litany, while the Altus and Tenor partbooks simply provide "sancte" to avoid an allusion to the French king.

45 On the life of Maximilian II, see, for example, Fichtner, *Emperor Maximilian II* and Edelmayer and Kohler, *Kaiser Maximilian II*. For a biography of the second-born son, Ferdinand II, see, for example, Hirn, *Erzherzog Ferdinand II. von Tirol*.

46 Anna was also the name of the mother of Anna Jagiellon (Anne de Foix-Candale). She was raised in the French court at Blois, part of a temporary alliance between the Jagiellon dynasty and the French. This relationship was dissolved with the Habsburg double marriage pact.

47 Wegman, "Musical Offerings in the Renaissance."

48 Marie recommended (and Ferdinand accepted) Pieter Maessens for the post. Maessens assumed the duties of vice-Kapellmeister on March 1, 1543. He was appointed Kapellmeister on January 1, 1546 upon Bruck's retirement. See Dunning, "Maessens, Pieter."

49 Kellman, "Two Sixteenth-Century Palatine Manuscripts," 30 and Kellman, "Vatican City, Biblioteca Apostolica Vaticana, MSS Palatini Latini 1976–79," 132.

Kellman has suggested (in private communication) that the word *registrum* may be likened to the word "diary" or "journal," which, if true, would alter the meaning of the inscription atop the table of contents and perhaps have implications for determining the sponsor of the partbooks. *Registrum*, however, is more likely an uncomplicated bureaucratic term simply meaning "register." The word *libri* must be inferred in this instance ("register *of the book…*"). My thanks to Leofranc Holford-Strevens for his kind assistance with this terminology.

50 Horn, *Jan Cornelisz Vermeyen*, I:7–9. The order to Vermeyen requests that portraits of the emperor, the king and queen of Hungary, and their children (especially their physiognomy) be made "as close to life as possible" (*plus près du vif que possible*). See Brussels, Archives Générales du Royaume, Reg. no. 1806.

51 The other composers who worked mainly in France were Johannes Prioris, Mathieu Gascongne, Antoine de Févin, and Pierre Moulu. Several others spent part of their lives in France or at the French court (Compère, Ghiselin, Josquin, Ockeghem, Brumel, Divitis, and Richafort). See Table 1 in *The Treasury of Petrus Alamire*, 33.

52 Kellman, "Josquin and the Courts of the Netherlands and France," 200–1.

53 After the "Anne group" come three additional subsections: one with works for the Virgin Mary, ending with a prayer to Christ (nos. 8–13); another focusing on the crucified Christ, ending with a work for Mary (nos. 14–23), and finally, a large group of Song of Songs settings allegorizing Mary and Christ (nos. 24–37). See Kellman, "Vatican City, Biblioteca Apostolica Vaticana, MSS Palatini Latini 1976–79," 130. In some sense, the emphasis on Mary and Christ fits better with a comparison to the book of hours, also popular in the early sixteenth century.

54 For instance, in his *Oraciones et alia pulcra ad sanctam Annam*, humanist Johannes von Lambsheym inserted Anne's name into the traditional Salve Regina prayer (emphasis added): "Salue *Anna*, mater misericordie … Ad te clamamus exules filij eue in angustijs constituti … O clemens, O pia, O dulcis mater *Anna*" ("Hail *Anne*, mother of mercy … To thee do we cry poor banished children of Eve … O clement, O loving, O sweet mother *Anne*"). One might also point to representations of the St. Anne Trinitarian that conflate mother and daughter as matrons. On Lambsheym's prayer and others that substitute the name of Anne for Mary, see Nixon, *Mary's Mother*, 47–52.

55 These prayers were found in the *Vita gloriosissime matris Annae christipare virginis Marie genetricis ab ascensio in compendium redacta ex historia suavissima eiusdem matris Anne ab religiosissimo viro F. dorlando ordinis Carthusiensis in zelem theuthonice prius edita,* published with Ludolph of Saxony, *Vita Jesu Christi,* 767. This "Rosarium" was also published in a popular tract by the most important advocate for St. Anne devotion in the Rhineland, Benedictine abbott Johannes Trithemius. See his *De laudibus sanctissimae matris Annae*. Scholarship has also noted that advocates for St. Anne were frequently champions of the Rosary devotion. See Wallert, Tauber, and Murphy, eds., *The Holy Kinship*, 9.

56 For this particular Rosary devotion to St. Anne, see The Hague, Koninklijke Bibliotheek, MS 135 E 19, fol. 19v, with illumination of the St. Anne Trinitarian. A study of this manuscript is provided in Broekhuijsen, *The Masters of the Dark Eyes*, 43, 167–8.

57 Bérenger, *A History of the Habsburg Empire*, 175.

58 On the Catholic league, see, for example, Kühn, *Die Geschichte des Speyerer Reichstag 1529*, 25–7, 244–5 and Pettegree, *The Reformation World*, 156. On Marie's religious leanings and those sympathetic to Protestantism in the court retinue, see Fichtner, *Ferdinand I of Austria*, 74–8. On the moderate religious stance of Ferdinand and Charles, see Chisholm, "The *Religionspolitik* of Emperor Ferdinand I (1521– 1564)" and Bérenger, *A History of the Habsburg Empire*, 150.

59 Evans, *The Making of the Habsburg Monarchy, 1550–1700*, 19.

60 Erasmus, *The Correspondence of Erasmus*, XIII:172.

61 Goetz, "Die geheimen Ratgeber Ferdinands I (1503–1564)," 462, 476, 483–5, 488.

62 Erasmus, *Poems*, LXXXVI:407–10, with poem and a translation at LXXXV:8–13.

63 The motet is first in both the *Liber secundus: quatuor et viginti musicales quatuor vocum Motetos habet* (Paris, 1534) and *Motettorum IV vocum 'Liber secundus', editio secunda* (Venice, 1545).

7 The French Royal Trinity, Biblical Humanism, and Chanted Mass Propers for St. Anne

1 On the living arrangements and interactions between Louise and her husband's mistress and their respective families, see Cholakian and Cholakian, *Marguerite de Navarre*, 11.

2 For Louis XII's handling of Louise and her family after the death of Charles, see Maulde-La-Clavière, *Procédures politiques du règne de Louis XII*, 716–27.

3 Knecht, *Renaissance Warrior and Patron*, 3.

4 Capefigue, *François Ier et la renaissance*, I:63.

5 Cholakian and Cholakian, *Marguerite de Navarre*, 43; Knecht, *Renaissance Warrior and Patron*, 114.

6 Marguerite also wrote poetry, though not music, for *rondeaux* and *chansons spirituelles*. For a brief reference to Marguerite's interest in music, the kinds of compositions she created, and references to music and music making in her literary works, see Marguerite of Navarre, *Selected Writings*, 282 and Pendle, ed., *Women and Music: A History*, 73.

7 For an edition, see Marguerite of Navarre, *The Heptaméron*. On the autobiographical potential of the novellas, see Cholakian and Cholakian, *Marguerite de Navarre*, 21–48.

8 On the politics of Marguerite's marriage prospects, see Ripart, "Les Mariages de Marguerite."
9 Her only surviving daughter, Jeanne III of Navarre (b. 1528), would eventually give birth to a future king of France, Henry VI. Marguerite's only son, Jean (b. 1530), died within six months of his birth.
10 Jourda, *Marguerite d'Angoulême*, II:1009–10. For a revised assessment of the relationship between Marguerite and Francis, see Stephenson, *The Power and Patronage of Marguerite de Navarre*, 113–48.
11 On Louise's extensive library, see the catalog compiled by Sheila Edmunds in Bagliani, ed., *Les manuscrits enluminés des comtes et ducs de Savoie*, 220–4.
12 On the correspondence in poetic verse among Marguerite, Francis, and Louise, see Knecht, *Renaissance Warrior and Patron*, 109–12 and Matarasso, *Queen's Mate*, 202.
13 Orth, "Madame Sainte Anne," 204; Cholakian and Cholakian, *Marguerite de Navarre*, 17.
14 On Louise's powerful influence on internal affairs in France (even outside of her stints as regent), see Knecht, "'Our Trinity!,'" 76–9.
15 By the early fourteenth century, the *rex christianissimus* designation was used to assert France's superiority to Rome as a uniquely Christian kingdom. See Beaune, *The Birth of an Ideology*, 172–93.
16 In an ancient ritual recalling the customs of consecrating kings in the Old Testament, the anointing of the French monarch with oil at the coronation gave him, in the words of Robert Knecht (*Renaissance Warrior and Patron*, 90), "a quasi-sacerdotal character."
17 See Prinet, "Les variations du nombre des fleures de lys" and Spiegel and Hindman, "The Fleur de Lys Frontispieces to Guillaume de Nangis' *Chronique abrégée*." A zealous subscriber to the Royal Trinity model, Charles V of France arranged for his coronation expressly on Trinity Sunday. See Delachenal, *Histoire de Charles V*, III:23–5.
18 For instance, during Francis's imprisonment in Madrid following his 1525 capture, Louise and Marguerite jointly wrote a letter to the incarcerated Francis, noting how "our Trinity" (*nostre trynyté*) was designated by God to remain united as one and would not be whole without its third part, which of course was not functional during his detention. See Champollion-Figeac, *Captivité du roi François Ier*, 142. Similar sentiments on the indivisibility of the Royal Trinity can be seen in an epistolary exchange (in verse) in 1527 between Francis and Marguerite (ibid., 537), as the latter married for the second time and feared the breakup of "our Trinity" (*nostre trinité*). For more on the history of the analogy, see Lecoq, *François Ier imaginaire*, 393–6 and Reid, *King's Sister*, I:85, fn. 1.
19 Paris, Bibliothèque nationale de France, MS nouv. acq. lat. 83, fol. 2v. For a reproduction, see Lecoq, *François Ier imaginaire*, 396.
20 Orth, "Madame Sainte Anne," 216.

21 For a full-length study, see Forrester, *La Vierge à l'enfant avec sainte Anne, Léonard de Vinci, 1492–1519*.
22 See, for example, Peter, "La Réception de Luther en France au XVIe siècle" and Higman, "Luther et la piété et de l'église gallicane."
23 Jourda, *Marguerite d'Angoulême*, II:1067 and Reid, *King's Sister*, I:2–4.
24 On the 1521 heresy hunt by conservatives, see Clerval, *Registre des procès-verbaux de la Faculté de théologie de Paris*, 354–425.
25 On Louise's counter-heresy commission and the reduction of the biblical humanists to a fringe movement, see Reid, *King's Sister*, I:23, 235–40.
26 Porrer, *Jacques Lefèvre d'Etaples and the Three Maries Debates*, 39–40.
27 Du Moulin's life of the Magdalene (*Vie de sainte Madeleine*) survives as Bibliothèque nationale de France, MS fr. 24955. For brief discussions of this *vita*, see Orth, "Louise de Savoie et le pouvoir du livre"; Orth, "Madame Sainte Anne," 207; and Porrer, *Jacques Lefèvre d'Etaples and the Three Maries Debates*, 40–2.
28 These three women were (1) the unnamed sinful woman who washed Christ's feet with her tears (Luke 7:36–50); (2) Mary, the sister of Martha who anointed Jesus with a precious ointment (Luke 10:42; John 12:1–8); and (3) Mary of Magdala who was present at Christ's crucifixion and resurrection (Matthew 27:56–28:10; Mark 15:40–16:10). On the third personage, see also Luke 23:55, 24:1, 24:9–10, 14:4 and John 19:25, 20:1–14, 18.
29 For the citations of these commentators in the second edition of the Magdalene treatise, see Lefèvre d'Etaples, *De Maria magdalena*, 2v–3r, 16v–17r, and 18r–v.
30 For a summary of the objections to Lefèvre's initial treatise, see Porrer, *Jacques Lefèvre d'Etaples and the Three Maries Debates*, 85–103.
31 Lefèvre d'Etaples, *De Maria magdalena*, fols. 65v–67v.
32 Ibid., fol. 62v.
33 Discussions of Du Moulin's works can be found in Lecoq, *François Ier imaginaire*, 80–5 and Matarasso, *Queen's Mate*, 201.
34 Beda, Noël. *Apologia p[ro] filiabus [et] nepotibus beatae Annae*. Paris, 1520.
35 Porrer, *Jacques Lefèvre d'Etaples and the Three Maries Debates*, 123–4.
36 The full text of the *Determinatio* can be found in Clerval, *Registre des procès-verbaux*, 299–301.
37 Paris, Bibliothèque de l'Arsenal, MS 4009. On the date of the *Petit livret*, see Holban, "François du Moulin de Rochefort et la querelle de la Madeleine," 166; Lecoq, *François Ier imaginaire*, 336; and Orth, "Progressive Tendencies in French Manuscript Illumination, 1515–1530," 98–100.
38 Paris, Bibliothèque de l'Arsenal, MS 4009, fol. 5r.
39 Orth, "Madame Sainte Anne," 208.
40 The interrogation of the various Marys and the extensive calculations about the age of the "sons of Zebedee" can be seen most vividly in Paris, Bibliothèque de l'Arsenal, MS 4009, fols. 13r, 15r, and 38v.
41 For a discussion of the politics of this treatise, see Orth, "Madame Sainte Anne," 200–12.

42 Fols. A7–A8. "Laquelle est apocriphe et mensongere combien que les theologiens de Paris l'ayent par long temps approuée. En parlant en reverance de vous MADAME ceulx qui l'ont dyt ont menti. Car Saincte Anne bonne et pudicque vefue fut contante d'ung seul mari savoir est de Joachim pere seulement de la vierge marie."

43 Orth, "Madame Sainte Anne," 214.

44 The gray robe could indicate that the author is a Franciscan, but Franciscans were also known to wear brown. The Master of Claude of France, however, represented the Franciscan St. Anthony of Padua with a gray habit (Paris, École Nationale Superieur des Beaux-Arts, M. 94). If the author were a member of the Faculty of Theology at the University of Paris, he would likely have worn a black garment. My thanks to Margaret Hadley for helping decipher the clothing in this image.

45 On the history of the Order of St. Michael, particularly its costumes and membership, see Boulton, *The Knights of the Crown*, 427–47. Orth's identification of the nobleman as Francis can be found in her "Manuscrits pour Marguerite," 96, fn. 16. The unidentified man's genuflection before Marguerite's throne would seem uncharacteristic of the French king.

46 The significance of Francis's gift of Berry to Marguerite is explained in Stephenson, *The Power and Patronage of Marguerite de Navarre*, 12, 79–83, 171 and Reid, *King's Sister*, I:96–7.

47 Fol. 2v–3r. "Nous verrons l'eglise millitante pascifiee les Roys et princes de la xpiante unys et assemblez pour soustenir nostre saincte foy catholique dessoubs l'obeissance de la tres saincte et sacree Romanie eglise mere et maistresse de toutes autres eglises. Dont a bon droit elle nous a este presignee et prefiguree per ladicte saincte anne mere des troyes nobles maries signifiantes les troyes partyes du monde esquelles toutes eglises signiffies par les sept filz sont construistes et ediffices. Puis doncques que du temps quilz estoient vivans au monde paix universelle regnoit." ("We see the Church Militant calmed, the kings and princes of Christianity united and assembled for support our holy catholic faith under the submission of the most holy and sacred Roman church, mother and mistress of all other churches. Of which in good right, it has been prefigured through the aforesaid St. Anne, mother of the three noble Marys signifying the three parts of the world in which all churches represented by the seven sons are built. Since therefore at the time that they were living in the world, universal peace reigned.")

48 The first five marginal texts (from top to bottom) are drawn from Genesis 7:2; Job 42:8; Romans 15:10; John 10:16; and Zechariah 4:10. The remaining two citations, adjacent to the miniature on the left, are nonbiblical. The invocation "Benedicat vos altissimus et sitis sicut columne [recte: columbe] septem civitatis refugii" ("Blessed are you most high, and may you be as the seven doves of the City of Refuge") derives from the story of Joseph and Asenath, an apocryphal extension of the book of Genesis. The final marginal annotation has no known source: "In

her sterility, Anne signified the synagogue; in her fecundity, the universal church militant" (*Anna in sterilitate synagogam in fecunditate universalem ecclesiam militate persignavit*). The passage above the miniature alludes to Genesis 29 and the seven-year periods that Jacob served to marry Rachel.

49 Fols. 5r–6v.

50 Fol. 6r. The miniature is rubricated with the following text (attributed to Augustine), equating the enemy with Satan: "Nunquid tu percusisti superbum vulneristi draconem. PSA C° LI° dictum est de dyabolo quia leo et draco est. Leo propter impetum. Draco propter insidias" ("Surely if you beat the proud one, you wound the dragon. Psalm 151. This is said from the devil, who is lion and dragon. The lion on account of his violence; the dragon on account of his deceits."). The reference to Psalm 151 alludes to the supernumerary psalm attributed to David after the slaying of Goliath, an allegory for the present situation.

51 Chapter 6 mentioned that John Zapolya, claimant to the Hungarian throne, entered into an alliance with the Ottoman sultan Suleiman against the Austrian Habsburgs, at the same time that he was actively conspiring with Francis I. During Francis's captivity after the Battle of Pavia, Louise of Savoy also sought an alliance with the Ottoman sultan in an effort to form an international coalition against the Habsburg Empire. See Knecht, *Renaissance Warrior and Patron*, 227–31.

52 Fols. 3r–4v. "Je vous supplie tres humblement ma dame qu'il vous plaise prier monseigneur reverendissime mon seigneur le legat que son plaisir soit de aproner ladicte messe d'auctre apostolicque." ("I humbly beg you my Lady that it please you to ask the most reverend monseigneur my lord the legate that his pleasure be to recommend this Mass to apostolic others [other churches].").

53 The alliterative *ferme foy* in the vernacular recalls the assonance of the tenor *Firma fide fidens* from a motet encountered in Chapter 6 (*Theodoce matrem/ Firma fide fidens*). This tenor points to a responsory of the same name from the widespread Office AH 25.18, suggesting that the idea of "firm faith" connected with St. Anne was neither a late development nor a keyword in reform theology.

54 Fol. 6v.

55 2 Esdras – called 4 Esdras in the Vulgate so as not to confuse it with the canonical book of Nehemiah (called 2 Esdras in the Vulgate) – has no relationship to the book of Ezra from the Old Testament, although it borrows the protagonist, through whom God speaks. In the first two chapters of 2 Esdras (from which the Introit is drawn), God rebukes Israel for previous disloyalty. Particularly notable in the second chapter of 2 Esdras is that it serves as the source of some of the Latin Requiem texts (2 Esdras 2:34–5). The collection of Jewish texts found in 2 Esdras, chs. 3–14 has attracted the most scholarly attention and has been securely dated to the late first or early second century. See Raymond E. Brown et al., eds., *The New Jerome Biblical Commentary*, 1062–3.

56 A survey of numerous missals from late medieval France confirms the rather stable transmission of Mass Propers for St. Anne, some of them already borrowed from masses for the Virgin Mary and for the Common of Virgins. The Gradual *Propter veritatem* from the Common of the Blessed Virgin Mary is often in the masses for St. Anne, as is the Communion antiphon *Diffusa est gratia*. The Offertory *Filiae regum* is often sung in the Mass for the Common of Virgins. The Introit *Gaudeamus omnes* is technically proper to St. Anne, though variants may be traced to the Masses for Virgins and Martyrs. The uniformity of these Proper chants for St. Anne – along with *Alleluia. Veni electa* – can be observed in a survey of several missals at the Bibliothèque nationale de France, namely MSS lat. 830, 861, 865A, 872, 876, 1098, 8885, 14448, 15615, and 17310.

57 Fol. 7r: "reges et principes christiani nobis unire et pascificare eiusque generosam prolem ad tue sacre fidei augmentum concedere digneris."

58 Isaiah 65:23, 66:12.

59 The Offertory contains an F clef, and the Communion begins with an F clef, but abandons it almost immediately.

60 Besides the elaborate initial for the Introit (with the coat of arms within the "N" of *Noli timere*), calligraphic initials begin each of the five remaining Proper chants. All initials, except for the one accompanying the Tract (fol. 15r), are drawn in pencil on a yellow background.

61 The antiphon *Luce splendida fulgebis* (CAO 3638) for the Common of Kings is found in just one unnotated medieval liturgical book, a ninth-century antiphoner from Compiègne (Paris, Bibliothèque nationale de France, MS lat. 17436). A portion of the text can also be found set in a verse for the Matins responsory *Plateae tuae Jerusalem* (CAO 7390). Finally, the text was set as a seventh-mode Gradual in Du Fay's plainchant settings for the Recollection of Feasts for the Blessed Virgin Mary. See Haggh, "The Aostan Sources," 370–1.

62 The music of *Exsurge iherusalem* may be compared with the Gradual *Specie tua et pulchritudine tua* found in *Graduale sacrosanctae romanae ecclesiae de tempore et de sanctis*, [60–1]. The urge to retext *Specie tua* is a curious one, because its text already contains royalist overtones (*prospere procede et regna*) that would be appropriate for the politically active sister of the king.

63 Chartres, Bibliothèque municipale, MS 529, fol. 145r; Provins, Bibliothèque municipale, MS 12 (olim 24), fols. 3r and 239r. The Alleluia is transcribed in Schlager, *Alleluia-Melodien*, VIII:145.

64 For a detailed study of the eighth-mode tracts, see Hornby, *Gregorian and Old Roman Eighth-mode Tracts*.

65 The position of *Commovebo celum* at the end of the mass was apparently not a mistake in the copying process. Two pieces of codicological evidence support this claim. First, there is a space carved out of the staves for a calligraphic "C" to begin the chant *Commovebo celum* (fol. 15r), perhaps part of the original copying plan. Moreover, the end of the chant contains a widely drawn (or extended) final note, resembling a maximal long in mensural notation. This note is followed by

a small sketched decoration, a clear indication of finality akin to a double bar, not found at the ends of the other five chants in the manuscript.

66 The shape of this incipit concords with the chants given in Example II.11.1 (f group) of Hiley, *Western Plainchant*, 112.

67 Stevens, *Words and Music in the Middle Ages*, 292–307 and Andrew Hughes, "Word Painting in a Twelfth-Century Office."

68 As Christopher Page has explained, sharp modal clarity and a restrained style were much in keeping with the ideals of chant composition that were achieved as part of eleventh-century reforms. See Page, *The Christian West and Its Singers*, 417–22.

69 Fol. 3r. Also on fol. 2v: "Laquelle fut legitimement mariee a troys marys. Et d'un chascun diceulx eut une fille. Et les troyes filles eurent sept filz." ("She rightfully married three husbands. From each of them came a daughter; and the three daughters had seven sons.")

70 Orth, "Manuscrits pour Marguerite," 89.

71 Isaiah 66:10–13. "Rejoice with Jerusalem, and be glad with her, all you that love her: rejoice for joy with her, all you that mourn for her. That you may suck, and be filled with the breasts of her consolations: that you may milk out, and flow with delights, from the abundance of her glory. For thus saith the Lord: Behold I will bring upon her as it were a river of peace, and as an overflowing torrent the glory of the Gentiles, which you shall suck; you shall be carried at the breasts, and upon the knees they shall caress you. As one whom the mother caresseth, so will I comfort you, and you shall be comforted in Jerusalem."

72 Marguerite apparently established communication with Briçonnet out of concern for her husband's safety in his new military assignment in northeast France, but the bishop and the duchess also had mutual concern for monastic reform. For a complete edition of the letters, see *Guillaume Briçonnet, Marguerite d'Angoulême: Correspondance*. On the significance of the correspondence with Briçonnet, see Stephenson, *The Power and Patronage of Marguerite de Navarre*, 149–84; Cholakian and Cholakian, *Marguerite de Navarre*, 66–103; and Reid, *King's Sister*, I:181–248.

73 Stephenson, *The Power and Patronage of Marguerite de Navarre*, 155–6.

74 Cholakian and Cholakian, *Marguerite de Navarre*, 80.

75 *Guillaume Briçonnet, Marguerite d'Angoulême: Correspondance*, II:172–82.

76 Fol. 2r.

77 Fol. 3r.

78 Fol. 5r.

79 On the Concordat, see *Ordonnances des rois de France*, I: no. 91.

80 Knecht, *Renaissance Warrior and Patron*, 85–6.

81 Fols. 3v, 5v.

82 In 1523, five hundred forty staff members served the king alone, with another two hundred forty in the service of Louise of Savoy. See Bibliothèque nationale de France, MS. fr. 7853, fols. 255r–262r. Louise and Marguerite had smaller

household staffs, though still with dozens of women attending them. See Knecht, *Renaissance Warrior and Patron*, 120.

83 Reid, *King's Sister*, I:108. The mendicant's spirit was very much with the Royal Trinity after the friar's death; Louise, in fact, wrote in her journal that she paid a fee for his canonization, which was completed in July 1519.

84 Farge, *Orthodoxy and Reform in Early Reformation France*, 118–20.

85 On De Ceva's preaching and his support from the royal court, see Renaudet, *Préréforme et humanisme*, 570–4 and Reid, *King's Sister*, I:109. De Ceva's sermons for Advent were published in *Sermones prenatalicii, sive de adventu*.

86 Bernardin is mentioned in passing in Armstrong, *The Politics of Piety*, 89.

87 On Thenaud's life and works, see, for example, Thenaud, *Le Triumphe des vertuz*, xvii–xxiv.

88 *Le Triumphe de vertuz* comprises a series of smaller treatises ("Le triumphe de Prudence," "Le triumphe de Force," etc.) spread across two manuscripts – Paris, Bibliothèque nationale de France, MS fr. 144 and Paris, Bibliothèque de l'Arsenal, MS 3358. Thenaud's 1508 treatise for Marguerite is entitled *Margarite* [sic] *de France* and survives in London, British Library, Add. 13969.

89 Thenaud's ambassadorial travels to the Levant in 1512 are recorded in his *Le voyage d'outremer*. There is no mention of any churches visited with the name St. Anne.

90 For Thenaud's astrological interests, see Holban, "Le Vrai Jean Thenaud." On the cabalistic treatises, see Knecht, *Renaissance Warrior and Patron*, 150. On the movement more generally, see Brann, *Trithemius and Magical Theology*, 253 and Hamilton, "Humanists and the Bible," 106.

91 Orth ("Madame Sainte Anne," 223, fn. 29) dismissed an attribution to Thenaud made by Marie Holban ("Le Vrai Jean Thenaud," 194), because Holban dated the manuscript to the time of Anne of Brittany (d. 1514); however, Orth reentertained the possibility of an attribution to Thenaud in "Manuscrits pour Marguerite," 96, fn. 16. The document that Holban was discussing was a "Messe des Trois Maries," not properly a "Mass for St. Anne." Holban presumably would not have erred in understanding the dedicatee of the *Mass for St. Anne* because Marguerite's title is clearly presented in the dedicatory image; therefore, these are likely two different masses. Unfortunately, Holban never cited the source of Thenaud's alleged "Messe des Trois Maries," so one is unable to examine further if the Franciscan humanist had a role in each manuscript. Thenaud also took an interest in astrology and horoscope-type prognostication, as demonstrated by Orth, "Francis du Moulin and the Journal of Louise of Savoy," 55–6. This aspect of his writing does not emerge in the *Mass for St. Anne*.

Postlude

1 Luther, *Werke, Kritischer Gesammtausgabe*, I:415. "Ipsa pene supra quam B. Virgo extollitur."

2 That the veneration of St. Anne in the fifteenth century was a response to the propagation of the Immaculate Conception is a view that originated in Falk, "Die Verehrung der h. Anna im 15. Jahrhundert," and was amplified in Kleinschmidt, *Die heilige Anna*, esp. 65.

3 The only source that has not been the subject of musicological inquiry is the anonymous *Mass for St. Anne* (Paris, Bibliothèque nationale de France, MS fr. 1035), discussed in Chapter 7.

4 Duffy, "The Jena Choirbooks."

5 For an edition of Dunstaple's motet, see Bukofzer, ed., *John Dunstable: Complete Works*, 70–3. This motet might have a connection to a prayer "Gaude felix Anna," which was well known in England. See Fein, "Mary to Veronica," 995–1000.

6 For an edition of Jacquet's motet, see Meconi, ed., *Fortuna desperata*, 122–5.

7 On the relics and reliquaries in general, see Kleinschmidt, *Die heilige Anna*, 393–404. The city of Düren – located between Aachen and Cologne – became a major destination for pilgrims when the church acquired a portion of the skull of St. Anne in 1510. As the legend has it, the church acquired the relic after a mason stole it from a Dominican institution in Mainz. Düren apparently experienced a great economic boon from the infusion of devotees who sought the precious relic. Residents of Düren also had their own peculiar customs related to St. Anne. For this singular case in the history of devotion to St. Anne, see Gatz, "Die Dürener Annaverehrung bis zum Ende des 18. Jahrhunderts" and Webb, *Medieval European Pilgrimage*, 137, 152. Due west of Düren, the city of Ghent was home to a confraternity of St. Anne in the mid-fifteenth century, and this organization endowed weekly polyphonic masses, a curious achievement given the scarcity of complete surviving masses in polyphony from this period. See Wegman, "Ghent."

8 See Bonaventure's commentary on the *Sentences* of Peter Lombard, lib. III, dist. IX, art. 1, q. 2, in Bonaventure, *Opera Omnia*, III:203.

Bibliography

Select Manuscripts

Bologna, Civico Museo Bibliografico Musicale, MS Q15.
Brussels, Bibliothèque royale de Belgique, MSS 228, 6428, 9126, 9236, 9551, 10389, 10974, 15075, IV.922.
Cambridge, Magdalene College, Pepys Library, MS 1760.
Cambridge, Fitzwilliam Museum, MS 159.
Chicago, Newberry Library, MS 83.
Copenhagen, Royal Library, L.N. MS 30.
Évreux, Bibliothèque municipale, MS lat. 89.
Ghent, Poor Clares, MS 8.
Graz, Universitätsbibliothek, MS 30 (olim 38/9).
Jena, Thüringer Universitäts- und Landesbibliothek, Chorbuch MSS 3, 4, 5, 7, 30, 34, 35.
London, British Library, MS Royal 8 G.vii.
London, British Library, MS Stowe 12.
London, Royal College of Music, MS 1070.
Mainz, Bischöfliches Dom- und Diözesanmuseum, Codex C.
Mechelen, Archief en Stadsbibliotheek, MS s.s., "Livre de choeur."
Montserrat, Biblioteca del Monestir, MS 773.
New York, Pierpont Morgan Library, MSS M.50, M.175, M.1166.
Oxford, Bodleian Library, MSS Lat. liturg.a.8, Lat. liturg.b.5.
Oxford, Bodleian Library, MS Laud Misc. 93.
Oxford, Bodleian Library, MS Rawlinson C. 489.
Paris, Bibliothèque de l'Arsenal, MSS 3358, 4009.
Paris, Bibliothèque nationale de France, MSS fr. 144, 1035, 5616, 7853.
Paris, Bibliothèque nationale de France, MSS lat. 830, 861, 865A, 872, 876, 1090, 1098, 8885, 9473, 9474, 10482, 12044, 14448, 15182, 15615, 17310, 17436.
Paris, Bibliothèque nationale de France, MS nouv. acq. lat. 83.
Torino, Biblioteca nazionale, MS J.II.9.
Vatican City, Biblioteca Apostolica Vaticana, MSS Palatini Latini 1976–9.
Vienna, Österreichische Nationalbibliothek, Musiksammlung, MS Mus. 15941.
Vienna, Österreichische Nationalbibliothek, MS Supplementum Musica 15496.

Prints Cited

Beda, Noël. *Apologia p[ro] filiabus [et] nepotibus beatae Annae.* Paris, 1520.

De Ceva, Boniface. *Sermones prenatalicii, sive de adventu.* Paris, 1518.

Erasmus of Rotterdam. *Rhythmus iambicus in laudem Annae, aviae Iesu Christi* in *Epigrammata.* Basle, 1518.

Glareanus, Henricus. *Dodecachordon.* Basel, 1547.

Lefèvre d'Etaples, Jacques. *De Maria magdalena, Triduo Christi, et ex tribus una Maria, disceptatio.* Paris, 1518.

Liber quartus XXIX. musicales quatuor vel quinque parium vocum modulos habet. Paris, 1534.

Liber secundus: quatuour et viginti musicales quatuor vocum Motetos habet. Paris, 1534.

Ludolph of Saxony. *Vita Jesu Christi.* Antwerp, [no date].

Luther, Martin. *An den christlichen Adel deutscher Nation.* Wittenberg, 1520.

―― *Wider den neuen Abgott und alten Teufel, der zu Meissen soll erhoben werden.* Wittenberg, 1524.

Motetti de la corona. Libro primo. Venice, 1514.

Motetti de la corona. Libro primo. Rome, 1526.

Motettorum IV vocum 'Liber secundus', editio secunda. Venice, 1545.

Trithemius, Johannes. *De laudibus sanctissimae matris Annae.* Mainz, 1494.

Editions

Acta Sanctorum. 68 vols. Brussels, 1965–70.

Agricola, Alexander. *Opera omnia.* 5 vols. Ed. Edward R. Lerner. Corpus mensurabilis musicae 22. Rome, 1961–70.

Bonaventure. *Opera Omnia.* 10 vols. Quaracchi, 1882–1902.

Castiglione, Baldassare. *The Book of the Courtier.* Trans. Charles S. Singleton. New York, 1959.

Collections complètes des mémoires relatifs à l'histoire de France. 130 vols. Ed. M. Petitot et al. Paris, 1819–29.

Commynes, Philippe de. *Mémoires.* Ed. Joël Blanchard. Paris, 2004.

D'Auton, Jean. *Chroniques de Louis XII.* 4 vols. Ed. René de Maulde la Clavière. Paris, 1889–95.

Data, Isabella and Karl Kügle, eds. *The Codex J.II.9, Torino, Biblioteca Nazionale Universitaria: Facsimile Edition with Introductory Study.* Ars Nova 4. Lucca, 1999.

Denemarken, Jan van. *Die Historie, die ghetiden ende die exemplen vander heyligher vrouwen Sint Annen.* Anvers, 1491.

Die Korrespondenz Ferdinands I. 3 vols. Ed. Wilhelm Bauer, Robert Lacroix, Christiane Thomas, and Herwig Wolfram. Veröffentlichungen der

Kommission für neuere Geschichte Österreich. Vols. 11, 30–1, 58. Vienna, 1912–77.

Elliott, J. K., ed. *Apocryphal New Testament: A Collection of Apocryphal Christian Literature in an English Translation*. Oxford, 1993.

Erasmus, Desiderius. *The Correspondence of Erasmus*. 13 vols. Ed. Wallace K. Ferguson. Trans. R. A. B. Mynors and D. F. S. Thomson. Toronto, 1974.

"De Vidua Christiana." *Collected Works of Erasmus: Spiritualia*, vol. 66. Ed. John W. O'Malley. Trans. Jennifer Tolbert Roberts. Toronto, 1988.

Poems. Ed. Harry Vredeveld. Trans. Clarence Miller. *Collected Works of Erasmus*. Vols. 85–6. Toronto, 1993.

Festa, Costanzo. *Opera omnia*. 8 vols. Ed. Alexander Main and Albert Seay. Corpus mensurabilis musicae 25. Neuhausen-Stuttgart, 1962–9.

Fortuna Desperata: Thirty-six Settings of an Italian Song. Ed. Honey Meconi. Middleton, 2001.

Gombert, Nicholas. *Opera omnia*. 11 vols. Ed. Joseph Schmidt-Görg. Corpus mensurabilis musicae 6. Rome, 1951–75.

Graduale sacrosanctae romanae ecclesiae de tempore et de sanctis. Paris, 1961.

Guillaume Briçonnet, Marguerite d'Angoulême: Correspondance, 1521–1524. Ed. Christine Martineau, et al. 2 vols. Geneva, 1975.

Jansen, Sharon L., ed. and trans. *Anne of France: Lessons for My Daughter*. Woodbridge, UK and Rochester, NY, 2004.

John Dunstable: Complete Works. Ed. Manfred F. Bukofzer. Rev. ed. prepared by Margaret Bent, Ian Bent, and Brian Trowell. *Musica Brittanica* 8. London, 1970.

Kellman, Herbert, ed. *London, British Library, MS Royal 8.G.vii*, Renaissance Music in Facsimile 9. New York, Garland, 1987.

La Rue, Pierre de. *Opera Omnia*. 9 vols. Ed. Nigel St. John Davison, J. Evan Kreider, and T. Herman Keahey. Neuhausen-Stuttgart, 1989.

Lassus, Orlande de. *Motets for Three to Twelve Voices from Magnum opus musicum (Munich, 1604)*. Ed. Peter Bergquist. Middleton, 2006.

Le Livre d'heures du duc Louis de Savoie. Ed. Clément Gardet. Annecy, 1960.

Lettres de Louis XII et du cardinal George d'Amboise. 4 vols. Ed. Jean Godefroy. Brussels, 1712.

Lhéritier, Jean. *Opera Omnia*. Ed. Leeman Perkins. Corpus mensurabilis musicae 48. Rome, 1969.

Luther, Martin. *Dr. Martin Luther's sämmtliche Werke*. 67 vols. Ed. J. G. Plochmann. Erlangen, 1826–57.

Werke, Kritischer Gesammtausgabe. 65 vols. Weimar, 1883–1966.

Makhairas, Leontios. *Recital Concerning the Sweet Land of Cyprus, entitled "Chronicle."* 2 vols. Ed. and trans. Richard Dawkins. Oxford, 1932.

Maldeghem, R-J van, ed. *Trésor musical: collection authentique de musique sacrée & profane des anciens maîtres Belges, recueillie et transcite en notation moderne*. Brussels, 1865–93. Repr. in 6 vols. Vaduz, Liechtenstein, 1965.

Marguerite of Navarre. *The Heptaméron*. Trans. with introduction by P. A. Chilton. New York, 1984.

Selected Writings: A Bilingual Edition. Ed. and trans. Rouben Cholakian and Mary Skemp. Chicago, IL, 2008.

Molinet, Jean. *Chroniques de Jean Molinet (1474–1506)*. 3 vols. Ed. Georges Doutrepont and Omer Jogodogne. Brussels, 1935–7.

Ockeghem, Johannes. *Collected Works*. 8 vols. in 3. Ed. Dragan Plamenac and Richard Wexler. New York, 1947–92.

Omont, Henri, ed. *Heures d'Anne de Bretagne: a reproduction réduite des 63 peintures du Manuscrit latin 9474 de la Bibliothèque nationale*. Paris, 1906.

Ordonnances des rois de France: règne de François Ier. 9 vols. Paris, 1902–92.

Pipelare, Mathaeus. *Opera Omnia*. 3 vols. Ed. Ronald Cross. Corpus Mensurabilis Musicae 34. Rome, 1967.

Pizan, Christine de. *The Book of the City of Ladies*. Ed. Natalie Zemon Davis. Trans. Earl Jeffery Richards. New York, 1988.

Le Livre des Trois Vertus: Édition critique. Ed. Charity Cannon Willard and Eric Hicks. Paris, 1989.

A Medieval Woman's Mirror of Honor: The Treasury of the City of Ladies. Trans. Charity Cannon Willard. Ed. Madeleine Pelner Cosman. Tenafly, NJ, 1989.

The Prayer Book of Anne de Bretagne: MS M.50, The Pierpont Morgan Library, New York. Commentary by Roger Wieck with a contribution from K. Michelle Hearne. Lucern, 1999.

Segovia, Juan de. *Septem allegationes et totidem avisamenta pro informatione partum Concilii Basiliensis …Circa Sacratissimae Virginis Mariae Immaculatam Conceptionem ejusque preservationem a peccato originali*. Brussels, 1664. Repr., 1965.

Schlagel, Stephanie, ed. *Si Placet Parts for Motets by Josquin and His Contemporaries*. Middleton, 2006.

Sherr, Richard, ed. *Selections from Motetti de la corona (libro primo) (Fossombrone, 1514)*. Vol. 4 of *Sixteenth-Century Motet*. New York, 1992.

Tertullian. *De carne Christi liber, Treatise on the Incarnation*. Trans. Ernest Evans. London, 1956.

Thenaud, Jean. *Le triumphe des vertuz (ms. Ars. 3358, ff. 149–282) Second traité, Le triumphe de force*. Ed. Titia J. Schuurs-Janssen. Geneva, 2002.

Le voyage d'outremer (Egypte, Mont Sinay, Palestine), suivi de la relation de L'Ambassade de Domenico trevisan auprès du Soudan d'Egypte 1512. Ed. Charles Schefer. Geneva, 1971.

Treize livres de Motets parus chez Pierre Attaingnant en 1534 et 1535. 14 vols. Ed. A. Smijers. Paris, 1934–64.

Vaux, Pierre de. *Vita Sanctae Coletae (1381–1447)*. Ed. Charles van Corstanje et al. Leiden, 1982.

Vie de soeur Colette/Pierre de Vaux. Trans. Élizabeth Lopcz. Saint-Étienne, 1994.

Villani, Giovanni. *Cronica di Giovanni Villani.* 4 vols. Ed. F. G. Dragomanni. Florence, 1844–5.

Voragine, Jacobus de. *The Golden Legend: Readings on the Saints.* 2 vols. Trans. William Granger Ryan. Princeton, NJ, 1993.

Willaert, Adrian. *Opera omnia.* Ed. Hermann Zenck et al. Corpus mensurabilis musicae 3. Rome, 1950–.

Secondary Literature

Ainsworth, Maryan W. "Bernaert van Orley. Virgin with Child." *Flemish Paintings in America: A Survey of Early Netherlandish and Flemish Paintings in the Public Collections of North America.* Ed. Guy C. Bauman and Walter A. Liedtke. Antwerp, 1992.

Amann, Emile. *Le Protevangile de Jacques et ses remainements latins.* Paris, 1910.

Anderson, Michael Alan. "Enhancing the Ave Maria in the Ars *Antiqua*." *Journal of Plainsong and Medieval Music* **19** (2010), 35–65.

"'His Name Will Be Called John': Reception and Symbolism in Obrecht's *Missa de Sancto Johanne Baptista*." *Early Music* **39** (2011), 547–61.

"Symbols of Saints: Theology, Ritual, and Kinship in Music for John the Baptist and St. Anne (1175–1563)." 3 vols. PhD diss., University of Chicago, 2008.

Andersson, Christiane. "Religiöse Bilder Cranachs im Dienste der Reformation." *Humanismus und Reformation als kulturelle Kräfte in der deutschen Geschichte.* Ed. L. W. Spitz. Berlin and New York, 1980. Pp. 43–79.

Anne de Bretagne: une histoire, un mythe. Musée d'histoire de Nantes. Paris, 2007.

Armstrong, Megan C. *The Politics of Piety: Franciscan Preachers during the Wars of Religion, 1560–1600.* Rochester, NY, 2004.

Ashley, Kathleen. "Image and Ideology: Saint Anne in Late Medieval Drama and Narrative." *Interpreting Cultural Symbols: Saint Anne in Late Medieval Society.* Ed. Kathleen Ashley and Pamela Sheingorn. Athens, 1990. Pp. 111–30.

Ashley, Kathleen and Pamela Sheingorn, eds. *Interpreting Cultural Symbols: Saint Anne in Late Medieval Society.* Athens, 1990.

Atkinson, Clarissa. *The Oldest Vocation: Christian Motherhood in the Middle Ages.* Ithaca, NY, 1991.

Bacon, Paul. "Art Patronage and Piety in Electoral Saxony: Frederick the Wise Promotes the Veneration of His Patron, St. Bartholomew." *Sixteenth Century Journal* **34** (2008), 973–1001.

"A Mirror of a Christian Prince: Frederick the Wise and Art Patronage at the Electoral Saxon Court, 1486–1525." PhD diss., University of Wisconsin, 2004.

Bagliani, Agostino Paravicini, ed. *Les manuscrits enluminés des comtes et ducs de Savoie*. Torino, 1990.

Baumgartner, Frederic. *Louis XII*. New York, 1994.

Beaune, Collette. *The Birth of an Ideology: Myths and Symbols of Nation in Late-Medieval France*. Trans. Susan Ross Huston. Berkeley, CA, 1991.

Bell, Susan G. *The Lost Tapestries of the City of Ladies: Christine de Pizan's Renaissance Legacy*. Berkeley, CA, 2004.

Bellman, Fritz, Marie-Luise Harksen, and Roland Werner, eds. *Die Denkmale der Lutherstadt Wittenberg*. Weimar, 1979.

Bent, Margaret. "The Musical Stanzas in Martin Le Franc's *Le champion des dames*." *Music and Medieval Manuscripts: Paleography and Performance*. Ed. John Haines and Randall Rosenfeld. Burlington, VT, 2004. Pp. 91–127.

Bérenger, Jean. *A History of the Habsburg Empire*. Trans. C. A. Simpson. London, 1997.

Besserman, Lawrence L. *The Legend of Job in the Middle Ages*. Cambridge, MA, 1979.

Blackburn, Bonnie. "Messages in Miniature: Pictorial Programme and Theological Implications in the Alamire Choirbooks." *The Burgundian-Habsburg Court Complex of Music Manuscripts (1500–1535) and the Workshop of Petrus Alamire*. Ed. Bruno Bouckaert and Eugeen Schreurs. Leuven, 2003. Pp. 161–84.

——— "The Virgin in the Sun: Music and Image for a Prayer Attributed to Sixtus IV." *Journal of the Royal Musical Association* **124** (1999), 157–95.

Bloch, R. Howard. *Etymologies and Genealogies: A Literary Anthropology of the French Middle Ages*. Chicago, IL, 1983.

Blockmans, Wim. "The Devotion of a Lonely Duchess." *Margaret of York, Simon Marmion, and "The Visions of Tondal."* Ed. Thomas Kren. Los Angeles, CA, 1992. Pp. 29–46.

Bloxam, M. Jennifer. "Cantus Firmus." NG, V:73.

——— "In Praise of Spurious Saints: The 'Missae Floruit egregiis' by Pipelare and La Rue." *Journal of the American Musicological Society* **44** (1991), 163–220.

——— Review of *Opera Omnia*, vols. 1–3. *Notes* **51** (1994–5), 407–10.

——— "Sacred Polyphony and Local Traditions of Liturgy and Plainsong: Reflections on Music by Jacob Obrecht." *Plainsong in the Age of Polyphony*. Ed. Thomas Forrest Kelly. Cambridge, 1992. Pp. 140–77.

Bonime, Stephen. "Anne de Bretagne (1477–1514) and Music: An Archival Study." PhD diss., Bryn Mawr College, 1975.

——— "The Musicians of the Royal Stable under Charles VIII and Louis XII (1484–1514)." *Current Musicology* **25** (1978), 7–21.

Boom, Ghislaine de. *Marguerite d'Autriche-Savoie et la Pré-Renaissance*. Paris, 1935.

Boorman, Stanley. *Ottaviano Petrucci: A Catalogue Raisonné*. Oxford, 2006.

Borkowsky, Ernst. *Das Leben Friedrichs des Weisen: Kurfürst zu Sachsen*. Jena, 1929.

Bossuyt, Ignace et al., eds. *Cui dono lepidum novum libellum?: Dedicating Latin Works and Motets in the Sixteenth Century.* Leuven, 2008.

Bott, Gerhard, ed. *Martin Luther und die Reformation in Deutschland.* Frankfurt am Main, 1983.

Boulton, D'Arcy Jonathan Dacre. *The Knights of the Crown: The Monarchical Orders of Knighthood in Later Medieval Europe, 1325–1520.* New York, 1987.

Boyce, James. "Cantica Carmelitana: The Chants of the Carmelite Office." 2 vols. PhD diss., New York University, 1984.

Boyd, George. "The Development of Paraphrase Technique in the Fifteenth Century." *Indiana Theory Review* **9** (1988), 23–62.

Boynton, Susan. *Shaping a Monastic Identity: Liturgy and History at the Imperial Abbey of Farfa, 1000–1125.* Ithaca, NY, 2006.

Bradley, Robert John. "Musical Life and Culture at Savoy: 1420–1450." 2 vols. PhD diss., City University of New York, 1992.

Brandenbarg, Ton. "Saint Anne: A Holy Grandmother and Her Children." *Sanctity and Motherhood: Essays on Holy Mothers in the Middle Ages.* Ed. Anneke B. Mulder-Bakker. New York, 1995. Pp. 31–65.

"St. Anne and Her Family: The Veneration of St. Anne in Connection with Concepts of Marriage and the Family in the Early Modern Period." *Saints and She-Devils: Images of Women in the Fifteenth and Sixteenth Centuries.* Ed. Lène Dresen-Coenders. Trans. C. Sion. London, 1987. Pp. 101–27.

Brandi, Karl. *Die Deutsche Reformation und Gegenreformation.* 2 vols. Leipzig, 1927–30.

Brann, Noel L. *Trithemius and Magical Theology: A Chapter in the Controversy over Occult Studies in Early Modern Europe.* Albany, NY, 1999.

Brecht, Martin. *Martin Luther: His Road to Reformation, 1483–1521.* Trans. James L. Schaaf. Philadelphia, PA, 1985.

Brinkmann, Bodo, ed. *Cranach.* London, 2007.

Brobeck, John T. "The Motet at the Court of Francis I." PhD diss., University of Pennsylvania, 1991.

"Musical Patronage in the Royal Chapel of France under Francis I (r. 1515–1547)." *Journal of the American Musicological Association* **48** (1995), 187–235.

"Style and Authenticity in the Motets of Claudin de Sermisy." *Journal of Musicology* **16** (1998), 26–90.

Broekhuijsen, Klara H. *The Masters of the Dark Eyes: Late Medieval Manuscript Painting in Holland.* Turnhout, 2009.

Brown, Cynthia Jane, "Like Mother, Like Daughter: The Blurring of Royal Imagery in Book for Anne de Bretagne and Claude de France." *The Cultural and Political Legacy of Anne de Bretagne: Negotiating Convention in Books and Documents.* Ed. Cynthia Jane Brown. Cambridge, 2010. Pp. 101–21.

The Queen's Library: Image-Making at the Court of Anne of Brittany, 1477–1514. Philadelphia, PA, 2011.

Brown, Howard Mayer. "In Alamire's Workshop: Notes on Scribal Practice in the Early Sixteenth Century." *Datierung und Filiation von Musikhandschriften der Josquin-Zeit.* Ed. Ludwig Finscher. Wiesbaden, 1983. Pp. 15–63.

"The Mirror of Man's Salvation: Music in Devotional Life about 1500." *Renaissance Quarterly* **43** (1990), 744–73.

Brown, Howard Mayer and T. Herman Keahey. "Févin, Antoine de." NG, VIII:752–3.

Brown, Howard Mayer and Thomas G. MacCracken. "Mouton, Jean." NG, XVII:239–51.

Brown, Rawdon, ed. *Calendar of State Papers and Manuscripts, Relating to English Affairs, Existing in the Archives and Collections of Venice, and in Other Libraries of Northern Italy, Vol. II: 1509–1519.* London, 1867. Repr. Nendeln, Liechtenstein, 1970.

Brown, Raymond E., Joseph A. Fitzmyer, and Roland E. Murphy, eds. *The New Jerome Biblical Commentary.* Englewood Cliffs, NJ, 1999.

Bruchet, Max. *Marguerite d'Autriche duchesse de Savoie.* Lille, 1927.

Bruck, Robert. *Friedrich der Weise als Förderer der Kunst.* Strasbourg, 1903.

Bryden, John and David Hughes. *An Index of Gregorian Chant.* 2 vols. Cambridge, 1969.

Capefigue, Jean-Baptiste Honoré Raymond. *François Ier et la renaissance, 1515–1547.* 4 vols. Paris, 1845.

Cattin, Giulio. "The Texts of the Offices of Sts. Hylarion and Anne in the Cypriot Manuscript Turin J.II.9." *The Cypriot-French Repertory of the Manuscript Turin J.II.9: Report of the International Musicological Congress, Paphos 20–25 March, 1992.* Ed. Ursula Günther and Ludwig Finscher. Neuhausen-Stuttgart, 1995. Pp. 249–301.

Census-Catalogue of Manuscript Sources of Polyphonic Music 1400–1550. 5 vols. Renaissance Manuscript Studies. Neuhausen-Stuttgart, 1979–88.

Champollion-Figeac, Aimé. *Captivité du roi François Ier.* Paris, 1847.

Charland, Paul-Victor, *Madame saincte Anne et son culte au moyen age.* 2 vols. Paris, 1911–13.

Chevalier, Ulysse, ed. *Repertorium Hymnologicum.* 6 vols. Louvain, 1892–1912.

Chisholm, M. A. "The Religionspolitik of Emperor Ferdinand I (1521–1564): Tyrol and the Holy Roman Empire." *European History Quarterly* **38** (2008), 551–77.

Cholakian, Patricia F. and Rouben C. Cholakian. *Marguerite de Navarre: Mother of the Renaissance.* New York, 2006.

Christensen, Carl C. *Princes and Propaganda: Electoral Saxon Art of the Reformation.* Kirksville, 1992.

Christoforaki, Ioanna. "Patronage, Art, and Society in Lusignan Cyprus c. 1192-c.1489." 2 vols. PhD diss., Oxford University, 2000.

Clerval, Jules-Alexandre. *Registre des procès-verbaux de la Faculté de théologie de Paris.* Paris, 1917.

Cobham, Claude Delaval. *Excerpta Cypria: Materials for a History of Cyprus.* Cambridge, 1908.

Cognasso, Francesco. *Amedeo VIII*. Turin, 1930. Repr. Milan, 1991.

I Savoia. Milan, 1971.

Collenberg, Wipertus Rudt de. "Les Lusignan de Chypre: Généalogie compile principalement selon les registres de l'Archivio Segreto Vaticano et les manuscrits de la Biblioteca Vaticana." *Epeteris* **10** (1979–80), 85–319.

Constable, Giles. "Twelfth-Century Spirituality and the Later Middle Ages." *Medieval and Renaissance Studies 5: Proceedings of the Southern Institute of Medieval and Renaissance Studies, Summer,* 1969 (1971), 27–60.

Constas, Nicholas. *Proclus of Constantinople and the Cult of the Virgin in Late Antiquity: Homilies 1–5*. Boston, MA, 2003.

Corblet, Jules. *Hagiographie du Diocèse d'Amiens*. 5 vols. Paris, 1868–75.

Crum, Roger J. and David G. Wilkins. "In the Defense of Florentine Republicanism: Saint Anne and Florentine Art, 1343–1575." *Interpreting Cultural Symbols: Saint Anne in Late Medieval Society*. Ed. Kathleen Ashley and Pamela Sheingorn. Athens, 1990. Pp. 131–68.

Curnow, Maureen Cheney. "The Livre de la Cité des Dames of Christine de Pisan: A Critical Edition." PhD diss., Vanderbilt University, 1975.

Cutler, Anthony. "Sacred and Profane: The Locus of the Political in Middle Byzantine Art." *Arte profana e arte sacra a Bisanzio*. Ed. Antonio Iacobini and Enrico Zanini. Rome, 1995. Pp. 315–38.

D'Ancona, Mirella Levi. *The Iconography of the Immaculate Conception in the Middle Ages and Early Renaissance*. New York, 1957.

Datz, Günther. *Die Gestalt Hiobs in der Kirchlichen Exegese und der 'Arme Heinrich' Hartmanns von Aue*. Göttingen, 1973.

Debae, Margaret. *La bibliothèque de Margaret d'Autriche: Essai de reconstruction d'après l'inventaire de 1523–24*. Leuven, 1995.

"La Bibliothèque de Marguerite d'Autriche, Duchesse de Savoie." *Les Manuscrits enluminés des comtes et ducs de Savoie*. Ed. Agostino Paravicini Bagliani. Turin, 1991. Pp. 147–70.

La Librairie de Marguerite d'Autriche. Brussels, 1987.

Delachenal, Roland. *Histoire de Charles V*. 5 vols. Paris, 1909–31.

Delogu, Daisy, "Advocate et moyenne: Christine de Pizan's Elaboration of Female Authority." *Désireuse de plus avant enquerre: Volume en homage à James Laidlaw. Actes du VIe colloque international sur Christine de Pizan (Paris, 20–24 juillet 2006)*. Ed. Liliane Dulac, Anne Paupert, et al. Paris, 2008. Pp. 57–67.

Denis, Valentin. "Saint Job, patron des musiciens." *Revue belge d'archéologie et d'histoire d l'art* **21** (1952), 253–98.

Diehl, George Karl. "The Partbooks of a Renaissance Merchant. Cambrai: Bibliothèque municipale, MSS 125–128." PhD diss., University of Pennsylvania, 1974.

Dörfler-Diercken, Angelika. *Die Verehrung der heiligen Anna in Spätmittelalter und früher Neuzeit*. Göttingen, 1992.

Vorreformation Bruderschaften der hl. Anna. Heidelberg, 1992.

Duby, Georges. *The Knight, the Lady, and the Priest: The Making of Modern Marriage in Medieval France.* New York, 1983.
   Love and Marriage in the Middle Ages. Trans. Jane Dunnett. Chicago, IL, 1994.
   "Structures de parenté et noblesse dans la France du Nord aux X^{ie} et XIIe siècles." *Hommes et structures du moyen âge.* The Hague, 1973. Pp. 267–86.
Duffy, Kathryn. "The Jena Choirbooks: Music and Liturgy at the Castle Church in Wittenberg under Frederick the Wise, Elector of Saxony." 5 vols. PhD diss., University of Chicago, 1995.
   "Netherlands Manuscripts at a Saxon Court." *The Burgundian-Habsburg Court Complex of Music Manuscripts (1500–35) and the Workshop of Petrus Alamire, Colloquium Proceedings: Leuven 25–28 November 1999.* Ed. Bruno Bouckaert and Eugeen Schreurs. Leuven, 2003. Pp. 215–23.
Dugdale, William. *Monasticon Anglicanum: A History of the Abbies and Other Monasteries, Hospitals, Frieries, and Cathedral and Collegiate Churches, with Their Dependencies, in England and Wales.* 6 vols. Ed. John Caley, Henry Ellis, and Bulkeley Bandinel. London, 1817–30.
Dunning, Albert. "Maessens, Pieter." NG, XV:576.
Durtelle de Saint-Sauveur, Edmond. *Histoire de Bretagne des origines à nos jours.* 2 vols. Paris, 1975.
Edbury, Peter. *The Kingdom of Cyprus and the Crusades.* Cambridge, 1991.
   The Lusignan Kingdom of Cyprus and Its Muslim Neighbors. Nicosia, 1993.
Edelmayer, Friedrich and Alfred Kohler. *Kaiser Maximilian II: Kultur und Politik im 16. Jahrhundert.* Munich, 1992.
Edmunds, Sheila. "The Medieval Library of Savoy." *Scriptorium* **24** (1970), 318–27.
Edwards, Warwick. "Alexander Agricola and Intuitive Syllable Deployment." *Early Music* **34** (2006), 409–26.
Eichberger, Dagmar. "The Culture of Gifts: A Courtly Phenomenon from a Female Perspective." *Women of Distinction: Margaret of York, Margaret of Austria.* Ed. Dagmar Eichberger. Leuven, 2005. Pp. 287–95.
   Leben mit Kunst, Wirken durch Kunst: Sammelwesen und Hofkunst unter Margarete von Österreich, Regentin der Niederlande. Turnhout, 2002.
   "Margaret of Austria: A Princess with Ambition and Political Insight." *Women of Distinction: Margaret of York, Margaret of Austria.* Ed. Dagmar Eichberger. Leuven, 2005. Pp. 49–55.
   "Margaret of Austria's Portrait Collection: Female Patronage in Light of Dynastic Ambitions and Artistic Quality." *Renaissance Studies* **10** (1996), 258–73.
   ed. *Women of Distinction: Margaret of York, Margaret of Austria.* Leuven, 2005.
Eichberger, Dagmar and Lisa Beaven. "Family Members and Political Allies." *Art Bulletin* **77** (1995), 225–48.
Engelbrecht, Christine. "Die Psalmsätze des Jenaer Chorbuches 34." *Internationalen musikwissenschaftlichen Kongress Köln, 1958.* Cologne, 1959. Pp. 97–9.
Evans, Joan. *Art in Medieval France, 987–1498.* Oxford, 1969.

Evans, R. J. W. *The Making of the Habsburg Monarchy, 1550–1700: An Interpretation.* Oxford, 1984.

Esser, Werner. "Die Heilige Sippe: Studien zu einem spätmittelalterlichen Bildthema in Deutschland und den Niederlanden." PhD diss., Rheinischen Friedrich-Wilhelms-Universität, 1986.

Falk, Franz. "Die Verehrung der h. Anna im 15. Jahrhundert." *Der Katholik. Eine religiöse Zeitschrift zur Belehrung und Warnung* 58 (1878), 60–76.

Farcy, Louis de. *Monographie de la cathédrale d'Angers.* 4 vols. Paris, 1901–26.

Farge, James K. *Orthodoxy and Reform in Early Reformation France: The Faculty of Theology of Paris, 1500–1543.* Leiden, 1985.

Fassler, Margot. "Mary's Nativity, Fulbert of Chartres, and the *Stirps Jesse*: Liturgical Innovation circa 1000 and Its Afterlife." *Speculum* 75 (2000), 389–434.

Fein, Susanna. "Mary to Veronica: John Audelay's Sequence of Salutations to God-Bearing Women." *Speculum* 86 (2011), 964–1009.

Fichtner, Paula S. *Emperor Maximilian II.* New Haven, CT, 2001.

Ferdinand I of Austria: The Politics of Dynasticism in the Age of the Reformation. New York, 1982.

The Habsburg Monarchy, 1490–1848: Attributes of Empire. New York, 2003.

Fleming, Peter. *Family and Household in Medieval England.* New York, 2001.

Forney, Kristine K. "Music, Ritual and Patronage at the Church of Our Lady, Antwerp." *Early Music History* 7 (1987), 1–57.

Forrester, Viviane. *La Vierge à l'enfant avec sainte Anne, Léonard de Vinci, 1492–1519.* Paris, 2000.

Franke, Birgit. *Assuerus und Esther am Burgunderhof: Zur Rezeption des Buches Esther in den Niederlanden (1450–1530).* Berlin, 1998.

Friedländer, Max J. and Jakob Rosenberg, eds. *The Paintings of Lucas Cranach.* Rev. ed. Ithaca, NY, 1978.

Friesen, Ilse. "Luther and St. Anne in the Art of the Northern Renaissance." *Art and Interreligious Dialogue: Six Perspectives.* Ed. Michael Bird. Lanham, MD, 1995. Pp. 1–17.

Gabory, Emile. *Anne de Bretagne: duchesse et reine.* Paris, 1946.

Gatz, Erwin. "Die Dürener Annaverehrung bis zum Ende des 18. Jahrhunderts." *St.-Anna in Düren.* Ed. Gatz. Mönchengladbach, 1972. Pp. 162–9.

"Zur Geschichte der Annaverehrungen." *St.-Anna in Düren.* Ed. Gatz. Mönchengladbach, 1972. Pp. 149–60.

Gelfand, Laura D. "Margaret of Austria and the Encoding of Power in Patronage: The Funerary Foundation at Brou." *Widowhood and Visual Culture in Early Modern Europe.* Ed. Allison Levy. Burlington, VT, 2003. Pp. 145–59.

"Regency, Power, and Dynastic Visual Memory: Margaret of Austria as Patron and Propagandist." *The Texture of Society: Women in Medieval Flanders.* Ed. Ellen Kittell and Mary Suydam. New York, 2003. Pp. 203–25.

Gélis, Jacques. *History of Childbirth: Fertility, Pregnancy, and Birth in Early Modern Europe.* Trans. Rosemary Morris. Boston, MA, 1991.

Gerken, Robert. "The Polyphonic Cycles of the Proper of the Mass in the Trent Codex 88 and Jena Choirbooks 30 and 35." 3 vols. PhD diss., Indiana University, 1969.

Gerken, Robert, ed. *Three Mass Proper Cycles from Jena 35.* Madison, WI, 1982.

Giaccaria, Angelo. "Il codice franco-cipriota J.II.9 e le vicende del fondo manoscritto della Biblioteca Nazionale Universitaria di Torino." *Miscellanea di studi 4, in onore di Alberto Basso.* Ed. Isabella Data. Turin, 1996. Pp. 7–12.

Gijsel, Jan. *Die unmittelbare Textüberlieferung des sogenannte Pseudo-Matthäus.* Verhandelingen van de Koninklijke Academie voor Wetenschappen. Letteren en Schone Kunsten van Belgie, Klasse der Letteren 43, no. 96. Brussels, 1981.

Gill, Miriam. "Female Piety and Impiety: Selected images of Women in Wall Paintings in England after 1300." *Gender and Holiness: Men, Women and Saints in Late Medieval Europe.* Ed. Samantha J. E. Riches and Sarah Salih. London, 2002. Pp. 101–20.

Godt, Irving. "Renaissance Paraphrase Technique: A Descriptive Tool." *Music Theory Spectrum* **2** (1980), 110–18.

Goetz, Helmut. "Die geheimen Ratgeber Ferdinands I (1503–1564). Ihre Persönlichkeit im Urteil der Nuntien und Gesandten." *Quellen und Forschungen aus italienischen Archiven und Bibliotheken* **42/3** (1963), 453–94.

Gómez, María A., Santiago Juan-Navarro, and Phyllis Zatlin, eds. *Juana of Castile: History and Myth of the Mad Queen.* Lewisburg, 2008.

Goody, Jack. *The Development of the Family and Marriage in Europe.* Cambridge, 1983.

Grossman, Maria. *Humanism in Wittenberg 1485–1517.* Nieuwkoop, 1975.

Guéry, Charles. *Histoire de L'Abbaye de Lyre.* Évreux, 1917.

Günther, Ursula and Ludwig Finscher, eds. *The Cypriot-French Repertory of the Manuscript Turin J.II.9: Report of the International Musicological Congress, Paphos 20–25 March, 1992.* Neuhausen-Stuttgart, 1995.

Gurlitt, Cornelius. *Die Kunst unter Kurfürst Friedrich dem Weisen.* Dresden, 1987.

Haggh, Barbara. "The Aostan Sources of the Recollectio festorum Beatae Mariae Virginis by Guillaume du Fay." *International Musicological Study Group Cantus Planus: Papers Read at the Third Meeting, Tihany, 1988.* Budapest, 1990. Pp. 355–75.

——. "Binchois and Sacred Music at the Burgundian Court." *Binchois Studies.* Ed. Andrew Kirkman and Dennis Slavin. Oxford, 2000. Pp. 11–25.

——. "The Celebration of the 'Recollectio Festorum Beatae Mariae Virginis', 1457–1987." *Studia Musicologica Academiae Scientiarum Hungaricae* **30** (1988), 361–73.

——. "Music, Liturgy, and Ceremony in Brussels 1350–1500." PhD diss., University of Illinois at Urbana-Champaign, 1988.

Haliczer, Stephen. *The Comuneros of Castile: The Forging of a Revolution, 1475–1521*. Madison, WI, 1981.

Hamilton, Alastair. "Humanists and the Bible." *The Cambridge Companion to Renaissance Humanism*. Ed. Jill Kraye. Cambridge, 1996. Repr., 2003. Pp. 100–17.

Hankeln, Roman, ed. *Political Plainchant? Music, Text and Historical Context of Medieval Saints' Offices*. Ottawa, 2009.

Haug, Andreas. "Neue Ansätze im 9. Jahrhundert." *Die Musik des Mittelalters*. Ed. Carl Dahlhaus and Hermann Danuser. Laaber, 1991. Pp. 94–128.

Heal, Bridget. *The Cult of the Virgin Mary in Early Modern Germany: Protestant and Catholic Piety 1500–1648*. Cambridge, 2007.

Heartz, Daniel. *Pierre Attaingnant: Royal Printer of Music: A Historical Study and Bibliographical Catalogue*. Berkeley, CA, 1969.

Heide, Klaas Dirk van der. "Polytekstuele religieuze muziek aan het Bourgondisch-Habsburgse hof als spiegel van het laat-Middeleeuws wereldbeeld." PhD diss., University of Utrecht, 1998.

Heidrich, Jürgen. *Die Deutschen Chorbücher aus der Hofkapelle Friedrichs des Weisen: Ein Beitrag zur mitteldeutschen geistlichen Musikpraxis um 1500*. Sammlung Musikwissenschaftlicher Abhandlungen, 84. Baden-Baden, 1993.

Herlihy, David. *Medieval Households*. Cambridge, 1985.

Higman, Francis. "Luther et la piété et de l'église gallicane: Le Livre de vraye et parfaicte oraison." *Revue d'histoire et de la philosophie religieuse* **63** (1983), 91–111.

Hiley, David. *Oxford, Bodleian Library, MS. Lat. liturg. b. 5*. Ottawa, 1995.

Western Plainchant: A Handbook. Oxford, 1993.

Hill, George Francis. *A History of Cyprus*. 4 vols. Cambridge, 1940–52.

Hirn, Josef. *Erzherzog Ferdinand II. von Tirol: Geschichte seiner Regierung und seiner Länder*. 2 vols. Innsbruck, 1888.

Hoffman, Werner, ed. *Luther und die Folgen für die Kunst*. Munich, 1983.

Holban, Marie. "François du Moulin de Rochefort et la querelle de la Madeleine." *Humanisme et Renaissance* **2** (1935), 147–71.

"Le Vrai Jean Thenaud." *L'Humanisme français au début de la Renaissance*. 14e colloque internationale de Tours. Paris, 1973. Pp. 193–205.

Holburn, Hajo. *A History of Modern Germany*. 3 vols. New York, 1959–69.

Hoppin, Richard. "The Cypriot-French Repertory of the Manuscript Turin, Bibliotheca Nazionale, J.II.9." *Musica Disciplina* **11** (1957), 79–125.

ed., *The Cypriot-French Repertory of the Manuscript Torino, Biblioteca Nazionale, J.II.9*. 4 vols. Corpus mensurabilis musicae 21. Rome, 1960–3.

ed., *Cypriot Plainchant of the Manuscript Torino, Biblioteca nazionale J.II.9: A Facsimile Edition with Commentary*. Dallas, TX, 1968.

Horn, Hendrik J. *Jan Cornelisz Vermeyen: Painter of Charles V and His Conquest of Tunis*. 2 vols. Doornspijk, 1989.

Hornby, Emma. *Gregorian and Old Roman Eighth-Mode Tracts: A Case Study in the Transmission of Western Chant.* Burlington, VT, 2002.

Hufton, Olwen. *The Prospect before Her: A History of Women in Western Europe, 1500–1800.* New York, 1996.

Hughes, Andrew. "Chants in the Rhymed Office of St. Thomas of Canterbury." *Early Music* **16** (1988), 185–201.

― *Late Medieval Liturgical Offices: Resources for Electronic Research: Texts.* Toronto, 1994.

― *Late Medieval Liturgical Offices: Resources for Electronic Research: Sources and Chants.* Toronto, 1996.

― "Late Medieval Rhymed Offices." *Journal of the Plainsong and Mediaeval Music Society* **8** (1985), 33–49.

― "Modal Order and Disorder in the Rhymed Office." *Musica Disciplina* **38** (1983), 29–51.

― "Rhymed Offices." *Dictionary of the Middle Ages.* 13 vols. Ed. J. R. Strayer. New York, 1982–9, X:375.

― "Word Painting in a Twelfth-Century Office." *Beyond the Moon: Festschrift Luther Dittmer.* Ed. Bryan Gillingham and Paul Merkley. Ottawa, 1990. Pp. 16–27.

Hughes, Michael. *Early Modern Germany, 1477–1806.* Philadelphia, PA, 1992.

Huglo, Michel. *Les tonaires: inventaire, analyse, comparaison.* Paris, 1971.

Huizinga, Johan. *The Autumn of the Middle Ages.* Trans. Rodney J. Payton and Ulrich Mammitzsch. Chicago, IL, 1996.

Iongh, Jane de. *Margaret of Austria, Regent of the Netherlands.* Trans. M. D. Herter Norton. New York, 1953.

Israel, Friedrich. *Das Wittenberger Universitätsarchiv, seine Geschichte und seine Bestände.* Forschungen zur Thürnigisch-sächsischen Geschichte, no. 4. Halle, 1913.

Ives, Eric. *The Life and Death of Anne Boleyn.* Malden, 2004.

Jammers, Ewald. "Vienna, Österreichische Nationalbibliothek, Musiksammlung, MS Mus. 15941." *The Treasury of Petrus Alamire: Music and Arts in Flemish Court Manuscripts 1500–1535.* Ed. Herbert Kellman. Ghent, 1999. P. 159.

Jas, Eric. "Jena, Thüringer Universitäts- und Landesbibliothek, MS 7." *The Treasury of Petrus Alamire: Music and Arts in Flemish Court Manuscripts 1500–1535.* Ed. Herbert Kellman. Ghent, 1999. P. 96.

Jas, Eric and Herbert Kellman. "Jena, Thüringer Universitäts- und Landesbibliothek MS 20." *The Treasury of Petrus Alamire: Music and Arts in Flemish Court Manuscripts 1500–1535.* Ed. Herbert Kellman. Ghent, 1999. P. 102.

Jones, Michael. "Les Manuscrits d'Anne de Bretagne, reine de France et duchesse de Bretagne." *Mémoires de la Société d'histoire et d'archéologie de Bretagne* **50** (1978), 43–81.

Jonsson, Ritva. *Historia: Études sur la genèse des offices versifiés.* Stockholm, 1968.

Jotischky, Andrew. *The Carmelites and Antiquity: Mendicants and Their Pasts in the Middle Ages.* Oxford, 2002.

Jourda, Pierre. *Marguerite d'Angoulême: Duchesse d'Alençon, reine de Navarre (1492–1549).* 2 vols. Paris, 1930.

Judd, Cristle Collins. "Josquin's Gospel Motets and Chant-Based Tonality." *Tonal Structures in Early Music.* Ed. Judd. New York, 1998. Pp. 39–54.

Junghans, Helmar. *Wittenberg als Lutherstadt.* Berlin, 1979.

Kalkoff, Paul. *Ablaß und Reliquienverehrung an der Schloßkirche zu Wittenberg unter Friedrich dem Weisen.* Gotha, 1907.

Kamerick, Kathleen. "Patronage and Devotion in the Prayer Book of Anne of Brittany, Newberry Library MS 83." *Manuscripta* **39** (1995), 40–50.

Popular Piety and Art in the Late Middle Ages: Image Worship and Idolatry in England, 1350–1500. New York, 2002.

Kantorowicz. Ernst H. *Laudes Regiae: A Study in Liturgical Acclamations and Mediaeval Political Theology.* Berkeley, CA, 1946.

Karras, Ruth Mazo. "'This Skill in a Woman is By No Means to Be Despised': Weaving and the Gender Division of Labor in the Middle Ages." *Medieval Fabrications: Dress, Textiles, Clothwork, and Other Cultural Imaginings.* Ed. E. J. Burns. New York, 2004. Pp. 89–104.

Kauffmann, Claus Michael. *The Legend of Saint Ursula.* London, 1964.

Kellman, Herbert. "Josquin and the Courts of the Netherlands and France: The Evidence of the Sources." *Josquin des Prez: Proceedings of the International Josquin Festival-Conference held at The Juilliard School at Lincoln Center in New York City, 21–25 June 1971.* Ed. Edward E. Lowinsky. London, 1976. Pp. 181–216.

"London, British Library MS Royal 8.G.vii." *The Treasury of Petrus Alamire: Music and Arts in Flemish Court Manuscripts 1500–1535.* Ed. Kellman. Ghent, 1999. Pp. 110–11.

"The Origins of the Chigi Codex." *Journal of the American Musicological Society* **11** (1958), 6–19.

"Two Sixteenth-Century Palatine Manuscripts: Answers for Oliver Strunk." *Remembering Oliver Strunk: Teacher and Scholar.* Ed. Christina Huemer and Pierluigi Petrobelli. Hillsdale, 2005. Pp. 27–42.

"Vatican City, Biblioteca Apostolica Vaticana MSS Palatini Latini 1976–79." *The Treasury of Petrus Alamire: Music and Arts in Flemish Court Manuscripts 1500–1535.* Ed. Kellman. Ghent, 1999. Pp. 130–2.

ed. *The Treasury of Petrus Alamire: Music and Arts in Flemish Court Manuscripts 1500–1535.* Ghent, 1999.

Kendrick, Robert L. "Intent and Intertextuality in Barbara Strozzi's Sacred Music." *Recercare* **14** (2002), 65–98.

Kerman, Joseph. *The Masses and Motets of William Byrd.* Berkeley, CA, 1981.

Kirkman, Andrew. *The Cultural Life of the Early Polyphonic Mass: Medieval Context to Modern Revival.* Cambridge, 2010.

"The Invention of the Cyclic Mass." *Journal of the American Musicological Society* **54** (2001), 1–47.

Kleinschmidt, Beda. *Die heilige Anna: Ihre Verehrung in Geschichte, Kunst, und Volkstum*. Düsseldorf, 1930.

Knecht, Robert. "'Our Trinity!': Francis I, Louise of Savoy and Marguerite d'Angoulême." *Gender, Power and Privilege in Early Modern Europe*. Ed. Penny Richards and Jessica Munns. Harlow, 2003. Pp. 71–89.

Renaissance Warrior and Patron: The Reign of Francis I. Cambridge, 1994.

The Valois: Kings of France, 1328-1589. London, 2004.

Kreitzer, Beth, *Reforming Mary: Changing Images of the Virgin Mary in Lutheran Sermons of the Sixteenth Century*. Oxford and New York, 2004.

Kren, Thomas and Scot McKendrick, eds. *Illuminating the Renaissance: The Triumph of Flemish Manuscript Painting in Europe*. Los Angeles, CA, 2003.

Kügle, Karl. "Glorious Sounds for a Holy Warrior: New Light on Codex Turin J.II.9." *Journal of the American Musicological Society* **65** (2012), 637–90.

"The Repertory of the Manuscript Torino, Biblioteca Nazionale J.II.9, and the French Tradition of the 14th and Early 15th Centuries." *The Cypriot-French Repertory of the Manuscript Turin J.II.9: Report of the International Musicological Congress, Paphos 20–25 March, 1992*. Ed. Ursula Günther and Ludwig Finscher. Neuhausen-Stuttgart, 1995. Pp. 151–81.

Kühn, Johannes. *Die Geschichte des Speyerer Reichstag 1529*. Leipzig, 1929.

L'Estrange, Elizabeth. *Holy Motherhood: Gender, Dynasty and Visual Culture in the Later Middle Ages*. Manchester, 2008.

"Penitence, Motherhood, and Passion Devotion: Contextualizing Anne de Bretagne's Prayer Book, Chicago, Newberry Library, MS 83." *The Cultural and Political Legacy of Anne de Bretagne: Negotiating Convention in Books and Documents*. Ed. Cynthia Jane Brown. Cambridge, 2010. Pp. 81–98.

"Sainte Anne et le mécénat d'Anne de France." *Patronnes et mécènes en France à la Renaissance*. Ed. K. Wilson-Chevalier. St-Étienne, 2007. Pp. 135–54.

Laskin, Myron and Michael Pantazzi. *European and American Painting, Sculpture, and Decorative Arts*. Ottawa, 1987.

Laurentin, Rene. "The Role of the Papal Magisterium in the Development of the Dogma of the Immaculate Conception." *The Dogma of the Immaculate Conception: History and Significance*. Ed. Edward O'Connor. Notre Dame, 1958. Pp. 271–324.

Le Fur, Didier. *Louis XII, 1498–1515: un autre César*. Paris, 2001.

Le Roux de Lincy, Antoine. *Vie de la reine Anne de Bretagne, femme des rois de France Charles VIII et Louis XII*. 4 vols. Paris, 1860–1.

Leaver, Robin A. *Luther's Liturgical Music: Principles and Implications*. Grand Rapids, MI, 2007.

Lecoq, Anne-Marie. *François Ier imaginaire: Symbolique & politique à l'aube de la Renaissance française*. Paris, 1987.

Legaré, Anne-Marie. "'La librairye de Madame': Two Princesses and their Libraries." *Women of Distinction: Margaret of York, Margaret of Austria*. Ed. Dagmar Eichberger. Leuven, 2005. Pp. 207–19.

LeMaire, Claudine. *Isabelle de Portugal: Duchesse de Bourgogne, 1397–1471.* Brussels, 1991.

Levi, Anthony. *Renaissance and Reformation: The Intellectual Genesis.* New Haven, CT, 2002.

Levy, Allison. "Widow's Peek: Looking at Ritual and Representation." *Widowhood and Visual Culture in Early Modern Europe.* Ed. Allison Levy. Burlington, VT, 2003.

Lipton, Emma. *Affections of the Mind: The Politics of Sacramental Marriage in Late Medieval English Literature.* Notre Dame, 2007.

Lockwood, Lewis. "Adrian Willaert and Cardinal Ippolito d'Este: New Light on Willaert's Early Career in Italy, 1515–21." *Early Music History* **5** (1985), 85–112.

Long, Michael. "Symbol and Ritual in Josquin's Missa di Dadi." *Journal of the American Musicological Society* **42** (1989), 1–22.

Ludolphy, Ingetraut. *Friedrich der Weise: Kurfürst von Sachsen 1463–1525.* Göttingen, 1984.

Luko, Alexis. "Unification and Varietas in the Sine nomine Mass from Dufay to Tinctoris." PhD diss., McGill University, 2007.

Lynch, Joseph H. *The Medieval Church: A Brief History.* London: Longman, 1992.

Madden, Charles. *Fib and Phi in Music: The Golden Proportion in Musical Form.* Salt Lake City, UT, 2005.

Marvin, Mary Beth Winn. "*Regret* Chansons for Marguerite d'Autriche by Octovien de Saint-Gelais." *Bibliothèque d'Humanisme et Renaissance* **39** (1977), 23–32.

Masseron, Alexandre. *Sainte Anne.* L' Art et les Saints, no. 19. Paris, 1926.

Matarasso, Pauline. *Queen's Mate: Three Women of Power in France on the Eve of the Renaissance.* Burlington, VT, 2001.

Maulde la Clavière, René de. *Procédures politiques du règne de Louis XII.* Paris, 1885.

McCarthy, Kerry. *Liturgy and Contemplation in Byrd's* Gradualia. New York and London, 2007.

Meconi, Honey. "Another Look at Absalon." *Tijdschrift van de Vereniging voor Nederlandse Muziekgeschiedenis* **48** (1998), 3–29.

"Foundation for an Empire: The Musical Inheritance of Charles V." *The Empire Resounds: Music in the Days of Charles V*. Ed. Francis Maes. Leuven, 1999. Pp. 18–34.

"Habsburg-Burgundian Manuscripts, Borrowed Material, and the Practice of Naming." *Early Musical Borrowing*. Ed. Meconi. New York, 2004. Pp. 111–24.

"La Rue, Pierre de." NG, XIV:282–9.

"Margaret of Austria, Visual Representation, and Brussels, Royal Library, Ms. 228." *Journal of the Alamire Foundation* **2** (2010), 11–36.

Pierre de la Rue and Musical Life at the Habsburg-Burgundian Court. Oxford, 2003.

Review of Pierre de la Rue, *Opera Omnia.* Ed. Nigel St. John Davison, J. Evan Kreider, and T. Herman Keahey. *Journal of the American Musicological Society* **48** (1995), 283–93.

Meyer, Kathi. "St. Job as a Patron of Music." *Art Bulletin* **36** (1954), 21–31.

Michaud-Fréjaville, Françoise. "Marguerite d'Angoulême: Reine de Navarre, Duchesse de Berry." *Marguerite de Navarre 1492–1992: Actes du colloque international de Pau (1992)*. Ed. Nicole Cazauran and James Dauphiné. Mont-de-Marsan, 1995. Pp. 45–57.

Michelant, Henri. *Inventaire des vaisselles, joyaux, peintures, manuscrits, etc. de Marguerite d'Autriche, régente et gouvernante des Pays-Bas, dressé en son palais de Malines, le 9 juillet 1523*. Brussels, 1871.

Moeller, Bernd. "A Luther Relic." *The Transmission of Ideas in the Lutheran Reformation*. Ed. Helga Robinson Hammerstein. Dublin, 1989. Pp. 47–64.

Mone, Franz Joseph. *Lateinische hymnen des mittelalters*. 3 vols. Freiburg im Breisgau, 1853–5.

Monson, Craig, "Byrd, the Catholics, and the Motet: The Hearing Reopened." *Hearing the Motet: Essays on the Motet of the Middle Ages and Renaissance*. Ed. Dolores Pesce. Oxford, 1997. Pp. 348–74.

Montgomery, Scott B. *St. Ursula and the Eleven Thousand Virgins of Cologne: Relics, Reliquaries and the Visual Culture of Group Sanctity in Late Medieval Europe*. Pieterlen, 2009.

Morgan, Nigel. "Texts of Devotion and Religious Instruction associated with Margaret of York." *Margaret of York, Simon Marmion, and "The Visions of Tondal."* Ed. Thomas Kren. Los Angeles, CA, 1992. Pp. 63–76.

Mowrey, Hannah. "The Alamire Manuscripts of Frederick the Wise: Intersections of Music, Art, and Theology." PhD diss., University of Rochester, 2010.

Muller, Theodor. *Sculpture in the Netherlands/Germany/France/Spain: 1400–1500*. Baltimore, MD, 1966.

Nixon, Virginia. *Mary's Mother: Saint Anne in Late Medieval Europe*. University Park, PA, 2004.

Oettinger, Rebecca. *Music as Propaganda in the German Reformation*. Burlington, VT, 2001.

Orth, Myra. "Francis du Moulin and the Journal of Louise of Savoy." *The Sixteenth Century Journal* **13** (1982), 55–66.

"Louise de Savoie et le pouvoir du livre." *Royaume de Fémynie: Pouvoirs, contraintes, espaces de liberté des femmes, de la Renaissance à la Fronde*. Ed. Kathleen Wilson-Chevalier and Eliane Viennot. Paris, 1999. Pp. 71–90.

"'Madame Sainte Anne': The Holy Kinship, the Royal Trinity, and Louise of Savoy." *Interpreting Cultural Symbols: Saint Anne in Late Medieval Society*. Ed. Kathleen Ashley and Pamela Sheingorn. Athens, 1990. Pp. 199–227.

"Manuscrits pour Marguerite." *Marguerite de Navarre 1492–1992: Actes du colloque international de Pau (1992)*. Ed. Nicole Cazauran and James Dauphiné. Mont-de- Marsan, 1995. Pp. 85–105.

"Progressive Tendencies in French Manuscript Illumination, 1515–1530: Godefroy le Batave and the 1520s Hours Workshop." PhD diss., New York University, 1975.

Owens, Jessie Ann. "Concepts of Pitch in English Music Theory, c. 1560–1640." *Tonal Structures in Early Music*. Ed. Cristle Collins Judd. New York, 1998. Pp. 183–246.

Ozment, Steven. *A Mighty Fortress: A New History of the German People*. New York, 2004.

The Reformation in the Cities: The Appeal of Protestantism to Sixteenth-Century Germany and Switzerland. New Haven, CT, 1975.

Page, Christopher. *The Christian West and Its Singers: The First Thousand Years*. New Haven, CT, 2010.

"Reading and Reminiscence: Tinctoris on the Beauty of Music." *Journal of the American Musicological Society* **49** (1996), 1–32.

Pearson, Andrea. *Envisioning Gender in Burgundian Devotional Art, 1350–1530: Experience, Authority, and Resistance*. Aldershot, 2005.

"Margaret of Austria's Devotional Portrait Diptychs." *Woman's Art Journal* **22** (2001–2), 9–25.

Pendle, Karin, ed. *Women and Music: A History*. Second ed. Bloomington, 2001.

Pérez, Joseph. *La révolution des 'Comunidades' de Castille (1520–1521)*. Bordeaux, 1970.

Peter, Rodolphe. "La Réception de Luther en France au XVIe siècle." *Revue d'histoire et de la philosophie religieuse* **63** (1983), 67–89.

Pettegree, Andrew. *The Reformation World*. New York, 2000.

Pfaff, Richard. *New Liturgical Feasts in Later Medieval England*. Oxford, 1970.

Picker, Martin. *Album de Marguerite d'Autriche: Brussel, Koninklijke Bibliotheek, MS. 228*. Facsimile Edition with Introduction. Peer, 1986.

The Chanson Albums of Margaret of Austria. Berkeley, CA, 1965.

Review of *Drie Missen van Pierre de la Rue*. Ed. Bernard Lenaerts and Jozef Robyns. *Journal of the American Musicological Society* **16** (1963), 262–6.

Planchart, Alejandro Enrique. "Connecting the Dots: Guillaume Du Fay and Savoy during the Schism." *Plainsong and Medieval Music* **18** (2009), 11–32.

Pölnitz, Götz Freiherr von. *Anton Fugger*. 2 vols. Tübingen, 1958–63.

Porrer, Sheila. *Jacques Lefèvre d'Etaples and the Three Maries Debates*. Geneva, 2009.

Powell, Thomas W. *The History of the Ancient Britons and Their Descendants*. Delaware, Ohio, 1882.

Powers, Harold. "Is Mode Real? Pietro Aron, the Octenary System, and Polyphony." *Basler Jahrbuch* **16** (1992), 9–53.

Prinet, Max. "Les variations du nombre des fleures de lys dans les armes de France." *Bulletin monumental* **75** (1911), 468–88.

Raby, F. J. E. *A History of Christian-Latin Poetry from the Beginnings to the Close of the Middle Ages*. Oxford, 1927.

Reames, Sherry, ed. *Middle English Legends of Women Saints*. Kalamazoo, MI, 2003.

Reames, Sherry. "Origins and Affiliations of the Pre-Sarum Office for Anne in the Stowe Breviary." *Music and Medieval Manuscripts: Paleography and*

Performance. Ed. John Haines and Randall Rosenfeld. Burlington, VT, 2004. Pp. 349–68.

Reid, Jonathan A. *King's Sister – Queen of Dissent: Marguerite of Navarre (1492–1549) and Her Evangelical Network*. 2 vols. Leiden, 2009.

Renaudet, Augustin. *Préréforme et humanisme à Paris pendant les premières guerres d'Italie (1494–1517)*. Second edition. Paris, 1953.

Reynolds, Christopher. "The Counterpoint of Allusion in Fifteenth-Century Masses." *Journal of the American Musicological Society* **45** (1992), 228–60.

——— "Interpreting and Dating Josquin's *Missa Hercules dux ferrariae*." *Early Musical Borrowing*. Ed. Honey Meconi. New York, 2004. Pp. 91–110.

Rifkin, Joshua. "A Black Hole? Problems in the Motet around 1500." *The Motet around 1500: On the Relationship of Imitation and Text Treatment*. Ed. Thomas Schmidt-Beste. Turnhout, 2012. Pp. 21–82.

Ring, Grete. *A Century of French Painting*. New York, 1949.

Ripart, Laurent. "Les Mariages de Marguerite." *Marguerite de Navarre 1492–1992: Actes du colloque international de Pau (1992)*. Ed. Nicole Cazauran and James Dauphiné. Mont-de-Marsan, 1995. Pp. 59–83.

Ritchey, Sara. "Spiritual Arborescence: The Meaning of Trees in Late Medieval Devotion." PhD diss., University of Chicago, 2005.

Robertson, Anne Walters. *Guillaume de Machaut and Reims: Context and Meaning in His Musical Works*. Cambridge, 2002.

——— "The Man with the Pale Face, the Shroud, and Du Fay's *Missa Se la face ay pale*." *Journal of Musicology* **27** (2010), 377–434.

——— "The Savior, the Woman, and the Head of the Dragon in the Caput Masses and Motet." *Journal of the American Musicological Society* **59** (2006), 537–630.

Robyns, Jozef. *Pierre de la Rue (circa 1460–1518), een bio-bibliographische Studie*. Brussels, 1954.

Rothenberg, David J. "The Most Prudent Virgin and the Wise King: Isaac's *Virgo prudentissima* Compositions in the Imperial Ideology of Maximilian I." *Journal of Musicology* **28** (2011), 34–80.

Roediger, Karl Erich. *Die geistlichen Musikhandschriften der Universitäts-Bibliothek Jena*. 2 vols. Jena, 1935.

Rudy, Kathryn M. "Women's Devotions at Court." *Women of Distinction: Margaret of York, Margaret of Austria*. Ed. Dagmar Eichberger. Leuven, 2005. Pp. 231–9.

Saenger, Paul. *A Catalogue of the Pre-1500 Western Manuscript Books at the Newberry Library*. Chicago, IL, 1989.

Sanborn, Helen J. *Anne of Brittany: The Story of a Duchess and Twice-crowned Queen*. Boston, MA, 1917.

Sanders, Eve Rachael. *Gender and Literacy on Stage in Early Modern England*. Cambridge, 1998.

Sargent-Baur, Barbara Nelson. *Brothers of Dragons: Job Dolens and François Villon*. New York, 1990.

Schabel, Chris, "Religion." *Cyprus: Society and Culture*. Ed. Angel Nicolaou-Konnari and Chris Schabel. Leiden, 2005. Pp. 157–218.

Schade, Werner. *Cranach: A Family of Master Painters*. Trans. Helen Sebba. New York, 1980.

Schiller, Gertrude. "The Tree of Jesse." *Iconography of Christian Art*. Trans. Janet Seligman. Greenwich, 1976.

Schlager, Karlheinz. *Alleluia-Melodien*. Monumenta monodica medii aevi 7–8. Kassel and New York, 1968–87.

Schmidt-Beste, Thomas. *Textdeklamation in der Motette des 15. Jahrhunderts*. Turnhout, 2003.

Schnitker, Harry. "Margaret of York on Pilgrimage: The Exercise of Devotion and the Religious Traditions of the House of York." *Reputation and Representation in Fifteenth-Century Europe*. Ed. Douglas Biggs, Sharon D. Michalove, and Albert Compton Reeves. Leiden and Boston, MA, 2004. Pp. 81–122.

Schuchardt, Christian, *Lucas Cranach des Ältern: Leben und Werke*. 3 vols. Leipzig, 1851–71.

Sebastian, Wenceslaus. "The Controversy after Scotus to 1900." *The Dogma of the Immaculate Conception: History and Significance*. Ed. Edward O'Connor. Notre Dame, 1958. Pp. 213–70.

Seifert, Herbert. "The Institution of the Imperial Court Chapel from Maximilian I to Charles VI." *The Royal Chapel in the Time of the Habsburgs: Music and Court Ceremony in Early Modern Europe*. Ed. Juan José Carreras López, Bernardo José García García, and Tess Knighton. Rochester, NY, 2005. Pp. 40–7.

Severis, Leto. *Ladies of Medieval Cyprus and Catherine Cornaro*. Nicosia, 1995.

Sheingorn, Pamela. "Appropriating the Holy Kinship: Gender and Family History." *Interpreting Cultural Symbols: Saint Anne in Late Medieval Society*. Ed. Kathleen Ashley and Pamela Sheingorn. Athens, 1990. Pp. 169–98.

"The Holy Kinship: The Ascendancy of Matriliny in Sacred Genealogy of the Fifteenth Century." *Thought* **64** (1989), 268–86.

"'The Wise Mother': The Image of St. Anne Teaching the Virgin Mary." *Gesta* **32** (1993), 69–76.

Sherr, Richard. "The Membership of the Chapels of Louis XII and Anne de Bretagne in the Years Preceding Their Deaths." *Journal of Musicology* **6** (1988), 60–82.

Shine, Josephine. "The Motets of Jean Mouton." 3 vols. PhD diss., New York University, 1953.

Silver, Larry. *Marketing Maximilian: The Visual Ideology of a Holy Roman Emperor*. Princeton, NJ, 2008.

Snyder, James. *Northern Renaissance Art: Painting, Sculpture, the Graphic Arts from 1350 to 1575*. New York, 1985.

Soisson, Jean-Pierre. *Margaret: Princesse de Bourgogne*. Paris, 2002.

Spalatin, Georg. *Friedrichs des Weisen: Leben und Zeitgeschichte*. Jena, 1851.

Spiegel, G. M. and S. Hindman. "The Fleur de Lys Frontispieces to Guillaume de Nangis' *Chronique abrégée*: Political Iconography in Late Fifteenth-century France." *Viator* **12** (1981), 381–407.

Stäblein, Bruno. *Die mittelalterlichen Hymnenmelodien des Abendlandes*. Monumenta monodica medii aevi 1. Kassel, 1956.

Steinberg, Leo. *The Sexuality of Christ in Renaissance Art and in Modern Oblivion*. New York, 1983.

Stephenson, Barbara. *The Power and Patronage of Marguerite de Navarre*. Aldershot, 2003.

Stevens, John. *Words and Music in the Middle Ages: Song Narrative, Dance and Drama 1050–1350*. Cambridge, 1986.

Stewart, Rebecca. "Jean Mouton: Man and Musician; Motets Attributed to both Josquin and Mouton." *Proceedings of the International Josquin Symposium, Utrecht 1986*. Ed. Willem Elders. Utrecht, 1991. Pp. 155–70.

Stinson, John. "The Turin Manuscript and Late Medieval Chant Reforms: Liturgy, Style and Composition." Paper read at the International Musicological Congress on the Cypriot-French Repertory of the Manuscript of Turin National Library J.II.9, Paphos, Cyprus, March 20–5, 1992.

Strohm, Reinhard. "European Politics and the Distribution of Music in the Early Fifteenth Century." *Early Music History* **1** (1981), 305–24.

Swarenski, Georg. "Cranachs Altarbild von 1509 im Städelschen Kunstinstitut zu Frankfurt." *Müncher Jahrbuch der bildenden Kunst* **2** (1907), 49–65.

Swing, Peter Gram. "Gascongne, Mathieu." NG, IX:553.

Tacconi, Marica S. *Cathedral and Civic Ritual in Late Medieval and Renaissance Florence: The Service Books of Santa Maria del Fiore*. Cambridge, 2005.

Tamussino, Ursula. *Margarete von Österreich: Diplomatin der Renaissance*. Graz, 1995.

Taverna, Donatella. *Anna di Cipro: l'eterna straniera*. Milan, 2007.

Terris, Paul. *Sainte Anne d'Apt: Ses traditions, son histoire d'après les documents authentiques*. Avignon, 1876.

Thomas, Jennifer. "Patronage and Personal Narrative in a Music Manuscript: Marguerite of Austria, Katherine of Aragon, and London Royal 8.G.vii." *Musical Voices of Early Modern Women: Many-Headed Melodies*. Ed. Thomasin K. LaMay. Burlington, VT, 2005. Pp. 337–64.

Thornton, David E. "Genealogies, Royal." *The Blackwell Encyclopaedia of Anglo-Saxon England*. Ed. Michael Lapidge, et al. Oxford, 1999. Pp. 199–200.

Thoss, Dagmar. "Flemish Miniature Painting in the Alamire Manuscripts." *The Treasury of Petrus Alamire: Music and Arts in Flemish Court Manuscripts 1500–1535*. Ed. Herbert Kellman. Ghent, 1999. Pp. 53–62.

Tilmans, Karin. "Sancta Mater versus Sanctus Doctus? Saint Anne and the Humanists." *Sanctity and Motherhood: Essays on Holy Mothers in the Middle Ages*. Ed. Anneke B. Mulder-Bakker. New York, 1995. Pp. 330–51.

Tilmouth, Michael and Richard Sherr. "Parody (i)." NG, XIX:145–7.

Tirro, Frank. "Royal 8.G.vii: Strawberry Leaves, Single Arch, and Wrong-Way Lions." *The Musical Quarterly* **67** (1981), 1–28.

Tolley, Thomas. "Monarchy and Prestige in France." *Viewing Renaissance Art*. Ed. Kim W. Woods, Carol M. Richardson, and Angeliki Lymberopoulou. New Haven, CT, 2007. Pp. 133–70.

Tournoy-Thoen, Godelieve. "Le manuscrit 1010 de la Biblioteca de Cataluña et l'humanisme italien à la cour de France vers 1500, II." *Humanistica Lovaniensa* **26** (1977), 1–81.

Treccani degli Alfieri, Giovanni. *Storia di Brescia*. 5 vols. Brescia, 1963–4.

Tremayne, Eleanor E. *The First Governess of the Netherlands: Margaret of Austria*. London, 1908.

Van Kerrebrouck, Patrick. *Les Valois*. Villeneuve d'Ascg, 1990.

Viollet, Paul. "Comment les femmes ont été excluses en France de la succession à la couronne." *Mémoires de l'Académie des Inscriptions et Belles-Lettres* 34, Part 2. Paris, 1893.

Vloberg, Maurice. "The Iconography of the Immaculate Conception." *The Dogma of the Immaculate Conception: History and Significance*. Ed. Edward Dennis O'Connor. Notre Dame, 1958. Pp. 463–504.

Walker, Alicia and Amanda Luyster, eds. *Negotiating Secular and Sacred in Medieval Art: Christian, Islamic, and Buddhist*. Burlington, VT, 2009.

Wallert, Arie, Gwen Tauber, and Lisa Murphy, eds. *The Holy Kinship: A Medieval Masterpiece*. Amsterdam, 2001.

Ward, Jennifer. *Women in Medieval Europe, 1200–1500*. London, 2002.

Warmington, Flynn. "A Master Calligrapher in Alamire's Workshop: Towards a Chronology of His Work." Paper presented at the 48th Annual Meeting of the American Musicological Society, Ann Arbor, November 4–7, 1982.

"A Survey of Scribal Hands in the Manuscripts." *The Treasury of Petrus Alamire: Music and Arts in Flemish Court Manuscripts 1500–1535*. Ed. Herbert Kellman. Ghent, 1999. Pp. 41–52.

Warren, Nancy Bradley. "Colette of Corbie." *Women and Gender in Medieval Europe: An Encyclopedia*. Ed. Margaret Schaus. New York, 2006. P. 155.

"Monastic Politics: St. Colette of Corbie, Franciscan Reform and the House of Burgundy." *New Medieval Literatures* 5. Ed. Rita Copeland, David Lawton, and Wendy Scase. Oxford, 2002.

Women of God and Arms: Female Spirituality and Political Conflict, 1380–1600. Philadelphia, PA, 2005.

Wathey, Andrew. "European Politics and Musical Culture at the Court of Cyprus." *The Cypriot-French Repertory of the Manuscript Turin J.II.9: Report of the International Musicological Congress, Paphos 20–25 March, 1992*. Ed. Ursula Günther and Ludwig Finscher. Neuhausen-Stuttgart, 1995. Pp. 33–54.

Watson, Arthur. *The Early Iconography of the Tree of Jesse*. London, 1934.

Wauters, Alphonse Jules. *Bernard van Orley*. Paris, 1893.

Webb, Diana. *Medieval European Pilgrimage, c. 700 – c. 1500*. Basingstoke, 2002.

Wegman, Rob C. "Agricola, Alexander." NG, I:225–6.

——— "Ghent." NG, IX:806.

——— "Musical Offerings in the Renaissance." *Early Music* **33** (2005), 425–37.

——— "New Music for a World Grown Old: Martin Le Franc and the 'Contenance Angloise'." *Acta Musicologica* **75** (2003), 201–41.

Wellens, Richard. "La revolte brugeoise de 1488." *Handelingen van Gennotschap voor Geschiedenis 'Societé d'Emulation' te Brugge* **102** (1965), 5–52.

Welsh, Jennifer. "Mother, Matron, Matriarch: Sanctity and Social Change in the Cult of St. Anne, 1450–1750." PhD diss., Duke University, 2009.

Welzel, Barbara. "Princeps Vidua, Mater Castrorum: the Iconography of Archduchess Isabella as Governor of the Netherlands." *Jaarboek Koninklijk Museum voor Schone Junsten Antwerpen* (1999), 158–75.

——— "Widowhood: Margaret of York and Margaret of Austria." *Women of Distinction: Margaret of York, Margaret of Austria*. Ed. Dagmar Eichberger. Leuven, 2005. Pp. 103–13.

Wentz, Gottfried, "Das Kollegiatstift Allerheiligen in Wittenberg." *Germania Sacra*. Ed. Fritz Bünger and Gottfried Wentz. Berlin, 1941. Section 1, Vol. 3, Pt. 2, 75–164.

Wessely, Othmar. "Arnold von Bruck: Leben und Umwelt mit Beiträgen zur Musikgeschichte des Hofes Ferdinands I. von 1527 bis 1545." Habilitationsschrift, University of Vienna, 1958.

Wiesflecker, Hermann. *Maximilian I: Die Fundamente des habsburgischen Weltreiches*. Vienna, 1991.

Willard, Charity Cannon. "Margaret of Austria: Regent of the Netherlands." *Women Writers of the Renaissance and Reformation*. Ed. Katharina M. Wilson. Athens, 1987. Pp. 350–62.

Wilmart, André. "Les Compositions d'Osbert de Clare en l'honneur de sainte Anne." *Annales de Bretagne* **37** (1926), 1–33.

Wilson, Stephen. *The Magical Universe: Everyday Ritual and Magic in Pre-Modern Europe*. London, 2000.

Wright, Craig. *The Maze and the Warrior: Symbols in Architecture, Theology, and Music*. Cambridge, 2001.

——— *Music and Ceremony at Notre Dame of Paris, 500–1550*. Cambridge, 1989.

——— "Musicology and the Fifteenth Century." *Journal of Musicology* **1** (1982), 39–43.

Zophy, Jonathan W. *The Holy Roman Empire: A Dictionary Handbook*. Westport, CT, 1980.

Index

Abraham, 55, 64, 162, 229, 241
Adjutorium nostrum, 144, 146, 150–4, 157, 159, 174–5, 176–7, 178, 179, 180, 201–2
Agricola, Alexander, 183, 184, 207
   Transit Anna timor, 179, 180, 183–5, 193, 198, 203, 204, 207, 214
Alamire, Petrus, 23, 66, 69, 104, 133, 134, 144, 145, 146, 178, 179, 185, 192, 194, 197, 201, 203, 205, 206–7, 248
All Saints Collegiate Church (*Allerheiligenkapelle*). *See* Castle Church (Wittenberg)
Alleluia V. Multiplicabitur, 234–5
Alma redemptoris mater, 72, 76
Alphaeus, husband of Mary Cleophas, 7, 113, 115
Amadeus VIII of Savoy, 30, 60, 62
Anna Jagiellon. *See* Anna, Queen of Bohemia and Hungary
Anna matrona nobilis, 180–3, 192, 193, 204
Anna of Austria, 202, 203, 205, 211
Anna, Queen of Bohemia and Hungary, 23, 145, 176, 178, 179, 183, 185, 193, 194, 196, 197, 201, 202, 203, 204, 205, 206, 207, 208, 210
Anna Weller von Molsdorf, 115
Anne de Beaujeu (Anne of France), 22, 84, 85, 87, 88, 143, 212
Anne of Brittany, Queen of France, 22, 23, 87, 107, 143, 144, 147, 152, 154, 157, 159–69, 171, 173, 174, 179, 183, 197, 201, 202, 204, 210, 212, 214, 226
Anne of Cyprus, 30, 39–40, 60, 61, 62, 197
Anne of France. *See* Anne de Beaujeu (Anne of France)
Anne of Lusignan. *See* Anne of Cyprus
Anne, Saint. *See* St. Anne
Antoine de Lalaing, Count of Hoogstraten, 99
Augsburg, 120, 145
Ave mater matris Dei, 189–92, 193, 204
Avogadro family (Brescia), 29, 30, 40, 59–60

Beda, Noël, 224, 243
Beisselius, Jodocus, 208

biblical humanism, 212–13, 220–5, 226, 227, 229, 239–40
book of hours, 7, 161, 164, 165, 171
Borssele, Anna van, 210
Bourdichon, Jean, 164, 165
Briçonnet, Guillaume, 216, 220
Bruck, Arnold von, 197, 205
Brussels, Royal Library, MS 228, 95–6
Burgundy, House of, 60, 61, 81–4, 91, 92, 94, 95, 107, 206

Carmelites, 75, 77, 79, 80, 98
Castle Church (Wittenberg), 22, 107, 110, 112, 113, 116, 117, 118, 120, 123, 124, 126, 127, 128, 131, 132, 135, 140, 141, 142, 247, 248
Catherine of Aragon, 145, 176, 178
Ceva, Boniface de, 245
Charles the Bold, Duke of Burgundy, 81, 83, 84
Charles V, Holy Roman Emperor, 18, 67, 88, 91, 101, 102, 103, 109, 135, 145, 176, 178, 184, 194, 196, 197, 198, 199, 206, 209, 210, 214, 242
Charles VIII, King of France, 22, 84, 87, 88, 96, 98, 107, 143, 160, 161, 162
Charles, Count of Angoulême, 213–4
Charles, Duke of Alençon, 215–16, 229, 241
Charles-Orland (Dauphin of France), 160, 167, 169, 171
Charlotte of Bourbon, Queen of Cyprus, 29, 39, 58
Chicago, Newberry Library, MS 83, 161–2, 164
Christine de Pizan, 49, 65, 85–6, 88, 89–90, 93, 97, 143
Clare of Assisi, 94, 95, 97
Claude of France, 144, 162, 163, 165, 169, 171, 173, 184, 185, 214, 221, 243
Clemens non Papa, Jacob, 77
Clement VII, pope, 198, 199
Cleophas, second husband of St. Anne, 6, 7, 18, 97, 113, 115, 116, 169, 223, 224, 225, 273n31
Colette of Corbie, 83, 94–5, 97, 98

341

Commovebo celum, 237
Cranach, Lucas (the Elder), 111, 112, 113, 142
    Altarpiece of the Holy Kinship, 113–16

Da Vinci, Leonardo, 218, 220, 223, 246
David, 55, 62, 64
Divitis, Antonius, 106, 144, 147
Dominicans, 98, 244
Du Fay, Guillaume, 61, 233
Du Moulin, Francis, 217, 221–2, 224–6, 239, 240, 243, 244
Dunstaple, John, 77, 248

Elizabeth, mother of John the Baptist, 6, 161, 218
Emerentia, mother of St. Anne, 9
Erasmus, Desiderius, 91, 197, 208, 209–10, 213, 220, 223
Esmeria, sister of St. Anne, 9

Felix Anna quedam matrona, 67, 72, 74, 76, 77, 79, 80, 100, 103
Ferdinand I, 18, 23, 145, 176, 179, 185, 193, 194, 196–7, 198–200, 201, 202, 203, 204, 205, 206, 207, 208, 209–10, 211
Ferdinand II, 202
Festa, Costanzo, 77
Févin, Antoine de, 106, 144, 188, 197
Finck, Heinrich, 197
Flanders, 81, 94
Florence, 17
Francis I, King of France, 88, 147, 163, 171, 181, 198, 206, 212, 213, 214, 216, 217, 218, 221, 223, 224, 228, 230, 242, 244, 245, 246
Francis II, Duke of Brittany, 87
Francis of Angoulême. *See* Francis I, King of France
Francis of Paule, 214, 245
Franciscans, 94, 98, 135, 227, 244–5
Frederick III, Holy Roman Emperor, 106–7, 200
Frederick the Wise, Elector of Saxony, 22, 67, 102, 103, 107–10, 111, 112, 113, 115, 116, 117, 118, 120, 124, 128, 132, 133, 135, 139, 141, 142, 175, 177, 199
Fugger, Raimund (the Elder), 145
Fulbert of Chartres, 20

Gascongne, Mathieu, 178
    Christus vincit, Christus regnat, Christus imperat, 199, 200, 202, 203, 205, 207, 210
Gaudium et leticia invenietur, 237–9, 240–1

Ghent, 81, 83, 90
Golden Gate of Jerusalem, 5, 62, 81, 100
Gombert, Nicolas, 77, 189

Haimo of Auxerre, 6
Hanelle, Jean, 29, 58, 60, 61
Hannah, mother of Samuel, 6, 54–5, 161, 210
Henry II of Navarre, 214, 216, 229
Henry VIII, King of England, 145, 176, 178, 214
Hey, Jean (Master of Moulins), 86
Holy Family, 142, 164, 165, 218, 223
Holy Kinship, 3, 7, 9, 10, 15, 17, 19, 23, 51, 59, 83, 95, 106, 110, 113, 115, 116, 142, 165, 167, 169, 210, 218, 220, 223, 224, 225, 226, 242, 243
Holy Roman Empire, 22, 108
Holy Trinity, 131, 171

Immaculate Conception, 10, 35, 98, 104, 120, 122, 125, 131, 132, 133, 134–9, 140, 141, 142, 180, 247

Janus I, King of Cyprus, 21, 26, 30, 39, 58
Jena, Universitätsbibliothek, MS 4, 133, 134, 135
Jena, Universitätsbibliothek, MS 5, 133, 134, 139
Jena, Universitätsbibliothek, MS 7, 69, 98, 102, 103, 104–6, 107, 109, 118, 122, 135, 139
Jena, Universitätsbibliothek, MS 30, 118, 122–3, 125–6, 128, 133
Jena, Universitätsbibliothek, MS 34, 118–20, 122, 123, 125, 126, 128, 133
Jerome, St. (Church Father), 6, 39, 222, 272n16, 272n18, 324
Jesse, root/rod of, 20, 52, 59, 62, 65
Joachim, husband of St. Anne, 5, 6, 7, 15, 47, 54, 62, 80, 81, 83, 97, 99, 100, 113, 142, 156, 186, 273n25, 311n42
Job, 97
John of Saxony. *See* John the Steadfast
John the Steadfast, 113, 115–16, 141, 200
Joseph. *See* St. Joseph
Josquin, 68, 106, 145, 147, 177
Juan of Castile. *See* Juan, Prince of the Asturias
Juan, Prince of the Asturias, 87, 88, 96, 178
Juana of Castile, 88, 102
Judah, 57, 64
Judith, 93–4
July 26, feast day, 9, 17, 35, 119, 154, 237, 273n25, 286n39

Kellman, Herbert, 179, 192, 197–8, 199, 201, 202, 203, 205, 206, 207, 208

La Rue, Pierre de, 66, 67–9, 70–1, 72, 96, 157, 198, 202
   Missa Conceptio tua, 133–9
   Missa de Sancto Job, 96, 97, 106
   O salutaris hostia, 67, 100–1
   St. Anne Mass, 22, 66–7, 68, 69–81, 91, 94, 96, 97, 98–9, 100, 101, 102, 104, 106, 107, 117, 118, 128, 133, 134, 154, 155
Lassus, Orlande de, 189
laudes regiae, 16–17, 199
Le Batave, Godefroy, 221, 224
Lefèvre d'Etaples, Jacques, 213, 218–20, 222–3, 224, 225–6, 239, 243, 244
Leo X, pope, 242, 243
London, British Library, MS Royal 8 G.vii, 145, 176, 177–8
Louis d'Orléans. *See* Louis XII, King of France
Louis II. *See* Louis Jagiellon
Louis Jagiellon, 194, 196, 205
Louis of Savoy, 30, 40, 60, 61, 62
Louis XI, King of France, 84, 213, 227, 245
Louis XII, King of France, 22, 88, 143, 144, 147, 152, 157, 161, 162, 164, 174, 175, 176, 179, 183, 184, 185, 201, 202, 212, 213, 214
Louise of Savoy, 85, 88, 163–4, 212, 213, 214, 216, 217, 218, 221, 222, 223, 224, 225, 226, 243, 244, 245, 246
Lusignan, House of, 26, 30, 32, 58–9, 60
Luther, Martin, 108, 110, 140–1, 142
Lyre antiphoner, with office for St. Anne (Évreux, Bibliothèque municipale, MS lat. 89), 37

Mainz, 75, 79
Margaret of Austria, 21, 67, 69, 81, 83, 84, 85, 86–94, 95–100, 101–2, 104, 106, 113, 133, 134, 135, 139, 143, 160, 178, 196, 198, 205–6, 208, 209
Margaret of Bourbon, 85, 212
Margaret of York, 81, 83, 90, 95
Marguerite of Angoulême, 212, 213, 214–16, 217, 218, 220–1, 226, 227, 228–9, 230, 239, 240, 241, 243, 244, 245
Marguerite of Navarre. *See* Marguerite of Angoulême
Marie of Hungary, 194, 196, 205, 207, 209
Mary. *See* Virgin Mary

Mary Cleophas. *See* Mary Iacobi, daughter of St. Anne
Mary Iacobi, daughter of St. Anne, 6, 62, 221, 222, 243
Mary Magdalene, 221–2, 223, 224, 240
Mary of Burgundy, 81, 84, 107
Mary Salome, daughter of St. Anne, 62, 113, 115, 116, 169, 221, 222, 223, 225, 243
Mass for St. Anne (anonymous), 213, 227–46
Master of Claude of France, 171, 173
Masters of the Dark Eyes, 208
Maximilian I, 17, 84, 87, 88, 89, 90, 91, 96, 104, 106, 107–9, 113, 143, 160, 184, 194, 200, 242
Maximilian II, 202
Mechelen, 67, 69, 81, 87, 90, 91, 95, 101, 102, 103, 108, 206, 209
Mechelen, Archief en Stadsbibliotheek, MS s.s., "Livre de choeur," 134, 135
Meit, Conrad, 93, 113
Melanchthon, Philip, 142
Mouton, Jean, 143, 144, 145, 146, 147–8, 150, 155, 157, 174, 181, 188, 191, 192, 206, 207
   Celeste beneficium, 21, 22, 143–6, 148–50, 152, 154, 155, 159, 160, 163, 164, 165, 173, 174, 175, 176–7, 178, 180, 185, 190–1, 193
   Non nobis Domine, 174, 192, 201, 202
   Quis dabit oculis nostris, 144, 174

Nativity of Mary, 20, 118, 119, 131, 156
New York, Pierpont Morgan Library, MS M.50, 167–9, 171
New York, Pierpont Morgan Library, MS M.1166, 171–4
Noli timere mater filiorum, 237

Odense Office for St. Anne (Copenhagen, Royal Library, L.N. MS 30), 35–7
Osbert of Clare, 38, 48

Palatini Partbooks (Vatican City, Biblioteca Apostolica Vaticana, MSS Palatini Latini 1976–9), 23, 145–6, 176, 178–80, 183, 185, 187, 189, 190, 192, 193, 197, 198, 201, 202–4, 205–7, 208, 209, 210, 211, 248
Paris, 74, 75, 140, 147, 220, 221, 222, 224, 226
Paris, Bibliothèque nationale, MS lat. 9473, 61–2
Paris, Bibliothèque nationale, MS lat. 9474, 164–7
Petit, Guillaume, 244

Philibert II of Savoy, 22, 85, 88, 89, 90, 93, 96, 97, 99, 212
Philip the Bold, Duke of Burgundy, 84
Philip the Fair (Philip I of Castile), 84, 87, 88, 90, 91, 177, 184, 198, 207
Philip the Good, Duke of Burgundy, 81, 83
Politics in sacred music, 3–5
Poor Clares, 83, 94
Poyer, Jean, 167, 171
Protoevangelium of James, 5, 6, 15, 50, 54, 210, 272n12, 272n16

Raphael, 218, 243
Reformation, 107, 108, 110, 140, 165, 197, 208–9, 212, 226, 249
Renée of France, 21, 162, 174, 201, 202
Rener, Adam, 109, 118
Richafort, Jean, 147, 198, 202
Rohan, Pierre de, 214
Romano, Giulio, 218, 243
Rosary, 2, 207–8, 307n55, 308n56

Salome, third husband of St. Anne, 6, 97, 223, 225
Sarah, wife of Abraham, 6, 55, 161, 162, 210, 241
Sarto, Andrea del, 218, 243
Savoy, House of, 30, 40, 60–4, 85, 88–9, 90, 212
Sermisy, Claudin de, 147, 150, 188
Sixtus IV, pope, 139
St. Anne
    and ancient lineage, 6, 19–20, 48, 53, 61, 62, 98, 183, 186, 189, 204, 210, 229, 230, 241, 249
    areas of intercession, 9–16
    and childbirth, 3, 11, 58, 99, 160, 204
    and children, 81, 99–100, 106, 204, 243, 249
    and the craft of weaving, 46–50
    as dynastic protectress, 11, 16, 17, 19, 21, 44, 50, 54, 59, 62, 66, 69, 94, 102, 106, 108, 178, 194, 200, 206, 210, 212, 232, 248
    and education of the Virgin, 14, 28, 60, 86, 116, 143, 165, 167–71, 173
    and fertility, 3, 11–12, 17, 22, 24, 50, 58, 61, 100, 160, 189, 190, 201, 203, 204, 210, 212, 231, 247
    and humanism, 14, 23–4, 175, 208
    legend of, 5–9, 156, 224, 247
    and marriage, 3, 14, 98, 99–100, 142, 143, 211, 247
    and motherhood, 15, 41, 50, 61, 80, 98, 99, 100, 142, 143, 154, 160, 163, 165, 173, 189, 193, 212, 213, 241, 246, 249
    and nature metaphors, 50–1, 57, 121, 186
    noble devotion to, 3, 17–20, 44, 50, 57, 64–5, 85, 95, 102–3, 106, 115, 121, 128, 142, 164–74, 175, 178, 212, 247, 248, 249
    and physical connection to Mary and Jesus, 49, 54, 61, 101, 142, 190, 210
    and three marriages, 6, 98, 106, 222–3, 226, 229, 239
    and wealth, 5
    and widowhood, 49, 98, 226
St. Anne Trinitarian, 10, 12, 23, 53, 61, 81, 111, 165, 212, 218, 273n29, 286n45, 302n56, 307n54, 308n56
St. Claudius of Besançon, 169
St. George, 176
St. Helena, 165, 167
St. Hilarion, 26, 28, 29, 32, 34, 38, 39, 41, 57, 58, 62
St. Joseph, 142
St. Margaret, 11, 94, 161, 162
St. René (Renatus), 152, 176, 201
St. Ursula, 165, 167
Stollanus, father of St. Anne, 9
Strigel, Bernhard, 17–19, 106, 210
Suleiman the Magnificent, 196, 197–8
Suzanne of Bourbon, 85

Thenaud, Jean, 245–6
Theodoce matrem/Firma fide, 185–9, 193, 204, 206
Three Marys, 7, 121, 123, 169, 222–3, 224, 225, 226, 229, 239, 240, 242, 243, 244, 246
Torgau, 109, 113, 141
Turin Codex (Torino, Biblioteca nazionale, MS J.II.9), 21, 26–30, 31, 32, 35, 58, 59, 60, 248
    Office for St. Anne, 21, 32–65

University of Wittenberg, 110, 116
Urban VI, pope, 9, 36

van Male, Zeghere, 78
Vermeyen, Jan Cornelisz, 194, 206
versified office, 30–1, 32, 46
    modal organization of, 34
Vienna, Österreichische Nationalbibliothek, Musiksammlung, MS Mus. 15941, 145

Virgin Mary, 7, 49, 50, 61, 72, 80, 97, 98, 99, 100, 113, 116, 119, 120, 125, 128, 131, 132, 135, 141, 162, 164, 169, 171, 180, 183, 186, 205, 208, 218, 220, 222, 223, 224, 225, 247
   appropriation of Marian symbolism, 1, 180, 208
   and salvation, 3, 223
Voragine, Jacobus de, 2, 7, 9, 10, 38, 54, 169

Walther, Johann, 141
Willaert, Adrian, 179
   Pater noster, 179, 207, 210
Wittenberg, 107, 108, 110, 111, 112, 117, 118, 124, 140, 141, 143

Zapolya, John, 196, 198, 206
Zebedee, husband of Mary Salome, 7, 113, 225, 310n40